Notable Quotables

A COMPENDIUM OF GEMS FROM
SALVATION ARMY LITERATURE

Notable Quotables

A COMPENDIUM OF GEMS FROM
SALVATION ARMY LITERATURE

Allen Satterlee

THE SALVATION ARMY SUPPLIES
Atlanta, Georgia

Acknowledgements

It is obvious that I could not complete this project without a lot of help from a lot of people. A simple line of acknowledgement here is hardly adequate, but I trust the spirit is appreciated. There are many who helped who are not mentioned but I had to limit my acknowledgements because of space.

My grandfather, Corps Sergeant-Major Monroe Satterlee, has not only served as a sterling example of Salvationism through his fifty years of soldiership, but precious to me in particular is that he allowed me to read his books. It was while sitting at his desk that my love for Army books was born.

Brigadier Lillian Blackburn gave me wonderful assistance by allowing me access to The School for Officers' Training Library in Atlanta. She has allowed me to interrupt her many times and has never been less than gracious.

Mr. Ralph I. Miller was the first person I talked to who really believed in this book. At a point when I was ready to give it up, his encouragement was invaluable.

Lt. Colonel Houston Ellis also encouraged me and helped me decide on the format of the book as well as material that should be included. His commitment to the ministry of books gives him an outreach to thousands.

This book has spanned two appointments. I wish to thank my office staff in Port Richey, Florida for their help in typing the manuscript, especially Rachael Ramoni and Naomi Satterlee. In Roanoke, Virginia I have been aided by Anita Young.

I have met only three or four of the authors quoted in this book. To all those I quote I thank you for writing and making my life richer through your insights.

Captain Allen Satterlee

With appreciation for typesetting
by The Scotch Type Shop, Inc.
Typeface: Garamond

Dedication

This book is dedicated to my family, my wife Esther, my children, Jacob, Sharon and Jonathan. They have inspired, shared and been the fulfillment of my dreams. God has made me a rich man.

Foreword

The Southern Territory is proud to present this awesome compendium of quotations from the vast realm of Salvation Army literature.

In it, the author – Captain Allen Satterlee – has unearthed gems from leaders of the past as well as significant statements from current Army leaders and Salvationist authors.

It is intended to be a valuable resource book, packed with notable quotations on a spectrum of subjects literally running from A to Z.

We pay tribute to the wisdom and wit of Godly men and women who have enriched Army literature and thereby enriched all of us. God grant that as we prepare for our ministry, we may find just the right quote to sharpen and strengthen messages on the love and mercy and power of Jesus Christ, the Author of our faith!

Andrew S. Miller
COMMISSIONER

Atlanta, Georgia
October, 1985

Preface

"The Salvation Army is primarily action oriented – not thought oriented." So explained one of my teachers in a class while I was in training. This, he went on to explain, was why there are not great volumes of theology or great schools of higher learning. While everyone else has been discussing what ought to be done about a problem, The Salvation Army has been solving it. Because of this action orientation there are few who take the luxury to spend time writing. The discipline of writing takes on a whole new meaning for the Salvationist who must down his pen to distribute the bread.

Despite this The Salvation Army has a rich legacy of literature. With poetry that sings and prose that paints vivid pictures we make no apologies for our literature. The biggest regret that I have with Army literature is that its circulation is so limited. Our books could take their place on anybody's bookshelf. One of my hopes is that this volume will whet the appetites of those who read for the books that are quoted.

We are the better because of books. I do not need to wonder how the Founder felt because he speaks to me directly in a book. The fire of Railton, the moving words of Brengle, the demand for action of Catherine Booth are all in my hand. Please turn off the television set and read.

Allen Satterlee

Table of Contents

Holiness	Mercy Seat	Promise
Holy Spirit	Miracles	Public Relations
Home	Mission	Purity
Honesty	Missionaries	Purpose
Hope	Money	Race
Humanism	Morality	Reading
Humility	Motherhood	Reality
Hypocrisy	Motivation	Rebellion
Idolatry	Music	Religion
Identity	Name of Jesus	Reluctance
Imagination	Nature	Renewal
Improvement	Needs	Repentance
Incarnation	Nurture	Reputation
Individuality	Obedience	Respect
Indwelling	Officership	Responsibility
Inspiration	Omnipotence	Resurrection
Intellect	Omnipresence	Revelation
Jesus Christ	Open Air	Revival
Joy	Opinion	Righteousness
Judgment	Opportunity	Sacraments
Justice	Patience	Sacrifice
Kindness	Peace	Salvation
Knowledge	Persecution	Salvation Army
Law	Perseverance	Salvationist
Laziness	Politics	Satan
Leadership	Potential	Science
Legalism	Power	Second Coming
Life	Praise	Security
Liquor	Prayer	Seeking
Loneliness	Preaching	Self
Love of God	Prevention	Self-Denial
Love (Human)	Presumption	Selfishness
Loyalty	Pride	Separation
Man	Priorities	Service
Marriage	Prison	Sex
Mercy	Procrastination	Silence

Simplicity
Sin
Social Work
Sorrow
Soul-Winner/Soul-Winning
Sovereignty
Spouse Abuse
Statistics
Stewardship
Strength
Success
Suffering
Suicide
Supernatural
Surrender
Talent
Tears
Temptation
Thanksgiving
Theology
Time
Tobacco
Tongues
Trials
Trinity
Trust
Truth
Tyranny
Unemployment
Uniform
Unity
Urban Life
Victory
Virgin Birth
Visitation
War Cry

Warfare (Earthly)
Warfare (Spiritual)
Weakness
Will
Wisdom
Witnessing
Woman
Work
Works
World
Worldliness
Worry
Worship
Writing
Youth
Zeal

Acceptance

Again, the man who is filled with the Spirit tolerates those who differ from him in opinion, in doctrine. He is firm in his own convictions, and ready at all times with meekness and fear to explain and defend the doctrines which he holds and is convinced are according to God's Word, but he does not condemn and consign to damnation all those who differ from him.

When the Holy Ghost Is Come
Samuel Logan Brengle

Achievement

Progress is the best antidote to backsliding and desertion.

Orders and Regulations
for Corps Officers

Great spiritual achievements depend upon faithfulness in small things.

The Armoury Commentary
The Four Gospels
Frederick Coutts, edit.

The world is inhabited by men who, although perhaps hollow spiritually, are sometimes capable of great achievement. It is one of civilization's greatest ironies that those men are impotent in the things that truly matter.

A Sense of God
Peter W. Stine

Action

While activity is impossible without life there can be no strong life, whether bodily or spiritual, without plenty of activity, and there can be no strong salvation soldiers without plenty of fighting.

Orders and Regulations
for Corps Officers

The narrow way, being also a straight way, must be the most direct way.

Powers of Salvation Army Officers
Florence Booth

Make your will, pack your box, kiss your girl, be ready in a week.

William Booth
The General Next to God
Richard Collier

Oh, my comrades, again I say what I have said before — when you see your duty, that is the moment of action. Don't let that moment slip, and so miss the power of it, for, perchance, you will never be as strong again.

Salvation Soldiery
William Booth

Faith must "work by love", emotion must be transmitted into action, and love to faithful, self-sacrificing service, else they become a kind of pleasant, a respectable, but nonetheless deadly debauchery.

When the Holy Ghost
Is Come
Samuel Logan Brengle

Peace is the offspring of a faith that is ceaseless in its activity — an activity that is the most perfect, and the mightiest of which man is capable, for through it unarmed men have subdued kingdoms, wrought righteousness, obtained promises, stopped the mouths of lions, quenched the violence of fire, escaped the edge of the sword, out of weakness were made strong, waxed valiant in the fight, turned to flight the armies of the aliens, women received their dead to life again.

Helps to Holiness
Samuel Logan Brengle

Read it (the Bible) not so that you may know, but that you may do.

Heart Talks on Holiness
Samuel Logan Brengle

We cannot share our love without action, without involvement, without doing.

Excursions in Thought
Jean Brown

The great need of the world, its lost condition, or the opportunity to be the hands, or the feet, or the mouth of the Lord is a sufficient call for anyone who has the opportunity or the talent to respond. The desire to serve God and the conviction of lost souls can take root in your heart and mind until it drives you to action.

When God Calls You
Edward Deretany

Our part is to be spontaneous, rather than sedate; rambunctious rather than ritualistic; fortissimo rather than pianissimo; light refracting glass rather than bomb shelter brick!

Marching On!
Ted Palmer

We are not a say it religion, not even a sing it religion; we are the Christian Church's ultimate do it denomination.

Marching On!
Ted Palmer

Dare ye still lie fondly dreaming,
Wrapped in ease and worldly scheming,
While the multitudes are streaming
      Downward into Hell?

attr. George Scott Railton
Salvation Army Song Book

It is scarcely possible for an organization to be devised beforehand to meet those peculiar circumstances which exist in society at various periods. God has contented Himself with the general direction to His servants to go everywhere and gather all they can out of the world unto His kingdom, leaving it to them to adapt their measures and invitations to the various classes whom they may have to deal with.

Heathen England
George Scott Railton

It is easy to thoughtlessly outrun God. Salvationists are confirmed activists, and therefore need to remember that activism is beset by a special peril. Too often through the years I have become so preoccupied with my own perfectly laudable business that Christ's call to inner peace and poise has been neglected. Christian action requires balancing at its deepest level by Christian living and understanding. Doing is comparatively easy, but living in Christ involves the total person and demands a conscious, sensitive response to the Spirit of God.

A Burning in My Bones
Clarence Wiseman

Age

But is it an abyss? Will it swallow me up and shall I be lost in its dark and silent depth? Is it not rather the sunkissed peaceful slope on the sunset side of life where my often overtaxed body can have a measure of repose, and my spirit, freed in part from the driving claims of the War, can have a foretaste of the Sabbath calm of eternity?

Ancient Prophets
Samuel Logan Brengle

If God should say to me, "I will let you begin over again, and you may have your youth back again," I should say, "O dear Lord, if you don't mind, I prefer to go on growing old!"

Samuel Logan Brengle
Peace Like a River
Sallie Chesham

O Lord, as old age overtakes me, save me from two evils; on the one hand, the querulous, critical faultfinding habits into which so many old people fall; and, on the other, the soft, gullible spirit. Keep my eyes wide open to the weakness, foolishness, sin of men; yet keep my heart tender and sympathetic and hopeful. Help me to be firm and steadfast in my loyalty to what truth is. Don't let me go astray the very least in my old age. Don't permit me to fall into even a little folly that, like a fly in a pot of ointment, will spoil the influence of a life devoted to Thee. Help me, O Lord.

Samuel Logan Brengle
Portrait of a Prophet
Clarence Hall

When I was a child a man of seventy seemed to be to be as old as the hills. I stood in awe of him. No words could express how venerable he was. When I looked up to him it was like looking to the snowy, suncrowned, stormswept heights of great mountains.

The Guest of the Soul
Samuell Logan Brengle

While the snows of seventy winters are on my head, the sunshine of seventy summers is in my heart. The fading, falling leaves of seventy autumns solemnize my soul, but the resurrection life upspringing in flower and tree, the returning songbirds, the laughing, leaping brooks and swelling rivers, and the sweet soft winds of seventy springtimes gladden me.

The Guest of the Soul
Samuel Logan Brengle

Even if we are slow on the uptake...for the will to do still exists when the power departs. The tenant remains youthful while the house decays.

Just a Moment, Lord
Flora Larsson

I wouldn't want to live my life over again, Lord.
There have been too many painful passages,
  too many struggles,
  too many disappointments...
I feel like the ship that is entering a long sought harbor, storm-worn, with sunblistered paint yet chugging along the old faithful engine toward a final docking.

Between You and Me, Lord
Flora Larsson

We who face the problems of the latter years,
    when frailty replaces energy,
    when memory starts to fail,
    when hearing and sight diminish,
    what word have You for us?
It comes crystal clear, so convincingly,
    "Lo, I am with you even until the end."

I'm Growing, Lord!
Flora Larsson

Aggressiveness

It is the dare in commerce that makes the big business. It is the dare in campaigning that wins trenches and pill boxes in commanding positions. It is the dare in the service of God that stamps one with the seal of leadership, attracts around one a fighting force, rallies and gives heart to the timid, overleaps obstacles, makes the devil turn and fly and wins the forlorn hopes of the Kingdom.

The Officer — 1918

That spirit of aggression which fights and struggles and wrestles, which thinks and schemes, prays and believes, and storms the ramparts of the impossible. And the strength of God is the very antithesis, is the death knell of that complacent contentment which says: "Oh, we are doing very well! We are holding our own and in fact making some little progress — so things are not so bad!"

Bramwell Booth
The Officer - 1917

If you want to do right, on pleasant or unpleasant lines, go straight at it; get satisfied as to what you ought to do, and then give up deliberating. Cease weighing the matter over, getting the advice of good, timid people, and at once commit yourself, in the most emphatic and public manner and if you don't act this way ten to one you won't act in the right way at all.

Salvation Soldiery
William Booth

3

Oh, the danger of settling down and waiting till the sinners come to you! Go after them...Go in for direct soul-saving; you do not exist to amuse or to educate the people...

William Booth
Mildred Duff
Madge Unsworth

Salvationists once startled the world as an assault force for Christ. Dare the Army now be content to be merely an army of occupation?

Rediscovering the Open Air
Lyell Rader

Ambition

Some officers seem to be thinking of themselves, their reputation, reward, and appreciation, instead of realizing that the battle is at the gates, and going forward in the fight. What can we hope from officers who regard their work as a ladder by which they can mount to distinction and a place of comparative ease?

Powers of Salvation Army
Officers
Florence Booth

Beware how you indulge that dangerous element of character — ambition. Misdirected, it will be everlasting ruin to yourself and, perhaps, to me also. Oh, my love, let nothing earthly excite it, let not self-aggrandizement fire it. Fix it in on the Throne of the Eternal, and let it find the realization of its loftiest aspirations in the promotion of His glory, and it shall be consummated with the richest enjoyments and brightest glories of God's own Heaven. Those that honor Him He will honor, and to them who thus seek His glory, will He give to rule over the nations, and even to judge the angels, who through a perverted ambition, the exaltation of self instead of God, have fallen from their allegiance and overcast their eternity with the blackness of darkness forever.

Catherine Booth
Catherine Booth, Mother
of The Salvation Army
Frederick Booth-Tucker

If a man has a money-making spirit, he will probably make money. If a man has an ambitious spirit, he will possibly vault to some higher grade of life than that in which he was born. If a man has a soul-saving spirit, he will certainly save souls. It matters little what his circumstances may be. Therefore, the business of everyone of us is to come into the possession of an absorbing passion for the salvation of men.

William Booth
History of The Salvation
Army — Volume Four
Arch Wiggins

Ambition for God can be as strong as selfish ambition, and therefore as open to disappointment. In all these and similar matters we are likely to feel as keenly as the man without religion.

Messages to the Messengers
Catherine Bramwell-Booth

Anger

The wrath of man is to praise God.

History of The Salvation
Army — Volume One
Robert Sandall

Anger is carnal when it is self-defensive. It is spiritual when it defends God, His purity and righteousness, His kingdom.

The Holy Spirit — Friend
and Counsellor
Milton S. Agnew

It is often harder to suffer in the right spirit than if one might blaze forth in righteous anger toward the instrument of injustice.

Messages to the Messengers
Catherine Bramwell-Booth

A man must have his spiritual eyes wide open to discern the difference between sinful temper and righteous indignation.

When the Holy Ghost Is Come
Samuel Logan Brengle

Sanctifying grace does not mean the abolition of temper but its control and re-direction. God will not take* a man's temper from him. Whey should He? A man without a temper is as useless as a knife without temper.

The Call to Holiness
Frederick Coutts

Remember, if you want to retain a clean heart, don't argue!

Commissioner Dowdle
Helps to Holiness
Samuel Logan Brengle

Your honor was at stake and I
   who love Your Name
Felt my blood boil with righteous wrath
   and indignation.
Hot and fast the words poured
   from my lips
As I upheld Your cause.
I looked into Your face
To catch Your glad approval of my zeal;
   But my glance fell
Before the quiet censure of Your eyes.

From My Treasure Chest
Flora Larsson

God is not shocked by our rage, nor is it hidden from Him even when we refuse to face ourselves. If truth is to be the foundation upon which we build our personalities it is better that we learn to stand naked in the Divine presence.

Our Rebel Emotions
Bernard Mobbs

The saving truth of Calvary is that God positively invites us to vent our rage and anger upon Him, not that we may remain forever in a state of childish peevishness, but that we may come to terms with our hostility because we have discovered a love that is stronger than our hatred.

Our Rebel Emotions
Bernard Mobbs

Contempt is soul-murder.

The Christian Charter
George S. Smith

Anxiety

And some of Your best songs
Are often sung
With instruments
One might call
Highly strung!

O Lord!
John Gowans

Is there a heart o'erbound by sorrow?
   Is there a life weighed down by care?
Come to the Cross, each burden bearing
   All your anxiety, leave it there.

Salvation Army Song Book
Edward H. Joy

Apathy

Indifference is the height of folly, and the extreme of wickedness.

Life and Death
Catherine Booth

Oh! what a great many blessings, how much light, how much instruction, and how much influence for good, many professing Christians lose for lack of a bit of trouble! And how many sinners will lose their souls from the same cause! No soul was ever saved yet who was TOO IDLE TO SEEK!

Life and Death
Catherine Booth

Satan has got men fast aleep in sin, and that is his great device to keep them so. He does not care what we do, if he can do that.

Life and Death
Catherine Booth

What a deal there is of going to meetings and getting blessed, and then going away and living just the same, until sometimes we, who are constantly engaged in trying to bring people nearer the heart of God, go away so discouraged that our hearts are almost broken.
We feel that people go back again from the place where we have led them, instead of stepping up to the place to which God is calling them. They come and come, and we are, as the Prophet says, unto them a

5

very pleasant instrument or a very un-pleasant one, as the case may be; and so they go away, and do not get anything. They do not make any DEFINITE ADVANCE. We have not communicated unto them any spiritual gifts. They merely have their feelings stirred, and consequently, they live the next week exactly as they have lived the last, and go down under tempta-tion just as they did before.

Papers on Godliness
Catherine Booth

We must not give up because the devil is learning to oppose us more successfully with indifference than by stirring people up to persecute.

Messages to the Messengers
Catherine Bramwell-Booth

Frequently in meetings and conventions the people all suppose Jesus is in the com-pany, and yet there may not be one that is personally conscious of His presence. They take it for granted that He is with someone else, and lo! He may not be in their midst at all. He has not been persever-ingly, importunately, humbly and be-lievingly sought for and invited to come, and so He has stayed behind.

Heart Talks on Holiness
Samuel Logan Brengle

There are some people who imagine that living by faith means living by chance; they obey the injunction "Take no thought for the morrow" by taking no thought.

The Armoury Commentary
The Four Gospels
Frederick Coutts, edit.

Assurance

God does not leave His real people with-out assurance of their saintship.

Life and Death
Catherine Booth

Assurance means a deep sense of settle-ment, of peace and purpose and accep-tance by God — and an increasing sense of love for all of life.

Peace Like a River
Sallie Chesham

The assurance of faith is to be found only in the possibility of doubt.

Reason to Believe
Harry Dean

I shall not fear though darkened skies may gather round me.
The God I serve is One Who cares and un-derstands.
Although the storms I face would threaten to confound me,
Of this I am assured:
  I'm in His hands!
I'm in His hands. I'm in His hands.
Whate'er the future holds,
I'm in His hands.
The days I cannot see
Have all been planned for me.
His way is best, you see.
I'm in His hands.
What tho' I cannot know the way
  That lies before me?
I still can trust and freely follow
  His commands.
My faith is firm since it is He
  That watches o'er me.
Of this I'm confident:
  I'm in His hands.
In days gone by my Lord has always
  proved sufficient,
When I have yielded to the law of
  love's demands.
Why should I doubt that He would
  evermore be present
To make His will my own?
  I'm in His hands.

Stanley E. Ditmer

Atheism

It was like preaching in Hell, for the atheism of East London in those days was an atheism which hated the very name of God.

The Salvation Army —
Its Origin and Development

If your outward life, harmonious with God's purposes, is not the outcome of your inner life infidelity brands your spirit just as infidelity defames the manhood of him who is secretly unfaithful to his wife.

Powers of Salvation Army
Officers
Florence Booth

Never hear a backslider bring his infidel arguments out. If he begins to spread them before you, tell him plainly to his face that he knows they are all rubbish and twaddle, and that there is nobody in his parish who knows it better than he does. Infidelity–with backsliders at any rate–is a thing of the head rather than the heart.

The General's Letters
William Booth

Atonement

We believe that the Lord Jesus Christ has, by His suffering and death, made an atonement for the whole world, so that whosoever will may be saved.

Salvation Army Doctrine #6

This human body served Jesus for the more than thirty years of His earthly life as the source of human life and vitality from which His ministry, His teaching, His example should flow forth, and in which He would be tried with all the temptations common to man. But ultimately, and actually primarily, it was to serve as the once-for-all Sacrifice for the sins of man.

The Better Covenant
Milton S. Agnew

How counteth God, when all is said and done?
Stars only cost Him breath; but souls, His only Son.

Lillian Blackburn
It's Beautiful
Dorothy Breen, Edit.

That there is no remedy for it but His remedy. No rains in all the heavens to wash it, no waters in all the seas to cleanse it away, no fires in Hell itself to purge its defilement. The only hope was in the blood of His sacrifice.

Bramwell Booth
Trumpets of the Lord
Catherine Bramwell-Booth,
Editor

...we do mean that Jesus Christ, by the grace of God, did actually offer on Mount Calvary, for the sins of the world, such a sacrifice as made it possible for God, consistent with the honor of His law, and the well-being of mankind, to pardon, sanctify, and glorify every man who sincerely turns to Him in repentance, obedience and faith.

The Founder's Messages
to Soldiers
William Booth

Bless God, in dying for me, He died for mine! — in dying for thee, He died for thine! — and in dying for one, He died for all!

Heart Messages
Emma Booth-Tucker

The Atonement distinguishes Christianity from all other religions. In *them*, man gropes after God. In *the Atonement*, God comes seeking and finding man.

Robert Hoggard
The Salvationist and
the Atonement
John Waldron, edit.

It is not our theories of the Atonement that save us, but the Atonement itself.

Doctrine Without Tears
John Larsson

We are all hopeless moral and spiritual bankrupts. We face the tragedy of life's insolvency — the factors we cannot balance, our wasted capital, our disappointing or bitter dividends. And ahead of us as the African says, is "the river of lastness" where death is the ferryman who cries, "Debit! Debit! All debts and no credit! Here you must pay your debts!" Into this hopeless reckoning comes Christ, the

Reconciler, compensating for over-inadequacy, finding the missing factors, building again our wasted reserves, supplying the equation which balances and integrates the disordered life. He reconciles life's accounts and meets our deficit with Divine forgiveness.

Albert Orsborn
The Salvationist and
the Atonement
John Waldron, Edit.

His death's claim, His love has a plea;
   O, it is wondrous love!

Emmanuel Rolfe
The Salvation Army Song Book

O sinner, see for you and me
   He freely suffers in our stead
And lo! He dies upon the tree;
   Behold, He bows His sacred head!

George S. Smith
Salvation Army Song Book

Attitude

We cannot be wholly responsible for an individual's attitude towards ourselves—he can refuse to be reconciled, but we are wholly responsible for our attitude toward him.

The Soldier's Armoury
The Four Gospels
Frederick Coutts, Edit.

Whenever people think more of appearance than attitudes, pretense is never far away.

The Soldier's Armoury
The Four Gospels
Frederick Coutts, Edit.

B

Backsliding

We believe that continuance in a state of salvation depends upon continued obedient faith in Christ.

Salvation Army Doctrine #9

Come, oh come, backslider, hear your Father,
Hear, oh hear how lovingly He pleads,
"Come, oh come, my heart and arms are open
You to receive and meet all your needs."
Up, brother, up from swine and dirt and hunger
Bread, and to spare, you'll find when you get home.
From love and peace and pardon stay no longer
Nor further in sin's barren desert roam.

Gems for Songsters Vol. 1
Anonymous

It is possible, terribly possible, for us not to make God cease to love us, but to put ourselves outside the place where His love is effectual.

More Than Conquerors
Milton S. Agnew

Abroad o'er life's harvest field scattered they lie,
Their blades caked with rust, clogged with soil;
Each plough tells the story of one who looked back,
A ploughman who turned from the toil.
O the rusty old ploughs on the Lord's harvest fields!
The land choked with weeds, rank and tall!

The harvest that might have been, now lost for aye
By a ploughman turned back from his call!

Flora Larsson
The Book of Salvationist Verse
Catherine Baird

No one can tell when Judas made his first
Surrender to himself.
But at some point along the way with Christ,
The light of loyalty had weakened,
Waned.
Thus, when he came to his immortal hour,
The fragile flame went out.

Reflections
Catherine Baird

It is not the difficulties which spoil men. It is not devils that silence them. It is not even temptations to selfishness which destroy them. What does overthrow some of them is going back on God — going back on their vows; doing violence to the Holy Ghost, and silencing the inward voice — the living word which He has given them to declare to the souls of men.

Bramwell Booth
Trumpets of the Lord
Catherine Bramwell-Booth

Am I what once I was?
 Have I that ground maintained
Wherein I walked in power with Thee,
 And Thou my soul sustained?

Herbert Booth
Salvation Army Song Book

Saviour, hear me while before Thy feet,
I the record of my sins repeat,
Stained with guilt, myself abhorring,
Filled with grief, my soul outpouring;
Canst Thou still in mercy think of me,

Stoop to set my shackled spirit free.
Raise my sinking heart and bid me be
Thy child once more?

Herbert Booth
Salvation Army Song Book

"Ah! Who is this?" he (William Booth) asked, almost whispering, conjuring up a vision of a man suddenly in view. "What is this man doing? He is counting. Coming up close to us, a hellish gleams in his eyes, he whispers, 'See, see, one, two, three, four, five, six, seven, eight, nine, ten, twenty, thirty!'" Then like a lost soul his cry rang out, 'Ah! That WAS WHAT I SOLD HEAVEN FOR — THAT WAS WHAT I SOLD MY SOUL FOR. See those lights gleaming up yonder. There is the gate of Heaven, there is the throne of God, shining in the faraway distance. Ah, for this I sold it all, I sold it all!' That is Judas, the prince of backsliders. And if ever you to Hell, he will come to you, and count his silver over in your ears — AND YOU WILL SHOW HIM THE PRICE YOU HAVE PAID FOR YOUR SOUL TOO!"

The General Next to God
Richard Collier

By a backslider, I mean, one who has known the forgiveness of sins, felt the power of the Holy Ghost in the changing of his heart and life, rejoiced at the prospect of Heaven, and gone about doing good; but who has by disobedience and unbelief fallen again under the power of sin, and gone back like a sow that was washed to be pleased and occupied with the amusements, pleasures, works and anxieties of the world.

The General's Letters
William Booth

Never hear a backslider bring his infidel arguments out. If he begins to spread them before you, tell him plainly to his face that he knows they are all rubbish and twaddle, and that there is none in his parish who knows it better than he does. Infidelity — with backsliders at any rate — is a thing of the head rather than the heart.

The General's Letters
William Booth

There is backsliding. Going back on your pledges; breaking your vows to the Lord; deserting the Flag; leaving your comrades to struggle forward as best they can; throwing up your hope of Heaven, and crucifying your Saviour afresh. This is a shameful and distressing change.

The Founder's Messages
to Soldiers
William Booth

The Devil has prepared a secret staircase for them with a cunningly devised trapdoor at the base. Sometimes he has garlanded the fatal steps with the flowers of this world's inducements, and almost unconsciously the redeemed of the Lord, the callen and chosen instruments of Christ, have taken the first step which has led to those following, until at length the last step into uttermost worldliness and selfishness has been taken and their names have been blotted out of the Lamb's Book of Life; their daring deeds are only a tale that is told relating to the past; the battlefield that has witnessed their courage and sacrifices knows them no more; under the Blood and Fire flag their names are unspoken, and so far as present history is concerned, they have not been heard of again.

Heart Messages
Emma Booth-Tucker

They once walked in white raiment; they once rejoiced in a Full Salvation; they were once empowered and fired for service; they once wielded the sword in battle for their Lord; they once brought weary spirits to the footstool of the Cross; they did exploits and scaled mountains and overcame principalities and powers, and despite discouragements and difficulties and sorrows, they followed the Lamb, they fought the fight. But that day has gone.

Heart Messages
Emma Booth-Tucker

Why this backsliding in the life of this once bright and promising young convert? Why the barren appearance of this once flourishing Corps? Why the sudden blight upon this lovely heart and home? Why the leader fallen? Why the follower lost heart? Why the energy no more the ardor chilled, the sympathies dried up, the courage departed as in a single night, the promise of life that filled, one thinks, even Heaven with expectation and earth with hope, blighted, blasted, destroyed?

Heart Messages
Emma Booth-Tucker

I've seen the bright path, with its light clear and shining,
Directing my footsteps in ways straight and plain,
But now, all alone and my love still declining,
I wonder if ever I'll see it again.
I sigh and I cry for its rays, oh, so cheering,
But dark is my soul and no light is therein,
Oh come, for I feel that eternity's nearing
And shine once again, and dispel all my sin.

R.S. Bradbook
Gems for Songster #2

Have I ceased from walking close beside Thee?
    Have I grieved Thee with an ill-kept vow?
In my heart of hearts have I denied Thee?
    Speak, dear Lord, O speak and tell me now.

Will J. Brand
Salvation Army Song Book

A dead shepherd of the sheep. A dead watchman of the city. A dead teacher of the unlearned. A dead nurse of little children. A dead physician of souls. A dead ambassador of Heaven. DEAD! Moving about, but dead! Occupying an important place, and so excluding any other who might fulfill its functions, but dead! What could be sadder? What so ghastly?

Resurrection Life and Power
Samuel Logan Brengle

Backsliding usually begins through neglected or hurried secret prayer.

Heart Talks on Holiness
Samuel Logan Brengle

It is not by some huge wickedness, some Judas-like betrayal, some tempting and lying to the Holy Ghost, as did Ananias and Sapphira, that we grieve Him, but by that which most people count little and unimportant; by talk that corrupts instead of blessing and building up those that hear, by gossip, by bitterness, and uncharitable criticisms and faultfinding.

When the Holy Ghost Is Come
Samual Logan Brengle

The higher and more intense the life the more carefully must it be guarded, lest it be endangered and go astray. It is so in the natural world and likewise in the spiritual world.

When the Holy Ghost Is Come
Samuel Logan Brengle

The Holy Spirit is not capricious and fickle. He has to strive long to get into your heart, and He will strive long before He will leave it, unless you willfully harden your heart and drive Him from you.

Helps to Holiness
Samuel Logan Brengle

When professing Christans bear hard upon backsliders, it is usually only a question of time when they themslves backslide.

The Soul-Winner's Secret
Samuel Logan Brengle

Avoiding the folly of morbid introspection, we need, as Jesus said, to keep a watch on ourselves, resisting the easy degeneration of flabby bodies, and dulled spirits, a degeneration which is often camouflaged by tame respectability.

The Soldier's Armoury
The Four Gospels
Frederick Coutts, Edit.

In vain you strive to drown the thought
Of what you might have been.
Earth's pleasures are too dearly bought,
It's sorrows all too keen!
Backslider, hear! God speaks your name,
It is not yet late;
The Lord in mercy tarries yet,
He has not closed the gate.

Mildred Duff
Salvation Army Song Book

The heart that once has Jesus known
And turned away again,
Finds soon the joys of sin are flown
Though sharp the sting remain.
The soul that once has walked with Him,
Then left His guiding light,
Can only find earth's glitter dim,
Its promise quenched at night.

Mildred Duff
Salvation Army Song Book

Knowing my failures, Knowing my fears,
Seeing my sorrow, Drying my tears,
Jesus recall me, Me reordain,
You know I love You, Use me again.

Jesus Folk
John Gowans

Two years after leaving Egypt the people
were at Kadesh, and 38 years later they
were back at the same place. It is always
tragic to be out of the will of God.

Search the Scriptures
Robert Hoggard

How many do you think I sent to Hell
while I was backsliding?

The Old Corps
Edward Joy

Has the veil of flesh thickened
    so as to shut You out?
Have the shutters of my mind
    snapped together?
Have I carelessly left the blinds
    drawn on the windows of my soul?

Just a Moment, Lord
Flora Larsson

Poor backslider, thou hast driven,
Jesus from thy heart and home;
Once thou hadst a hope of Heaven
Now thy life is filled with gloom.
Still, with pardon and compassion,
He is knocking loud today;
If thou dar'st refuse salvation,
He from thee may turn away.

John Lawley
Salvation Army Song Book

Shepherd of souls that have strayed in the
night,
Scatter our darkness and restore our sight!

Erring and desolate, wounded within,
Help our returning, pardon our sin.
Sad and perverted are our ways,
Yet for Thy comforts yearning,
Homeward now returning,
We beseech Thy healing grace.

The Beauty of Jesus
Albert Orsborn

One act of sin committed by a believer
does not mean that he is thereby cast out
of the family of God. He can and should
and usually will repent and be restored.
But if he does not, the tolerated sin will
invite further sin, with disastrous consequences.

Studies in Sanctification
Edward Read

Those who are on the heights of grace,
must not stoop to the level of mere nature.
If they do, they imperil their future happiness, and probably sacrifice the salvation
of their souls.

Catherine Booth
Mrs. Booth
W.T. Stead

The corruption of the best is the victory of
the worst.

A Burning in My Bones
Clarence Wiseman

Beauty

We never see a blooming girl with rosy
cheeks and laughing eyes and bewitching
curls for whom some mother has not
gradually faded and given her own bloom
and beauty and youth.

Ancient Prophets
Samuel Logan Brengle

There was something inside that made a
difference; then there was how you attended to beauty outside yourself; and then
there was the matter of beauty on yourself.

Peace Like a River
Sallie Chesham

Whoever says that holiness has no place for beauty knows neither the nature of holiness nor the nature of beauty.

The Call to Holiness
Frederick Coutts

Belief

The moment men really see that life is not merely a broken thread, or a socket without an eye, and that death is not just a trapdoor to nothingness, they begin — yes! In that very moment they begin — to look ahead, to look up, to think, to believe, to see that they may rise even to the heights of Heaven or sink to the abyss of Hell. Nay, they begin to see that they must rise to the one or sink to the other.

Bramwell Booth
Trumpets of the Lord
Catherine Bramwell Booth, Edit.

Previously not all the promises in the Bible could induce me to believe; now not all the devils in hell could persuade me to doubt.

Catherine Booth
Mrs. Booth
W.T. Stead

"He that believeth shall be saved." It is not to him that hears, to him that desires, to him that feels, to him that agonizes, to him that consecrates. But it is promised and assured and given to him that believes.

Salvation Soldiery
William Booth

Without the believing and the loving, how impossible all real Salvation Army work is!

Messages to the Messengers
Catherine Bramwell-Booth

Bible

We believe that the Scriptures of the Old and New Testaments were given by inspiration of God and that they only constitute the Divine rule of Christian faith and practice.

Salvation Army Doctrine #1

In the hands of Jesus and in the light of Christian revelation the Old Testament has a glory which it does not display when standing alone.

Handbook of Doctrine

It is the testimony of one generation after another that through the Scriptures God finds the soul of man and the soul of man finds God.

Handbook of Doctrine

The man who says that he can see nothing in the Bible is not judging the Bible but himself.

Handbook of Doctrine

We had God in man two thousand years ago; now we need the Bible in man.

The Founder's Messages
to Soldiers
William Booth

The Word of God is of little avail, the Apostle says, unless it be mixed with faith in them that hear, and I verily believe that it is often made equally ineffective because it is not mixed with faith in those who speak it.

Bramwell Booth
Privilege of All Believers
John Waldron, Edit.

Don't imagine that these supposed contradictions will be an excuse for you at the Judgment Seat. It is not many weeks since a gentleman said to me, "While you Christians are quarrelling, there's hope for us sinners. One teaches one thing and another another, till a poor fellow doesn't know what he is to believe." Ah! that is a comfortable way to put it down here; but when you get to the Bar of God, He will say to all such, "Thou wicked and slothful servant, why didst thou not go to My Book for thyself, and be at the trouble to know my will?"

Life and Death
Catherine Booth

He has got the Church, nearly as whole, to receive what I call an "Oh, wretched man that I am" religion. He has got them to lower the standard which Jesus Christ

13

Himself established in this Book — a standard not only to be aimed at, but to be attained unto — a standard of victory over sin, the world, the flesh, and the Devil, real, living, reigning, triumphing Christianity.

Aggressive Christianity
Catherine Booth

Previously not all the promises in the Bible could induce me to believe; now not all the devils in Hell could make me doubt.

Catherine Booth
Mrs. Booth
W.T. Stead

"Mates, I never read a word of the Bible afore I gi' my heart to God, but now I read it every day and it seems to me just like a lovely rose opening its petals."

Quoted in
Friendship With Jesus
Florence Booth

I want to see a new translation of the Bible into the hearts and conduct of living men and women. I want an improved translation — or transference it might be called — of the commandments and promises and teachings and influence of this Book to the minds and feelings and words and activities of the men and women who hold on to it and swear by it and declare it to be an inspired Book and the only authorized rule of life.

The General's Letters
William Booth

Suppose we woke tomorrow morning and found that every Bible at present in existence had been taken out of the world? Or suppose — which would amount to the same thing — that, all at once, we discovered that every page in our Bibles had become blank paper? What a mourning and lamentation there would be, and justly so. People who had never thought it worth the trouble to read, and disbelieved would mourn. Even people who had read and disobeyed would feel they had lost what could never be replaced.

The Seven Spirits
William Booth

This Book is a fire escape by which men can be pulled out of the raging fire of sin; a lifeboat by which they can be rescued from the stormy waves of everlasting destruction; a ladder up which they can climb to the golden gates of the City of God.

William Booth
The Founder Speaks Again
Cyril Barnes, Edit.

You may go through life with the Bible under your arm and yet finish up in the bottomless abyss, spending your eternity in Hell reading over and over again the words that might have got you to the heart of God on earth and to the home of God in the skies.

William Booth
The Armoury Commentary
The Four Gospels
Frederick Coutts, Edit.

God has put His heart on paper.

Frederick Booth-Tucker
The Officer — 1893

Set forth within the sacred Word,
   The path of life is plainly shown;
The ways of God its lines record,
   For every soul of man made known,
The truth, of all our hopes the ground,
Is here within its pages found.
The Scriptures living words express
And point the way to holiness.

Will J. Brand
Salvation Army Song Book

How can I prove the inspiration of the Bible? By the way it answers to the heart of man. The key that fits an intricate lock was evidently made for that lock. The Bible meets me at every point of my moral and spiritual need.

Ancient Prophets
Samuel Logan Brengle

I am a lonely man, and yet I am not lonely. With my Bible I live with the prophets, priests and kings; I walk and hold communion with apostles, saints and martyrs, and with Jesus, and mine eyes see the King in His beauty and the land that is afar off.

Ancient Prophets
Samuel Logan Brengle

If the Bible does not settle the question for us, it cannot be settled.

Love-Slaves
Samuel Logan Brengle

No man can read the Bible thoughtfully without either hating it or hating his sins.

When the Holy Ghost Is Come
Samuel Logan Brengle

It is not one text more than another, but a WHOLE BIBLE that blesses me, assures me, warns and corrects and comforts me. A hundred promises whisper to me. I never know when one of the promises — perhaps one that I have not met for days or even months — may suddenly stand before me, beckon me, speak to me tenderly, comfortingly, authoritatively, austerely; speak to me as though God were speaking to me face to face.

The Guest of the Soul
Samuel Logan Brengle

Precious things are deeply hidden. Pebbles and stones and autumn leaves abound everywhere, but gold and silver and precious stones are hidden in the bowels of the earth; shells cover the seashore, but pearls are hidden in its depths. And so with truth. Some truth may lie on the surface of the Bible, but those that will altogether satisfy and distinguish us and make us wise unto salvation are found only after diligent search, even as hid treasure.

Heart Talks on Holiness
Samuel Logan Brengle

Read and study it as two young lovers read and study each other.

Heart Talks on Holiness
Samuel Logan Brengle

Read and study the Word not to get a mass of knowledge in the head, but a flame of love in the heart...Read it not that you may know, but that you may do.

Heart Talks on Holiness
Samuel Logan Brengle

So the worker for souls may read ten thousand books, may be able to quote poetry by the yard, may be acquainted with all the facts of science and history, and may even be a professed theologian, but unless he be a diligent student of the Bible, he will not permanently succeed as a soul-winner.

The Soul-Winner's Secret
Samuel Logan Brengle

The Bible is God's recipe for making holy people. You must follow the recipe exactly, if you want to be a holy Christlike person.

Helps to Holiness
Samuel Logan Brengle

The most convincing proof of the inspiration of the Bible that I can offer to an unbeliever is a redeemed life, lived in the power and sweetness of the Spirit; a life that matches the Bible.

Ancient Prophets
Samuel Logan Brengle

The reason why people get mixed up over the Bible is because they have not the Holy Spirit to show them the meaning. A young or humble Christian who is full of the Holy Ghost can tell more about the real, deep, spiritual meaning of the Bible than all the doctors of divinity and theological professors in the world who are not baptized with the Holy Ghost.

Samuel Logan Brengle
The Center of the Circle
John Waldron, Edit.

The Spirit quickens that which is already in the mind and memory, as the warm sun and rains of spring quicken the sleeping seeds that are in the ground, and only those. The sun does not put the seed in the soil, nor does the Holy Spirit without our attention and study put the Word of God in our minds.

When the Holy Ghost Is Come
Samuel Logan Brengle

The staple diet of the saints should be the promises seasoned with the commandments to give them a healthy relish.

The Soul-Winner's Secret
Samuel Logan Brengle

15

The sun does not need learned astronomical treatises to prove its existence, nor a candle of man's making to enable it to be seen. All it needs is that men should have eyes to see. It is its own evidence. So the Bible carries its own evidences of inspiration.

Ancient Prophets
Samuel Logan Brengle

While others debate about the inspiration of the Word, let us eat it, drink it, preach it, and live thereby, and we shall live in the power of "an endless life".

Ancient Prophets
Samuel Logan Brengle

We shall be able to use the Bible as an armory. It will be our chief weapon when we fight for god, our chief when Satan assails. Its truths will protect us. From it we shall learn the doctrines of sin, redemption and eternal life. We shall use this truth to bring salvation and spiritual health to other souls

All things New
William Burrows

The Gospel of Jesus is infinitely more than good advice — it is good news.

The Armoury Commentary
The Four Gospels
Frederick Coutts, Edit.

The purpose of Bible reading is to make us more sensitive to God who meets us in the whole of life.

The Armoury Commentary
The Four Gospels
Frederick Coutts, Edit.

What the Old Testament declared, the New Testament underlines.

In Good Company
Frederick Coutts

The Gospel is too good not to believe.

Reason to Believe
Harry Dean

The Bible should be our practical help in our everyday life. We can find ourselves in no circumstances where advice and help cannot be gleaned from its pages, if only we know where to look. Other people, we read, have been this way before. Some found a path; we can follow in their track. Some slipped and lost their foothold; we will avoid that danger spot. As we study, we see how people succeeded — and why; how people failed — and why. Thus God's unchanging laws in dealing with humanity are revealed to us.

Mildred Duff
Mildred Duff
Madge Unsworth

One of the chief reasons for misunderstanding the Bible is failure to view it as a whole. Stand back, so to speak, as when viewing the work of a master artist and, in that grand perspective, mystery and miracle, poetry and parable, history and biography fall into proper place, and there emerges the most amazing drama ever presented to the mind of man.
This drama stretches from eternity to eternity, makes all history its stage, and embraces in its action God and all humanity. It centers around the presence of evil and suffering in the world, and with utter frankness shows how the problem originated, staying with it until it is completely solved.

Searching the Scriptures
Robert Hoggard

Our holy religion is connected both with a Book and a Person...I have an unspeakable pity for those whose religious consciousness does not include a deep, glowing love for Christ. "Lo I am with you always", said Jesus, "even unto the end of the world"... The old woman was right when she corrected her pastor who quoted it as a promise — "no sir, that is not a promise; it is a fact!"

Fuel for Sacred Flame
T. Henry Howard

As long as the Bible stands, error cannot be sure of tomorrow.

First Called Christians
Gustave Iseley

"Show me your orders." And we do. We open our Bible.

Marching On!
Ted Palmer

The Salvation Army has served God with authority and success over the years because it is motivated by the Word of God, structured according to the principles of those same Scriptures, and ready to evaluate what it is doing or not doing according to God's commandments in the Bible.

Marching On!
Ted Palmer

It is a holy Bible, written by a holy God, to make us a holy people.

Allister Smith
The Privilege of All Believers
John Waldron, Edit.

We act without discipline and live without restraint, and then look to the Bible to rescue us, to provide a stamp of approval for our questionable behavior. The Bible is intended as a light to cut the darkness; it is to be a guide, not an afterthought.

A Sense of God
Peter W. Stine

Bitterness

The dark valleys of bitterness and loneliness are often better for us than the land of Beulah.

Bramwell Booth
Trumpets of the Lord
Catherine Bramwell-Booth, Edit.

Bitterness will be the only water of Hell.

George Scott Railton
The Officer — 1893

Boredom

Don't be afraid of boring him. Let him be bored. People who won't serve God ought to be bored. Bore him till he gives in.

Catherine Booth
Mrs. Booth
W.T. Stead

Buildings

If you can only induce them to frequent a building of your own so much the better; but to persist in holding forth your own conventicle to hundreds when you can gather thousands in the theatre or music hall across the way, would be folly indeed!

Twenty-One Years
Salvation Army
George Scott Railton

Our buildings are God's spiritual hospitals.

Maiden Tribute
Madge Unsworth

C

Calling

Is he truly saved? Has he got sound mental powers? Is he well and free from bodily defects? Is his education at a standard which at least corresponds to the average around him? If the answer to these questions is in the affirmative, could it be that his plea that he lacks God's call is in reality an indication that he does not want to accept it?

Chosen to be a Soldier

No call can be more important than that to officership. It is a matter which must be decided irrespective of the likes or dislikes of the person concerned. It is God who calls, and He is able to make His will so plain that the one He singles out for the unique honor of being His messenger will not need to doubt it.

Chosen to be a Soldier

If God is calling you to become a Salvation Army Officer, you will never find any peace or power till you become one. Never! "Oh but," you say, "I don't know what He will want next." No, we none of us know that, but we know that we shall be safe in His hands. He wants all we are, all we acquire and all we can do to the end of our days.

Catherine Booth
The General Next to God
Richard Collier

Now, then, to be — what? An Officer, perhaps. Well, you will never be happy anymore if you hold back — never. As I said to somebody the other day, you might as well try to be happy in perdition, as to be happy in this life while you have that call in your soul and are refusing to obey it.

Life and Death
Catherine Booth

Is it consistent to leave home in answer to the call of God, and then to return?

Powers of Salvation
Army Officers
Florence Booth

If, my comrades, you are not satisfied as to the call of Jehovah — not sure what He wants you to do in the matter — go and deliberate, consider, enquire, pray, but, when the light has come, and you see clearly the Divine will and the guiding hand, cease enquiring — the time for asking questions has gone by, and the hour of action has arrived. Away to your post.

Salvation Soldiery
William Booth

If you are cut out for being an Officer, an Officer you must be, an Officer you will be, or it will be so much the worse for you both here and hereafter.

The General's Letters
William Booth

"Not called," did you say? Not heard the call, I think you should say. He has been calling loudly ever since He spoke your sins forgiven — if you are forgiven at all — entreating and beseeching you to be His ambassador. Put your ear down to the Bible, and hear Him bid you go and pull poor sinners out of the fire of sin. Put your ear down to the burdened, agonized heart of humanity, and listen to its pitying wail for help. Go and stand by the gates of Hell, and hear the damned entreat you to go to their father's house, and bid their brothers, and sisters, and servants and masters not to come there. And then look the Christ in the face, whose mercy you profess to have

19

got, and whose words you have promised to obey, and tell Him whether you will join us heart and soul and body and circumstances in this march to publish His mercy to all the world.

The General's Letters
William Booth

To attempt to perform the sacred functions of an evangelist without the deep conviction of a call would lead to profanity and failure. No one can stand the strain of living up to so high a vocation without the spiritual resources needed to execute its demands. Is there a more pathetic sight than to watch someone struggling to "hold down" a job for which there has been no Divine endowment?

George Smith
When God Calls You
Edward Deratany

Now, my brethren, do you hear the voice of God in some form or another? Does He speak to you, so that you know it is He calling you forward in the path of duty and sacrifice and consecration and service? That is the Divine commission you have.

Salvation Soldiery
William Booth

If God called you to the Army (and He certainly did), He called you to it as a whole; that your life might be devoted to its interests, and to the building up of His Kingdom within its ranks. Surely, your faith in that call should not waver, nor your obedience to it fail, because it seems likely that your work in it may be of a different character from that which you anticipated? Does the real joy of the fully consecrated soul begin at the point when we can say, "Lord, I am in Thy hands, up to the measure of strength, for any work, at any time, in any place?

Messages to the Messengers
Catherine Bramwell-Booth

She afterwards explained that for months before she yielded, she realized she was called — called by voices too powerful and too appealing to ignore; called to leave the foolish, fading fancies of time for the everlasting gain and glory of eternity; called to arise and follow into paths of service, where each golden moment should be used in sowing, so that in eternity she and others might reap; called to live today for tomorrow, that today might be filled with the satisfaction that nothing of earth can give, and the morrow with everlasting reward.

Heart Messages
Emma Booth-Tucker

And, no doubt, He leads most men by His providence to their life work; but the call to preach the Gospel is more than a providential leading; it is a distinct and imperative conviction.

When the Holy Ghost
Is Come
Samuel Logan Brengle

Again, the call may come as a quiet suggestion, a gentle conviction, as though the gossamer bridle were placed upon the heart and conscience to guide the man into the work of the Lord. The suggestion gradually becomes clearer, the conviction strengthens until it masters the man, and if he seeks to escape it, he finds the silken bridle to be one of stoutest thongs and firmest steel.

When the Holy Ghost
Is Come
Samuel Logan Brengle

Does God call you? Be not disobedient to the heavenly vision. Stay not in the order of your going. Let nothing hinder you. Go and God will be with you as He was with Moses and Paul, and as the years speed by you will increasingly thank God that no business prospects, no fond friendships, no lust of power or love of scheduled ease kept you from the battle's front with its burdens and bitter conflicts and fierce sorrows and soul-satisfying triumphs. One soul joining in the anthem of the redeemed ones around the Throne, saved from Hell through your labors, will pay you for all your toils; one look at the face of Jesus will reward you for all your privations. What care Peter and John and Paul now, if they did lose all to follow Jesus, and did suffer and die for the men they sought to save? And what will you care?

Heart Talks on Holiness
Samuel Logan Brengle

The man whom God calls cannot safely neglect or despise the call. He will find his mission on earth, his happiness and peace, his power and prosperity, his reward in Heaven, and probably Heaven itself, bound up with that call and dependent upon it. He may run away from it, as did Jonah, and find a waiting ship to favor his flight; but he will also find fierce storms and billowing seas overtaking him, and big mouthed fishes of trouble and disaster ready to swallow him.

When the Holy Ghost
Is Come
Samuel Logan Brengle

There is a threefold ministry to which we are called: the ministry of service, the ministry of sacrifice, and the ministry of suffering.

Ancient Prophets
Samuel Logan Brengle

My calling as an officer is to serve the Lord Jesus Christ — not limiting that service only to responsibilities designated for me, but simply being obedient to those opportunities which the Lord so readily presents. I find there are so many. The task is to discern priorities.

Mrs. Major Dudley Coles
This Was Their Call

The call to service cannot yield place to any human consideration.

The Armoury Commentary
The Four Gospels
Frederick Coutts, Edit.

When Christians are untrue to their calling, the initiative passes to other hands.

The Armoury Commentary
The Four Gospels
Frederick Coutts, Edit.

To receive the call to preach is to be entrusted with a treasure; the urge to preach is an appreciation of the value of the treasure; the worthwhileness of that preaching is achieved only as that treasure is delivered as it was first entrusted.

When God Calls You
Edward Deratany

...to serve the present age — not to flabbergast or bamboozle it — my calling to fulfill.

Erik Leidzen
This Man Leidzen
Leslie Fossey

When leaders place a commercial value upon their high calling, they inevitably become "as other men" and spiritual disaster follows.

Search the Scriptures
Robert Hoggard

That sacred call; that glorious hazard of one's all; that love and devotion to our Lord; that pledge to live and die beneath the flag with the fiery star, are not marketable. These values are above price, neither bought nor sold, cannot be measured by law or finance, but are known and honored by God.

The House of my Pilgrimage
Albert Orsborn

Most young people choose what *they* will do for God. But the Word of God insists, "Ye have not chosen Me, but I have chosen you." For a Christian to assert his own will in opposition to the mind of Christ is not just crazy, it is high treason!

God has a plan for every life. We are expected to know His will for our lives. He has promised to reveal it to us unmistakably as though a Voice had spoken, "This is the way, walk ye in it."

Called to Life Service
Lyell Rader

Whilst my call was not blinding it certainly has been and continues to be binding.

Derrick Tribble
This Was Their Call

It is never wise to act hastily when one's calling is at stake. The Holy Spirit must be granted time to penetrate the smokescreen of rationalization we instinctively create in such circumstances, in the hope of justifying our selfish motives. Any serious contemplation of a divine call should exclude selfish consideration and look instead at the Lord who calls.

A Burning in My Bones
Clarence Wiseman

Officers are not called by the Army but by the Lord of the Army. Neither are their appointments made by the Army. Even though the Army is responsible for distributing appointments, it does so only under the guidance of the Lord through the Holy Spirit. Unless the path of witness and service leads through Jesus Christ, it becomes a blind alley.

A Burning in my Bones
Clarence Wiseman

Change

The more men change, the surer God will be; the more they forget, the more He will remember; the further they withdraw, the nearer He will come.

Bramwell Booth
The Trumpets of the Lord
Catherine Bramwell-Booth

The sun, the astronomers tell us, is burning itself away. The everlasting hills are only everlasting in a figure; for they, too, are crumbling day by day. Time is writing wrinkles on the whole world and all that is therein. But, above it all, I see standing — my unchanging God.

Bramwell Booth
The Trumpets of the Lord
Catherine Bramwell-Booth

The wild rose can only be a wild rose, a thistle can only be a thistle; to man only God gave the power to change his way.

Messages to the Messengers
Catherine Bramwell-Booth

What a calamity it must be when a husband's affection for his wife, or a daugh-ter's love for her mother, changes into indifference, hatred, or something more dreadful still. It seems to me that there is only one change which could cause more pain to a human heart, and that would be if the Savior were to change.

The Founder's Messages
to Soldiers
William Booth

Character

God wants to build us up in holy character, but holy character is for eternity and is many sided, and therefore must be subjected to manifold testings. We must be taught by both pain and pleasure, we must learn how to abound and to suffer need. And in this we shall often be plunged from the heights to the depths, and hurled from the depths to the heights again.

Heart Talks on Holiness
Samuel Logan Brengle

A man reveals his natural bent not in some prepared statement but in his unstudied responses.

The Armoury Commentary
The Four Gospels
Frederick Coutts, Edit.

To see the true character of a man, look into his heart when he faces imminent and inevitable death.

Search the Scriptures
Robert Hoggard

A man deserves to be called great-hearted only as his character shows kindness added to courage, and humility added to achievement.

Christ's Cabinet
William McIntyre

We must yet climb on and up to reach Christ's full appreciation of the worth of man. With Him the only real human worth is character, not the size of the body, brains, bank accounts, titles, houses, automobiles, or fashions. Character is the charter and proclamation of worth with Jesus.

Christ's Cabinet
William McIntyre

You take care of your character and God will take care of your reputation.

Clifton Sipley

If character is capable of degeneration it is also capable of regeneration.

Meditations for the
Ordinary Man
George B. Smith

Children

Only the lowly and the wise
Hear the victory in infant cries!

Reflections
Catherine Baird

God expects all parents that they work with Him in the making of their children into men and women after the pattern of their Lord. The little child is the clay in the mother's hands — she is the potter; it is the father's workshop — he is the worker.

Bramwell Booth
Trumpets of the Lord
Catherine Bramwell-Booth

Children brought up without love are like plants brought up without sunshine.

Catherine Booth
Mrs. Booth
W.T. Stead

Regenerate the parents, and you will save the children

Catherine Booth
The Words of Catherine Booth
Cyril Barnes

A father who never dandles his child on his knee cannot have a very keen sense of the responsibilities of paternity.

In Darkest England and the Way Out
William Booth

Ah! hope sings in my soul! There is another generation coming along — a generation that is being nursed at the breast and rocked at the cradle on purpose to fulfill this saving mission; who, amidst their toys, and lessons, and alphabets, and arithmetic, and grammar are being fired with a Soldier's ambition. In their boyish and girlish imaginings and plannings and castle building they are being inspired with their ambition and filled with that purpose — that highest and holiest purpose of living and fighting and dying in the suffering track of their Master.

The General's Letters
William Booth

God speed the rising race! Mothers and fathers, captains and lieutenants, sergeants and soldiers, help the little ones! Spend time and money and strength in teaching and training them. Possess their minds with the trust. Teach them your music, and hurry them on in every possible way to get ready for the flight!

William Booth
God's Army
Cyril Barnes

I want you to know that the children are His property. They belong to Him. He has bought and paid for them with His precious blood. They are not given you to be your playthings, or to feed your vanity, or to add to your income, or to render you some personal service merely, regardless of the Kingdom of God. Your children are the property of Jesus Christ. They are intended to follow in His footsteps, and to be lovers of souls and saviors of men. I want you to realize that Jesus Christ loves you, children. When He said, "Suffer the little children to come unto me" — and He is saying still — He meant *your* children. He loves *them*.

The Founder's Messages to Soldiers
William Booth

Perhaps it is through thinking that I might have been a Captain myself, or perhaps a Divisional Officer, if there had been anybody to make me a Junior Soldier; or, perhaps it is through having seen the children of so many of my neighbors, and some of our Soldiers, grow up to be drunkards and ne'er-do-wells, for want of being taken hold of when they were young.

Sergeant-Major Do-Your-Best
William Booth

If half or a quarter of the labor devoted to the old were given to the young, we should reap twice the fruits; nay, possibly sevenfold. It is easier to bend a sapling than to bend an oak.

Heart Messages
Emma Booth-Tucker

He stands among us today; we who are in the forefront of the fray, upon whose spirits the burden of the war presses, and upon whose ears the clash and crash of a thousand claims hourly fall. And amid all our plans and schemes for the ingathering of the parents, He pleads on behalf of the children "Let them come! Forbid them not! Unto Me!"

Heart Messages
Emma Booth-Tucker

The largest lake would soon evaporate but for the streams that are continually pouring their waters into it. Nay, the ocean itself would dry up but for those perpetual supplies. The river, in turn, borrows its water from a thousand tiny fills, and these again owe their existence to insignificant snowflakes and raindrops. It is the same with the children. There is not a church or nation in the world which would not come to a speedy end, if it were not perpetually recruited by the children. Cut off from your Corps, or from the Army, this source of increase — allow (as we too frequently do) even our own Army children to go to swell the ranks of surrounding organizations — and our future is surely doomed.

Heart Messages
Emma Booth-Tucker

Do not choose ease and wealth and worldly power and fame for your children, but rather choose the lowly way of the Cross

Heart Talks on Holiness
Samuel Logan Brengle

If parents have trained their children so wisely as to hold their deep affection, while commanding their highest respect, there will come a time when a look will be weightier than law, and the character of the loved and esteemed parent will exert a greater authority to mold and fashion the child in righteousness than anything a parent can say or do.

Ancient Prophets
Samuel Logan Brengle

A child is in the twilight; things are as yet dim, mysterious; but it is the twilight, remember, of dawn, not of evening

Mildred Duff
Mildred Duff
Madge Unsworth

'Tis better by far to seek Him in childhood's tender days,
Before the heart is hardened by traveling sin's dark ways;
For evil surely severs the mind and heart from Him;
Who wants to make us happy by keeping us from sin.

Frederick G. Hawkes
Salvation Army Song Book

If the highest virtue is to be childlike, then the most dispicable sin must be to mistreat a child...Then you see this ugly evil arising that we call, for want of a better name, "child abuse". Indescribable, unbelievable horror, it's a sin against human nature itself. The basic mothering and fathering instincts are destroyed. I suspect that in the eyes of Jesus this must be the most despicable sin on record — spiritually, socially, physically or intellectually – destroy the life of a child.

O Boundless Salvation
John D. Waldron

Christian

Our glory and strength are found, not in splendid temples and vast cathedrals, but in union with Christ in sharing His cross, in bearing His burdens, in possessing His lowly, loving, sacrificial Spirit. If we have this Spirit we shall go from strength to strength; we shall pass on a heritage of faith and love and holy example to our children. We shall have a crown of life, a crown of life that fadeth not away. We shall see Jesus. We shall be like Him — and we shall be satisfied.

Samuel Logan Brengle
The Holy Spirit – Friend and Counsellor
Milton S. Agnew

True Christian living not only is good but looks good.

The Call to Holiness
Frederick Coutts

There is no general way of being a Christian — there are many specific ways.

A Burning in My Bones
Clarence Wiseman

Christianity

Christianity is as much a spirit as a practice, and herein it differs from all other religions and ethical systems, inasmuch as the practice of it is impossible without the infusion of the living spirit of the Author. A man must live, by Christ and in Christ, a supernatural life before he can exemplify the principles, or practice or precepts of Christianity; they are too high for unrenewed human nature, it cannot attain unto them.

Catherine Booth
Mrs. Booth
W.T. Stead

The only kind of Christianity which is of any value today is the personal, fully-surrendered and sanctified kind, which, in spirit, completely separates from the world and is set in opposition to selfish aims and ambitions.

George Carpenter
The Privilege of All Believers
John D. Waldron, Edit.

The virility of Christianity as a religion, surrounded and challenged by a score of other religions, stands or falls with its ability or inability to perform miracles in the lives of its adherents.

Out of the Depths
Clarence W. Hall

Dying paganism tries hard to infiltrate into dawning Christianity.

Henri Bacquet
Congo Crusade
Albert Kenyon

We do not accept the doctrine of the Apostolic succession in the same way that some do, and yet we do believe in the Apostolic succession – the succession of men who have the Apostolic spirit, the spirit of self-emptiness, the power of witnessing, men who know facts, who can talk about facts, who realize that Christ is risen, and who want to tell the world of the Saviour whom they love.

Christ's Cabinet
William McIntyre

Christlikeness

Christlikeness is the best one-word definition in the English language for holiness.

The Southern Spirit
Andrew S. Miller

The clearness of our vision will decide our likeness to the Model.

Messages to the Messengers
Catherine Bramwell-Booth

A spark from the fire is like the fire. The tiniest twig on the giant oak or the vine and is in that respect like the oak or the vine. A drop of water on the end of your finger from the ocean is like the ocean; not in size, of course, for the big ships cannot float upon it nor the big fishes swim in it: but it is like the ocean in its essence, in its character, in its nature. Just so, a holy person is like God.

The Way of Holiness
Samuel Logan Brengle

Holiness consists in having something taken from us and in having our spiritual nature made over in the image of Jesus.

Heart Talks on Holiness
Samuel Logan Brengle

The closer we come to the pattern given by Jesus, the more and more important other people become to us.

Religion With a Punch
George Carpenter

25

Christmas

If the Babe had not lain in the manger, then the Man would not have been nailed to the tree, and the Lamb that was slain would not have taken His place on the Everlasting Throne.

Bramwell Booth
Trumpets of the Lord
Catherine Bramwell-Booth, Edit.

Jesus, a Saviour born,
    Without:
Without the inn, refused with scorn.
    Cast out:
Cast out for me, my Saviour King,
Cast out to bring this lost one in.

Bramwell Booth
Papers on Godliness
Catherine Booth

The Divine condescension never appears so new and so real to us as when we stand at the side of this lowly cradle. Here are no high sounding doctrines, no hard words, no terrible commands, no faroff thunders of a new Sinai, no rumblings of a coming judgment. Here we see Jesus and Jesus only. God joined in that Babe His great strength to our great nothingness.

Bramwell Booth
Trumpets of the Lord
Catherine Bramwell-Booth, Edit.

Only one sight is lovelier under Heaven than a soul turning in its confessed weakness and heartbroken sorrow to Jesus, and that is the sight so peculiarly representative of Christmas, that which involves the love and effort of others in the sinner's behalf.

Heart Messages
Emma Booth-Tucker

We cannot now look out across the snows of nineteen centuries upon that first Christmas scene of long ago and say that wrought that victory, or that glory did it, or that honor did it, or that wealth did it, for every bell that rings, and every lip that sings carols the fact that the victory which over-came was the victory of love, and love demonstrated in the personality of a little Christ.

Heart Messages
Emma Booth-Tucker

While some smile, others weep; perhaps not openly, yet the tears are nonetheless bitter because unrevealed. Sorrow never tires, never sleeps, never dies. It is always there, and its shadows seem the gloomier from the brilliant contrast presented by the light and glow of Christmas cheer.

Heart Messages
Emma Booth-Tucker

When He comes
At midnight,
He does not
Ask a tree;
A creche,
A star
A candle —
Only me.

Wind Chimes
Sallie Chesham

Christmas reminds us that as we are loved of God we can afford to let go our defensive isolation.

The Soldier's Armoury — The Four Gospels
Frederick Coutts, Edit.

For the shepherds the most astonishing thing about that night which was so full of surprises must have been the commonplace scene of the manger. Surely the splendor of the angelic appearance, and the ecstacy of the heavenly chorus, must have been but the prelude to something more "out of this world". But no! Bethlehem had nothing more unusual to show than a mother weary from the labor of childbirth, an anxious, vigilant father, and a Baby unfortunate enough to be born in a stable. Yet in this ordinary situation the shepherds did not experience an anticlimax; they discovered God.

The Soldier's Armoury — The Four Gospels
Frederick Coutts, Edit.

When the time had fully come — and God is never a moment early or late — there appeared, not the horses and chariots of military might nor the awesome sight of angelic hosts bent on battle, but a helpless little Babe lying in a manager!

Search the Scriptures
Robert Hoggard

Sever Christmas from Good Friday and the result would be to doom Christmas to nothing more than a time to be merry and gay based on lore.

The Creche and the Cross
Hulda C. Miller

Lord, help me to keep Christmas unhurried. Let me make a soft manger bed of worship in my heart for You and take time for adoration of the Babe of Christmas

Dear God
Virginia Talmadge

Churches

Salvationists do not see it as their God-given task to *protest* against the doctrines or practices of other Christians, but to *attest* the Gospel message about the saving work of Christ.

Chosen to be a Soldier

The Salvation Army does not compete with the Churches. It is a friend to the churchless.

Blood and Fire
Edward Bishop

Of the great Church of the living God, we claim, and have ever claimed, that we of The Salvation Army are an integral part and element — a living fruit bearing branch in the true vine.

Bramwell Booth
William Booth's First Gentleman
Harry Williams

Beware of imitating the churches. Keep seperate from them. Allow no interchange of pulpits. Permit no singing by outsiders on our platforms. If choirs, or others, wish to give you a service of song, let this be done in their own buildings or hire a hall

for the occasion. I call upon each of you to take your stand in these matters.

Friendship With Jesus
Florence Booth

You are sent to deal with all whose hearts you can unlock, but not to encroach upon the work of churches and chapels.

Powers of Salvation Army Officers
Florence Booth

Some Officers venture altogether too close to the methods of the denominations, and wherever that is done two things inevitably follow — a smaller number of penitents and a decline in the fighting spirit of the Soldiers!

Steward of God
Edward J. Higgins

We were not, and are not, opposed to the church, but we feel we were raised by God to present religion in a different way to the masses outside the church orbit.

The House of My Pilgrimage
Albert Orsborn

The other churches need us, not to come up with some pale imitation of what they do, but to complement their outreach by doing what only The Salvation Army can!

Marching On!
Ted Palmer

To be invited to take our posts on the bridge of the ship with other clergy is very flattering and may be thought necessary. To share fine food and conversation in the captain's lounge with other Christians is enriching and justifiable. But then, who is going to stand at the deck rails and throw out the lifeline to the drowning souls who can barely be seen in the dark waters of these times?

Marching On!
Ted Palmer

We don't judge other Christian groups based upon how convenient to or compatible with us they are: We accept them so long as God sees fit to permit their existence and their use of His name.

Marching On!
Ted Palmer

We are an army of soldiers of Christ, organized as perfectly as we have been able to accomplish, seeking no church status, avoiding as we would the plague, every denominational rut, in order perpetually to reach more and more of those who lie outside every church boundary.

Heathen England
George Scott Railton

Cleansing

From every stain made clean,
From every sin set free;
O blessed Lord, this is the gift,
That Thou hast promised me.
And pressing through the past
Of failure, fault and fear,
Before Thy Cross my soul I cast,
And dare to leave it there.

Herbert Booth
Salvation Army Song Book

My sins they are many, their stains are so deep,
And bitter the tears of remorse that I weep;
But useless is weeping, thou great crimson sea;
Thy waters can cleanse me, come, roll over me!

William Booth
Salvation Army Song Book

You cannot make a man clean by washing his shirt.

William Booth
Blood and Fire
Edward Bishop

One truth I learned, Lord,
Is that partial cleansing is worse than none.
One polished window shows up the grimy ones;
having begun, one has to finish.
My thoughts moved along that thread,
discovering its spiritual dimensions.
A word from Your Book came to my mind with singular comfort:
"He who has begun in you a good work will continue it."

Between You and Me, Lord
Flora Larsson

Deep were the scarlet stains of sin.
Strong were the bonds of fault within;
But now I stand both pure and free,
The Blood of Jesus cleanses me.

Olive Holbrook
Salvation Army Song Book

Light, life and love are in that healing fountain.
All I require to cleanse me and restore;
Flow through my soul, redeem its desert places,
And make a garden there for the Lord I adore.

Albert Orsborn
Salvation Army Song Book

Saviour, if my feet have faltered
On the pathway of the cross,
If my purposes have altered
Or my gold be mixed with dross,
O forbid me not Thy service,
Keep me yet in Thy employ,
Pass me through a sterner cleansing
If I may but give Thee joy!

Albert Orsborn
Salvation Army Song Book

Wash from my hands the dust of earthly striving;
Take from my mind the stress of secret fears;
Cleanse Thou the wounds from all but Thee far hidden
And when the waters flow let my healing appear.

Albert Orsborn
Salvation Army Song Book

Jesus, save me through and through,
Save me from self-mending;
Self-salvation will not do,
Pass me through the cleansing.

William Pearson
Salvation Army Song Book

Lord Jesus, if still I do not fully bow,
If anything wrong in myself I allow,
O search out and to me my evil ways show!
Lord, wash me, and I shall be whiter than snow.

George Scott Railton
Salvation Army Song Book

I can't imagine the angry waves, the violent winds and the whipping and lashing that broke the beach accessories, eroded big chunks of earth, sand and sod. The heaving and breathing of the ocean had washed up debris from years of living. The ocean had cleansed itself but it took a storm to do it.

Dear God
Virginia Talmadge

Purge the dark halls of thought,
Here let Thy work be wrought,
Each wish and feeling brought
Captive to Thee.

Leslie Taylor-Hunt
Salvation Army Song Book

Compassion

I do here declare that I will never treat any woman, child, or other person whose life, comfort or happiness may be placed within my power, in an oppressive, cruel or cowardly manner, but that I will protect such from evil and danger, so far as I can, and promote, to the utmost of my ability, their present welfare and eternal salvation.

The Articles of War

For God is now and God is here,
Not hidden in some shadowy sphere.
Who stoops to heed another's cry
Shall touch His hand and reach the sky.

Reflections
Catherine Baird

Should I be blind to human ills
    And deaf to human cries,
If I ignore imploring hands
    Or children's anguished eyes,
Though my name shine across the world,
    My dreams contented swell,
I shall wake up some bitter day
    To find myself in Hell.

Geoffrey Allen
Book of Salvationist Verse
Catherine Baird, Edit.

Go to the graveyard, the prison, the hospital, the lunatic asylum; go down into the slums and the dens of Hell on earth, where the Devil is transforming men and women into fiends and training little children to grow up to be damned; go and look and think until you feel, until your whole soul rises up and cries out to God: "Who is sufficient for these things?" Mingle your tears with the tears of those who weep; groan and travail and struggle with those who are in darkness; wring your hands for those who sink; say with Paul: "I would (even) wish myself accursed from Christ... for my kinsmen according to the flesh."

Bramwell Booth
Trumpets of the Lord
Catherine Bramwell-Booth, Edit.

Someone is weak and discouraged,
Someone is weary of life;
Someone is fighting hard battles,
All is confusion and strife.
My prayer when the daybreak is dawning,
Ascends on its heavenly way:
Thou Saviour of sinners, I pray Thee,
Help me to help someone today.

More Poems of a Salvationist
Irena Arnold

Show mercy. No soul ever was made poor by loving too much, or injured by forgiving too often.

Messages to the Messengers
Catherine Bramwell-Booth

Comrades, whatever other gifts you have, if you are to succeed, you must have hearts, and hearts that can feel.

Salvation Soldiery
William Booth

How many compassionate tears does this world get from you?

The Founder's Messages to Soldiers
William Booth

I must go, not only to those who need me, but to those who need me most.

William Booth
The Officer — 1893

I think sometimes that the Salvationists have been a sort of second edition of Jesus Christ weeping over Jerusalem, with the difference that through His compassion wrought in our hearts, our tears have been shed over the sins and miseries of the whole world.

International Congress Addresses — 1904
William Booth

It (the world) believes in the survival of the fit...The Salvation Army believes in the salvation of the unfit.

William Booth
History of The Salvation Army Volume 3
Robert Sandall

While women weep, as they do now, I'll fight; while little children go hungry, as they do now, I'll fight; while men go to prison, in and out, in and out, as they do now, I'll fight; while there is a drunkard left, while there is a poor lost girl upon the streets, while there remains one dark soul without the light of God, I'll fight — I'll fight to the very end!

William Booth
The Founder Speaks Again
Cyril Barnes, Edit.

Do not the needs and struggles of your own heart teach you to yearn for those who are only beginners?

Messages to the Messengers
Catherine Bramwell-Booth

Keep your hearts tender, even if it hurts more when it gets trampled on.

Messages to the Messengers
Catherine Bramwell-Booth

A tear may often win when every other force fails, and who can say but that what this world of sin and woe most needs, with its cold and indifferent millions, is not so much the courage or the faith or the ability of bygone Christians, but beyond and above all other things the heart made tender as was even the Lamb of God's by sanctified suffering!

Heart Messages
Emma Booth-Tucker

If the cleansed man is a superior, it makes him patient and considerate; if a subordinate, willing and obedient. It is the fruitful

root of courtesy, of compassion and of utterly unselfish devotion.

Heart Talks on Holiness
Samuel Logan Brengle

True charity has no fellowship with deeds of darkness. It never calls evil good, it does not wink at iniquity, but it is as far removed from this sharp, condemning spirit as light is from darkness, as honey is from vinegar. It is quick to condemn sin, but is full of saving, longsuffering compassion for the sinner.

When the Holy Ghost is Come
Samuel Logan Brengle

Who have been the mightiest and most faithful preachers of the gloom and terror and pain of a perpetual Hell? Those who have been the mightiest and most effective preachers of God's compassionate love.

When the Holy Ghost is Come
Samuel Logan Brengle

We may not be a part of this kind of organized thrust, but we can appoint ourselves one man listening teams. The world is full of voices crying out for help. Listen! Don't you hear the lonely man? Listen! Don't you hear the sorrow in that voice, the discouragement in that one, the bewilderment in that one?

It Seems To Me
Philip E. Collier

Make no mistake — it is easier to think lovingly of a crowd than actually to love an individual man, woman or child into the Kingdom.

The Armoury Commentary — The Four Gospels
Frederick Coutts, Edit.

These are human tragedies brought on by human beings. They can be as destructive as natural tragedies, or more so, and often as unavoidable. The Salvation Army cares for both kinds — the woes mankind inflicts on himself, and the ones that are the result of nature's erratic course.

A Gentle Warfare
Lawrence Fellows

Consecrated indeed must be the hands and hearts of those nurses and attendants who give their lives to cleaning and scrubbing inside and out those human rubbish heaps for whom cleanliness has long since lost it attraction

Out of the Depths
Clarence W. Hall

Do I matter?
That's a vital question for me, Master.
Among so many others does my life count for anything?
I believe it does, Lord, to You, the Creator of life itself
Who feels a pang of loss
When the heart of a sparrow stills.
You have granted me the gift of life,
    So I must matter to You.

I'm Growing Lord!
Flora Larsson

Except I am moved with compassion,
    How dwelleth Thy Spirit in me?
In word and in deed,
Burning love is my need;
    I know I can find this in Thee.

Albert Orsborn
Salvation Army Song Book

Great Son of God! Thy sympathies,
We thank Thy name, are still with men;
Not on the mountain height alone
But with the people in this plain;
Down on the hard and dusty road,
The pavement of our common life.
Where weary pilgrims lift the load
And hardpressed soldiers wage the strife.

The Beauty of Jesus
Albert Orsborn

Let's be hurt by the hurting of others. Let's shun anything and everything that might stain our holy Movement, except the stain of a tear.

Marching On!
Ted Palmer

May God send us a deep, all consuming concern for the souls of our neighbors, that shall rend our hearts, and bow our souls and make our lives one ceaseless flow of the sweetest, tenderest compassion

for the wretched blinded victims of sin, whose looks of horror and anguish before the Judgment Seat of Christ will otherwise recall to us many a listless, unfeeling prayer, and many a hard, emotionless speech.

George Scott Railton
G.S.R.
John D. Waldron, Edit.

What a royal quality is compassion! It has power to transform the small soul of man into a big hearted man. The compassionate souls are not only the salt of the earth; they are the world's true royalty — God's elite.

Charles Rich
The Officer's Review — 1936

Complacency

Our own great danger is of settling into ruts and being satisfied with a little when we might do more.

Frederick Booth-Tucker
The Officer — 1893

Compromise

A true Salvationist desires to have no part in conduct which:
(a) Comes short of a proper respect for another person,
(b) Results in guilty secretiveness,
(c) Brings into question his own Christian reputation.

Orders and Regulations for Corps Officers

Compromise with the world will not make it any better! Compromise with the world always fails. It pulls down the man who proposes it and never raises up anyone else.

Bramwell Booth
Trumpets of the Lord
Catherine Bramwell-Booth, Edit.

Alas! alas! for the man who wishes to please his friends and to please God into the bargain. God is likely to have a very poor place in the arrangements, and the man worse still.

Twenty-One Years' Salvation Army
William Booth

31

The Lord has called us to a great work. We must not be content with a small one.

William Booth
The History of The Salvation Army — Volume 1
Robert Sandall

Lowering the standard? No; raising it! Losing sight of the ideal? No; drawing near to complete the perfect details! But you see how the very capacity for this involves capacity for the opposite — susceptibility to evil influences. So the devil works.

Messages to the Messengers
Catherine Bramwell-Booth

A stick that is about straight is crooked.

Samuel Logan Brengle
Peace Like a River
Sallie Chesham

But for all its superficial attractiveness the line of least resistance is frequently the way of disaster.

The Armoury Commentary — The Four Gospels
Frederick Coutts, Edit.

Some people's love of peace makes them little but troublemakers; for their policy of peace at any price, causing them to leave undisturbed unjust situations, and to "patch up" quarrels without dealing with basic antagonisms, makes harmonious human relationships finally impossible.

The Armoury Commentary — The Four Gospels
Frederick Coutts, Edit.

Each temptation was the offer of a way easier than the Cross; it was an alternative to the way of love.

Power and Glory
Harry Dean

As we mix with our fellows and hear of their experiences of life, it becomes evident that with sadly too many there is a great struggle between ideals and actualities... how often the highest is neglected.

Fuel for Sacred Flame
T. Henry Howard

Confession

The confession is as necessary as the believing. We insist upon this in the matter of justification and it is equally important in the matter of sanctification. If we do not testify definitely, humbly and constantly to the blessed experience, we put our light under a bushel and it goes out.

Heart Talks on Holiness
Samuel Logan Brengle

Confession to God is a primary need of the human heart.

The Mercy Seat
William Burrows

Confidence

One prayed — "Lord our knees shake, our hearts shake, our heads shake — then You say 'be still I am God'" — and we say 'we cannot be still we tremble so much' — then You say 'When you are quiet you are strong' — and we hold Your hand and all the shaking stops.

Quoted in
The House of My Pilgrimage
Albert Orsborn

Conflict

His business is not to argue; it is to offer the grace of God in time of need.

Orders and Regulations for Officers

The Army will not be party to encouraging divisions in the Church of God by pronouncing on views that must remain speculative and are no part of the universal Christian faith.

Chosen to be a Soldier

I am of Paul and I am of Apollos soon leads, so far as the actuality is concerned, to being nothing save wrangling and the devil.

Salvation Soldiery
William Booth

Remember that no good can ever be served by a conflict whether with the roughs or with the police. The best officers are those who can desperately attack the largest number of people with the least amount of disturbance of any sort from them.

William Booth
The History of the Salvation Army – Volume 2
Robert Sandall

Another common mistake is to spend all your powder and shot over some cantankerous, argumentative infidel or backslider, instead of giving him a broadside and passing on.

Frederick Booth-Tucker
The Officer — 1893

Arguments about religion or politics almost always generate more heat than light.

It Seems to Me
Phillip Collier

Conscience

Conscience is a witness of God's own appointment; it stands, as it were, an impartial judge between God and the sinner. You cannot bribe your conscience even now to swerve one iota from the light that is in it — you cannot make it say that is right which it feels is wrong. You may refuse to listen to it, and you may act contrary to its teaching; but it will mutter its condemnation even here. What an *awful witness* to be against you in the day of wrath!

Life and Death
Catherine Booth

Conscience is an INSEPARABLE COMPANION: it goes with us wherever we go, and notes whatever we do. It is with us all through life, and in death: and when the soul and body part, the soul and conscience do not part, but go together into the next world; so that its record exists for every moment of our lives, from the dawn of reason to the last thought in death.

Life and Death
Catherine Booth

The conscience is not the voice of God within us — there are too many shades of

conscience for that to be possible — it is a voice of God and right in our hearts.

From My Treasure Chest
Flora Larsson

Deep within the heart of him,
A goaded conscience tortured him.
An ancient venom, old as Adam's race,
Worked ceaselessly within his sinful mind.

Memoirs of Peter
Arthur Pitcher

Consecration

I dedicate myself to Thee,
O Master, who hast chosen me;
My every selfish aim denying,
I give my all on Thee relying;
   Take Thou my life and use me as Thy will;
   In deep submission I dedicate myself to Thee.

Brindley Boon
Book of Salvationist Verse
Catherine Baird, Edit.

Jesus calls where'er the suffering
Bear their anguish all alone,
Homeless, loveless, lost and fainting,
Needing bread, yet offered stone;
Calls for intellect and will,
Calls for dedicated skill.

Reflections
Catherine Baird

If you want to understand how much the Lord will give you, kneel down. Come and give your all first. He never gives the sugar plum *until* we've done the lesson. He never shows us the light *until* we've gone through the tunnel. He didn't show Abraham the ram *until* he had taken the knife to slay his son.

On the Banks of the River
Bramwell Booth

You may bring Him your gifts, and your head-faith, and your church creeds, and your dead formal services, or whatever else you like, but He will not accept them, and in the day of judgment He will say, "You never gave me your heart!"

Life and Death
Catherine Booth

Canst Thou my poor treasure take
And my heart Thy temple make;
Can my sins for Thy dear sake,
Be washed away?

Herbert Booth
Salvation Army Song Book

Every day it seems plainer to me that nothing tremendous will be accomplished till we have a force of people willing to dash pearls to atoms, trample on worldly pleasure, wealth, ease, reputation and all else and even life itself.

The General's Letters
William Booth

For a full salvation you must bring an undivided consecration.

Salvation Soldiery
William Booth

Giving God the best means receiving the best. Many people who have really not had time to think a great deal about themselves as individuals, but who have consistently been giving to God their best, will be surprised to find how beautiful they themselves have become. That, partly, is the reason why real saints seldom know that they are saints. It is as though God bestows His beautifying touches on our souls when we are wholly taken up with making something else as good as we know how for Him.

Messages to the Messengers
Catherine Bramwell-Booth

What have you to give? Your young heart's love; its faith, its prayers, and its praise. How shall you give? As you will be advised in different ways from time to time. Sparingly? As people shall deserve it of you? Think; if you had only received from God what you deserved! Will you give in harmony with the giving of others; or generously, honorably; that is, as you promised, keeping faith with your own heart's intentions? Will you give bountifully — more than people have deserved of you; freely — without thought of getting anything for yourself in return, though you often will, for it is marvellously true that with what measure ye mete, it shall be measured to

you again? Will you give courageously; in spite, that is, of other people's sneers or ridicule? To be generous in your opinion of praise of another when some are criticizing and minimizing their work, demands real courage. Give "not meanly"; that is, when you have a chance of bestowing your love and care, do it as though there were enough and to spare, not as though you were giving as little as possible.

Messages to the Messengers
Catherine Bramwell-Booth

But standing here in spite on Mount Calvary, we see and feel that to be like Him we must spend ourselves as unreservedly in His cause as the worldling is spent in the cause of self; that we must toil for Him as the miser toils for himself; sacrifice for Him as the explorer does for science.

Heart Messages
Emma Booth-Tucker

Sixty-five years old today. Lord, here and now and forever, I consecrate my spared life to Thy service to be, to do, to think, to plan all that Thou dost desire. Take me, make me, break me, but do not forsake me, or suffer me to forsake Thee!

Diary of Frederick Booth-Tucker quoted in
William Booth's First Gentleman
Harry Williams

When from sin's dark hold Thy love had won me,
    And its wounds Thy tender hands had healed,
As Thy blest commands were laid upon me,
    Growing light my growing need revealed.
Thus I sought the path of consecration
    When to Thee, dear Lord, my vows were given;
And the joy which came with full salvation,
    Winged my feet and filled my heart with heaven.

Will J. Brand
Salvation Army Song Book

We have put all on the altar to get it. We must keep all on the altar to keep it.

Heart Talks on Holiness
Samuel Logan Brengle

I cannot pray that others may do the Lord's will unless and until I myself am already committed to that will. I must say, "Here am I; send me"before I begin to pray that my fellow believers may answer God's call.

The Armoury Commentary — The Four Gospels
Frederick Coutts, Edit.

If I could live one more life I would give it to God in exactly the same way.

Mildred Duff
Mildred Duff
Madge Unsworth

'Tis true; the power of fearing is my own;
But e'en that gift must needs at first be given
From every ownership and right I'm driven,
My sacred stewardship remains alone.

Erik Leidzen
This Man Leidzen
Leslie Fossey

You must all be as good as you can. You must all work as hard as you can. You must keep the flag flying as high as you can. Do good to all men, and let mercy and justice triumph throughout the world.

Edward J. Higgins
Storm Pilot
William G. Harris

Here I lay me at Thy bleeding feet,
    Deepest homage now I give to Thee;
Hear Thy whispered love within my soul;
    Jesus, Thou art everything to me.

Edward H. Joy
Salvation Army Song Book

This is where I failed many times, and I have found scores of other souls who have failed on this very point. They come sincerely to the altar, definitely laying their gift there, a living sacrifice; but when the knife is felt, the realization of the dying comes upon them as they feel the hurt and understand fully what it means, they shrink and draw back.

Kate Lee
The Privilege of All Believers
John D. Waldron

Jesus can do wonders with meager material placed unreservedly in His hands.

Christ's Cabinet
William McIntyre

As you tread the road to Calv'ry, some may bring their tears,
Some may help to ease the burden which upon you bears.
But the great renunciation you must make alone!
There the heart must break
For our Redeemer's sake,
And the gift must be your own.

The Beauty of Jesus
Albert Orsborn

My life must be Christ's broken bread,
    My love His outpoured wine,
A cup o'erfilled, a table spread
    Beneath His name and sign,
That other souls, refreshed and fed,
    May share His life through mine.

Albert Orsborn
The Salvation Army Song Book

There are times when we dare not say, even to our closest supporters, all that is in our consecration. In our work as colaborers with Christ we have to take very lonely paths..

The Silences of Christ
Albert Orsborn

His responsibility — to spark the flame,
    Ours — to be willing to be lit;
His responsibility — to empower the light,
    Ours — to shine where the darkness is deepest.
His responsibility — to provide the fuel for burning,
    Ours — to keep in touch with the source.

God's Whispers in my Heart
Shirley Pavey

35

I'm set apart for Jesus,
To be a king and priest;
His life in me increases,
Upon His love I feast.
From evil separated,
Made holy by His blood.
My all is consecrated
Unto the living God.

William Pearson
Salvation Army Song Book

No place on earth I own,
No field, no house be mine;
Myself, my all I still disown,
My God, let all be Thine.
Into Thy gracious hands
My life is ever placed;
To die fulfilling Thy commands
I march with bounding haste.

George Scott Railton
Salvation Army Song Book

Bring your time and bring your talents,
Bring the gift which costs you pain;
Bring your best, your dearest treasure
Let God have His own again.

Barbara Stoddart
Salvation Army Song Book

Consistency

We must not divorce conduct from character, or works from faith. Our lives must square with our teaching. We must live what we preach. We must not suppose that faith in Jesus excuses us from patient, faithful, laborious service.

When the Holy Ghost is Come
Samuel Logan Brengle

Living the Gospel is always more meaningful than merely talking about it.

The Armoury Commentary — The Four Gospels
Frederick Coutts, Edit.

What a man is, will count for more than the message he utters. For him a flame will go forth that warms, or a deadly chill will freeze the atmosphere. It is the power of God burning in and through the true lover of souls which accomplishes the end.

Kate Lee
The Officer — 1919

Ah, my child, do not belittle your light
because of its size;
Its power lies not in its dimensions
But rather, in its constancy of shining.

God's Whispers in my Heart
Shirley Pavey

Contentment

A man may be gratified with that which is base, but he can be satisfied only by the highest.

Love-Slaves
Samuel Logan Brengle

O that in me this mind might be,
The will of God be all my joy,
Prepared with Him to go or stay,
My chief delight His sweet employ.

Edward H. Joy
Salvation Army Song Book

Conversation

God did not give us words to use idly; they are too powerful and contain too many possibilities. A word may be a dagger, a bullet, a balm, a poison, a serpent, a mine of wealth, a dynamite bomb. It can build or blast a reputation. Then what right have we to be playing with such engines of power without understanding them? Unless you learn to weigh well your words, you are as dangerous as would be a child entrusted with the throttle valve of a mountain locomotive.

The Officer — 1919

That which lies in the well of your heart will come up in the bucket of your speech.

The Officer — 1917

The tongue is like a mint; it may turn out base counters of little or no value, stamped with the sign of earth and earthy things, or coins of pure gold, bearing the image of the Divine. The tongue of the sanctified man or woman may send into circulation words of priceless value.

Bramwell Booth
Trumpets of the Lord
Catherine Bramwell-Booth

Too much talk ruins heaps of people.

Catherine Booth
Words of Catherine Booth
Cyril Barnes

Wise people are seldom great talkers.

Catherine Booth
Words of Catherine Booth
Cyril Barnes

One thing we would just for a moment touch upon, and that is the importance of hurtful words. Oh, how much harm has come to the Kingdom of God, how much spiritual wreckage among the weak and trembling babes in Christ, how many sheep have been driven from the fold never to return to its precincts of security and precious possibility by thoughtless words, words of unkindness, words of calumny — not meant, perhaps, as this, but thoughtlessly spoken, and therefore resulting in the same cruel havoc! Words of cowardice, where words of faithful warning and holy convincing were needed. Words of impatience, where tender entreaty would have won the day. Truly, how great fire a little matter kindleth, and surely if we would have the tender epitaph written across our lives, that we never hurt another, we must beware the magnitude of good and evil that can result from the words we daily speak.

Heart Messages
Emma Booth-Tucker

Here, in the marketplace of words,
Help me, O Lord, to be an honest merchant.

Walking With The Wind
Sallie Chesham

The premeditated word might be deceptive, but the spontaneous utterance — being the overflow of heart and mind — shows the nature of the inner life. "Second thoughts" may be best, but first thoughts declare what we are.,

The Armoury Commentary — The Four Gospels
Frederick Coutts, Edit.

Unresponsive listening results in unrealized spiritual deafness.

The Armoury Commentary — The Four Gospels
Frederick Coutts, Edit.

Words as well as men can be converted.

The Call to Holiness
Frederick Coutts

For words have power! They do not fall on empty air, to be carried away by a passing breeze. They have a life of their own. They pierce deep into sensitive souls, into depressed spirits, into impressive minds. They can provide the right growing ground or they can hinder, devitalize and cripple. A whole lifetime ahead someone may remember a remark we made quite casually today; remember it with gratitude for the boost it gave, or blame us for dampening out a spark of initiative, a good resolve, or jeering at the thought of some act of kindly service.

From My Treasure Chest
Flora Larsson

Swearing is the sin of speech; the explosive expletive is a safety valve to the carnal nature; it is tolerated chiefly because it only seems to harm the influence of the one who swears.

The Christian Charter
George B. Smith

Some people have a way of saying things that hurt and sting,
They're always finding fault with everyone and everything,
The world is full of bitterness according to their views:
Their presence is obnoxious, they would give us all the blues.

Some people have the happy knack of saying pleasant things,
And, oh, the joy and comfort to a body's heart it brings!
It sweetens all the world for us, we feel life is worth while
When pleasant words are spoken and we're greeted with a smile.

More Poems of a Salvationist
Irena Arnold

37

Conversion

It does not signify how we are trained or what were the particular circumstances of our antecedent life: there comes a crisis, a moment when every human soul which enters the Kingdom of God has to make its choice of that Kingdom in preference to everything else that it holds and owns as its world; when it has to renounce its world — all that would constitute the worldly and temporal benefits of that soul — it has to give up all that and embrace and choose God and His righteousness and His Kingdom.

Catherine Booth
Mrs. Booth
W. T. Stead

Bad men were being made good, and in a few weeks their names — these nobodies from working class homes, some with criminal records and many more profane gin swillers — would appear as Lieutenants in charge of mission stations, themselves now writing of their converts.

William Booth's First Gentleman
Harry Williams

Conversion is the pivot of The Salvation Army.

Mrs. Booth
W. T. Stead

Conversion does not make a man different from what God made him; it can only make him what God intended him to be, and that is different from what he has made of himself.

Meditations for the Ordinary Man
George B. Smith

One should never treat as common the miracle of the New Birth.

A Burning in My Bones
Clarence Wiseman

Conviction

What is conviction? Mere opinion is not conviction; prejudice is not conviction; personal preference is not conviction; fanaticism is not conviction. Convictions spring and bloom from truths received into the heart and rooted there.

Powers of Salvation Army Officers
Florence Booth

To hold only convenient convictions, to voice only acceptable views, is to place an insurmountable stumbling block in our pathway, to insure that we will never wholeheartedly believe anything.

The Armoury Commentary — The Four Gospels
Frederick Coutts, Edit.

No church is stronger than the convictions that motivate its people!

Search The Scriptures
Robert Hoggard

A small man may entertain strong opinions; a great man cherishes strong convictions. Opinions cost only breath; convictions may well cost blood.

Manpower for the Master
Bramwell Tillsley

Corps Work

He must not only feel that he is responsible for commanding the Corps, but that he is responsible to God for the salvation of every unsaved man, woman and child in the town or district in which he is appointed.

Why and Wherefore
Bramwell Booth

The salvation or sanctification of souls should be aimed at in every meeting. That is the main object of all Army meetings, and no Officer or Soldier should be satisfied unless this end is accomplished.

Why and Wherefore
Bramwell Booth

It is impossible for a man to be desperately in earnest without making a mark upon somebody. No matter how crooked the corps, how cold the soldiers, how hard the sinners, if you are only a flame of fire you will burn your way through opposing circumstances, and are bound to make advance.

Evangeline Booth
The Officer — 1893

Lay it to heart, my comrades, that an Officer's success and power are manifest in the raising and maintaining of a fighting force. You will not be on the active list forever. Indeed, the year is fixed when your part in the rank will be played out. What we each can do in the fighting line to build up the Kingdom of God will soon be accomplished. Then other voices will issue the orders; other hands will wipe away the tears of the penitent, other brains and hearts will plan for the goodness and happiness of the soldier. Someone else will work for the holiness of the corps. But your works will follow you. They will be seen in the fighting qualities of the soldiers you have trained, in the power and spirit of the Officers who replace you. The Officers who will take the places of those now in command are being raised by their predecessors today.

Powers of Salvation Army Officers
Florence Booth

If an officer is tempted to say that he is not called to do business, but to save souls, he should remember that the business of his corps is an important part of the work of saving souls; indeed that a corps cannot be carried on without it. He should also consider that none is so suited to attend to this business as he who is separated from the ordinary concerns of life.

William Booth
Powers of Salvation Army Officers
Florence Booth

If you want an active, generous, fighting, daredevil Corps, able and willing to drive Hell before it, that Corps must be possessed and that fully, by this spirit of life. Nothing else can effectively take its place. No education, learning, Bible knowledge, theology, social amusements, or anything of the kind will be a satisfactory substitute. The Corps that seeks to put any of these things in the place of life will find them a mockery, a delusion, and a snare; will find them to be only the wraps and trappings of death itself.

The Seven Spirits.
William Booth

Isn't that just what I've been telling you — that the way to make friends and get money for the Corps is to go and get the poor lost creatures saved?

Sergeant-Major Do-Your-Best
William Booth

The best qualification for managing a corps must be to help to make one, and to help to work one.

Salvation Soldiery
William Booth

What is a Salvation Army Corps? To this I reply, that it is a band of people united together to attack and Christianize an entire town or neighborhood.

Salvation Soldiery
William Booth

A Corps Officer has the honor to be chosen for service similar to that our Founder undertook when he first turned to the unchurched masses of the East End of London. To him is committed the spiritual responsibility for the town or part of the town in which he is stationed. He is there to preach in the streets to the people who will not go to places of worship, and by every lawful means to compel them to his hall for help at closer range. He is there to visit the sick, to seek out the drunkard, to visit the police court, to encourage, and lift and lift again the weak and stumbling. He is there to answer letters from anxious parents, to hunt up straying sons and daughters, to rebuke sin; in outbreaks of infectious disease and catastrophes to administer comfort and help to the sorrowing and bereaved; to instruct children; to shepherd and inspire the band of Salvationists already attached to the Corps; to raise money for furtherance of the Army's work. Indeed, little which affects the well being of the populace lies outside the sphere of The Salvation Army Corps Officer.

The Angel Adjutant
Minnie Lindsay Carpenter

Our work is not to gather up fragments of other societies or organizations, or to build up a body out of the limbs of other bodies, but to create a new people for God out of the raw material around us.

Fuel for Sacred Flame
T. Henry Howard

The great, bleeding, throbbing heart of the Salvation Army is to be found in the Corps. Here it is that the weary sinner comes for rest. Here it is that the drunkard expects to find a conquering power; here the thief comes for forgiveness, the harlot for purity, the murderer for the Holy Blood that can wash away bloodstain. Here also comes the cynical, the unbelieving, the one who thinks he has gone too far. For one and all of these hearts there is one key, the one Jesus used...love. On this key, are to be found the prongs of kindness, sympathy, understanding. And, comrades, you may be assured that it will unlock any heart, however hard and resisting.

Henry Milans
Out of the Depths
Clarence W. Hall

Has my corps got the devil on the run? Has it grabbed the attention of sinners, sat them under the ministry of the Holy Spirit through God's Word, and seen them fall at the Mercy Seat in heartfelt repentance? Or have we been losing our 100% purpose as the public was dropping half the name?

Marching On!
Ted Palmer

Some of these corps, particularly the smaller ones, were like oysters. They opened up to emit a pearl, in the shape of a convert who was destined to become an outstanding officer, and then closed up again soon after, sometimes never to reopen.

The History of The Salvation Army — Volume 4
Arch Wiggins

Courage

Where courage lives there also lurks defeat.

Reflections
Catherine Baird

Where are you now when the Son of God is crucified? Where are you now when the interests of truth, righteousness, benevolence, and holiness are trembling in the balance? Have you courage now to stand up for right? If not, you would have it then, for "he that is faithful in little will be faithful in much." Are you today for Jesus or Barabbas?

Catherine Booth
The Life of Catherine Booth
Frederick Booth-Tucker

By courage I mean that quality which makes a man do his duty he sees before him, although the doing of it may be painful, and the consequences of doing it may be more painful still.

William Booth
The Founder Speaks Again
Cyril Barnes

Courage has no banners,
Courage has no drums,
But softly, when the heart asks God,
Courage always comes.

Wind Chimes
Sallie Chesham

Courage is not the absence of fear, but its conquest.

The Armoury Commentary – The Four Gospels
Frederick Coutts, Edit.

As the sound of an approaching crowd reached Him, Jesus rose to meet His foes, for this was no retreat. Right to the very end He took the initiative, selflessly giving Himself, in the realization that there can be no Messiahship without suffering and no salvation without atonement.

Power and Glory
Harry Dean

Creativity

In meetings, as in other phases of salvation warfare, an officer is free to adopt any plans whatever, provided they are likely to accomplish the object in view and are in harmony with Bible teaching and with the spirit, practice and regulations of the Army.

Orders and Regulations for Officers

Is it time we invented some new device, or have we given up using the old ones? How is it that our meetings go on, and we pray and preach often only to twenties and thirties, while people perish by the thousand – broken, enslaved, degraded by their sins?

Messages to the Messengers
Catherine Bramwell-Booth

We in the Army have learned to thank God for eccentricity and extravagance, and to consecrate them to His service. We have men in our ranks who can rollick for the Lord. Often they have blundered and occasionally they land us in awkward places. Some of them have been very rough and uncouth, and all that...

Bramwell Booth
The History of The Salvation Army – Volume 1
Robert Sandall

Resourceful, therefore, applied to the Salvation Army officers, must mean a new source, contrivance, device for soul-saving.

Messages to the Messengers
Catherine Bramwell-Booth

Every child possesses a creative instinct in one direction or another; it is very important that this should be encouraged and developed...A child must not only have something to do, something to make; there must be someone to admire the finished work.

Florence Booth
Fighting for the King
Catherine Bramwell-Booth

Creator

We believe that there is only one God, who is infinitely perfect – the Creator, Preserver and Governor of all things – and who is the only proper object of religious worship.

Salvation Army Doctrine #2

Dust! If one had searched the whole sphere of existence, could there have been found anything more unlikely, more unpromising, out of which to produce so noble a result? But that He might be glorified, that He might show forth His power, that none might share the honor with Him, He took dust and made man!

Bramwell Booth
Trumpets of the Lord
Catherine Bramwell-Booth, Edit.

Criticism

And there's a bunch who are spiteful,
Who snap and snarl like a dog;
They wonder why they have no power,
And sit around like a log;
They grumble and growl at the Captain,
They find fault, they sulk and they pout;
When the Lamb's Book of Life shall be opened
God's Word says they'll have to stay out.

Early Salvation Army Song
Combat Songs of The Salvation Army
Sallie Chesham

As it takes a good man to believe in goodness, a truthful man to believe in truth – a habitual liar cannot accept another man's word – it takes a man full of the Holy Spirit to recognize His presence in the life and work of another. Spiritual life is only spiritually discerned. Failure to perceive God's handiwork in the effort of another is more likely a judgment upon ourselves than on the other man.

The Officer's Review – 1932

His duty is to the ideal Army, as God wishes it to be, and he will find that if he strives wholeheartedly to be faithful to this ideal, he will have neither time nor mind to criticize the shortcomings of others.

Chosen to be a Soldier

In speaking of another's faults,
Pray don't forget your own;
Remember those in homes of glass,
Should seldom throw a stone;
If you have nothing else to do,
But talk of those who sin,
'Tis better you commence at home,
And from that point to begin.

Early Salvation Army Song
Combat Songs of The Salvation aRmy
Sallie Chesham

It is usually not so much the greatness of our trouble as the littleness of our spirit which makes us complain.

The Officer – 1919

They grumble at our music,
    They grumble at our drum,
They grumble at our marching,
    To make the people come;
They grumble at our uniform,
    They say it's all display,
But still we are the people
    Who are bound to win the day.

They grumble if we visit them,
    They grumble if we don't,
They grumble of we speak to them,
    They grumble if we won't
And say that in a year or two,
    The Army will decay,
But still we are the people
    Who are bound to win the day.

They grumble if we weep or sing,
    They grumble all the while;
And what is most peculiar,
    They grumble if we smile;
But still we keep on smiling,
    In spite of what they say,
For with God we're the people
    Who are bound to win the day.

Combat Songs of The Salvation Army
Sallie Chesham

Our Captain is a busy man,
    As busy as can be,
His mind is exercised about things
    Too deep for you and me.
He deals with facts and figures,
    For he's business through and through;
He's busy thinking up the things
    Headquarters ought to do.

Jack Addie
Combat Songs of The Salvation Army
Sallie Chesham

Do I my comrade slight,
Or deny him his place?
Do I exaggerate his faults
Or speak behind his face?

Herbert Booth
Companion to the Song Book
Gordon Avery

As I tells my comrades, if some of 'em aren't exactly what we would like 'em to be, it won't make 'em any better by pulling 'em to pieces.

Sergeant-Major Do-Your-Best
William Booth

Perhaps in all kinds of dumb and unbeautiful ways many have cried, and some still cry, for that smile of recognition that should bring them new inspiration. But, no; the captain was too busy seeing faults that badly needed correcting, and so the approving look was not given; and who knows how many have sunk silently down defeated?

Messages to the Messengers
Catherine Bramwell-Booth

Turn from the questioning of other people's holiness to the living out of your own.

Messages to the Messengers
Catherine Bramwell-Booth

Instead of looking at those who have fallen, shall we not look at those who have stood? Instead of losing heart and faith because of those who have thrown down the sword and fled from the field, shall we not shout for joy and emulate those who were faithful unto death, who came up out of great tribulation with robes washed in the Blood of the Lamb? Why not shout victory for joy, and triumph with Joseph in his victory rather than sneer and lose faith in God and man, and thus suffer defeat with David in his fall? Why not look at the beloved John and rejoice, rather than at the traitor Judas and despair?

Love-Slaves
Samuel Logan Brengle

Nothing more surely makes manifest a man's spiritual blindness and deadness and hardness of heart than his hiding behind others and confessing their faults instead of his own, and nothing will more surely confirm him in blindness and sin.

Love-Slaves
Samuel Logan Brengle

Think about your own evils. This will be far more profitable to you than to think about his, and will be infinitely more likely to make a better man or woman of you.

Heart Talks on Holiness
Samuel Logan Brengle

Nothing exposes our superficiality as much as our judgment of others.

The Armoury Commentary — The Four Gospels
Frederick Coutts, Edit.

The important thing about the Gospel is that all who hear have a responsibility to acknowledge its benefits. Too many think that their obligation is fulfilled by criticizing.

The Armoury Commentary — The Four Gospels
Frederick Coutts, Edit.

We know neither the hidden weakness in the person we admire nor the secret goodness in the person we condemn. Nor do we know the strains and stresses which others have to combat.

The Armoury Commentary — The Four Gospels
Frederick Coutts, Edit.

The worst thing I must bear
It seems to me,
Is not the critic's comment
But his spite.

O Lord!
John Gowans

I do love sinners, yet, 'tis strange. O Lord, how difficult I find the awkward saints!
The love I feel for those outside Your fold seems somehow lacking when it is Your own who irritate me.
We expect so much of those who name Your Name that we forget the human vessel's frailty
and our sight is jaundiced,
by our ready misconception of motives
seen alone by You
and judged at their true worth.

From My Treasure Chest
Flora Larsson

Some of us consider ourselves a long way in our spiritual education when we can take just reproof and righteous accusation kindly. We have first to learn this most difficult lesson for ourselves, and then we have to teach it by rule and practice to others. But few can manifest this exclusively Christian grace of silence under false accusation.

The Silences of Christ
Albert Orsborn

How can my brother know Your love
when he finds no love in me?
How can he reach Your outstretched hand
with but my greedy hand to see?
What can he know of tenderness from my
harsh and strident tone
Shrilly counting his poor, sad sins, and
making his failings known?

Dorothy Phillips
It's Beautiful
Dorothy Breen, Edit.

Most of us possess the curious capacity of being able to look at ourselves from outside ourselves, as it were, though too often with very little consequence beyond a bit of prideful preening while we overlook our flaws. It is difficult to be sufficiently honest and objective to recognize our own weaknesses and failures, though usually we are not slow to decry them in others. A sharpened critical faculty and the ability to laugh at oneself are essential corollaries of constructive self-examination.

A Burning in My Bones
Clarence Wiseman

Cross

Believers must do more than associate themselves with Calvary as those who look upon the Sinbearer who suffers there for them. They are called to identify themselves with Him on the Cross, as being crucified with Him and fully united with Him, and He with them, so that His death means the death of their old nature, leading to a new life in the power of the Resurrection.

Handbook of Doctrine

Men are not saved by believing in a doctrine, nor are they saved by the Cross of wood upon which Christ suffered. Salvation comes through Him who suffered there and ever lives to save.

Handbook of Doctrine

Thus while the Cross stands as a sign of God's will to save men, it also stands as a symbol of man's opposition to the disturbing Lordship of Christ. Each man must decide for himself what the Cross is to mean to him.

Handbook of Doctrine

The Cross points two ways — backwards, when God passed by sins, and forward, when He conquers them.

More Than Conquerors
Milton S. Agnew

So He came
To grips with nail and sword and angry men,
His weapon Love — and Love — and Love again.

Reflections
Catherine Baird

The dumb, whose lips responded to My touch,
Raised not his voice on My behalf
The lame man stood afar not followed Me,
Up the steep slopes of Calvary.
And he whose eyes first saw the light in Me,
Stood with the multitude gazing in
Vulgar curiosity
While I lifted up — and bled — and died.
O Soul, I too have known defeat.

Reflections
Catherine Baird

Dark Gethsemane,
Darker Calvary,
Surely Jesus suffer'd this for me;
Bore the mocking jeer,
Faced the angry sneer
Jesus, dare I suffer for Thee?

G. Bomwick
Gems for Songsters #1

Unless you accept His Cross, He will prepare for you a coffin.

Bramwell Booth
Trumpets of the Lord
Catherine Bramwell-Booth, Edit.

Oh how men will sing about the Cross, amuse and ornament themselves with the Cross, weep oceans of tears about the Cross, which means painful and ignominious death, not only to the Master who hung upon it, but to the loves and lusts He died to destroy; but as to making it the tree on which they are crucified, on which they die to the power, and charm, and fascination of a vain, fashionable, frivolous, God-hating world, that is quite another thing.

Salvation Soldiery
William Booth

But now love conquered power. Love held on. Alone — in the dark — amid the leers — despite the pain! With a breaking heart, a bleeding body, and 'neath the weight of a world, He held on — He held on — He held on!

Heart Messages
Emma Booth-Tucker

They would have believed if He had come down. We believe because He stayed up.

William Booth
The Armoury Commenrtary — The Four Gospels
Frederick Coutts, Edit.

A Man, with all humanity's keen shrinking from the Cross, and yet a Savior! For every trembling limb is offered as a sacrifice for sin; every nerve and fiber throbs with love and aching longing for mankind. And alone and single-handed that Monarch Heart upbears the weight eternal of suspended millions. Nor does He flinch, for every nail and thorn adds but fresh links to love's stong chain which binds Him to a world for which He dies.

Heart Messages
Emma Booth-Tucker

Calvary is a big place, and all the world can meet upon its heights.

Heart Messages
Emma Booth-Tucker

The Cross! The real, the rugged, the personal, the everyday, the for-Jesus Christ's-sake Cross, which goes contrary to flesh and blood, which costs us the nails of sacrifice, the thorns of suffering, the spear of persecution. The Cross that leads us out into the streets and alleys when self would stop at home. The Cross that goes after the lowest and worst, when self says, "Let them alone." The Cross that raises up a standard for the hopeless, when all others forsake them and flee. The Cross, our calling, our hope, our victory and our song. Oh, sister-Christians, saints and sinners, behold the Cross!

Heart Messages
Emma Booth-Tucker

On the Cross of Calvary,
  Jesus died for you and me;
There He shed His precious Blood,
  That from sin we might be free.
O the cleansing stream does flow,
And it washes white as snow!
  It was for me that Jesus died
    On the Cross of Calvary.
      On Calvary, on Calvary!
      It was for me that Jesus died
        On the Cross of Calvary.

Sarah Graham
Salvation Army Song Book

Calvary is a big place, and all the world can meet upon its heights.

Heart Messages
Emma Booth-Tucker

The sinner desires the crown without the Cross; the saint is willing for the Cross without the crown.

Life of Catherine Booth — Volume 2
Frederick Booth-Tucker

It came;
The cross, the cries, the pain, the shame,
But 'twas not I
Whom they led forth to die;
It was the one I loved!

Fighting for the King
Catherine Bramwell-Booth

If the future of The Salvation Army is to be spiritually radiant and all conquering, we must not simply endure the Cross, but glory in it.

Ancient Prophets
Samuel Logan Brengle

And here is the Gospel — the Cross reveals that men are no longer only under God's law, but within God's love.

The Armoury Commentary — The Four Gospels
Frederick Coutts, Edit.

For Jesus' glory and victory lay not on the far side of Calvary, but in the very cross itself.

The Armoury Commentary — The Four Gospels
Frederick Coutts

God can turn even the evil of men to His redeeming purpose — as is shown by the way in which the worst of man's actions, the crucifixion of Jesus, was transformed into the means of man's redemption.

The Armoury Commentary — The Four Gospels
Frederick Coutts

What a strange paradox this is, that a Cross of agony should become a Cross of healing!

The Armoury Commentary — The Four Gospels
Frederick Coutts, Edit.

His wounds are not His main appeal to us, for His sorrow was more than physical pain. His great agony was the knowledge of what men were, the realization of how deeply sin was entrenched in human hearts, sin from which He had come to save them. Jesus suffered in Gethsemane before any lash had touched His flesh; indeed it was then that Calvary's victory was won.

Power and Glory
Harry Dean

The Cross reveals the power of the love of God that cannot be shattered because it is indestructible. It reveals the power of the holiness of God, by revealing the way of our sins — for they were ordinary, everyday sins that crucified Christ — appear in His sight. It reveals the power of the mercy of God, for by means of the Cross He pledges His forgiveness to all who truly repent.

Power and Glory
Harry Dean

The Cross was to be the revelation of true power, the power of light. The love we see there is the only unbreakable power, for it did not break then, when human sin had done its utmost and manifested its utter ugliness and shame. Here lies our confidence; always the final word is with love.

Power and Glory
Harry Dean

While He was not responsible for the evil in men that made the Cross inevitable, He chose to use man's natural character in the overall purpose of His Father God.

Power and Glory
Harry Dean

See now, His shoulder bears the Cross
On which extended
He's to die;
My endless gain is in His loss.

F.W. Fry
Gems for Songster #1

When I'm compelled
To contemplate Your Cross,
Your agony,
And can escape no more
The fact of loss,
It's infamy.
Your broken body
Seems to me to say
That Love is best.
But he who loves
Must pay!

O Lord!
John Gowans

I heard a voice so gently calling;
  Take up thy cross and follow me,
A tempest on my heart was falling,
  A living cross this was to be.
I struggled sore, I struggled vainly,
  No other light my eyes could see.

Agnes Heathcote
Salvation Army Song Book

The Cross is the divine answer to all lawlessness.

Search the Scriptures
Robert Hoggard

God's name was glorified in Christ when death's relentless power He defied.

The Creche and the Cross
Hulda C. Miller

On every hill our Savior dies
  And not on Calvary's height alone;
His sorrows darken all our skies,
  His griefs for all our wrongs atone.
Present He is in all men's woes,
  Upon a worldwide Cross is hung,
And with exceeding bitter throes
  His world-embracing heart is wrung.

Albert Orsborn
The Salvationist and the Atonement
John D. Waldron, Edit.

On the very ground where angels of peace poured their tears of sorrow and healing, evil men execute a devil's dance of new quarrels and conflicts. But the place of God's peace offer to man is unchanging, it is the "eternal yea or nay". There stands the Cross, in the midst of our turmoil and sin, with its loving and unchanging message, "Be ye reconciled to God!"

Albert Orsborn
The Salvationist and the Atonement
John D. Waldron, Edit.

There was no precedent for Calvary; there has been no repetition of it. It is unique and final.

Albert Orsborn
The Salvationist and the Atonement
John D. Waldron, Edit.

We mourn that e'er our hearts should be
One with a world that loves not Thee;
That with the crowd we passed Thee by
And saw, but did not feel, Thee die.
Not till we knew our guilt and shame
Did we esteem the Savior's name.

Albert Orsborn
Salvation Army Song Book

Dying love! creation trembled,
And the sun withheld its light
All the hosts of hell assembled
With the Son of God to fight.
Still in love He cried, "Forgive them!"
As His Spirit took its flight.

Mrs. Adjutant Parsons
Gems for Songsters #1

CROSS

This strange thing happened: As more and
more people were saved and transformed,
as martyrdom failed to destroy them, and
ridicule failed to deter them, the ages
began to pay tribute to that instrument of
their salvation. They washed from it the
blood — from its rugged horror, took from
it its rusty nails; they gilded it and glamor-
ized it, and the cross lost its foolishness
and became fashionable.

Arthur Pitcher
The Salvationist and the Atonement
John D. Waldron, Edit.

Jesus could have revoked at any moment
His Cross — He died *on* a cross, not *from*
it.

The Christian Charter
George B. Smith

47

Death

The Salvation Army has always affirmed that man is the highest expression of God's creation, and that every human personality is to be respected and safeguarded for this reason. On this truth, The Salvation Army's ministry of healing for body, mind and spirit is founded, and compassion for those who suffer is fundamental in all its social services.

Death is not regarded in isolation, but in the perspective of eternal life. Thus the Salvationist, with deep respect for the sanctity of human life, recognizes the inevitability of death. For this reason, The Salvation Army is opposed to euthanasia, that is any deliberate procedure to terminate life, as contrary to God's law. Man has a right to die with dignity, and this is important in the treatment of a dying patient. Where it is clear to the medical professional that "brain death" has occurred, we see no justification for artificial means for sustaining life.

Salvation Army Position Statement —
Euthanasia and the Artificial Prolongation of Life
United States Commissioners' Conference
October, 1975

The end of the journey is not therefore contemplated as something dark and somber. The faithful soldier does not die. He is Promoted to Glory.

Chosen to be a Soldier

And should I be afraid of Death?
The pall of darkness and abating breath?
More surely would I fear to stand
Upon the shores of my fair native land.

Poems
Catherine Baird

Death did but sink the ship
And set the captain free

To step ashore
Then to explore
God's land of great discovery.

Book of Salvationist Verse
Catherine Baird

The tomb is but the porch of a temple in which we shall surely stand, the doorway to the place of an abiding rest.

Bramwell Booth
Trumpets of the Lord
Catherine Bramwell-Booth, Edit.

The waters are rising, but so am I. I am not going under, but over. Don't be concerned about your dying; only go on living well and the dying will take care of itself.

Catherine Booth
Life of Catherine Booth — Volume 2
Frederick Booth-Tucker

When our days are gone we'll find death is not night at all, but breaking sun.

Songs of the Evangel
Evangeline Booth

Yes! to the grave, But the crown as well.
A comrade's gone, But in Heav'n to dwell;
Sorrow's night is ended, Jesus' cause defended,
Gone the heavenly choir to swell.

Herbert Booth
The Officer — 1893

But heavenly wisdom rose superior to human understanding, and in the evening time, when summer's day was fairest and her night was sweetest with the accents of the harvester's rich thanksgiving, the angel clasped the flower to her breast and gathered it from storms and strifes of earth's uncertainties to realms of changeless love beyond!

Heart Messages
Emma Booth-Tucker

Other things sacrificed in life's battling journey we can for the most part bring back again, or redeem, but after the dividing line of life's border has been crossed, and the cold waves of Jordan's stream have tolled over the departing feet, there is no filling the gap by earth's consolations; and although kindly time and other loved ones may do much to staunch the quivering wound that death has made, the grave of the truly loved remains green in the heart until we clasp our darlings gone before on the Resurrection Morn.

Emma Booth-Tucker
The Salvationist and the Atonement
John D. Waldron

Widowhood represents what has always seemed to be the keenest form of human sorrow. Alone — heartbroken — left! One link in life's chain is broken and every future hope and promise lie shattered at the widow's feet! One presence is missing, and her loneliness is only emphasized by the remaining crowd. One chair is vacant, and life's sunniest spheres are changed into a weary wilderness, a dreary desert.

Heart Messages
Emma Booth-Tucker

Death is, to all alike, the common end of life's probation. Saint and sinner pass through its portals carrying with them nothing but their character; the panorama of their every deed and phonogram of every word, with which, and with which alone, to appear before the Judgment Throne.

Life of Catherine Booth — Volume 2
Frederick Booth-Tucker

The winning post of life — to those who win — is death. It is here that humanity gathers to watch the last hours of the handful of swiftfooted spirits who in each age outrun their fellows, whether in the realm of war, or politics — of thought, of doubt or piety; and a grand career is either illumined by the radiance of its final triumph or enveloped in a sombre pall by its defeat. The finishing touch is put to an already perfect picture, or the artist's own hand mars the landscape with dingy daub.

Life of Catherine Booth — Volume 2
Frederick Booth-Tucker

Four hundred million Chinamen look back and down, worshipping their ancestors. Two hundred million Hindus long to be lost in vague consciousness because active life to them is full of terrors but, since Jesus was resurrected, the Christian is jubilant with hope. The grave has no terrors for him, for he knows he will never lie down in it — it only receives his castoff body. He will live because his Lord lives. He will never die, but will someday simply move out of the tenement of his perishing body and be forever with the Lord. His friends who die in the Lord are not dead, but living, robed in splendor, throned in light, washed from every stain, and freed from every throb of pain. Blessed be God for the streams of light pouring forth from the open and empty grave of Jesus, flooding the future with joyous hope — hope that smites the face with radiance and that maketh not ashamed. Hallelujah!

Resurrection Life and Power
Samuel Logan Brengle

The bird in the cage lives in the atmosphere. When the cage is opened and the bird flies forth, it still lives in the atmosphere, but without limitations. Our body is our cage. We live and move and have our being in God while in the body, but when we escape from it, and leave it empty, we still live in God.

Resurrection Life and Power
Samuel Logan Brengle

There is something about death that is awful, and from which men shrink, and yet, since Jesus has died and gone down into the grave and risen again, the terror is lost to the Christian. Still, it is probable that if allowed to choose most Christians and all sinners would say, "Let us go to Heaven like Enoch did".

Heart Talks on Holiness
Samuel Logan Brengle

To our sainted dead the coffin is not a narrow and locked prison, but an easy couch of sleep; the grave is not a bottomless abyss, but an open door through which the dear one has passed into the presence of the King, into the unveiled vision of

Jesus and the unbroken joys and fellow-ships of the saints made perfect; a door of escape from the limitations and tears and toils and temptations and tortures of time into the ageless blessedness of eternity where "God shall wipe away all tears from their eyes; and there shall be no more death, neither sorrow, nor crying, neither shall there be any more pain" (Rev. 21:4). To faith death simply means that the appointed task in this world's harvest field is done, and the dear one has gone home; the day's lessons have been learned, and the Father has come to take His children home from school; or some evil was coming which God in His wisdom did not see it best to turn aside, but from before which He saw fit to snatch His loved one.

Resurrection Life and Power
Samuel Logan Brengle

Devotion to the dead is poor compensation for disloyalty during their life.

The Armoury Commentary — The Four Gospels
Frederick Coutts, Edit.

Death is always an interruption. It puts a period in the middle of a sentence of an unfinished book.

Footsteps to Calvary
Henry Gariepy

But death's my friend,
Why greet him with a frown?
He's only Life
Dressed in another gown!

O Lord!
John Gowans

We secretly admire
Someone,
But stupidly
We wait
Till death has put
A world between
Their eyes and ears
And ours.
And only when they've gone
We find
That we have
Speaking powers!

O Lord!
John Gowans

How wonderful 'twill be to live with God,
When I have crossed death's deep and swelling flood;
How wonderful to see Him face to face
When I have fought the fight and won the race!

Theodore H. Kitching
Salvation Army Song Book

Grant me one favor, Master.
Let my light flicker until the end,
Until the flame sinks into final rest.

Just a Moment, Lord
Flora Larsson

Is there any comfort for such a loss! Yes, there is. With all my heart I believe that what we call death is only transition, only the opening — and shutting — of a door, and that on the other side of that door is life, joyous, full, abounding life, rich in ways unimaginable to our finite minds. Your child, my child is there, awaiting our coming.

From My Treasure Chest
Flora Larsson

Out of the great unknown we come, one by one. Back into the beyond we are gathered when our lifespan is at an end.

From My Treasure Chest
Flora Larsson

They have met the last foreman and the last fight,
And now walk unhindered, in heavenly light.
No message may reach us from that blest abode,
But we know they are safe in the keeping of God;
So rest we our hearts, and kiss we the rod.

The Beauty of Jesus
Albert Orsborn

In the flame of the play of my life
When I take that last curtain call,
It is my wish, as I leave earth's stage,
To know His Kingdom had claimed my all.

God's Whispers in My Heart
Shirley Pavey

Promoted from the infantry of earth to the cavalry of the skies.

George Scott Railton
Life of Catherine Booth — Volume 2
Frederick Booth-Tucker

The souls that had put off salvation
"Not tonight, I'll get saved by and by
No time now to think of religion"
At last they had found time to die.

Richard Slater
Gems for Songsters #2

Debt

Debt is a great evil. It destroys a man's peace, makes him feel like a slave, and has a bad effect upon his example.

Chosen to be a Soldier

Every officer should understand the evils of debt and adhere to the standing rule of the Army — no debt!

Orders and Regulations for Officers

The Corps Officer is required to keep his corps free from debt whatever sacrifice may be involved.

Orders and Regulations for Corps Officers

Deceit

The art of deception is to be able to appear true!

Catherine Booth
Life of Catherine Booth — Volume 1
Frederick Booth-Tucker

How do You regard half-truths, Master?
In your reckoning do two half-truths equal a whole truth
Or do they add up to one big, whopping lie?
I hope the former, but I fear the latter.
And my fear is greater than my hope.

Just a Moment, Lord
Flora Larsson

Decision

Every spark of light you get without obeying it, leaves your soul darker. Every time you come up to the verge of the Kingdom and don't go over, the less the probability that you ever will.

Papers on Godliness
Catherine Booth

We can only measure our work for God by our success in bringing men to the point of personal decision.

Friendship With Jesus
Florence Booth

The most difficult decisions to make are not between good and evil but between the good and the best.

The Armoury Commentary — The Four Gospels
Frederick Coutts, Edit.

Slight effects may sway great decisions.

Mildred Duff
Madge Unsworth

Great resolves are often best taken alone, with God only for counselor. No matter how good or well intentioned the disciples were, if their advice or opinion had been asked, which of them would have seen beyond the Cross?

The Silences of Christ
Albert Orsborn

Desire

Uncontrolled thought will lead to unsanctified desire, and thence to unholy action.

Bramwell Booth
Trumpets of the Lord
Catherine Bramwell-Booth, Edit.

Teach me, O Lord, that in the place
To which desire has been the only guide,
Desire will ever be unsatisfied.

Fighting for the King
Catherine Brawell-Booth

As pants the hart for streams in desert dreary

So pants my soul for Thee, O Thou life-giving One.

Catherine Booth-Clibborn
Salvation Army Song Book

Despair

But ah, sometimes I come with heavy eyes and heavier heart,
Bruised by defeat — bereft of self-esteem;
Battered the gleaming sword I proudly bore,
Beggar, I dare not lift my eyes,
To Thee instead, I raise appealing hands,
And God, I love Thee most
When in that mournful hour
Thou stoopest to restore poor sinful me.

Poems
Catherine Baird

In the perilous night of black despair,
Jesus of Nazareth entered there.

Poems
Catherine Baird

I have been much depressed since you left — worse than usual; but it is of no use reasoning with myself when these fires of despondency are on me. I must hold on and fight my passage through, and when I get to Heaven the light and joy will be all the greater contrast.

Catherine Booth
Life of Catherine Booth — Volume 2
Frederick Booth-Tucker

All the saints of old had hours of darkness and depression, many of them going through seas of anguish. And as with the saints of old, so is it with the saints of modern times. It is not sinful to weep and be cast down, if in our distress we do not give way to unbelief and despair and wrongdoing.

Purity of Heart
William Booth

Nothing can be done with a heart whose chief occupation is despair.

William Booth
Maiden Tribute
Madge Unsworth

There is a November time, perhaps, in every man's history when everything is gloomy, and nothing seems to bring sunshine to the people's hearts, so twisted and perverted they have become. Cross currents will sometimes run so strongly that, try as you will, you cannot reach the desired haven of the people's affections.

Salvation Soldiery
William Booth

One picture I could not banish: the beautiful face and golden head of the little fifteen year-old mother, appearing in the filthy, dark, box-like room as a jewel amid the ruins; the fast and bitter tears falling on the human mite dead in her arms; the despair in the frightened blue eyes as she said, "Look there is no place for us in life, or in death: no place for my baby or me. Where can I hide my baby? Where can I hide myself?"

Songs of the Evangel
Evangeline Booth

My unbelieving heart found it always easier to turn to the human than to the Divine. God led me by a way in which I thought no other soul had traveled; and when in the darkness there seemed no light, when in my sorrow no sympathy from an understanding heart was within reach, then I cried to God: not the cry of words nor of mind only, nor of determination only but the cry of my whole being, "Save me, or I perish!"

Messages to the Messengers
Catherine Bramwell-Booth

If you sit down with a pad and pencil to figure the problem out, leaving Jesus Christ out of the account you will be driven to despair.

Christ's Cabinet
William McIntyre

Disappointment

There was the same dissatisfaction, the same disquiet in his soul that there is in every human soul till it finds God, and which nothing else can ever satisfy; because God has made us for Himself, and until we find the end of our being we can never rest; we are like Noah's dove, wandering hither and thither and finding no rest for the soles of our feet.

Life and Death
Catherine Booth

Ambition for God can be as strong as a selfish ambition, and therefore as open to disappointment. In all these and similar matters we are likely to feel as keenly as the man without religion.

Messages to the Messengers
Catherine Bramwell-Booth

Can disappointment
Have its uses
Really?
A dream of mine has crashed,
I loved
Dearly,
I built a structure
Upon golden dust
With stainless steel
They said would
Never rust
And now the ruin
Lies about my feet.
My cruel disappointment
Is complete.
But now that I'm emerging
From the shock
At least I've learnt
To build next time
On rock!

O Lord!
John Gowans

Discipline

What is required of the salvation soldier is not blind unintelligent obedience, but a self-discipline which enters into every aspect of life, and is in direct contrast to the self-indulgent world.

Chosen to be a Soldier

"Ah, but", you say, "if I shut my door on my sons, what will become of them?" I answer no worse, and nine chances to one not half as bad as will become of them if you go on making the path of the transgressor easy to them. God's way is that the rebellious shall suffer. You try to come between God's rod and your children's sins, consequently you help them down the incline of evil faster than they could otherwise go.

Catherine Booth
Mrs. Booth
W.T. Stead

It is a law that liberation comes by limitation, we are chastened to be perfected.

Ancient Prophets
Samuel Logan Brengle

Correction is as much essential part of our spiritual education as encouragement.

The Splendour of Holiness
Frederick Coutts

Spiritual perception, like musical appreciation and artistic taste, is the result of long training and inner discipline. Disloyalty to truth always blunts our perception; obedience refines and heightens it.

The Armoury Commentary — The Four Gospels
Frederick Coutts, Edit.

Strong discipline has its inspiration in strong doctrine.

Search the Scriptures
Robert Hoggard

Every leader of God's people has to learn how to administer rebuke properly. He has, indeed, often to be a living rebuke.

The Silences of Christ
Albert Orsborn

Doubt

Unbelief is not the matter of failure to accept that which a man has never heard but rather the rejection of what he has heard.

More Than Conquerors
Milton S. Agnew

It seems to me that our position should not be so much that of knocking at the door of Heaven to ask God to come and do something for us, as that of knocking at the door of our own hearts to beseech them to put away all their stupid pre-

judices and all their obstinate unbelief —
to put away that unbelief which when
beaten away from one hiding place does
not give in and give up the controversy,
but goes and hides behind another bush,
and when it is dislodged from that, it is
only to seek another shelter — carrying
on a sort of guerilla warfare which is always dodging and always being beaten,
but never giving in.

Salvation Soldiery
William Booth

Doubt paralyzes prayer.

When the Holy Ghost is Come
Samuel Logan Brengle

The last thing a soul has to give up, when
seeking salvation or sanctification, is "an
evil heart of unbelief". This is Satan's
stronghold. You may drive him from all
his outposts, and he does not care much;
but when you assail this citadel, he will resist with all the lies and cunning he can
command. ·

Samuel Logan Brengle
At the Center of the Circle
John D. Waldron, Edit.

About any event which men have continued denying for nineteen centuries we
should doubt their denials!

The Armoury Commentary — The Four Gospels
Frederick Coutts, Edit.

The assurance of faith is to be found only
in the possibility of doubt.

Reason to Believe
Harry Dean

The real opposite to faith is not doubt, as
some imagine, but denial. It is on doubt
that faith lives; it is the hard black coal that
feeds the fire of faith.

Reason to Believe
Harry Dean

The tree of unbelief bears bitter fruit.

Search the Scriptures
Robert Hoggard

We need not be ashamed of our doubts
any more than we need to be ashamed of
the growing pains of adolescence.

Manpower for the Master
Bramwell Tillsley

I was beginning to doubt my doubts.

A Burning in My Bones
Clarence Wiseman

Duty

It is true that you obtain salvation by faith
in Jesus Christ, but it is equally true that
you can only maintain it by keeping the
commandments of God. It is therefore a
ruinous delusion to pretend to have a religion of any value whether for this world
or for the next, if all the time you know
that you are neglecting your duty.

The Founder's Messages to Soldiers
William Booth

Nothing can relieve you from the duty of
fighting for the salvation of dying souls
around you.

Purity of Heart
William Booth

The duties of a good citizen must not be
evaded. Caesar must receive what is
Caesar's — though never that which is
God's.

The Armoury Commentary — The Four Gospels
Frederick Coutts, Edit.

I'm bound to the wheel of duty, Master;
It whirls round, carrying me in its dizzy
turnings.
I long at times for freedom must go on.
I say, "Stop", but it doesn't stop.
I say "Can't"...
but I find I can because I must.

Just a Moment, Lord
Flora Larsson

E

Easter

Pentecost confirmed what Easter had asserted – that God was still on the throne.

The Splendor of Holiness
Frederick Coutts

With the social upheavals in our present-day culture, many hearts are seized with fear. That first Easter began with a group of frightened men and women. Easter is the story of how those anxious and fearful people were transformed into a vibrant, courageous, witnessing community. They were emptied of their fears through the Good News: "Christ is risen!" Because he lives, we fear not!

Orval Taylor
Good News

The Bible says Christ arose. Almost 2,000 years of human belief say Christ arose. The testimony is not only historical; it is experiential. The Holy Ghost brings conviction and convincing to millions in our day. Christ did die; He was buried but He did arise. The resurrection is most certain. Hallalujah, Christ arose!

Norman S. Marshall
The War Cry

Easter left the disciples changed men! First, we see a picture of utter failure, indecision, fear and flight. Shortly afterward, we see confident, decisive people emptied of their fears through the irresistible preaching of Jesus Christ. The good news is "Christ is risen" and with Him we can live with courage and hope, free from anxiety and fear because God is alive in the world.

Orval Taylor
Good News

Education

Do you say, "but we are educating the masses?" I answer, "It is vain to expect the needed moral reform from the schoolmaster. the more educated, the more dangerous, unless you also make them good."

The Salvation Army in Relation to
the Church and State
Catherine Booth

If He sent me to seek a lost sheep in the wilderness, or to pull an ox out of some pit into which he had stumbled in the night, I should endeavor to gain any information not already in my possession which my Employer might possess concerning the duty which He commissioned me to discharge, and I should equally endeavor to use measures as I was already familiar with and which seemed appropriate to the occasion. He has sent me to seek lost men and women and children wandering in the wilderness of sin and misery, and to pull the wretched backsliders and drunkards and harlots out of the horrible pit into which they have fallen, and to stimulate all true Blood and Fire soldiers to take part in the same blessed task; and while relying on Him for the supply of that wisdom and strength which I possess not, I still feel that it is only reasonable that I should use such knowledge, such arguments, such songs, and such other measures as I already have knowledge of, or which I can by thought and enquiry obtain, and which appear likely to secure that accomplishment of my end.

The Officer – 1893
William Booth

Our schools help to enable a starving man to tell his story in more grammatical language than that which his father could have employed, but they do not feed him, or teach him where to go to get fed.

In Darkest England and the Way Out
William Booth

The better informed, the wiser and more cultivated we are, provided we're dedicated wholly to God and set on fire with spiritual passion, the more effectually can we glorify God and serve our fellowmen.

Ancient Prophets
Samuel Logan Brengle

Soldiers are disciples, not religious robots.

Marching on!
Ted Palmer

Effort

People die and go to hell because nobody will be at the trouble and expense to save them. Let the countryside turn out. Put a way through. Know no impossibilities. If you cannot reach the perishing souls one way, try another. Try every way, and then try them all over again. Never be beaten. You must succeed. Make your mind up to it, and it shall be done.

Salvation Soldiery
William Booth

A great trick of the devil is to lead people to think they will get it by doing something, but a man might as well try to lift himself over the fence by his own bootstraps as to transform himself into the divine nature by works. He can get it no more by works than he can change the color of his eyes by works. He can no more rid himself of an inherited temper, or get lust out of his heart, or hatred, or pride, by getting baptized, by going to church, by joining the Army, by putting on the uniform, by reading the Bible, by doing any or every religious work, than he can get scrofula out of his blood by doing these things or add one cubit to his stature.

Heart Talks on Holiness
Samuel Logan Brengle

We are never nourished from His word by being given our food, so to speak, "ready cooked." We have to work for it!

Mildred Duff
Mildred Duff
Madge Unsworth

Christ left the multitude and went up into a mountain, and his disciples came to Him, and he taught them – indicating that the only people He could teach were those who took the trouble to climb.

Christ's Cabinet
William McIntyre

Emotion

Get the right kind of religion and it will make you feel. If you have not the right kind of feeling, I am afraid you have not the right kind of religion.

Papers on Godliness
Catherine Booth

Sentimentalism will have no resurrection; it will rot with the grave clothes.

Catherine Booth
The Officer — 1893

My tempers are fitful, my passions are strong,
They bind my poor soul and they force me to wrong;
Beneath thy blest billows deliverance I see,
O come, mighty ocean, and roll over me!

Salvation Army Song Book
William Booth

This feeling has, no doubt, been in large measure the result of realization. Perhaps realization is only another word for feeling, for what is realization but the consciousness – that is, the inward knowing that things are what they appear? As some have heard me say; "How can a man realize the existence of God, the forgiveness of sins, the value of his soul, the terrors of Judgment Day, the glories of heaven and the anguish of hell without the feelings that correspond with those tremendous truths?" When truths are known to be what they seem, the heart will be stirred and feelings must be the inevitable result.

William Booth
How to Preach
Charles Talmadge, Edit.

One touch, one word, one look, one tear – it matters little what the manifestation; if but strong feeling drives the arrow home, how deep a place that arrow often finds!

Heart Messages
Emma Booth-Tucker

After all, the world is not lost for want of brainless people, who do not think, but rather for want of heartless people who do not feel.

The Officer – 1893
Frederick Booth-Tucker

It is a sad fact that in an age when men and women are seeking emotional stimulus in every form of sport and amusement, when the thrills of the race track and the suspense of drama increase the tension almost to the breaking point, when folk seek erstwhile excitement in a weekly gamble, some believers become more and more afraid of emotionalism and less and less willing to persuade men to come to God.

The Mercy Seat
William Burrows

Yet there can be no doubt that men enslaved by sinning seldom find conversion in "cold blood." It is a surge of emotion which carried them forward to repentance and, the step once taken, God gives them strength to win through.

The Mercy Seat
William Burrows

Ecstasy is not always a good thing; it sometimes has a tendency to sweep one's feet off the ground. Too often, it begets the fanatic, the wild-eyed one, the impractical visionary. When religion goes to the head instead of the heart, the effects are always disastrous. Though our hearts may soar, the place for our feet is on the ground.

Out of the Depths
Clarence W. Hall

As to emotion: Well, what are we speaking about? If you mean emotionalism, the exploitation of high feeling for religious or any other ends, we want none of it! What comes with the flood goes out with the ebb. If we have in mind the excitement of the films, or the sports arena, or the latest temporary madness, "rock and roll," we never used such stimulations. When we speak of emotion we mean a deep stirring of the soul wrought within us by the Spirit of God.

The House of My Pilgrimage
Albert Orsborn

Empathy

Some, I know, are struggling; their faith is weak, their winters are long, and it ought not to be so. I believe if we talked more about these things to each other it would be an immense help. There would be less doubting and more faith; less of the season of spiritual inertia, and more the activity of spring; holiness of heart, and so God's favor and blessing, quickening into life and fruitfulness all the best in us.

Messages to the Messengers
Catherine Bramwell-Booth

I have not many hopes about Heaven; but this is one of them: that with freedom from the flesh will come the possibility of such communion with the spirit of another as shall make us able to enter into each other's feelings, and to know the measure of the cup of sorrow or joy each drank alone.

Messages to the Messengers
Catherine Bramwell-Booth

Our spirits tread the same road, our feet grow weary on the same stretches, and we stumble over the same places!

Messages to the Messengers
Catherine Bramwell-Booth

The Father's heart of love was pierced by the thorns that pierced the head of the Son. the Father's heart was hurt with the nails that pierced the hands and feet of the Son. The Father's heart was thrust through with anguish at the guilt and sins of men when they thrust the spear into the heart of Jesus. The Father suffered with and in the Blessed Son.

The Guest of the Soul
Samuel Logan Brengle

There is not a cry of anguish, not a heart-ache, nor a pang of spiritual pain in all the world that does not reach His ears and touch His heart, and stir all His mighty sympathies. But especially does He suffer and sympathize with His own believing children.

Heart Talks on Holiness
Samuel Logan Brengle

Those chosen by God to lead His people must discover how to relate to them in a direct and personal way, entering into their sorrows and joys as Jesus did, sharing their struggles and aspirations, and standing by them in stresses and storms of life. It is utterly impossible to conduct the care of souls from the keyboards of a typewriter or the end of a telephone. Neither business strategies, nor persuasive communications can compensate for lack of personal contact in a spirit of genuine love, nor fill the vacuum created by the absence of sensitive shepherding.

A Burning in My Bones
Clarence Wiseman

Envy

I beseech you, do not dwell unduly in your moments of reflection upon the eloquence, the organizing gifts, the pastoral abilities of your comrades in the war. They would rather be failures than you should be provoked to jealousy by their success. They'd rather point you to the Master, without whom they can do nothing. It is not for us to ponder over what Barnabas does, how he came to be where he is, how he brings to the Army such God-glorifying results. These things will have a savor of death unto death if they take their eyes off Jesus. We shall begin to sink in the distressful waters of envy, that cruel sea whose depths are unplumbed and whence drowning men are rarely rescued.

The Officer's Review – 1933

Envy fed the fire that burst into flame in the first murder. Envy moved his brethren to sell Joseph into slavery and prostrate their father with grief. And it was "because of envy" the rulers delivered Jesus up to Pilate.

Transformed Christians
Milton S. Agnew

Jealousy is unmitigated misery. Some emotions – like hatred, pride or lust – carry with them at least some things of pleasure and release. The envious person is, however, always in toils of anguish. To feel jealous is invariably humiliating.

Our Rebel Emotions
Bernard Mobbs

Moral indignation is often jealousy with a halo.

The Christian Charter
George B. Smith

Error

One of the truest evidences of real wisdom is the ability to see our mistakes. To fail to do this puts you on the way to join the folk who think themselves martyrs, when other folk can only think them fools.

Messages to the Messengers
Catherine Bramwell-Booth

Nearly all error is founded and built upon a broken and disconnected and misplaced fragment of truth. Thus the devil quoted Scripture to Christ, with his plausible "it is written." The Judaizing teachers quoted the commands of God regarding circumcision. The bare hook will attract no fish, therefore it must be concealed and baited with a plausible fragment of truth. The appearance of a wolf will cause the whole flock of sheep to flee, therefore he must be disguised in a clever imitation of a sheep. The angel of light will attract and deceive, when the appearance of Satan undisguised will cause alarm.

Frederick Booth-Tucker
The Officer – 1919

He is tolerant of those who differ from him in opinion, in doctrine. He is firm in his own convictions, and ready at all times with meekness and fear to explain and defend the doctrines which he holds and is convinced are according to God's Word. But he does not condemn and consign to damnation all those who differ from him. He is glad to believe that men are often better than their creed, and may be saved in spite of it; that, like mountains whose bases are bathed with sunshine and clothed with fruitful fields and vineyards while their tops are covered with dark clouds, so men's hearts are often fruitful in the graces of charity, while their heads are yet darkened by doctrinal error.

Samuel Logan Brengle
Portrait of a Prophet
Clarence W. Hall

The great heresy of the ages is not manifested so much in false doctrine as in failing love and consequent false living.

Ancient Prophets
Samuel Logan Brengle

Very often heresy is the exaggeration of a neglected truth.

Reason to Believe
Harry Dean

Modern apostasy denies the exceeding sinfulness of sin and the efficacy of the shed blood of Christ. It substitutes reformation for transformation, emphasizes environmental and educational factors, and leaves the sinner in his sin.
Apostasy in not error due to ignorance but the deliberate rejection of revealed truth by a professing Christian, usually under the guise of superior intellectual attainment.

Search the Scriptures
Robert Hoggard

Human mistakes are swallowed by the divine intention.

My Best Men are Women
Flora Larsson

Heresies always seem very attractive to the human mind. This is partly because every respectable heresy contains a sizeable grain of truth and partly because it is usually far easier to understand than the orthodox line. It fascinates because it gives the impression of having solved the difficult problems.

Doctrine Without Tears
John Larrson

Eternity

It is religious cant which rids itself of the importunity of suffering humanity by drawing unnegotiable bills payable on the other side of the grave.

William Booth
The General Next to God
Richard Collier

Eternity is not coming. Eternity is here. We are enwrapped with it. Its arches cover us as do the heavens above us. It enfolds us as does the atmosphere about us.

Resurrection Life and Power
Samuel Logan Brengle

Not living death,
but deathless living
Forevermore.

Walking With the Wind
Sallie Chesham

Belief in God's love is our strongest reason for believing in life beyond the grave.

The Armoury Commentary – The Four Gospels
Frederick Coutts, Edit.

"Eternal" does not just mean lasting forever, for there is no time scale in eternity. Eternal life is that kind of quality of life which belongs to God and is characteristic of Him. It is a life where love rules supremely and from which selfishness has been banished.

The Armoury Commentary – The Four Gospels
Frederick Coutts, Edit.

Eternity, eternity, that boundless, vast forever!
In heaven above, where all is love, I'll spend it with my Savior;

For though the storms beat fierce and wild
Upon life's restless sea,
'Tis Jesus waits upon the shore,
And He will welcome me.

Gems for Songsters #1
S.L. Fidler

Oh, as I read the story
From birth to dying cry
A longing fills my bosom
To meet Him by and by.

Gems for Songsters #2
W. A. Hawley

But in my heart, my caterpillar heart,
I dream...dream of the day when I shed my
cumbrous clothing,
Say good-bye to my clodfootedness,
Rise from my chrysalis-coffin,
And on flashing wings skim the eternities
Of the upper sphere.

Just a Moment, Lord
Flora Larsson

They are gone on a journey, and one may
know
The Way that the heav'n bound travellers
go;
We may watch as they enter the shadowy
dale,
At the gates of the land where delights
never fail.
But there we must wait till God lifts the
veil.

The Beauty of Jesus
Albert Orsborn

In that world we shall all have to spend
our time either at a holiness meeting or a
meeting of unholiness.

George Scott Railton
The Privilege of All Believers
John D. Waldron

Evangelism

A corps officer should understand that he
is sent by God and the Army to all the un-
converted, non-churchgoing people in his
district, especially to the most needy and
depraved among them.

Orders and Regulations
for Corps Officers

Nor will the officer be content if the work
of the Army is better understood, or if his
youth sections flourish, or if he secures
more time on the mass media for the Army's
message, unless these become the means
whereby young and old alike personally
commit themselves to Jesus as Savior and
Lord.

Orders and Regulations for Officers

Oh, we have a grand salvation plan,
    Of which I'm going to tell,
The grandest ever made by man,
    To rescue souls from Hell.
Salvation human and divine,
    Of soul and body, too.
We'll have eternity in time
    When the General's dream comes true.

Old Salvation Army Song
Combat Songs of The Salvation Army
Sallie Chesham

The soldier knows that Christ is a mighty
Savior. He therefore has strong faith for
the salvation of sinners for whom there is,
humanly speaking, little hope.

Chosen to be a Soldier

All the world for Christ our Master!
    He has bought us with his blood;
O my comrades, march on faster,
We shall bring the world to God.

James Bateman
Salvation Army Song Book

An Army, a corps, a division, an officer, a
campaign, which does not make men,
which does not restore them to the likeness, and add them to the kingdom of
Christ, may do many wonderful things, but
it is not working the great work of God.

Bramwell Booth
Trumpets of the Lord
Catherine Bramwell-Booth

Christ did not come to civilize the world,
but to save it and to bring it back to God.

Catherine Booth
The Words of Catherine Booth
Cyril Barnes

I would lead Hallelujah Bands and be a damn fool in the eyes of the world to save souls.

Catherine Booth
The General Next to God
Richard Collier

We teach them that we are to compel men to come in, that we are to seek by our own individual power and by the power of the Holy Ghost in us to persuade men, that the Gospel idea of preaching is not merely laying the truth before men, for the exercise of their intellectual faculties; but that a teacher and savior has something more to do than this – that he ought to be possessed of sufficient Divine influence to thrust his message in upon the heart, to make the soul realize and feel his message. This is our great characteristics – pressing the Gospel upon the attention of men.

The Salvation Army in Relation to Church and State
Catherine Booth

Why we might give the world such a time of it that they would get saved in very self-defense, if we were only up and doing, and determined that they should have no peace in their sin.

Aggressive Christianity
Catherine Booth

The World for God! The World for God!
For this, dear Lord, give to my soul consuming fire!
Give fire that makes men heroes,
Turns weakness into might,
The fire that makes the courage to suffer for the fight.
The fire that changes fearing to Pentecostal daring,
The fire that makes me willing for Christ to live or die.
For, behold! on a hill – Calvary! Calvary!

Songs of the Evangel
Evangeline Booth

The world for God, the world for God;
  I give my heart, I'll do my part;
The world for God, the world for God,
  I give my heart, I will do my part.

The Salvation Army Song Book
Evangeline Booth

Test your work by the question – am I bringing souls into right relationships with Jesus? Your test question should not be, am I making Salvationists? though it is important that you should make Salvationists, and you will do this if you are true to our purpose. Your life is dedicated to bring sinners to Jesus.

Friendship With Jesus
Florence Booth

DOES SALVATION TRAVEL AS FAST AS SIN? See how wickedness spreads. Talk about a prairie fire – it is nothing to it! How it devours everything before it.
Does salvation keep pace with the increase in population? Make the calculation in your most favored Christian cities, and you will find we are terribly behind in the race. Do we keep pace with the devils in energetic and untiring labor?
Do we go as fast as death? Is he not always stealing a march on us?
Oh, say no more! We'll close our ears, my comrades, to this cold, unfeeling, stony-hearted utterance of unbelief. LET US GO FASTER!

The General's Letters
William Booth

I must go, not only to those who need me, but to those who need me most.

William Booth
How to Preach
Charles Talmadge

If any one still wants a reply, let him ask the lost souls in Hell whose brothers and sisters are following them there. Let him go and ask the Bloodwashed throng in heaven, whose eyes are wide open at last, to the value of salvation. Let him anticipate the Judgment Day and in spirit stand before the Throne and propose, if he dare, the question to Him who sits thereon. Methinks from Hell and Heaven and from the Great White Throne, the answer would come back, "More speed! Go faster!"

The General's Letters
William Booth

If the people will not come to see us, the greater is the necessity and urgency that will be laid upon us to go to them. And to them we Salvationists must and will go.

William Booth
How To Preach
Charles Talmadge

Men cannot be turned from Satan to God by gentle phrases and lavender water. To save men is a desperate, agonizing, wounding business.

The Seven Spirits
William Booth

My humanity and my Christianity, if I may speak of them in any way as separate one from the other, have cried out for some more comprehensive method of reaching and saving the perishing crowds.

In Darkest England and the Way Out
William Booth

Now, as I have explained to you before, by red-hot religion I mean hearts made hot with love for God, for comrades, for perishing souls, for noble work, and for every other good thing possible to men or women on earth or in Heaven.

William Booth
How To Preach
Charles Talmadge

Now look at them. It is not whether you can please them, send them away satisfied, get a good collection, induce them to come again; the first and foremost thing with you is to save and sanctify and inspire them with the burning love of Jesus Christ.

William Booth
How To Preach
Charles Talmadge

Perfect your improvements. Machinery and steam and electricity are all right – welcome and invaluable handmaidens of The Salvation Army...carry us if you can on the wings of the wind, only let us fly the news of mercy at home, abroad, round the world, everywhere. It has been long done in sentiment, in poetry, in oratory, on platforms, in figures of speech...Oh! may God let The Salvation Army do it in reality!

William Booth
The History of The Salvation Army – Volume 2
Robert Sandall

Persecute the sinners – force them to get saved.

The Officer – 1893
William Booth

Reason with them about the salvation of their souls as if Jesus Christ stood by listening to what you say.

Sergeant-Major Do-Your-Best
William Booth

The ordinary church idea of saving souls is to wait for an open door – to get into an open box one day in the seven and talk to those who come; if they choose to listen, very well; if not, it can't be helped.

The Officer – 1893
William Booth

Thousands who would stand up and FIGHT FOR A FEVER AMONGST THEIR CATTLE, scouting the idea that it was of God, routing out every cesspool and hotbed of the disease, localizing the malady, and stamping it out of existence, if asked to fight the deadly contagion of sin, to shut up the public houses, close the brothels, shield the little children, and use all means taught in the Bible, and suggested by the Holy Ghost, to clear the neighborhood of sin, would be shocked at the very idea.

The General's Letters
William Booth

To me men, especially the worst, possess the attraction of gold mines.

William Booth
The General Next to God
Richard Collier

We are moral scavengers netting the very sewers. We want all we can get, but we want the lowest of the low.

William Booth
Rediscovering the Open Air
Lyell Rader

Go for souls and go for the worst!

William Booth

Why are only ones and twos saved? Not because of any decree to save ones and twos only, but because only ones and twos go out to save them. A crowd that understands its business, and knows how to take hold of God, and how to deal with men, will catch a crowd. Let us go out in crowds to this scavenging business. Come along!

Salvation Soldiery
William Booth

It is the timidity and delicacy with which men attempt God's work that often accounts for their failure. Let them speak out boldly like men, as ambassadors of heaven, who are not afraid to represent their King and they will command attention and respect and reach the hearts and consciences of men.

When the Holy Ghost is Come
Samuel Logan Brengle

We got some nobody saved and God uses that nobody to reach somebody who becomes "Great in the sight of the Lord."

Ancient Prophets
Samuel Logan Brengle

The world of godlessness is never won by being ignored; it needs to be invaded and captured for Christ.

The Salvationist at Work
Fred Brown

That part of the church of Christ known as The Salvation Army is perfect when fulfilling her appointed end – seeking in the highways and byways for the maimed and halt and lame so that they may share in the feast of good things prepared by Him who keeps open house for sinners. This is not easy work for the Army and, busy with her task her dress may be soiled, her face flushed, her accent not always impeccable, her grammar shaky under stress of emotion, her appearance not always so collected as others of the Lord's servants, but she is perfect in His household in that she is accomplishing that good thing which is His will for her.

The Call to Holiness
Frederick Coutts

The obligation to turn men from this darkness to the light rests not upon them but on us. Error will not correct itself. Lost sheep do not return to the fold of their own accord. The lost coin could not find itself. The owner had to sweep diligently until she found it. The man who is outside the Kingdom of God does not wander in by chance. He has to be sought in the highways and byways. If he follows his own bent he will only wander still farther into the far country.

Essentials of Christian Experience
Frederick Coutts

Have we become keepers of the aquarium rather than fishers of men?

Refuge in the Secret Place
Edward Deratany

Lost interest? O Lord, where would I be
If some caring soul had lost interest in me?
Open my eyes, Lord; please help me to see
That lost interest in souls means lost interest in Thee!

Lauretta J. Keene
It's Beautiful!
Dorothy Breen, Edit.

And this word it reaches nations;
    Not the rich or learned or clever
Only shall by Him be rescued,
    O praise God! 'tis "whosoever!"

Salvation Army Song Book
William McAlonan

And still there are fields where the laborers are few,
    And still there are souls without bread.
And still eyes that weep where the darkness is deep.
    And still straying sheep to be led.

Salvation Army Song Book
Albert Orsborn

The door of salvation will not swing open to the multitudes if rust and ineffectiveness have sealed it up.

Marching On!
Ted Palmer

The Salvation Army is a "bottom of the barrel" Army. Whoever is so low as to be rejected or forgotten is automatically within our circle of concern.

Marching On!
Ted Palmer

I've heard the call for workers,
The world's great need I see,
O send me to the rescue,
I'm here, my Lord, send me!

W. Walker
Salvation Army Song Book

Too long at ease in Zion
   I've been content to dwell,
While multitudes are dying
   And sinking into Hell,
I can no more be careless,
   And say there's naught to do,
The fields are white to harvest
   And laborers are few.

W. Walker
Salvation Army Song Book

Evil

I can conceive what we often term as evil existing without sin, but I cannot conceive sin as existing without evil, and a personal devil seems to me to be related to the mystery of sin.

Samuel Logan Brengle
Peace Like a River
Sallie Chesham

If it were fully possible to rationalize evil, this would mean evil is in itself a reasonable thing.

Reason to Believe
Harry Dean

What is seen to be good satisfies our reason, and what is seen to be bad disturbs us. As soon as we recognize the goodness of something, we no longer ask "Why?" Goodness itself is sufficient explanation; it provides a legitimate claim to existence. But evil outrages both our moral sense and our reason. Evil has no meaning. The rationality of existence is inseparable from the problem of evil, which baffles the reason and causes us to say, "It doesn't make sense."

Reason to Believe
Harry Dean

Nothing is so much alive with vengeful energy as evil coiled and stored in personality.

Meditations for the Common Man
George B. Smith

All Christians are vulnerable to the evil of the world. Only a passionate love for the Lord and constant sensitivity to the leadings of the Spirit can preserve us against the eroding pressure.

Clarence Wiseman
The Privilege of All Believers
John D. Waldron, Edit.

Evolution

It all began, the General (William Booth) explained, poker faced, in a patch of mud. After a long time — "ages and ages and ages" — out of the mud came a fishy creature something akin to a shrimp. Time yawned — "ages and ages and ages" — before the shrimp turned into a monkey. And then? "ages and ages and ages passed," Booth would drawl, his eyes now twinkling, "before the monkey turned into — an infidel!"

The General Next to God
Richard Collier

Failure

He (the officer) will be willing to be dedicated to failure. In the divine economy this could be the way to God-glorifying success.

Orders and Regulations for Officers

Soldier — Where courage lives,
There also lurks defeat,
Where'er defeat, a chance to
Rise again!

Reflections
Catherine Baird

If we fail in anything, it is not for us to say that our failure proves the Lord's will. It may just prove the contrary. God's will is always, and everywhere, that sin should be destroyed, that devils should be sent back to hell, and that all men should be saved. If we fail through the unfaithfulness of those about us, let us admit it, and that our failure is of the devil, and go to work and get things altered and mended.

The General's Letters
William Booth

God knows how to make yesterday's failure the secret of today's success.

Messages to the Messengers
Catherine Bramwell-Booth

The man who fails is the man who does less than he can do, be the circumstances what they may.

Frederick Booth-Tucker
The Officer — 1893

There is no short cut to success save through an ocean of failures: The man who at last succeeds is the man who has often failed, but has gone on. The man who never fails is the man who never succeeds.

Frederick Booth-Tucker
The Officer — 1893

Know, then, that all failure has its beginning in the closet, in neglecting to wait on God until filled with wisdom, clothed with power, and all on fire with love.

Helps to Holiness
Samuel Logan Brengle

To lose God is the sum of all loss. If we lose Him we lose all. If we lose all and still have Him, we shall in Him again find all.

Ancient Prophets
Samuel Logan Brengle

The secret of all failures, and of all true success, is hidden in the attitude of the soul in its private walk with God. The man who courageously waits on God is bound to succeed. He cannot fail. To other men he may appear for the present to fail, but in the end they will see what he knows all the time; that God was with him, making him, in spite of all appearance, "a prospering man".

Helps to Holiness
Samuel Logan Brengle

Keep me from thundering, and sundering,
Bombing my neighbor because of my
   bruises.
A person must know how to fail.

Walking With the Wind
Sallie Chesham

It is significant that the first parable was that of the Sower, which illustrated Jesus' acceptance of the fact of failure. There were many reasons why the seed had not brought forth the fruit, and even when it did produce, results were not in equal measure.

Power and Glory
Harry Dean

One of the evidences of the authenticity and credibility of the Scriptures is the frankness with which the failures of its heroes are recorded.

Search the Scriptures
Robert Hoggard

The disposition of so many has been to aim high but to fail on the ground work. They neglect the preparation of mind, and attention to elemental efficiency, leading to the heights. So the lower level seems to be crowded and the higher level is all to thin.

William McIntyre
The Officer's Review — 1933

As long as men are sinners who need salvation there will be failures.

The Person of Jesus Christ
John A. Morrison

If, after all, it seems as if you were doomed to suffer loss, you must be willing to lose, and that never so much as when you seem just about to win. God requires the duty. If its performance brings no return, that is God's affair, not yours. The soldier who has obeyed every order comes back from defeat, as from victory — with honor.

George Scott Railton
G.S.R.
John D. Waldron, Edit.

Is Satan interested in high standards? I think he often is. Not in doing them, of course, but in setting them. One of his favorite devices with holiness-seekers is to set standards so high that no one could attain them, and then to condemn the conscientious struggler for failing. There could be few better ways to breed disillusionment or despair.

Studies in Sanctification
Edward Read

Better fall short of the ideal a thousand times than decide that there are no ideals.

Meditations for the Common Man
George B. Smith

Mine to smile in face of failure,
    Thine to gladden my defeat;
Mine to kneel and drink of Marah;
    Thine to make its waters sweet.

Susie Swift
Salvation Army Song Book

Some people live on top of the world while others live with the world on top of them.

Manpower for the Master
Bramwell H. Tillsley

Faith

Faith and works should travel side by side, step answering to step, like the legs of men walking. First faith, and then works; and then faith again, and then works again — until you can scarely distinguish which is the one, and which is the other.

The Founder's Messages to Soldiers
William Booth

Saving faith does not mean just that with his mind one accepts the teachings about Christ as true. It means that he is willing to stake his life and his eternal fate upon Christ's promise to receive him, the sinner; to forgive his every sin, and to be his personal Savior for time and eternity.

Chosen to be a Soldier

One great fact about faith is that it is not subject to any of the other laws of our world. Faith knows no class — learned and ignorant are one here; it can be exercised by each alike. It knows no special temperament, no special age — the child can believe and receive equally with the man. Faith has no past. Faith unlocks every door.

Bramwell Booth
The Privilege of All Believers
John D. Waldron, Edit.

What is faith? It is giving myself to God, "risking" myself (if we may use such a term, when there is no risk about it), risking my all, for this life and for the next, on the truthfulness and the goodness of God, and daring to live and act contrary to everybody around me, knowing that all that God has said is true.

Life and Death
Catherine Booth

Nothing fills all hell with dismay like a reckless daredevil shouting faith. Nothing can stand before a man with genuine shout in his soul!

Catherine Booth – Clibborn
Peace Like a River
Sallie Chesham

Faith reveals and interprets God's dealings. Faith brings the unseen and eternal world nearer to us and makes it more real than the world of time and sense. Like any earthly light, faith glows most brightly when it shines in the darkest places. It defies the darkness.

Friendship with Jesus
Florence Booth

By faith, I mean, in its general sense, the belief of what God has said, and by saving faith, I mean the trust of the soul to and in Christ as the only and all-sufficient Savior for time and eternity.

Salvation Soldiery
William Booth

The confidence that moves the mountains of misery and vice; that raises to life the dead in trespasses and sins; that makes us the masters of passion and pride, and empowers us to walk in the way of holiness, is faith in God alone.

The Founder's Messages to Soldiers
William Booth

Faith, simple faith, unmixed faith in God's promises, can no more exist in the same heart with sorrow than can fire and water or light and darkness consort together — one extinguishes the other.

The Soul-Winner's Secret
Samuel Logan Brengle

God never leads us in such a way as to do away with the necessity of faith.

When the Holy Ghost is Come
Samuel Logan Brengle

God's wisdom and ability to make all things work together for our good are not to be measured by our understanding, but to be firmly held by our faith.

When the Holy Ghost is Come
Samuel Logan Brengle

Great faith sees God and fights manfully against all odds, and though the enemy apparently triumphs, wins moral and spiritual victory, as did Christ on Calvary, and as did the martyrs who perished in flame.

Ancient Prophets
Samuel Logan Brengle

What though the treacherous road may wind,
Faith in my heart assures my mind;
E'en when His face I do not see,
The hand of Jesus reaches me.

Oliver Holbrook
Salvation Army Song Book

Let us receive this truth; let us truly believe it; let us rest in it, trusting our God to reconcile the contradictions, to unravel the tangle and weave the threads into a satisfactory pattern.

Fuel for Sacred Flame
T. Henry Howard

Faith is the end of our resources and the beginning of God's.

From My Treasure Chest
Flora Larsson

The real saint has arrived safely in the harbor of implicit faith in God.

From My Treasure Chest
Flora Larsson

Perhaps the most serious thing that can happen to a soldier of Christ is that he should lose the art of simple believing.

The Silences of Christ
Albert Orsborn

Give me the faith that claims the power,
  That stubborn devils cannot turn,
That lion teeth cannot devour,
  That furnaces can never burn;
That never fears the tyrant's frown,
That wins and wears a martyr's crown.
Give me faith that clearly sees
  What worldy eyes cannot behold,
That knows the way the Lord to please
  That can His secret ways unfold;
That gives up greatness for the good,
That wins the fight with Fire and Blood.

William Pearson
Salvation Army Song Book

The faith that saves is the faith that brings the life and power of God into the soul — a faith that makes the proud man humble, the impatient man patient, the haughty man lowly in heart, the stingy man open-handed and liberal, the lustful man clean and chaste, the fighting, quarrelsome man meek and gentle, the liar truthful, the thief honest, the light and foolish sober and grave, a faith that purifies the heart, that sets the Lord always before the eyes, and fills the soul with humble, holy, patient love toward God and man.

Helps to Holiness
Samuel Logan Brengle

While faith stands waiting and trembling, taunted by mocking devils and all manner of suggestions to doubt, it is hard not to flinch; but flinching will prove as fatal to the revelation of Jesus to your souls as a movement will prove to your picture when before a photographer's camera.

Heart Talks on Holiness
Samuel Logan Brengle

Faith is deepened every time we exercise it. We must use what faith we have, not waste time regretting its limitations.

The Armoury Commentary — The Four Gospels
Frederick Coutts, Edit.

Faith never contradicts reason; it transcends it, sees beyond it.

The Armoury Commentary — The Four Gospels
Frederick Coutts, Edit.

The truth is that when faith goes out by the door, superstition comes in at the window.

Essentials of Christian Experience
Frederick Coutts

Often faith is a state of tension. It is making an affirmative answer to a total view of life that many facts appear to deny and, seeing it is faith and not certainty, it is always open to challenge.

Reason to Believe
Harry Dean

Faith loves the stars too dearly to be fearful of the night.

Stuff That Makes an Army
William G. Harris

Faith does not minimize difficulties but does magnify God.

Manpower for the Master
Bramwell H. Tillsley

A man doesn't obtain more than he believes in.

To the Point
Bramwell Tripp

Despair will grip us unless we have faith in a Power beyond our own muscles, trust in an intelligence beyond our own minds, and confidence in a destiny beyond our own devising. We can go on weaving the threads of our lives on the loom of life only if we believe that the eventual pattern will have form and meaning.

To the Point
Bramwell Tripp

Faithfulness

Stand by your covenant and it shall be God's responsibility to bring you through.

Messages to the Messengers
Catherine Bramwell-Booth

Difficulties disappear for the man who is faithful.

The Call to Holiness
Frederick Coutts

Great spiritual achievements depend upon faithfulness in small things.

The Armoury Commentary — The Four Gospels
Frederick Coutts, Edit.

I shall not need for man to say,
Of my closed work, that this or that
Was born of pure sincerity,
And fitted for eternity;
If, by God's grace before I die,
The voice within shall testify;
"Counted faithful."
This will suffice, though I should stand
By a small task, for a pure heart
May yet be great in simple ways;
Through unromantic working days
My labor, led by truth's pure light;
Then, comforted, reflect at night,
"Counted faithful".
Oh! it were joy to give my Lord
A full, completed working day.
But if He bids me hand to Him
A half day work, my heart; what then?
What then, my heart? Just as before!
Then this there can be nothing more —
"Counted faithful".

The Beauty of Jesus
Albert Orsborn

What a work the Lord has done,
    By His saving grace;
Let us praise Him, every one.
    In His holy place.
He has saved us gloriously,
Lead us onward faithfully
Yet He promised we should see
    Even greater things.

Albert Orsborn
Salvation Army Song Book

Fanaticism

Fanaticism is without mercy. It has caused people in all ages to feel justified in seeking blood often by torturing those who would not conform to their particular religious opinions or modes of worship.

Friendship With Jesus
Florence Booth

Formalism will leave your house cold and freezing; fanaticism will burn your house down.

Samuel Logan Brengle
Portrait of a Prophet
Clarence W. Hall

Fasting

Christian fasting is concerned with more than food — with the need for Christian discipline in every detail of life.

The Armoury Commentary — The Four Gospels
Frederick Coutts, Edit.

Fasting, in the spiritual realm, is a parallel to pruning in the realm of nature. Just as we lop off some of the branches of a tree in order that some of the others may be more vigorous, and lessen the number of buds on a rose bush that we may have better blooms, so it has to be in the concern of the soul.

The Christian Charter
George B. Smith

Fear

The spirit tries to influence men more by appealing to their hopes than to their fears.

Life and Death
Catherine Booth

Fear destroys peace of mind, and robs life of love, rest, and beauty. Many go without present necessities, would not dream of buying a few flowers to transform their room, because fear goads them to grab and save, to be poor in the present in order to provide against a future of poverty.

Friendship With Jesus
Florence Booth

Is not prudence with many people only another word for cowardice?

The General's Letters
William Booth

71

No man can be happy while there is a fear in him that something is wrong.

Salvation Soldiery
William Booth

As for me, I am determined to be of good courage. God has been better to me than all my fears and the fears of all my friends.

Helps to Holiness
Samuel Logan Brengle

Our dungeon may be that of our own fears and misgivings.

Essentials of Christian Experience
Frederick Coutts

If I were asked to name the three main causes of lack of peace in the human heart I should say they were fears of the future, resentments against others and a guilty conscience.

From My Treasure Chest
Flora Larsson

One of the greatest difficulties that God has had with His people in a time of crisis has been the spirit of fear — the fear of man. In all the early Bible characters there seems to be some degree of fear. At the Red Sea, when the panicking Israelites said, "Let us go back!" Moses jumped to his feet and cried, "Stand still!" Then, to the fearing, another voice from the blue was heard, "Go forward!" The fear nots of the Bible stand out like great beacon lights — like the search lights that play at night for the guidance of airplanes.

William McIntyre
The Officer's Review — 1934

Observation seems to show that men who fear no foe are sometimes very much afraid of their friends.

The Silences of Christ
Albert Orsborn

Fellowship (Human)

Brief is our journey through the years,
  And fleeting are our longest days;
We cherish every laden hour
  And linger o'er familiar ways;
For toil and grief, or joy and gain,
  When blessed by God, are sanctified,

And friendships forged through serving Him,
  With each new test, are purified.

Catherine Baird
Salvation Army Song Book

Put a burning coal or stick by itself and the fire will often go out, and it will be cold and black; but put several sticks or coals together and they will burn brightly. And it is so with hearts full of the holy fire.

The Way Of Holiness
Samuel Logan Brengle

The best neighbors I know anything about are my two hands. They have lived on opposite sides of the street for many, many years, and they have never had a row. If my left hand is hurt, my right hand immediately drops all other business and rushes across the way to comfort it, help it out of its trouble. If one happens to hurt the other, the hurt one doesn't get in a huff and say, "Here, I will not stand for that; you can't treat me that way," and get into a fight. No, no. They are good neighbors. My two hands are members of one another. And Christians should be like that. They are members of Christ's body. They should be as loving, as forbearing, as sympathetic and helpful toward each other as are my two hands.

Samuel Logan Brengle
Portrait of a Prophet
Clarence W. Hall

The religion of Jesus is social. It is inclusive, not exclusive. We can have the glory only as we are united. We must be one in spirit with our brethren. Let division come and the glory departs. Let the unity of brotherly love continue, and the glory abides.

Samuel Logan Brengle
At the Center of the Circle
John D. Waldron, Edit.

An Army convert has no need to look far for new companions. At the penitent form the seeker places himself where Salvation Army comrades can help him — where the Ethiopian can meet his Phillip, Saul his Ananias, and the sinner the penitent form sergeant — this wise and kindly person of the same sex has traced the ways of God in his own, and many another's life during countless seasons of prayer, and places his experience at the disposal of the penitent.

The Mercy Seat
William Burrows

Army comradeship must be among the richest in the world, for the one flag unites men and women of all nations, and the uniform does away with the need of personal presentation.

My Best Men Are Women
Flora Larsson

The Lord is often revealed to a group as He is not to one alone. There is a sweet social side to religion that is missed by the man living entirely to himself. He may manage to keep the first of the two great commandments, "Love the Lord thy God," but how can he love his neighbor "as himself" without rubbing elbows with him?

Christ's Cabinet
William McIntyre

Fellowship With God

For the faithful knew now that death
Was neither evil nor fearful.
They understood the green pastures,
Still waters, protection
Are laden tables where the inner wealth
Of communion with the Eternal, and known to
Those who follow the Good Shepherd on
His perilous journey to seek the lost,
And on their journey Home
Forever in the House of the Lord.

Reflections
Catherine Baird

Spiritual authority always expresses intimate fellowship with God.

The Armoury Commentary — The Four Gospels
Frederick Coutts, Edit.

Fellowship suggests something of an atmosphere, where the soul lives and moves with the Divine; or of light, where the divine illumination falls on life's ways and problems — even right up to the vestibule of eternity, when the portals open

to let the soul exchange its fellowship of faith for face-to-face intercourse with its Lord.

Fuel for Sacred Flame
T. Henry Howard

Spirit of Eternal Love,
Guide me, or I blindly rove;
Set my heart on things above,
Draw me after Thee.
Earthly things are paltry show —
Phantom charms, they come and go.
Give me constantly to know
Fellowship with Thee.

The Beauty of Jesus
Albert Orsborn

Flag (Salvation Army)

Every army has its colors,
    And the soldiers hold them dear;
They will stand by and protect them,
    Facing death midst ringing cheer.
Let the army of salvation
    Rally at their Captain's call
Driving back the power of darkness;
    Do not let the colors fall.

Combat Songs of The Salvation Army
Sallie Chesham

It (the flag) is emblematic of the aggressiveness of salvation warfare and is a reminder of God's dealings with the Army in the past.

Chosen to be a Soldier

The flag is emblematic of the aggressiveness of salvation warfare and of important spiritual truths which underlie and prompt all Salvation Army effort.

Orders and Regulations for Officers

As Israel's history cannot be separated from her religion, so the Army flag, first among the military symbols adopted by the Founder, cannot be detached from Salvation Army history.

The Banner of Love
Catherine Baird

Just as my faith lives not in Palestine,
Nor rests upon the thrill of Mile End
Waste,
So this my flag is memory of the real.
It is the symbol, the reflected truth;
Beyond itself, it loyalty provokes.

Albert E. Mingay
Book of Salvationist Verse
Catherine Baird

The Salvation Army flag is never flown at
half-mast, for in all circumstances the love
of which it speaks is victorious.

The Banner of Love
Catherine Baird

I am dying under the Army flag; it is yours
to live and fight under.

Catherine Booth
Mrs. Booth
W. T. Stead

The flag is a symbol first of our devotion
to our great Captain in heaven and to the
great purpose for which He came down
and shed His blood that He might redeem
men and women from sin and death and
Hell! Secondly, this flag is emblematical of
our faithfulness to our great trust. Jesus
only wants faithful soldiers in order to win
the heathen for His inheritance and the uttermost parts of the earth for His possession. May God help us to be faithful. Faithful to conscience, to principles, to man
and to God. This flag is also an emblem of
victory! In this war of ours victory is sure.
But by what power is this victory to be
achieved? By The Holy Ghost!

Catherine Booth
The History of The Salvation Army — Volume 2
Robert Sandall

There's no voice so fondly calling,
  There's no face that I could see,
No melody so enthralling
  As that first flag given to me.

Poems
Evangeline Booth

They bid me choose an easier path,
  And seek a lighter cross;
They bid me mingle with Heaven's gold
  A little of earth's dross;
They bid me, but in vain, once more
  The world's illusions try;

I cannot leave the dear old flag,
  'Twere better far to die.
I answer, life is fleeting fast,
  I cannot, cannot wait;
For me my comrades beckoning stand
  Beyond the pearly gate;
I hear their hallelujahs! grand,
  I hear their battle cry;
O do not leave the dear old flag,
  'Twere better far to die!

Frederick Booth-Tucker
Salvation Army Song Book

O flag of hallowed memories a thousand
times retold.
The chronicles of twice-born men beneath thy shade enrolled;
Glad trophies won from Satan's power
who fight nor count the odds,
Contented that the wounds be theirs, they
claim the victory God's.

Will J. Brand
Salvation Army Song Book

There is a flag that flies for freedom,
A flag that flies for liberty,
Let's march beneath its floating colors,
Share the victory.
It calls the people of all nations
To find salvation full and free;
I love its message and its meaning,
It's the flag for me.

There is a flag that calls to service,
The flag of yellow, red and blue;
It calls to men of deep compassion
And of courage, too.
Will you enlist beneath its colors
And dedicate yourself anew?
Beneath the flag of selfless service
There's a place for you!

The Blood of the Lamb
John Gowans

I'll be true! I'll be true!
  True to my colors, the yellow, red and
blue.
I'll be true! I'll be true!
  True to my Savior in the Army.

Gustavus Grozinsky
Salvation Army Song Book

When you have seen the old Standard wave nightly amidst a yelling, fiendish mob; when you have seen it still held aloft in spite of every attempt to lower it; when you have seen your comrades bruised and bleeding in defense of it – then you will understand the sacredness which hallows it to those who have such memories. A Salvation Army march without a flag seems an incomplete affair.

The Old Corps
Edward H. Joy

The flag of the Lord is now thrown to the breeze,
And God calls His warriors true,
To sacrifice their ease,
And over all lands and seas
To bear His yellow, red and blue.

T.C. Marshall
Gems for Songsters #1

Army Flag! Thy three-fold glory
Greets the rising of the sun;
Radiant is the way before thee,
Rich trophies to be won.
Onward in the cause of Jesus!
Witness where the dawning glows,
Flying on the wings of morning,
Follow where the Savior goes!

The Beauty of Jesus
Albert Orsborn

This flag never set people against each other; never caused bloodshed; never provoked divisions. It has brought together the sons and daughters of all nations in the bond of peace.

The House of My Pilgrimage
Albert Orsborn

Formalism

Those who have not the Holy Spirit, or who do not heed Him, fall easily and naturally into formalism, substituting lifeless ceremonies, sacraments, genuflections and ritualistic performances for the free, glad, living worship inspired by the indwelling Spirit. They sing, but not from the heart. They say their prayers but they do not really pray.

When the Holy Ghost is Come
Samuel Logan Brengle

If I were asked to put into one word what I consider to be the greatest obstacle to the success of Divine Truth, even when uttered by sincere and real people, I should say, STIFFNESS.

Papers on Godliness
Catherine Booth

Forgiveness

The noblest vengeance is forgiveness.

The Officer – 1919

Forgiveness is as natural to love as fragrance is to flowers.

Bramwell Booth
Trumpets of the Lord
Catherine Bramwell-Booth

'Tis hard to tell how keen sin's woe;
Ask of the crowd its depth that know,
And turn to Him who loved you so,
He'll freely all forgive.

Songs of the Evangel
Evangeline Booth

Show mercy. No soul was ever made poor by loving too much, or injured by forgiving too often.

Messages to the Messengers
Catherine Bramwell-Booth

There is no covering for evil but that of pardon. Forgetfulness and concealment are but poor substitutes – narcotics, from the effects of which the miserable victim must, sooner or later, awaken to discover that his state is indeed worse than his first. The sinner requires not a change of name, but a change of character.

Life of Catherine Booth – Volume 2
Frederick Booth-Tucker

There are those who need to hear the message of divine pardon before they can appreciate the message of divine power.

Arnold Brown
The Privilege of All Believers
John D. Waltron, Edit.

The life that is wholly forgiven needs to be wholly possessed.

The Call to Holiness
Frederick Coutts

When I receive
Your pardon in my soul,
I only see
An atom of the whole.
I glimpse the essence
Of a love so wide
That none who really seek it
Are denied!

O Lord!
John Gowans

Perhaps, after all, it is prodigals who get nearest to the real Father heart. Having been forgiven much, they love much, and know intimately.

Out of the Depths
Clarence W. Hall

The curtain has descended forever on the sadder acts; God Himself has rung it down, and there will be no further attempt to peep backstage. The grim clouds of tragedy have passed by.

Out of the Depths
Clarence W. Hall

The foundation of religious experience is a clear sense of sins forgiven.

Fuel for Sacred Flame
T. Henry Howard

I have no claim on grace;
I have no right to plead;
I stand before my Maker's face
Condemned in thought and deed.
But since there died a Lamb
Who, guiltless, my guilt bore,
I lay fast hold on Jesus' name,
And sin is mine no more.

Albert Orsborn
Salvation Army Songbook

Forgiveness is not only an act of grace; it's an act of justice.

Meditations for the Ordinary Man
George B. Smith

This spirit of forgiveness is a delicate essence distilled from the gift of God's pardoning love.

Meditations for the Ordinary Man
George B. Smith

True forgiveness is the silence of a forgiving heart. It is a feeling of goodwill which transcends the logic of fact.

The Christian Charter
George B. Smith

Freedom

There is no delusion more common among men than the belief that liberty, which is a good thing in itself, is so good as to enable those who possess it to dispense with all other good things. But as no man lives by bread alone, neither can nations or factories or shipyards exist solely upon unlimited freedom to have their own way.

Darkest England and the Way Out
William Booth

For God imposes liberty
To take my own way. Liberty
To scorn the secret judgment conscience makes,
Reject God's laws and substitute the fakes
That pride or lust or merely love of self
Dictates to bind me, turn my gold to pelf;
Bold God would purify and prove, until
His likeness shone from it, I reach the goal
For which God formed me, made me a living soul.

Fighting for the King
Catherine Bramwell-Booth

Thank you, God, for the miracle of flight. Teach me to fly, to spread my wings, to soar high so I can see wide.

Dear God
Virginia Talmadge

Fruit

Godliness is measured by fruitfulness.

The Holy Spirit — Friend and Counsellor
Milton S. Agnew

You are sowing to the flesh; but do you see what the harvest must be — *must be*? For God has so made you, that if there were no material hell, while you exist and remain guilty, you must be a hell to yourself.

Life and Death
Catherine Booth

Our hearts may be as pure as the heart of an archangel, and we may love with perfect love, and yet our conduct may be misjudged and we be accounted by others as being anything but fully saved.

Heart Talks on Holiness
Samuel Logan Brengle

Every gift of the Spirit which a believer may claim to possess must be judged by its power to produce a more Christlike character.

The Call to Holiness
Frederick Coutts

Seeds now we are sowing, and fruit they must bear,
For blessing or cursing, for joy or despair;
Though we may forget them, the things of the past
Will work out God's sentence upon us at last.

Richard Slater
Salvation Army Song Book

I became alarmed at the possibility of myself being a withered branch. What a tragedy it would be to have an organization contact, but be out of touch with the divine; to be disconnected from the True Vine, though still held up high; to have a secure position, and yet, if taken down from it and placed in fresh soil, be incapable of growth and fruit-bearing — for disconnected dead branches cannot produce anything.

George Walker
The Officer's Review — 1934

It is no more possible to plant a stick in the ground, hang a bunch of grapes on it, and call it a vine, than it is to ascribe external activities that do not spring from a heart indwelt by the Lord as fruit of the Spirit!

The Desert Road to Glory
Clarence Wiseman

Future

If we are to better the future we must disturb the present.

Catherine Booth
The Life of Catherine Booth — Volume 2
Frederick Booth-Tucker

We strain our eyes, peering into the future, wondering what its issues will be and what it holds for us and ours. Our loved ones and friends die and pass out of our sight. Life weakens, its full tides ebb, the sun is setting, the night is falling, and we stand by a silent, shoreless sea where we look in vain for a returning sail, and upon which we must launch alone. And we cling to life and shrink back with fear and lo! He comes walking on the water and says, "It is I. Be not afraid!"

Guest of the Soul
Samuel Logan Brengle

To concentrate exclusively in the here and now is neither necessary or right. The believer can live fully in "time present" because "time future" is assured — it is in the safe hands of Christ.

Reason to Believe
Harry Dean

God wisely keeps from us the sight of our shattered dreams that tomorrow sometimes brings.

Out of the Depths
Clarence W. Hall

The future may prove to be the biggest challenge that Salvation Army courage has ever faced. Will we continue to preach on the street corners and knock on strange doors when the pagan society of tomorrow has rejected us because we're too religious for its tastes? Will we continue to be God's righteous remnant (the five or ten for whose sake God is willing to save a city from destruction) even when holiness becomes a crime? Will we walk into "deathful" situations as have the soldiers, missionaries, and chaplains before us and trust God for courage as they did?

Marching On!
Ted Palmer

The future belongs to the consecrated, not to the comedian.

The Christian Charter
George B. Smith

G

Gambling

The Salvation Army is acutely aware of the suffering and deprivation visited upon countless thousands of persons as the result of gambling. Our basic spiritual motivation, as well as our social welfare experience, indicate that many of those who gamble tend to disregard their primary responsibilities in life and frequently they embarrass and deeply hurt their loved ones and dependents thereby.

The Salvation Army sees in gambling a basic unfairness, for its allure is in the prospect of getting something for nothing. Since all gambling is motivated by selfishness, it runs counter to the Christian experience of love, respect and concern for one's fellow man. Its continued practice often leads to grosser excesses and tends to undermine the personality and character of the gambler.

The Salvation Army is unalterably opposed to gambling and regards any attempt to legalize it as morally wrong. Official sanction and public acceptance of this evil would, in the opinion of The Salvation Army, be contrary to the great principles upon which this country was founded and contrary to the Christian principles to which we subscribe.

Salvation Army Position Statement
Commissioner's Conference
October, 1964

Gambling violates the fourfold duty of man:

a. It is a sin against God, since it is to misuse and waste my substance and my brains, for which I shall have to give account.

b. It is a sin against myself, since its corroding influence turns me into a selfish, grasping man.

c. It is a sin against my neighbor, since it is an effort to profit at his expense. Even if gambling profits the pocket, someone else must lose.

d. It is a sin against society, since it inflicts vast evils upon the community.

Frederick Coutts
The Officer's Review — 1933

Betting is money promised for no real equivalent.

George Scott Railton
G.S.R.
John D. Waldron, Edit.

Gifts (Giving)

If there is in any heart but one drop of that burning passion which stripped the skies of its brightest and best, and gave the Son of God that none need perish, it MUST give. Give, if it means to suffer; give, if it means to lose; give, in life; give, in death; give forever throughout eternity!

Love Is All
Evangeline Booth

What have you to give? Your young heart's love; its faith, its prayers, and its praise. How shall you give? As you will be advised in different ways from time to time — sparingly? As people shall deserve it of you? Think if you had only received from God what you deserved! Will you give in harmony with the giving of others; this is, as you promised, keeping faith with your own heart's intentions? Will you give bountifully — more than people have deserved of you; freely — without thought of getting anything for yourself in return, though you often will, for it is marvelously true that with what measure ye mete, it shall be measured to you again? Will you give courageously; in spite, that is, of other people's sneers or ridicule? To be generous in your opinion or praise of another when some are criticizing and minimizing their work, demands very real courage. Give "not meanly"; that is, when you have a chance of bestowing your love and care, do it as though there were enough and to spare, not as though you were giving as little as possible.

Messages to the Messengers
Catherine Bramwell-Booth

What we cannot give to God, we must give up.

Arnold Brown
The Privilege of All Believers
John D. Waldron, Edit.

He measures giving always by its quality; His concern is not how much we give, but why we give and how much is left.

The Armoury Commentary — The Four Gospels
Frederick Coutts, Edit.

Cast thy bread upon the waters and it shall return after many days as hot buttered toast!

Elijah Cadman
A Goodly Heritage
Wilfred Kitching

At the end, Lord, You will not ask what I have saved, but what I have given.

Just a Moment, Lord
Flora Larsson

It is a simple philosophy: all one's gifts are dedicated to serve God and mankind under the Army flag, and the glory and honor of such service lies in the fact that the balance between giving and getting is always weighted on the heavenly side.

My Best Men are Women
Flora Larsson

I have not much to give Thee, Lord,
    For that great love which made Thee mine;
I have not much to give Thee, Lord,
    But all I have is Thine.

Richard Slater
Salvation Army Song Book

In God's economy our giving is a recognition of His absolute claim to the total wealth of mankind.

Meditations for the Ordinary Man
George B. Smith

Though your all is very little,
    Cast it in God's treasury;
Jesus always recognizes,
    What is given cheerfully.

Barbara Stoddart
Salvation Army Song Book

Glory

The one unchanging command ever to be remembered is: "Give to Jesus glory!"

Orders and Regulations for Officers

Being made pure, being sanctified, brings His glory into our lives in a never ending cadence. We constantly are being changed from glory to glory – His glory, not ours.

The Better Covenant
Milton S. Agnew

Glory is not going to be revealed to us, not toward us, but in us. We shall be like Him. There is no higher glory. Union with God is the highest glory of both God and saint.

More Than Conquerors
Milton S. Agnew

When God has been deprived of His glory, men are also deprived of theirs.

More Than Conquerors
Milton S. Agnew

Jesus, Light of God, so holy,
Fan my life into a flame.
Through the candle of my spirit,
Radiate Your glorious name.

God's Whispers in my Heart
Shirley Pavey

I would go up to the mount of the Lord where the vision is too big for my heart to hold.

Dear God
Virginia Talmadge

Nothing is lost that glorifies the Savior's name.

The Desert Road to Glory
Clarence Wiseman

God

We believe that there is only one God who is infinitely perfect, the Creator, Preserver and Governor of all things, and who is the only proper object of religious worship.

Salvation Army Doctrine #2

God's unchangeableness is not like the rigidity of a machine, but is the attribute of a person whose nature, while unchanging, finds expression in an infinite variety of ways.

Handbook of Doctrine

If you do let us, all of us, officers, and rank and file, down somewhere with cords, into some dungeon, out of sight, forever, God will remain, and He is the difficulty.

Salvation Soldiery
William Booth

God is infinite, and your little mind and heart cannot exhaust the wonders of His wisdom and goodness and grace and glory in one short lifetime.

Helps to Holiness
Samuel Logan Brengle

A man's conception of holiness is governed by the character of the God he worships.

The Call to Holiness
Frederick Coutts

Just as the oneness of a piece of mineral or vegetable life is surpassed by the oneness of animal life, which in turn is surpassed by the richer oneness of human life, so that in turn is transcended by the unimaginable richness of Him whom we call Father, Son and Holy Spirit.

In Good Company
Frederick Coutts

Earthly kings need thrones to raise them up: God is prepared to stoop.

Power and Glory
Harry Dean

God is the Great Unrecognized whom most men look at without seeing.

Reason to Believe
Harry Dean

Old Testament religion did not begin with the concept of transcendence, but with the vital encounter between Jahweh and men. For the early Israelites God was not the God of the distant heavens but the God of their fathers, Abraham, Isaac and Jacob. He was present in their flesh and blood history. Old Testament religion belongs essentially here, not there; to the near, not the far; to the now, not the then. It is this sense of immediacy that needs to be rediscovered.

Reason to Believe
Harry Dean

In talking to people burdened by nervous suffering one repeatedly finds that they labor under an image of God, which, if applied to a fellow human being, would constitute him the most unattractive person imaginable.

Our Rebel Emotions
Bernard Mobbs

Man feels that nothing is under control until it is timed, measured, calculated. Like a boy trying to capture the sun with a butterfly net, we try to put a limit on God to crunch Him into our symbols. But though we may define God, we cannot confine Him.

Meditations for the Ordinary Man
George B. Smith

Thou art love's unfathomed ocean,
 Wisdom's deepest, clearest sea,
Heaven's and earth's salvation portion,
 Parent of Eternity;
 Grace and glory
In abundance flow from Thee.

Lillian Watkins
Salvation Army Song Book

Goodness

I have one passion. It has eaten at my brain and at my heart. It has sapped all my physical resources. It has absorbed all thought, all plans, all desires. It has risen above blunders, lightened all troubles. It has held me back from a thousand errors and unctionized a thousand achievements. This controlling force has been a passion for God and goodness.

Evangeline Booth
The General Was a Lady
Margaret Troutt

I suppose it is a pleasant sensation to feel that you are rich. I do not know what that pleasure is so far as my own experience goes. Earthly riches were never my portion. I suppose it is a pleasant thing to know that you are great and powerful in the sight of men. Of this I have had some little experience. It must be a pleasant thing, I fancy, to realize that you are wise and that you are considered such. It must be an unpleasant thing to be counted a fool, and more unpleasant still to know that you are one. But, in my estimation, it is a far greater satisfaction to feel that you yourself, are really and truly good, and engaged in the work of making other people good; and that you are, by the blessing of God, doing the Christlike work with success.

The Founder's Messages to Soldiers
William Booth

Goodness is better than greatness.

Guest of the Soul
Samuel Logan Brengle

Holiness makes one good all the time; not only in conduct, but also in character; not only in outward act, but also in inward thought and wish and feeling, and those who are content with anything below this, will miss the blessing.

Heart Talks on Holiness
Samuel Logan Brengle

A clever man may think he knows how clever he is, but a good man does not know how good he is. His eye is not turned inward upon any self-induced image but outward and upward to his Lord.

No Continuing City
Frederick Coutts

Goodness is love with its sleeves rolled up.

The Call to Holiness
Fredrick Coutts

Gossip

All our members shall be specially careful of each other's reputation, watch lovingly over each other's welfare, and promote it so far as lies in their power:

1. By prayer for each other,
2. By sympathy and practical help in the time of poverty, affliction, bereavement, or any other kind of tribulation.
3. By never allowing evil to be spoken of them unrebuked, by anyone, in their absence.

Christian Mission Pledge
The History of The Salvation Army — Volume 1
Robert Sandall

I know some who say they love Jesus; for hating they cannot be beat!
When it comes to the neighborhood gossip,
They never will take a back seat.
They tell you the latest in scandal,
And add a little bit more;
They sure will be lonesome in Heaven,
For no scandal can enter its door.

Combat Songs of The Salvation Army
Sallie Chesham

Salvationists must avoid gossip, criticism of individuals or religious denominations, discussion of party politics, argument, quarreling or anything disagreeable.

Orders and Regulations for Corps Officers

Some folks go out to tea,
And their tongues go pretty free
In discussing things they see
This side of Jordan.
They enlarge upon them all,
And bad names their neighbors call,
They'll get a mighty fall,
Over Jordan.

Combat Songs of The Salvation Army
Sallie Chesham

Be no party to any evil speaking about anyone; resolutely refuse to listen to a word that is unkind until you have made it clear that you will report everything to the person condemned and bring his slanderers to repeat their story before his face. Make no exception to this rule; have done with the whole pestilential business except on these terms.

Bramwell Booth
Trumpets of the Lord
Catherine Bramwell-Booth, Edit.

Nothing more quickly infects the whole man with the poison of doubt and hatred — the very spirit of Hell itself — than this practice of evil-speaking. It tarnishes everything it touches and blackens what it cannot consume. It fosters selfishness, destroys sympathy and kills love outright. Talk against one man long enough, and you will come to hate all men.

Bramwell Booth
Trumpets of the Lord
Catherine Bramwell-Booth

What is slander? It is the spreading of statements calculated to damage an individual for the mere gratification of personal spite and envy.

William Booth
The Founder Speaks Again
Cyril Barnes, Edit.

Things we hear are often not worth taking notice of, and folk who form their opinions by what "they say" seldom have opinions worth taking into account.

Messages to the Messengers
Catherine Bramwell-Booth

It is not by some wickedness, some Judas-like betrayal, some tempting and lying to the Holy Ghost, as did Ananias and Sapphira, that we grieve Him, but by that which most people count little and unimportant; by talk that corrupts instead of blessing and building up those that hear, by gossip, by bitterness, and uncharitable criticisms and faultfindings.

When the Holy Ghost is Come
Samuel Logan Brengle

Myriads of souls have backslidden; multitudes, almost persuaded, have turned back into darkness; many revivals have been quenched; and many houses of God have become spiritual sepulchres, all because of evilspeaking.

Heart Talks on Holiness
Samuel Logan Brengle

Taste gave place to talk.

Excursions in Thought
Jean Brown

It might be a good thing, Master,
 if we got tongue trouble
 when we misuse the gift of speech,
 or a rash spread on our lips
 when we had told lies
 or uttered cruel slander!
It would at least convince us that we had sinned.
We couldn't get away with so much!

I'm Growing, Lord
Flora Larsson

Gossip thrives on opposition, but dies of neglect when a soul lives above it.

The Silences of Christ
Albert Orsborn

Please, Lord, lock our lips against talk that plays tag.

Dear God
Virginia Talmadge

The Army grapevine is ubiquitous; throughout the world it disseminates information with astonishing efficiency, though at times it gets garbled in the process.

A Burning in My Bones
Clarence Wiseman

Government

Organization is essential to success and constantly needs the vitalizing and impelling force of the Holy Spirit, without which it would be useless.

Orders and Regulations for Corps Officers

Did a committee build the ark, emancipate the Israelites, or even command, or judge, or govern them after they were emancipated?

Salvation Soldiery
William Booth

It has never been intended that The Salvation Army should be governed merely by printed orders and regulations; a living army which fights can only be directed from hour to hour through the agency of living men, who make themselves thoroughly familiar with all its regulations and affairs and act accordingly.

William Booth
The History of The Salvation Army — Volume 2
Robert Sandall

Let every man fight as he is led, or every regiment charge up the hill and storm the redoubt, or do any deadly, murderous deeds according as they are resolved upon after discussion, and votes and majorities, and where will you be?

Salvation Soldiery
William Booth

There cannot be a greater mistake in this world than to imagine that men object to being governed. They like to be governed provided that the governor has his "head screwed on right" and that he is prompt to hear and ready to see and recognize all that is vital to the interests of the commonwealth. So far from there being an innate objection on the part of mankind to being governed, the instinct to obey is so universal that even when governments have gone blind, and deaf, and paralytic, rotten with corruption and hopelessly behind the times, they still contrive to live on. Against a capable government no people rebel. Only when stupidity and incapacity have taken possession of the seat of power do insurrections break out.

In Darkest England and the Way Out
William Booth

Nevertheless there must be regulations — they are a necessity. What is done must be done in some particular fashion, and if one way of doing it is better·than another, it must be the wisest course to discover that better way and to describe it in plain language, so that we may be able to walk in it until a still better becomes known. Regulation signifies that, so far as our knowledge extends, the particular course of action required by it is the best known to date.

William Booth
The History of The Salvation Army — Volume 2
Robert Sandall

They call the government of The Salvation Army a host of hard names — autocracy — but I reply to them that it is the government that God Himself invented. It was the government of Eden; it is the family government. It is the patriarchal government; it is the government of the Mosaic economy. Moses was the General, yet his people

were free. I say it is going to be the government of Heaven.

William Booth
The History of The Salvation Army — Volume 2
Robert Sandall

The danger of every religious organization has ever been that it becomes in time a rule of the pen, the desk, the counter, and red tape, till the spirit of the movement is swallowed up by its regulations.

Frederick Booth-Tucker
The Officer — 1893

Organization must not be overdone, lest the workers become like David in Saul's armor; lest their power be exhausted in routine; lest they become like a mighty engine that has not sufficient power to run it.

The Soul-Winner's Secret
Samuel Logan Brengle

The greatest danger to any religious organzation is that a body of men should arise in its ranks, and hold its positions of trust, who have learned its great fundamental doctrines by rote out of the catechism, but have no experimental knowledge of their truth inwrought by the mighty anointing of the Holy Ghost, and who are destitute of "an unction from the Holy One".

When the Holy Ghost is Come
Samuel Logan Brengle

Of necessity, in any army there must be generals and other commanding officers. However, they are all part of the fighting force. God never delegates only those in command to do the fighting, nor does He maintain a standby army. He has no reserves and there is never a discharge from the ranks.

When God Calls You
Edward Deretany

Orders and regulations are intended to be to a Salvation Army Officer what rails are intended to be to a well ordered railway. Rails are certainly not intended to curtail the power or restrict the usefulness of a locomotive. On the contrary, they direct the use of its energies and enable it to produce results, which apart from the rails, could never be obtained. For while the locomotive is capable of developing power quite apart from the double lines of steel rails on which it runs, it could not take the train from, say, New York to Boston, without them no matter what strains were put upon the boiler in generating power.

Edward Higgins
The Officer's Review — 1932

Grace

We believe that we are justified by grace through faith in our Lord Jesus Christ and that he that believeth hath the witness in himself.

Salvation Army Doctrine #8

The statement that man's sinful state is not in harmony with God's purposes for him prepares the way for the good news that this can be remedied by God's redeeming work in Christ. If man is subject to the wrath of God, he is also the object of God's redeeming grace..

Handbook of Doctrine

Grace is impelling in its nature of urgency. But it is not compelling. Jesus said, "And I, if I be lifted up from the earth, will draw all men unto Me." (John 12:32). The word is draw, not drag. His grace is a magnet. It is not a chain.

The Security of the Believer
Milton S. Agnew

If a man has to work for it, it is not grace, but rather a payment.

More Than Conquerors
Milton S. Agnew

From a secret armory
The grace of Jesus strengthens me.

Olive Holbrook
Salvation Army Song Book

Not the depth of my sin
But the breadth of His grace;
Not the darkness within,
But the light of His face;
Not my weakness of faith
But the surge of His power.

From My Treasure Chest
Flora Larsson

I have no claim on grace;
I have no right to plea
I stand before my Maker's face,
Condemned in word and deed.
But since there died a Lamb
Who, guiltless, my guilt bore,
I lay fast hold of Jesus' name
And sin is mine no more.

The Beauty of Jesus
Albert Orsborn

Any time which still is mine by grace, shall be dedicated to pay installments on a still recurring debt.

Memoirs of Peter
Arthur Pitcher

God's grace is not conditioned by the worth of its object.

The Desert Road to Glory
Clarence Wiseman

Grace is a one-word summary of all Christ's work.

The Desert Road to Glory
Clarence Wiseman

Growth

What a deal there is of going to meetings and getting blessed, and then going away and living just the same, until sometimes we, who are constantly engaged in trying to bring people nearer to God, go away so discouraged that our hearts are almost broken. We feel that people go back again from the place where we have led them, instead of stepping up to the place to which God is calling them. They come and come, and we are, as the prophet says, unto them a very pleasant instrument or a very unpleasant one, as the case may be; and so they go away, and do not get anything. They do not make any definite advance. We have not communicated unto them any spiritual gift. They merely have their feelings stirred and, consequently, they live the next week exactly as they lived the last, and go down under the temptation just as they did before.

Papers of Godliness
Catherine Booth

85

Everything that has life begins small. The largest oak was once enfolded in an acorn. The most skillful musician in the world one time did not know one note from another. The most learned man now living once did not know A from Z. Moses was once a helpless babe in a floating ark of bulrushes. The General was once a young convert. But they grew and increased. If there is spiritual life in you, you will grow, if you will do with your might what your hands find to do.

Heart Talks on Holiness
Samuel Logan Brengle

No place
For my burdens
But gone,
Nowhere to travel
But on.
There's nothing
To keep me
From Glory —
So help me,
O Lord,
In Your love,
To march on!

Wind Chimes
Sallie Chesham

The Christian is free to grow in love to the extent that he repeatedly realizes the unfailing love of Christ.

The Armoury Commentary — The Four Gospels
Frederick Coutts, Edit.

The man surrendered to God's will
From sin and self set free
Rooted and grounded in God's Word
Is likened to a tree.
The storms of life will surely come
And others fail to stand
But he, because his roots go deep
Is upheld by God's hand.

Verna M. Davis
It's Beautiful
Dorothy Breen, Edit.

Guidance

The light behind my dreams was God's illumining.

Mrs. Captain Ann Ashworth
This Was Their Call

We start out in the morning, and we know not what person we may meet, what paragraph we may read, what word may be spoken, what letter we may receive, what subtle temptation may assail or allure us, what immediate decisions we may have to make during the day, that may turn us almost imperceptibly but nonetheless surely, from the right way. We need the guidance of the Holy Spirit.

When the Holy Ghost is Come
Samuel Logan Brengle

If God guides I can never be lost — not even if I am in a land I know not of. If all I do is as He directs, then there is no moment and no situation in which He cannot work for the furtherance of His redeeming purposes.

Essentials of Christian Experience
Frederick Coutts

Guilt

Guilt was with Judas. The wrath of God filled his conscience with such terror that he could not bear it, but hanged himself to be rid of the burden, forgetting that he was rushing into greater terror still.

Life and Death
Caterine Booth

Habit

Habit is habit, and cannot be thrown out of the window, but must be coaxed downstairs a step at a time.

Booth the Beloved
J. Evan Smith

Hate

Go on hating, night and day, in every place, under all circumstances. Bring this side of your nature well into play. Practice yourself in habits of scorn and contempt and loathing and detestation and revenge; but mind, let your hatred and revenge go in the right direction — the direction of sin, evil — the evil condemned by the Bible, the evil that Jesus Christ was manifested to destroy.

The General's Letters
William Booth

Our most intense animosity is directed towards that in other people which we dare not recognize in ourselves.

Our Rebel Emotions
Bernard Mobbs

Hatred is self-esteem *on fire*.

The Christian Charter
George B. Smith

The icebergs of calculated hate must melt in the warm zones of love.

Meditations for the Ordinary Man
George B. Smith .

Healing

Ah, Lord, when the crowd gathered round Thee for healing,
I pressed 'mong the number and put in my claim,
And virtue from Thee, Lord, was found at that moment,
I felt I was whole, and I blessed Thy dear name.

Combat Songs of The Salvation Army
Sallie Chesham, Edit.

All ardent Christians believe in divine healing. All healing is the work of God whether done by prayer and faith, or by the skilled surgeon's scalpel, or by suitable diet, exercise, medicine and drugs.

The Holy Spirit — Friend and Counsellor
Milton S. Angew

From the crushed buttercup
    Rises the new pale shootlet;
From the sad heart springs up
    Hope, out of love's last rootlet.
That which has life will heal;
    Only dead things stay broken.

Lily Sampson
Book of Salvationist Verse
Catherine Baird, Edit.

Time heals!
But only cleansed wounds!
Our sores must first be felt and seen,
Then handled by a master touch;
The gash must lose its poison and its pain
Ere damaged flesh can win its own again.

Violet M. Beckett
Book of Salvationist Verse
Catherine Baird, Edit.

I did not underestimate the faith-healing question. I think I understand it now. God did not want the Army to be taken up with it. That was not His way. He wanted them to stick to the saving of souls and to leave the bodies to Him, only doing them all the good we can.

Catherine Booth
The Life of Catherine Booth — Volume 2
Frederick Booth-Tucker

Yes! Yes! Yes! The voices of the redeemed of Heaven, and of every suffering conquering saint on earth, blend in loudest chorus of thrilling testimony that comfort and healing is to be found in the Cross — that 'neath its shelter shall be discovered the consolations and the treasures which are found in darkness, the gain which is to spring out of loss, the victory which by our poverty shall make others rich.

Heart Messages
Emma Booth-Tucker

Christ's manifesto was, and is, a program of healing and liberation.

The Armoury Commentary — The Four Gospels
Frederick Coutts, Edit.

I compare these happenings to slight accidents through an outside agency, say, a splinter in one's hand or grit in the eye; to be removed at once and forgotten; only harmful if left in and allowed to set up inflammation.

Mildred Duff
Mildred Duff
Madge Unsworth

Healer of wounds and bearer of all pain, Thy touch, Thy power are evermore the same.

Robert Hoggard
Salvation Army Song Book

When shall I come unto the healing waters?
Lifting my heart, I cry to Thee my prayer,
Spirit of peace, my Comfortor and Healer,
In whom my springs are found, let my soul meet Thee there.

From a hill I know,
Healing waters flow,
O rise, Immanuel's tide,
And my soul overflow!

Wash from my hands the dust of earthly striving;
Take from my mind the stress of secret fear;
Cleanse Thou the wounds from all but Thee far hidden,
And when the waters flow let my healing appear.

Light, life and love are in that healing fountain,
All I require to cleanse me and restore;

Flow through my soul, redeem its desert places.
And make a garden there for the Lord I adore.

Albert Orsborn
Salvation Army Song Book

Lord, here today my great need I am feeling;
Wilt Thou not visit my soul once again?
I long to feel Thy sweet touch and its healing;
Wonderful Healer, touch me again.

Touch me again, touch me again,
Wonderful Healer, touch me again.

Often I've pressed through the throng for the blessing
Which, through my doubting, I've failed to obtain;
Here once again to Thy feet I am pressing;
Wonderful Healer, touch me again.

Only in Thee can I find liberation,
Cleansing and freedom from sin's hidden stain;
Only in Thee can I find full salvation,
Wonderful Healer, touch me again.

William H. Woulds
Salvation Army Song Book

Health

The body and soul are near neighbors and they greatly influence each other.

William Booth
Ancient Prophets
Samuel Logan Brengle

Well, the Lord's will be done. I have done my best for my God and for the people with my eyes; now, if it is His will, I must do my best for Him without my eyes.

William Booth
The History of The Salvation Army — Volume 5
Arch Wiggins

A few hours of extra sleep, and a little less to eat, would save many a defeat and put to flight many a doubt.

Messages to the Messengers
Catherine Bramwell-Booth

Oh, it is easy to preach in full and robust health about "grace, fathomless as the sea; grace enough for me." But the test comes in proving and practicing it in danger, in broken health, in poverty, in loneliness and neglect, and in sore trial.

Samuel Logan Brengle
Peace Like a River
Sallie Chesham

When there is inward peace and an ending of frustration, doubt and worry; when God's love fills the heart; when one is free from the strivings of self and of personal ambition, then every faculty of body and mind feels the benefit. Eating and drinking, nerves and blood pressure, share to some degree in the spiritual blessing.

Allister Smith
The Privilege of All Believers
John D. Waldron, Edit.

Heaven

For me; There's a mansion there for me,
    Up in that Land so bright and grand,
With a victor's palm I'll take my stand;
    Ha, ha; he, he, I'm not going back, you see;
If anyone's going to be happy There,
    It's me, me, me, me, me.

Combat Songs of The Salvation Army
Sallie Chesham, Edit.

In the Bible we're told
    Of a city of gold,
Which Jesus has gone to prepare;
    Though earth passes away,
And all things here decay,
    All is beauty and permanence
There.

Combat Songs of The Salvation Army
Sallie Chesham, Edit

Numberless as the sands of the seashore,
Numberless as the sands of the shore!
    O what a sight 'twill be
    When the ransomed host we see,
As numberless as the sands of the seashore!

F.A. Blackmer
Salvation Army Song Book

Once the sword, but now the scepter,
    Once the fight, now the rest and fame;
Broken every earthy fetter,
    Now the glory for the cross and shame;
Once the loss of all for Jesus,
    But now the eternal gain.
Trials and sorrows here have now their

meaning found,
    Mysteries their explanation;
Safe forever in the sunlight gleaming,
    Of His eternal salvation.

Herbert H. Booth
Salvation Army Song Book

Heaven will be a deal more like earth than we think, and we shall not be so much altered.

Catherine Booth
Mrs. Booth
W.T. Stead

There may be a lot of people there. I believe there will be the same differences in people there that there are here, and those who like to sit in a corner, playing a harp all day, they will let them, perhaps; but the people who will prod about and look after things and help the good, they will let them.

Catherine Booth
Mrs Booth
W.T. Stead

Oh, I wish you would let me go — I want to go home.

William Booth
The Armoury Commentary — The Four Gospels
Frederick Coutts, Edit.

They shall come from the east,
They shall come from the west,
And sit down in the Kingdom of God;
Both the rich and the poor, the despised, the distressed,
They shall sit in the Kingdom of God.
And none will ask what they have been
Provided that their robes are clean,
They shall come from the east,
They shall come from the west,
And sit down in the Kingdom of God.

The Blood of the Lamb
John Gowans

The throng that stand before the throne with victor's palms and crowns
Have been on earth, for Jesus, valiant soldiers;
Their fight is o'er, death's stream they've crossed,
But still in Heaven resounds the song about the Blood of their Redeemer.

Richard Slater
Gems for Songsters #1

Hell

I would go on an errand to Hell, if the Lord would give me the assurance that the Devil should not keep me there.

Catherine Booth
Life of Catherine Booth — Volume 2
Frederick Booth — Tucker

But here, come and listen! Listen to the march of millions to endless misery! Tramp! Tramp! Tramp! There they go; from every land, more especially from Christian lands, for God's bowels of compassion must move towards the heathen multitude; through every town, down every street, from every home, the children, the fathers and mothers, the aged sires — on they go; up to the Judgment Seat, and then down to — Hell!

The General's Letters
William Booth

Where God is not! O awful thought,
  A realm deserted, cast aside,
With sin to full fruition brought
  And evil crowned and deified;
Where dread remorse and vain desire
Burn like an unconsuming fire.

Will J. Brand
Salvation Army Song Book

If you go to Hell, it will be over the mangled body of Jesus.

The Army Drum
Elizabeth Swift Brengle

From hope of Heaven, by sinning driven,
The anguish of the unforgiven
  No mortal tongue can tell.
Remorse, despair, their lot shall be,
Eternal storms sweep o'er that sea,
  No rest, no peace in Hell.

John Lawley
Salvation Army Song Book

Heritage

Nothing the world has to give could induce the Army to part with one shred of its own hallowed past or one particle of the truths for which it stands or one duty which it holds sacred. No, what we want with the world is to save it.

Bramwell Booth
Trumpets of the Lord
Catherine Bramwell-Booth, Edit.

The great message of the Army of the past to the Army of the future is this: That The Salvation Army exists for the whole world.

Bramwell Booth
Trumpets of the Lord
Catherine Bramwell-Booth, Edit.

The Army has only escaped from the old ruts in which it would have stuck fast and been incapable of accomplishing its great work by desperate fighting against itself. There is no prejudice, there is no regard for old-fashioned ideas and customs which has not been, and is not today, strongly and respectably represented within the Army itself. But regard for those things, as for all other human opinions and powers, has been struggled against and overcome, because the General has, from the first, a single eye, and that single eye will enable us, if necessary, to emancipate ourselves even further still, will make it as easy to abandon Army customs, as the custom which prevailed before the Army, whenever it may be proved to our satisfaction that, by so doing, we should more rapidly or completely attain the one great end in view.

Twenty-One Years Salvation Army
George Scott Railton

We have been trying and, we thank God, with no little success, to break loose from all the trammels of custom and propriety which may in any degree have hindered or hampered us in the past. The dreadful tendency to settle down is apparent in connection with all religious work. We mean to gain the ear of the people for our Master, and we are more determined than ever that no conformity to any Church forms or ideas shall hinder us.

William Booth
The History of The Salvation Army — Volume 1
Robert Sandall

What God wants the Army to be He will prompt and inspire in the people. It's no good my hanging on to my old-fashioned ideas.

Commissioner Catherine
Catherine Bramwell-Booth

No tradition, however hallowed and apparently sacrosanct, can displace the Christian's loyalty to Christ.

The Armoury Commentary — The Four Gospels
Frederick Coutts, Edit.

Tradition, excellent in itself, is like a map; and a map is not the destination, but a guide to it.

The Armoury Commentary — The Four Gospels
Frederick Coutts, Edit.

We deceive ourselves if we think we can live on the spiritual capital of our fathers in the faith.

The Armoury Commentary — the Four Gospels
Frederick Coutts, Edit.

We should no more waste our breath sighing for the return of the giants of the past unless with equal fervor we covet the Spirit by whose strength they subdued kingdoms, wrought righteousness and waxed valiant in the fight. We cannot praise the total devotion of our fathers in the past and, at one and the same time, refuse to make a like dedication of ourselves in the present.

Essentials of Christian Experience
Frederick Coutts

The greatest disservice we could render to the past would be to adhere slavishly to our early methods.

The House of My Pilgrimage
Albert Orsborn

History

Many hands, many hearts, many heads have toiled and prayed and planned to bring the Army where it now is. History will record but a small part of the events, and many of the actors will be completely forgotten, but from God's history, on the Great Muster Day, every heartache, every tear, every agonizing prayer, every day and night of toil will be read out and credited to the proper persons. God won the victory, and to Him we give glory. It was not an uninteresting fight.

The War Cry
Marching to Glory
Edward McKinley

A wide knowledge of history tends to sanity, to sobriety, and correctness of judgment of man and events, if we have seen God in history. We need such knowledge to give us perspective, to study us, to save us from sharp judgments, to insure us against cocksureness on one hand and despair on the other. Without this wide view, we are like a tiny boat on a tempestuous sea, tossed like a ship on the waves, but with it we are more like a great ship that rides serenely over the billows.

Ancient Prophets
Samuel Logan Brengle

We are prone to look upon past ages and distant places as peculiarly favorable to godliness. Usually the further back we go, the more godly seems the age and the more blessed seem the men.

Heart Talks on Holiness
Samuel Logan Brengle

History is to a community what memory is to an individual.

In Good Company
Frederick Coutts

The Christian sets the worst that history can do constantly in the context of the best that God can do.

The Armoury Commentary — The Four Gospels
Fredrick Coutts, Edit.

Against the changing panorama of human rule, and overruling the passions and powers of man, God pursues His eternal purposes. Man is not left to drift along. The divine plan is never behind schedule.

Search the Scriptures
Robert Hoggard

When God's own people take themselves out of the sphere of His directive will, He may carry out His announced designs through men and nations who know Him not.

Search the Scriptures
Robert Hoggard

When the dilemmas of history are held up to the light by those who stand humbly in the presence of the Creator, their place in the ultimate scheme of things gradually becomes clearer. Not only is it true that "the Lord God omnipotent reigneth," but it is equally true that God will vindicate His promise in the book of Revelation, "Behold, I am making all things new."

A Burning in My Bones
Clarence Wiseman

Holiness

We believe that it is the privilege of all believers to be "wholly sanctified" and that their "whole spirit and soul and body" may be "preserved blameless unto the coming of our Lord Jesus Christ" (I Thess. 5:23)

Salvation Army Donctrine #10

A holy life is made up of a number of small things. Little words, not eloquent speeches or addresses; little deeds, not miracles or battles, not one great heroic act of martyrdom make up the Christian life. The avoidance of little evils, little sins, little inconsistencies, little weaknesses, little follies, indiscretions, indulgences of the flesh, the avoidance of such little things as these goes far to make up at least the negative beauty of a holy life.

The Officer — 1923

There is something seriously wrong with the spiritual life of any Christian who does not earnestly strive to become wholly devoted and obedient to God, strong and upright, true, pure, kind, loving and humble — in one word, holy, like Jesus.

Chosen to be a Soldier

Practical holiness is not something that begins by doing, but by being. Holiness works from the heart out to the surface.

Transformed Christians
Milton S. Agnew

Conversion is becoming a Christian — the noun. Sanctification is becoming Christian — the adjective.

The Holy Spirit — Friend and Counsellor
Milton S. Agnew

Sanctification is not only the removal of that which destroys, but also the addition of that which constructs.

Transformed Christians
Milton S. Agnew

This, after all, is true holiness: the Spirit of power, plus the Spirit of love, plus the Spirit of a sound mind, all three in a balanced, adequate portion! Overemphasize power and you have despotism. Isolate love and you court sentimentality. Focus on sane things and you foster rationalism. On the other hand, eliminate power and you have impotent wishing. Subtract love and you promote a critical self-righteousness. Drop a calm, well balanced mind and you invite emotionalism.

Transformed Christians
Milton S. Agnew

If holiness is possible anywhere for anyone at any time, it is possible anywhere for everyone at all times.

Bramwell Booth
The Splendor of Holiness
Frederick Coutts

He has not promised salvation from *sorrow*, but salvation from *sin*; not salvation from *temptation*, but salvation from *defeat*; not a salvation which is so complete that no further progress is possible, but the power to run and not be weary, to walk and not faint.

Likeness to God
Florence Booth

Holiness is God's way of providing a remedy for sin — an antidote in this life for its poison, a healing for its disease, a restoration for its destruction.

Likeness to God
Florence Booth

You must be willing to seek holiness, not for the sake of any gain to yourself, but because you are willing that God's purpose shall be carried out in you.

Likeness to God
Florence Booth

A sanctified life means a gentle, tender spirit; it means a fearless, undaunted zeal; it means the accompanying manifestation of the Holy Ghost. It is the prelude and condition and assurance of power.

Salvation Soldiery
William Booth

From the beginning, one of the most important features of the work has been the teaching of holiness, as a pure and heavenly state, which can be attained by anybody and enjoyed in perfect peace amidst all the temptations and harassings of everyday life.

Twenty-one Years Salvation Army
William Booth

Holiness to the Lord is to us a fundamental truth; it stands in the front rank of our doctrines. We inscribe it upon our banners. It is with us in no shape or form an open debatable question as to whether God can sanctify wholly, or whether Jesus does save His people from their sins.

Salvation Soldiery
William Booth

There is a deliverance — a deliverance from all sin — that can last all the days of your life, if you live to be as old as Methusaleh; and if you get properly saved, I shall be very sorry for you to die at all.

Salvation Soldiery
William Booth

With many sincere souls I have no doubt that one of the most serious hindrances in this strife is the coupling of holiness with happiness, and thinking that if they are holy they will be happy all the time; whereas, the Master Himself was a Man of Sorrows, and lived, more or less, a life of grief.

The Seven Spirits
William Booth

The blessing still means just that: an all embracing confidence in God, and everyday renouncing of my right to choose anything apart from Him.

Messages to Messengers
Catherine Bramwell-Booth

Holiness of heart does not insure us against those untoward and painful things which try our faith, but it does prepare us for the trial.

The Guest of the Soul
Samuel Logan Brengle

Holiness is not some lofty experience, unattainable except to those who can leap to the stars, but it is rather a lowly experience, which lowly men in the lowly walks of life can share with Jesus, by letting His mind be in them.

Heart Talks on Holiness
Samuel Logan Brengle

Holiness is a state in which there is no anger, malice, blasphemy, hypocrisy, envy, love of ease, selfish desires for good opinion of men, shame of the Cross, worldliness, deceit, debate, contention, covetousness, nor any evil desire or tendency in the heart.

Helps to Holiness
Samuel Logan Brengle

Holiness is that state of our moral and spiritual nature which makes us love Jesus in His moral and spiritual nature. It does not consist in perfection of intellect, though the experience will give much greater clearness to a man's intellect and simplify and energize his operations. Nor does it necessarily consist in his perfection of conduct, though a holy man seeks with all his heart to make his outward conduct correspond to his inward light and love. But holiness does consist in complete deliverence from the sinful nature, and in the perfection of the spiritual graces of love, joy, peace, longsuffering, gentleness, truth, meekness and self-control or temperance

Heart Talks on Holiness
Samuel Logan Brengle

Holiness will make you hot enough to burn your way through your circumstances.

The Way of Holiness
Samuel Logan Brengle

It is impossible for us to walk like Him, to live like Him, unless we have a heart like Him.

Helps to Holiness
Samuel Logan Brengle

Just as a man wants his watch to keep perfect time, his gun to fire true, his friends to be steadfast, his children to be obedient, and his wife to be faithful, so God wants us to be holy.

Samuel Logan Brengle
At the Center of the Circle
John D. Waldron

The baptism of the Holy Ghost is to bring us into union with Christ, into loving fellowship with the Heavenly Father, to fit snugly into God's great, complex scheme of life, and equip us for such service or sacrifice as falls to our lot.

Samuel Logan Brengle
At the Center of the Circle
John D. Waldron, Edit.

The electic current cannot transform the dead wire into a live one quicker than the Holy Spirit can flood a soul with light and love, destroy the carnal mind, and fill a man with power over all sin.

When the Holy Ghost is Come
Samuel Logan Brengle

There is a union with Jesus in which the soul is not so anxious to escape Hell as it is to be free from sin, and in which Heaven is not so desirable as holiness.

Heart Talks on Holiness
Samuel Logan Brengle

Virtue goes out from holy people as perfume floats out from a rose, or warmth from a fire, or light from a flame.

The Way of Holiness
Samuel Logan Brengle

When a man is thus filled with the Holy Spirit he is not made into a putty man, a jelly fish, with all powers of resistance taken out of him; he does not have any less "push" and "go" than before, but all his natural energy is now reinforced by the Holy Spirit and turned into channels of love and peace instead of hate and strife.

When the Holy Ghost is Come
Samuel Logan Brengle

Holiness does not begin with an outward conformity of habit but with an inward receiving of the Spirit.

The Call to Holiness
Frederick Coutts

Holiness is an experience of grace for normal people living lives, set in families as God intended, and finding their highest happiness in the sanctification of their common joys.

The Call to Holiness
Frederick Coutts

Holiness is not a conscious rectitude, a continual watching of one's step lest the wrong foot be put forward first. Separation, by itself, is not enough. Holiness is not just doing things and not going places. I am not made good by what I do not do.

Frederick Coutts
The Privilege of All Believers
John D. Waldron, Edit.

It does not make any man less man. The witty man is not robbed of his wit, nor the balanced individual of his sense of humor, nor the articulate spirit of his capacity for self-expression. His understanding of his fellows is deepened. His sympathies are widened. What he has lost — and what he had been glad to lose — are those failings which hindered his development as a man. The life of holiness is one of fulfillment, not frustration.

The Splendour of Holiness
Frederick Coutts

The doctrine of holiness should always be considered in its proper setting — as an integral part of the redemptive purpose of God for men. Rightly understood it is the one serious attempt which believers may make (as God shall help them) to translate the spirit of Jesus into a recognizable pattern of Christian behavior.

The Call to Holiness
Frederick Coutts

The first aim which the doctrine of holiness sets before us is victory over sin, not immunity from temptation.

The Call to Holiness
Frederick Coutts

The New Testament doctrine of holiness is one of progress, not progress to Christ so much as progress in Christ — and this rule governs the whole of the way from earth to Heaven.

The Splendour of Holiness
Frederick Coutts

This is what holy living means — the dedication of as much as I possess to as much as I know of the will of God for me. And far from this total response cramping any man's style, it ennobles him who makes it and glorifies the God whose service is always perfect freedom.

Essentials of Christian Experience
Frederick Coutts

Where Christ is enthroned, there is true holiness.

The Call to Holiness
Frederick Coutts

A holy life is made up for me of a multitude of small things; little renunciations, to be decided by an overmastering desire for God's glory, which govern every incident and accident of life that I am called upon to face.

Mildred Duff
Mildred Duff
Madge Unsworth

Holiness is more than an act of cleansing, or even a baptism of light and feeling and heavenliness; it is a condition of life — a life to be maintained and enjoyed year after year, to the end.

Fuel for Sacred Flame
T. Henry Howard

Holiness is not intended to make human beings less or other than men or women by removing the faculties and powers that constitute such. No faculty or power or appetite with which nature endows itself is evil. The evil lies in their perversion. They have been used for a wrong end, and their

misuse has grown into an evil habit that conquers the better nature. They need to be renewed and restored to the God-given purpose.

Fuel for Sacred Flame
T. Henry Howard

Holiness confounds our critics; holiness attracts the seeker; holiness earns us the trust of the cynic. Holiness in us, in this sort of world, is the more convincing argument that Jesus Christ rose from the dead and lives and saves today.

Marching On!
Ted Palmer

But spiritual values are not instantaneous. There are not shortcuts to holiness of life, No chair lift up the mountain of character.

I'm Growing, Lord!
Flora Larsson

A man who says, "I am justified," is not proclaiming his own moral equity, but the moral equity of God. A man who says, "I am made holy," does not proclaim his own perfection, but the moral perfection of God.

George Scott Railton
The Privilege of All Believers
John D. Waldron, Edit.

To be holy: that is how to glorify God. Oh! When will our miserable struggles against sin and for the right cease? When shall we give up our wretched attempts to glorify God ourselves and leave Him to glorify Himself in our lives, given into His own hands?

George Scott Railton
The Privilege of All Believers
John D. Waldron, Edit.

He who is already resident is invited to become president.

Studies in Sanctification
Edward Read

Sanctification is not a step beyond Calvary; it is a lingering longer at Calvary.

Studies in Sanctification
Edward Read

Sanctification is to give you and me a heart like that of Jesus, overflowing with love that is natural and warm and human, permeated and enriched with the tenderness and passion of God.

Studies in Sanctification
Edward Read

It is not so important to know the character of holiness as to know the holiness of character.

Norman S. Marshall
The War Cry

If you think of holiness as separate from the Holy Spirit, you will lose all. It you fail to recognize, honor, love, trust, and obey the Blesser, you lose the beauty of the rose, or the sweetness when you take away the honey, or the music when you lose the musician.

Ancient Prophets
Samuel Logan Brengle

It does not produce a perfect head, but rather, a perfect heart!

Heart Talks on Holiness
Samuel Logan Brengle

Holy Spirit

"Grieve not the Holy Spirit of God" commands Paul. Now, only a dear friend can be grieved. Not a stranger: he might be annoyed. Not a chance acquaintance: he might be perplexed. Not a business partner: he might be offended. Only a loved one can be grieved.

The Holy Spirit — Friend and Counsellor
Milton S. Agnew

It was more important for the Holy Spirit to come than for Jesus to stay.

The Holy Spirit — Friend and Counsellor
Milton S. Agnew

Members of the Trinity share interrelated activities, of which God the Holy Spirit is administrator.

The Holy Spirit — Friend and Counsellor
Milton S. Agnew

All the lovers of Jesus should in these days seek fresh renewings and a greater fullness of the Holy Spirit. They should study what the Bible says about Him as a Person. He is not a mere influence, passing over us like a wind, or warming us like a fire. He is a Person, seeking entrance into our hearts that He may comfort us, give us heavenly wisdom, and fit us for holy and triumphant service.

Guest of the Soul
Samuel Logan Brengle

He who wants a meeting of life and power should remember that there is no substitute for the Holy Ghost. He is life. He is power. And if He is sought in earnest, faithful prayer, He will come, and when He comes the little meeting will be mighty in its results.

Helps to Holiness
Samuel Logan Brengle

If anyone could have looked at the state of the world at the time of our Lord's death he would surely have regarded the work which the apostles were commissioned to attempt as the most utterly wild and impracticable enterprise that the human mind could conceive. And it was so, but for one fact. That fact was the promise of the Comforter, the Holy Spirit, to be the great Helper in the undertaking.

When the Holy Ghost is Come
Samuel Logan Brengle

If you will seek light when you have light, you will find darkness and confusion; and if you begin to seek the Holy Spirit when you already have Him, you will grieve Him.

Helps to Holiness
Samuel Logan Brengle

The common mistake is to set up before our minds a wrong ideal — a sentimental Holy Ghost, all charity — an emotional Holy Ghost, all feeling — or a doctrinal Holy Ghost, all theory, instead of a practical Holy Ghost, who pardons, purifies and equips us for the war. What we want to

seek and obtain is the Holy Ghost according to The Salvation Army — that subtle
Something — or rather Someone — which
we love to call the Army Spirit, which enables our humblest comrades to succeed
and save souls, where the most learned
theologians have toiled in vain.

Frederick Booth-Tucker
The Officer — 1893

Indeed, I am persuaded that if an intelligent heathen who had never seen the
Bible, should for the first time read the
four Gospels, and the Acts of the Apostles,
he would say that the personality of the
Holy Spirit is as clearly revealed in the Acts
as is the Personality of Jesus Christ in the
Gospels.

When the Holy Ghost Is Come
Samuel Logan Brengle

The great work of this Holy Guest is to
exalt Jesus; to glorify Him who humbled
Himself unto the shamfeful and agonizing
death of the cross: to make us to see Him
in all His beauty; to knit our hearts to Him
in faith and love and loyalty, conform us to
His image, and fit us for His work.

Samuel Logan Brengle
At the Center of the Circle
John D. Waldron, Edit.

The Holy Ghost is the great, secret, silent,
inward Teacher, speaking to the ears of
the soul, whispering in the silences of the
night, instructing in the hours of prayer
and communion. We are dull and ignorant, making no assured progress in the
school of Christ, until the Comforter is
come.

Guest of the Soul
Samuel Logan Brengle

When Jesus came, a body was prepared for
Him, and through that body He did wondrous works: but when the other Comforter comes, He takes possession of those
bodies that are freely and fully presented
to Him, and He touches their lips with
grace; He shines peacefully and gloriously
on their faces; He flashes beams of pity
and compassion and heavenly affection
from their eyes; He kindles a fire of love in
their hearts, and lights the flame of truth

in their holy of holies in which His blessed
presence ever abides; and from that central citadel He works, giving the man who
has received Him power.

When the Holy Ghost Is Come
Samuel Logan Brengle

The gifts of the Spirit are not to be rated
more highly than the character of the
Spirit Himself.

The Splendour of Holiness
Frederick Coutts

The Holy Spirit is the creative Spirit without whom all it sterility and barrenness.

The Call to Holiness
Frederick Coutts

Elijah called down fire on Carmel; Paul
shook off a viper at Malta; Peter spoke with
another tonge at Pentecost. None of these
facts argue that I should do the same. The
Spirit gives special abilities selectively.

Studies in Sanctification
Edward Read

Men forget God the Holy Spirit not because
He has ceased to exist; rather, they have
lowered their eyes and so grope through
the fog of their own futile industries.

A Sense of God
Peter W. Stine

Home

Confessing Christ is nowhere more essential and nowhere a greater responsibility
than at home.

Chosen to Be a Soldier

Jesus makes our home a heaven,
  Sacred in the fireside warm;
After battling through the long day,
  Home's a shelter from the storm.

Let us make our home the threshold
  Of the City bright and fair,
Each other's joy possessing,
  Each other's burden share.

In the storm of deep affliction,
  Let us seek the heavenly balm.

In life's tempest just remember
  Prayer will make the storm a calm.

Arthur S. Arnott
Salvation Army Song Book

Before I pledge myself to my husband,
  I want to give myself once more to You.
I invite You, Lord, to be the first guest in
our home:
    invisible yet potential and present,
    witness to all we see and do,
    guide in all our decisions.

I'm Growing, Lord!
Flora Larsson

No home on earth have I,
  No nation owns my soul,
My dwelling place is the Most High,
  I'm under His control.
O'er all the earth alike
  My Father's grand domain,
Each land and sea with Him alike
  O'er all He yet shall reign.

With Thee, my God, is home;
  With Thee is endless joy;
With Thee in ceaseless rest I roam;
  With Thee, can death destroy?
With Thee, the east, the west;
  The north, the south are one;
The battle's front I love the best
  And yet: Thy will be done.

George Scott Railton
Salvation Army Song Book

Honesty

I do here declare that I will not allow myself any deceit or dishonesty; nor will I
practice any fraudulent conduct in my
business, my home or in any other relation
in which I may stand to my fellowmen; but
that I will deal truthfully and honorably
and kindly with all those who may employ
me or whom I may myself employ.

The Articles of War

People want to make it out that they are
dying for want of light. I say no. I won't
allow myself to have that reflection cast
upon Him. They are not dying for want of
light; they are dying for want of *honesty.*

Life and Death
Catherine Booth

While I speak to Thee
  Lord, Thy goodness show;
Am I what I ought to be?
  O Savior, let me know.
Have I a truthful heart,
  A conscience keen to feel
The baseness of a false excuse,
  The touch of aught unreal?

Herbert H. Booth
Salvation Army Song Book

Those aspects of our personalities which
we refuse to recognize always pose the
greatest threat to our integrity.

The Armoury Commentary — The Four Gospels
Frederick Coutts, Edit.

When friend or foe questioned Him
(Jesus) on vital issues, He never asked for
time to consider His reply and never qualified an answer with such a phrase as "in
all probability," His answers were immediate, original and complete.

Search the Scriptures
Robert Hoggard

Hope

The spirit tries to influence men more by
appealing to their hopes than to their fears.

Life and Death
Catherine Booth

Christian hope is not to be written off as a
form of wishful thinking. The letter to the
Hebrews describes it as an anchor "as sure
as it is firm". This anchor cannot drag because it is rooted in the very being of God.

Christ is the Answer
Frederick Coutts

Rob a man of his horizon, and you have
taken his all.

Out of the Depths
Clarence W. Hall

Our first business, therefore, is to awaken
hope.

Adelaide Cox
Maiden Tribute
Madge Unsworth

Humanism

In humanism man becomes his own measure and consequently his own god. This has been called "idolatry turned inside out." The more man regards himself as self-made, with no one to thank or blame save himself, the more likely he is to turn into a demon.

Reason to Believe
Harry Dean

The final terror of absolute humanism is that there is no other mind in the universe save the human mind. Mankind is forever alone. If that is true, nothing lies ahead save insanity.

Reason to Believe
Harry Dean

Modern man has all but forgotten how to call on God's name except in profanity, or except in extreme emergency — as though God were an ambulance service. Man's chief desire should be to please God and to acknowledge Him as the Source of wisdom, strength, power and knowledge. But this has been superseded by a humanistic viewpoint which says that "man is the measure of all things" and that God's part in human affairs is, at best, incidental. Even Adam and Eve, who had no precedent to follow (except, perhaps, Satan and his cohorts) soon discovered the seductive attraction of exercising their independence from God. As a result, they drowned out the music of the spheres with the cacaphony of their wills.

A Sense of God
Peter W. Stine

If a child is encouraged in early years to view himself as merely a physical thing, no more than a zoological fact as it were, and if he goes on from there to see truth, honesty, love and meaning as having no significant permanent value, then what sort of person will he become?

Clarence Wiseman
The Privilege of All Believers
John D. Waldron, Edit.

Humility

Does not the lowly origin of our comrades make them hesitate on the threshold of great efforts when they ought to leap forward in the strength of their God? Let them remember their Master, and take courage. Let them call to mind the unfashionable, uneducated, uncultivated surroundings of Nazareth. Let them bear in mind the humble service of the family life. Let them, above all, remember the gentle Mother and the meek and lowly One Himself, and in this remembrance let them go forward.

Bramwell Booth
Trumpets of the Lord
Catherine Bramwell-Booth, Edit.

But God did not send him forth on his own charges and in his own strength. He never does send forth His prophets. He equips them. He humbles them until there is no conceit or strength left in them.

Ancient Prophets
Samuel Logan Brengle

Will not people walk over us, if we do not stand up for our rights, you ask. I do not argue that you are not to stand up for your rights; but that you are to stand up for your higher rather than your lower rights, the rights of your heavenly life rather than your earthly life, and that your are to stand up for your rights in the way and spirit of Jesus rather than in the way and the spirit of the world.

When the Holy Ghost is Come
Samuel Logan Brengle

If honor comes, thank God and lay it at the torn feet of Jesus, and forget it, lest it ruin you.

Love Slaves
Samuel Logan Brengle

Let us be content to wash each other's feet and be ambitious only to be servants of all.

Samuel Logan Brengle
At the Center of the Circle
John D. Waldron, Edit.

The Holy Spirit may lead to a holy rivalry in love and humility and brotherly kindness and self-denial and good works, but

99

He never leads men into the swelling conceit of such exclusive knowledge and superior wisdom that they can no longer be taught by their fellow-men.

When the Holy Ghost is Come
Samuel Logan Brengle

Humility is to rise to one's full stature by the side of Jesus Christ, and then to realize what pygmies we are in His shadow. This cuts a man down to size, in other words, blesses him with a sense of proportion.

The Splendour of Holiness
Frederick Coutts

Meekness is possible only to the spiritually strong. The meek are invincible because they are freed from self-concern in their devotion to God's Kingdom. Instinctively viewing every experience (adversity, injustice, disappointment) in the light of eternal values, they recognize the emptiness and ultimate insignificance of what would otherwise have caused them distress and resentment. The only thing they ask for themselves is the opportunity to go on serving.

The Armoury Commentary — The Four Gospels
Frederick Coutts, Edit.

Meekness is strength controlled by love.

The Armoury Commentary — The Four Gospels
Frederick Coutts, Edit.

For 40 years as a scholar he learned to be somebody. For the next 40 years as a herdman he learned to be a nobody. Only then did God call him to become the great emancipator, legislator, warrior and poet.

Search the Scriptures
Robert Hoggard

And when the way is open for my King,
    'Tis mine to stand aside and hidden be;
Not mine to enter in the sacred place —
It is the place of the King of grace,
    And I must stand aside and hidden be.
It is my place to open wide the door.
    Only to open — not to enter in!
Not mine to sit upon the sacred throne;

Jesus the King must reign, and He alone.
    I must just open, and not enter in.

Ivy Mawby
Book of Salvationist Verse
Catherine Baird, Edit.

Hypocrisy

What worth the careful cunning of my weapons,
The pretty prowess of my mind and hand,
If to a sad bewildered world I'm showing
A bloodless Christ, a shapeless spectral Lord
Set on a pedestal of man's conception
And crowned with rich rhetoric's dainty hand?
Though He be dressed in garb and mighty thinking
And crowned with all the wisdom of the years,
If in His form appear no woundprints,
He is not Christ, the Savior of the world.

Poems
Catherine Baird

I contend, you had far better let a man alone in sin than give him a sham conversion, and make him believe he is a Christian when he is nothing of the kind.

Aggressive Christiantiy
Catherine Booth

Oh! what a laughing stock to hell is a light, frivolous, lukewarm professor. Oh! what a shame and puzzle to the angels in Heaven, and what a supreme disgust to God.

Papers on Godliness
Catherine Booth

Yours is not true repentance. Oh! There is nothing will be shown up at the last day more than the oceans of crocodile tears that have been shed by professed penitents making out God to be a liar, and throwing back the blame of people damnation on Him!

Life and Death
Catherine Booth

You can talk charity without having it; you can expound and display its priceless beauties, with its rightful place in your heart usurped by self; you can join your voice with the numerous exclamations of pity for the poor without giving any shoes for bare feet, or clothes for naked forms; you can bewail with great pathos the distresses of the hungry, but spare no money for loaves of bread; you can with effective eloquence picture the sin and fate of the wicked and be void of one drop of Calvary's compassion for their poor sinking souls.

Love is All
Evangeline Booth

Any form of religion that allows a man to keep a hope of Heaven while living in the conscious neglect of duty, is a hypocrisy, and perhaps the most dangerous form of hypocrisy ever invented, whether on earth or in hell.

The Founder's Messages to Soldiers
William Booth

Oh, these Pilates, these Pilates! What stumbling blocks they are to those who, ready to perish, are groping for the light! How much easier might we slay the giants of drink and uncleanness, of infidelity and crime, if it were not for those who profess to follow Him, and yet who follow Him not; who have the form without the power, the letter without the spirit! Men who are for the Crown without the Cross, wanting a friend in Heaven whose claims they deny, whose cause they forsake down here!

Heart Messages
Emma Booth-Tucker

There is nothing, I fear, easier of acquisition than the aspirations and the language of devotion while living a life the opposite of all they imply.

William Booth
The Armoury Commentary — The Four Gospels
Frederick Coutts

In one of His parables Jesus said that the Pharisee "prayed with himself". He was so self-centered he never escaped from himself. Only too well aware of his fellowmen watching his religious devotions, he was unaware of the fact that God was an absentee.

The Armoury Commentary — The Four Gospels
Frederick Coutts, Edit.

Self-deception is the first step to a life of pretense.

The Armoury Commentary — The Four Gospels
Frederick Coutts, Edit.

The Christian is not better when he is pious at his place of worship, but moody at home; conscientiously supports the Lord's work, but gives less than his best at work, shuns every appearance of evil, but never goes the "second mile"; thinks more of his reputation than his righteousness; considers himself good merely because he is not bad.

The Armoury Commentary — The Four Gospels
Frederick Coutts, Edit.

The repressed desire that others shall pay in full for sins we would like to have committed is often at the bottom of distorted presentation of judgment.

The Armoury Commentary — The Four Gospels
Frederick Coutts, Edit.

Professed humility can be inverted hypocrisy.

The Christian Charter
George B. Smith

I

Identity

Dear God, I thank you for me — for the person I am, the person I am becoming. I'm glad for my identity.

Dear God
Virginia Talmadge

Idolatry

Every life must have some center, and if the living God does not occupy this central place, then some lesser god will rule. The lordship of self, or of any other god the self chooses to serve, is a turning away from the true God.

Handbook of Doctrine

The failure to distinguish between creature and Creator leads to the elevation of holy places, objects, institutions or persons to dignity to which they have no claim, and eventually to a point where they receive adoration as though they themselves are the source of blessings which are solely derived from God.

Handbook of Doctrine

It is a fact that as man becomes degraded he degrades his God likewise. As he loses the likeness of God he makes unto himself gods in his own likeness, and loses the very pattern of morality and holiness. He thus makes unto himself gods which are immoral and unholy. That is the sordid history of idolatry.

More Than Conquerers
Milton S. Agnew

Any god that is capable of definition is an idol.

Reason to Believe
Harry Dean

Imagination

God, make my thoughts as big and high
And spacious as the wide clear sky.

Poems
Catherine Baird

Imagination builds worlds within our world. Imagination may guild life's prospect, tint its sky with morning rose, and enchant our way with the song of a thousand birds; but imagination is powerful also to loose the Devil's legions upon us, to haunt our pathway with dread and awful spectres, and to drape the morning itself with gloom and death.

Powers of Salvation Army Officers
Florence Booth

Isn't that Your glowing gift, Master?
    that in imagination we can escape
    to live in our own chosen country
    for a few brief moments?
My heart felt warmed and happy;
    the world a better place.

I'm Growing, Lord!
Flora Larsson

Improvement

Were I dying before your eyes in this very hall I should call on you, by all that was sacred on earth and in heaven, to improve yourself.

The Seven Spirits
William Booth

This and better will do.

Congress Addresses, 1904
William Booth

Have you heard the recent rumor
From the philosophic boomer
'Bout this poor old race of ours?
'Tis a cool insinuation that we've reached the comsummation and the zenith of our powers.

It is surely from confusion
They arrive at this conclusion
Jehovah's outstretched arm they must forget;
Well, I venture to assert though it be to my own hurt,
That we haven't done our best thing yet!

Just to make my meaning clearer
I will come a little nearer
As a corps we've had success
With our music and our story
We have helped to glory,
Thousands still we cheer and bless.
But we're surely not omniscient
Neither are we so efficient
That further up the hill we cannot get;
If we practice and we pray,
We with confidence can say
That we haven't done our best thing yet,
not yet!

Now attend to my conclusion
Out of chaos and confusion
God commanded form and life;
His Almighty hand controlling
Still preserved the planets rolling
In their courses free from strife.
By a mighty condescension
Passing mortal comprehension
He gave His best to pay the sinner's debt,
But with reverence sincere,
Yet with boldness I declare
The Father hasn't done His best thing yet,
not yet!

C. Coller
Gems from Songsters #1

Incarnation

We believe that in the person of Jesus Christ the divine and human natures are united so that He is truly and properly God and truly and properly man.

Salvation Army Doctrine #4

God condemned sin as entirely unnecessary. The design and object of the incarnation and the sacrifice of Christ was to condemn sin; not to tolerate it, but to exclude its power and its guilt from the soul.

More Than Conquerors
Milton S. Agnew

He not only brought a message from God, but was Himself the message from God.

The Better Covenant
Milton S. Agnew

The divine condescension never appears so new and so real to us as when we stand at the side of his lowly cradle. Here are no high sounding doctrines, no hard words, no terrible commands, no faroff thunders of a new Sinai, no rumblings of a coming judgment. Here we see Jesus and Jesus only. God joined in that Babe His great strength to our great nothingness.

Bramwell Booth
Trumpets of the Lord
Catherine Bramwell-Booth, Edit.

The mystery of God in the Babe was the beginning of the mystery of God on the Cross.

Bramwell Booth
Trumpets of the Lord
Catherine Bramwell-Booth, Edit.

That was the dignity of the Almighty strength allying itself with human weakness, in order to raise it. It was the dignity of eternal wisdom shrouding itself in human ignorance, in order to enlighten it. It was the dignity of everlasting, unquenchable love, baring its bosom to suffer in the stead of its rebellious creature — man. Ah! it was incarnate God standing in the place of condemned, apostate man — the dignity of love! love! love!

Aggressive Christianity
Catherine Booth

In Jesus we do not see a man struggling to become as godlike as he can, but God making Himself known within the framework of human life.

In Good Company
Frederick Coutts

It was certainly not the New Testament writers who dreamed up the story of God Incarnate, but Jesus Himself who provided the facts they felt compelled to set down.

The Armoury Commentary — The Four Gospels
Frederick Coutts, Edit.

Jesus, sinless Son of God, was taking His place alongside sinful men, not as one of them, but as One for them.

The Armoury Commentary — The Four Gospels
Frederick Coutts, Edit.

The life of Jesus was the result not of human evolution — He was not merely man at his best — but of Divine intrusion. To use spatial terms, the life of Jesus marks both the descent of God and the possibility of the ascent of man.

The Armoury Commentary — The Four Gospels
Frederick Coutts, Edit.

A cattle shed and manger, two weary peasants and a newborn Babe, and there we believe that God began the final revelation of Himself.

Power and Glory
Harry Dean

The dogmatic way is to say that God must be either one or many, Jesus must be either human or divine; but the real answer lies in a reverent acknowledgement of mystery. Those who seek to find clear, simple, logical definitions are the heretics. The orthodox believer takes the attitude that there is not much more in the Christian revelation than can be easily captured in a phrase of crystal clarity.

Reason to Believe
Harry Dean

God spoke in the Old Testament by inspiration. He speaks in the New Testament by incarnation.

Search the Scriptures
Robert Hoggard

When the time had fully come — and God is never a moment early or late — there appeared, not the horses and chariots of military might, not the awesome sight of angelic hosts bent on battle, but a helpless little Babe lying in a manger.

Search the Scriptures
Roobert Hoggard

Sometimes I get a glimpse of what it must have cost You,

this humiliation,
this self-imposed limitation,
coming down to our level —
You, the source of all life, limited in movement and power;
You, the immortal and eternal, binding Yourself with the chains of time.
You, the mighty ocean, willing to live as a single droplet;
You, Lord of all, becoming a village carpenter;
You, the sinless One, dying for our sins,
    Incredible, yet true!

Just a Moment, Lord
Flora Larsson

We know more than the angels know!
He went as far as our loss and gain,
Our living and giving, our infant birth,
And made Himself one with our joy and pain
In the warm dark womb of the earth.

The Beauty of Jesus
Albert Orsborn

Christ would not have become what we are unless we were capable of becoming what He is. He came down to our measurements in order to bring us up to His.

Meditations for the Ordinary Man
George B. Smith

The incarnation is an amazing mystery of Christianity. Once accepted as a fact, it leads to the acceptance of the life-giving force of Christ in the human heart. Once denied, it leaves no opportunity at all for a human heart to be truly Christian. It is, indeed, the gift of God.

Andrew S. Miller
Holiness Institute

Individuality

It is still step by step.
    There is no hitchhiking in the spiritual life,
    No thumbing a life with Peter or Paul,
    No chartering a denominational coach
    Or booking a seat
In an ecclesiastical jumbo jet bound
for Paradise.

Between You and Me, Lord
Flora Larsson

No man's private spiritual discoveries — neither Paul's nor Brengle's nor those of anyone else — are really shareable, nor are any intended to be a standard or a norm. God is not so lacking in originality or in respect for your uniqueness, as that.

Studies in Sanctification
Edward Read

Indwelling

Descend the heavens, Thou whom my soul adoreth,
    Exchange Thy throne for my poor longing heart;
For Thee, for Thee, I watch as for the morning;
    No rest, no joy I find when from Thee I'm apart.

Catherine Booth-Clibborn
Salvation Army Song Book

The holy breath evokes divine harmonies.

The Call to Holiness
Frederick Coutts

O patient Weaver! Never give up Your work!
No other hand can fashion good out of evil,
    beauty and joy out of life's roughage.
Take the threads of my life, imperfect as they are, and make them a part of a glorious whole.

Between You and Me, Lord
Flora Larsson

He is standing with us here, in the pain!
Will you let Him ease the load and the strain?
He's a Helper and Stay,
Not a Savior far away,
But, the Christ of every day —
Bless His name!

The Beauty of Jesus
Albert Orsborn

Inspiration

Inspiration observes no office hours.

In Good Company
Frederick Coutts

Had I waited for inspiration to lay hold on me, most of my songs would never have been written. I have found that inspiration is for the seeker, the ardent lover of the Master, who takes his Bible to his prayer room, crying, "Speak, Lord, for Thy servant heareth."

Albert Orsborn
Companion to the Song Book
Gordon Avery

Intellect

An officer who is genuinely dedicated to the service of God and man will lose no opportunity to enrich his own mind so that he may more effectively proclaim the glorious Gospel of the blessed God.

Orders and Regulations for Officers

To cease to learn is to cease to live.

Orders and Regulations for Officers

God wants your heart. Then He will enlighten your intellect.

Life and Death
Catherine Booth

If a mere intellectual perception of the truth were saving faith, the Devil would have been saved a long time ago, for he is one of the profoundest believers in the universe.

Life and Death
Catherine Booth

No mere intellectual beliefs can save men, because right opinions do not make right hearts.

Catherine Booth
The Life of Catherine Booth — Volume 1
Frederick Booth-Tucker

Polish is not power; education is not intellect.

The Salvation Army in Relation to Church and State
Catherine Booth

There is always a danger that those richly endowed with intellectual power, and those in positions which enable them to exercise great power, will be led away by the power that is their own and will fail to look to God. The enemy of souls knows well how to kindle self-confidence even in those who have given themselves to God and desire to serve Him. The Holy Spirit is only bestowed upon us to the degree in which we look away from ourselves.

Powers of Salvation Army Officers
Florence Booth

If God has no need of our brains He has less use for our ignorance.

No Continuing City
Frederick Coutts

To declare for Christ will not solve all our intellectual difficulties, but it does redeem life from sheer pointlessness.

A Sense of God
Peter W. Stine

Unhappily, some Christians feel that the child of God ought to live by faith alone, and ignore the cultivation of his intellect. True, faith is crucial; we grow by the discipline required in the abdication of our will to God's and by the lessons of patience learned before His will is made known. But we are also required to be worthy stewards, and to prepare ourselves for the rigors of living in a competitive and challenging society. We do ourselves and God's kingdom a great disservice if we deny the necessity for improving our minds.

A Sense of God
Peter W. Stine

J

Jesus Christ

We believe that in the person of Jesus Christ the Divine and human natures are united so that He is truly and properly God and truly and properly man.

Salvation Army Doctrine #4

We believe that the Lord Jesus Christ has by His suffering and death made an atonement for the whole world so that whosoever will may be saved.

Salvation Army Doctrine #6

The truth about the person of Jesus Christ cannot be stated without reference to His mission, and the true significance of His mission cannot be declared without reference to His nature.

Handbook of Doctrine

And, in Thy meadowlands I find,
    Deep-rooted, Christ, the living Vine.

Reflections
Catherine Baird

Yes, that is it! Christ the Savior! Not merely Christ the Helper of the poor, or the Feeder of the hungry, or the Father of the prodigals, or the Brother of the Magdalene, or the Comfort of the sorrowful; but Christ the Savior from condemnation and guilt, from stains and filth, from the love and power and presence of sin.

Bramwell Booth
Trumpets of the Lord
Catherine Bramwell-Booth, Edit.

He was standing for us, in our stead, suffering in His soul the infliction of the justice of God against sin. It was this which drank up His Spirit, and made Him utter that exceeding loud and bitter cry. Now, if the wrath of God were so terrible to the Son of God Himself as to put Him in such agony, what will it be to the undone sinner in the great day of wrath?

Life and Death
Catherine Booth

What was His purpose? The salvation of the world. Not the humiliation and the suffering and the agony and the death. These were the means by which only the end could be reached; if the end could have been gained by any less agonizing way, doubtless it would have been followed. He wanted to reach the dying millions and, by living a divine life before them, and pouring forth His divine Blood for them, to make the salvation of all possible, to make the salvation of multitudes sure.

William Booth
The Founder Speaks Again
Cyril Barnes, Edit.

The surging mob, the base calumnies, the cruel cries, the looming cross, the soul anguish, all served but clearer to write upon the world's dark need, in letters of unfading love, the Christ spirit.

Heart Messages
Emma Booth-Tucker

Be satisfied with Him by whatever way He may come, whether as King of kings and Lord of lords, or as a humble, simple peasant Carpenter. Be satisfied with Him, and He will more and more fully reveal Himself to your childlike faith.

Helps to Holiness
Samuel Logan Brengle

The Bible says Jesus is God. Jesus says so. Paul says so. The Church and all its creeds say so. The wisest Christian teachers say so. The saints and martyrs who have perished by flame and wild beast's fangs say so. The humble penitents, rejoicing in the assurance of sins forgiven, say so, and with mingling tears and smiles and heaven-lit faces, cry out with Thomas; "My Lord and My God!"

Samuel Logan Brengle
Portrait of a Prophet
Clarence W. Hall

Jesus is always Himself; He creates His own categories; He Himself gives the light by which He can be known.

The Armoury Commentary — The Four Gospels
Frederick Coutts, Edit.

To those with eyes to see and ears to hear, Jesus Himself is sign enough of His true identify.

The Armoury Commentary — The Four Gospels
Frederick Coutts, Edit.

In Jesus, God committed Himself to humanity and humanity became the vehicle of the divine.

Reason to Believe
Harry Dean

It is legitimate, and indeed necessary, for Christians to believe that wherever and whenever God speaks, Jesus embodies that truth. History divides at His coming because He is the Center of the religious life of man. He is the supreme revelation. While there can be no fuller revelation than Jesus, there can be a constantly developing revelation of Jesus.

Reason to Believe
Harry Dean

What to me are all the joys of earth?
    What to me is every sight I see,
Save the sight of Thee, O Friend of mine?
    Jesus, Thou art everything to me..

Edward H. Joy
Salvation Army Song Book

And does He not still traverse life's dusty road today,
Where men in life's grim struggle are driven to dismay?
Yea, mid the heedless onrush, with calm assuring mien
He walks: the ever-present Christ, the wondrous Nazarene.

Albert Mingay
The Merchant of Heaven

The beginning of the Christian doctrine is found in an axiomatic truth, but this truth is a person, and this person is Jesus Christ.

The Person of Jesus Christ
John A. Morrison

When first, as His follower, I saw the world mock, defy, abuse, scorn, bargain away, condemn my Lord, my nature cried out, "Smite, Lord! For Thy glory's sake, lest the world should read weakness in Thy surrender, smite the smiters!" But no. He dies. Down into the gulf He goes alone, followed by the curses of His enemies and the doubts and disappointed love of His friends. Is meekness, then, the conqueror, not might? Yes, assuredly; the Lamb will finally triumph over the beast.

The Silences of Christ
Albert Orsborn

It would take a Jesus to forge a Jesus.

Meditations for the Ordinary Man
George B. Smith

Without a cause men hated Christ; without a cause He loves them.

More than Conquerors
Milton S. Agnew

Joy

Our sweetest songs must be the songs we sing to those who cannot sing. Our deepest joy must be joy with the Father when the prodigals come home from the far country of backsliding and sin.

Bramwell Booth
Trumpets of the Lord
Catherine Bramwell-Booth, Edit.

Holy joy is a mighty power in dealing with backsliders.

The General's Letters
William Booth

If when slaves find freedom, and tradesmen make fortunes, and kindred, or friends, or neighbors are delivered from some threatened calamity, it is allowable to go mad with joy and to express it by hiring music, and beating drums, and letting off fireworks, and shouting till hoarse, and everybody says that is all right, then by the same rule, if you please, and whether you please or no, we are the slaves who have now our freedom, the people who have made our fortune; we are the men who have seen our kindred and friends and neighbors saved from damnation; and therefore, we have a right to be merry.

Salvation Soldiery
William Booth

It must be a joyful experience. Joy in the Holy Ghost is an oceanic current that flows unbroken through the holy, believing soul, though surrounded by seas of trouble and compassed about by infirmities and afflictions and sorrows.

The Soul-Winner's Secret
Samuel Logan Brengle

My God, enroll me in
Your company of joy!

Wind Chimes
Sallie Chesham

Christian joy is not an emotion which has to be worked up from the human end but is a blessing which descends unsought upon the man who is in right relationship with God.

The Call to Holiness
Frederick Coutts

Christian joy is the fruit of Christian obedience.

The Call to Holiness
Frederick Coutts

We are called not to unhappy holiness but to a holy happiness.

The Call to Holiness
Frederick Coutts

So in my summers
Teach me thrifty ways,
To store some joys
Against the winter days.

O Lord!
John Gowans

I saw calm seas, bright fields bedecked with flowers;
Joy and content to lighten working hours;
But more than all beauty of sound and sight,
He smiled on me, and life was pure delight.

Violet L. Halsey
The Merchant of Heaven

Jest yer fancy, no, jest yer fancy me gettin' into 'Eaven. Ain't it jest enough to make ye say, 'Alleluyer?, 'Tis enough to make me laugh, and laugh, and laugh. Me gettin' into 'Eaven!

The Old Corps
Edward H. Joy

How wonderful it is to talk with God
When cares sweep o'er my spirit like a flood;
How wonderful it is to hear His voice
For when He speaks the desert lands rejoice.

Theodore H. Kitching
Salvation Army Song Book

The radio played such happy tunes that I danced
    across the floor as I dusted,
    which resulted in very skimpy dusting, Lord,
    But You understand, don't You?

Just a Moment, Lord
Flora Larsson

However serious the business at hand, the Great Salvation War was never joyless.

Marching to Glory
Edward H. McKinley

Because we are serious about salvation, we must be serious about our joyfulness.

Marching On!
Ted Palmer

There's one gift that I believe every Salvationist has in a wonderful measure and that is the gift of joy. I've seen many odd things in my time. I don't think I've ever seen a gloomy member of The Salvation Army. The gift of joy is wonderfully yours and may that gift go on being yours. It isn't only that we convert people to Christianity and that they cheer up and discover in our holy faith what a deep secret of joy there is. No, isn't it also the other way around? That by sheer joy of Christian character and Christian life other people are infected and are led to come and join in something that is full of cost, full of deep sacrifice, but also the most joyful thing in this world or the next.

Michael Ramsey
God's Army
Cyril Barnes

Judgment

We believe in the immortality of the soul; in the resurrection of the body; in the general judgment at the end of the world; in the eternal happiness of the righteous; and in the endless punishment of the wicked.

Salvation Army Doctrine #11

But I beseech you to remember that you are your own destroyer. God has not done it; angels have not done it; the Devil has not done it, he has only tempted you, whereas a whole legion of devils could not have forced you. No; you yourself have done it — you are your own executioner.

Life and Death
Catherine Booth

Sinner, remember for every sin there is so much wrath. You can label it off as surely as you do the profits of your day's business. Everyday's forbearance, so much more wrath. You are heaping it up, treasuring it up. It is hovering over the path you tread like some great towering black mountain.

Life and Death
Catherine Booth

Whatever of the wrath of God sinners have ever felt here, it is light in comparison with what is to come hereafter — it is, as it were, only a sip from the top of that cup of fury, the dregs of which all the wicked of the earth shall wring out and drink.

Life and Death
Catherine Booth

The wasted grace, the wounded face
Of Christ thy Savior, hated and illtreated,
Will all be found within the sound of that
eternal sentence still repeated.
For down in the deepest vaults
The sorrows of sin are resounding
Over and over and over and over
And over again.

Herbert Booth
Gems for Songsters #1

You're drawing nearer the Judgment Day
You're drawing nearer, you're drawing nearer
And soon your soul will pass away

And soon your soul will pass away
The great white throne you then will see
And ever in joy or pain you'll be
Floating — floating out of the sea of eternity.

Herbert Booth
Gems for Songsters #1

Sins of years are all numbered,
    Blackest stains brought to light,
Broken pledges uncovered,
    None escape from His sight.
Unwashed hearts are rejected,
    Guilty souls rise alone,
When you stand in the light
    Of His great judgment throne.

How you'll wish you'd gone forward,
    Loving Jesus alone.
When you stand in the light
    Of His great judgment throne.

Lucy Booth-Hellberg
Salvation Army Song Book

Human judgments were mostly concerned with what a man did; God's judgment was concerned primarily with what a man was.

The Armoury Commentary — The Four Gospels
Frederick Coutts, Edit.

The verdict of God and history has reversed the judgment of man.

The Armoury Commentary — The Four Gospels
Frederick Coutts, Edit.

If we candidly and impartially judge ourselves we may thereby do ourselves and others great good, and so escape the judgment of God.

Ancient Prophets
Samuel Logan Brengle

The majesty of God's law can be measured only by the terrors of His judgments. God is rich in mercy, but He is equally terrible in wrath. So high is His mercy, so deep is His wrath..

Love-Slaves
Samuel Logan Brengle

We can no more avoid the judgment of God's violated law than we can avoid casting a shadow when we stand in the light of the sun, or than we can avoid being burned if we thrust our hand in the fire.

Love-Slaves
Samuel Logan Brengle

The penalty of sin is not the anger of Jesus, but the heartbreak of His love and suffering for us.

Footsteps to Calvary
Henry Gariepy

God's judgment is never inconsistent with His mercy.

Search the Scriptures
Robert Hoggard

"Mr. Mayor," he said, "they tell me you have sworn to 'sweep the Army into hell'. I've come to say to you, Mr. Mayor, that you are on the brink of eternity yourself, and that, before many weeks pass over your head, you may find yourself there. Prepare to meet your God, Mr. Mayor!"

The Old Corps
Edward H. Joy

Think of the gloom
Where hopeless eyes are weeping!
Think of the doom
Where mem'ry knows no sleeping!
Think once again
Of Satan's dreadful reaping;
Think how he curses man one by one,
Let not one soul near thee
Say, "No one cared for me."

The Beauty of Jesus
Albert Orsborn

Justice

Methinks the first sentence that is groaned out by the lost sinner as he sinks into perdition will be, "It is just."

Life and Death
Catherine Booth

Justice cannot be cut at right angles, kept in packets, and handed out from a drawer.

The House of My Pilgrimage
Albert Orsborn

Kindness

Among the evidences that we are really the ministers of God is kindness. It is a humble qualification, which often influences people more than gifts which are, perhaps, more sought after; and is just as necessary in the minister of Christ as in patience or pureness or knowledge or love.

Bramwell Booth
Trumpets of the Lord
Catherine Bramwell-Booth, Edit.

How beautiful, if those who have known us, fought perhaps side by side with us on life's varying bttlefields, witnessed our private walk, known our heart's aspirations and struggles, it may be, as well as our public efforts and achievements — how beautiful if they are able to say of us when the tender gloom of death surrounds us, or in the bright all-revealing light of eternity's everlasting day: "That man (or woman) never hurt me!"

Heart Messages
Emma Booth-Tucker

The fierce hurricane which casts down the trees of the forest is not so mighty as the gentle sunshine, which, from tiny seeds and acorns, lifts aloft the towering spires of oak and fir on a thousand hills and mountains.

When the Holy Ghost is Come
Samuel Logan Brengle

Just as it is beautiful in children to never speak about or appear to notice club-feet of hunchback or crosseyes of a little playmate, so it is lovely and Christlike in us to pass by faults and infirmities, and is evil not to do so.

Heart Talks on Holiness
Samuel Logan Brengle

Gentleness is strength controlled by love.

The Call to Holiness
Frederick Coutts

The more excellent way is: if you can't be kind, be quiet.

The Armoury Commentary — The Four Gospels
Frederick Coutts, Edit.

Gentleness is such an effective grace. It can lead and live where sterner virtues utterly fall. Gentleness and tenderness of spirit are not weakness. Harshness and coercion can breed only resentment; and overbearing authority can crush the spirit.

Dear God
Virginia Talmadge

Knowledge

How could KNOWLEDGE make up for LOVE,
How could KNOWING make up for BEING,
How could THINKING make up for FEELING,
How could the BRAIN — glorious as it is
— take the place of SOUL?

Love is All
Evangeline Booth

There is no question but that ignorance and stupidity have been the cause of three parts of the spiritual wrecks which strew the shores of time.

Love is All
Evangeline Booth

Teach your people. Teach them sound doctrine; if you do not give them the truth, somebody else will give them falsehood.

Salvation Soldiery
William Booth

Am I eager for learning and knowledge? Let me then continually seek to know Him, and in due time, in this world or in the next, I shall know all that is of value for me to know.

Heart Talks on Holiness
Samuel Logan Brengle

Familiarity with what the Bible says, with the doctrine and that standard, will avail nothing, unless it is translated into conduct, into character, into life. It is not enough to know, it is not enough to approve, but with our undivided will, with our whole being, we must choose to be holy.

Samuel Logan Brengle
The Privilege of All Believers
John D. Waldron, Edit.

Loveless knowledge is the antichrist of every age.

The Call to Holiness
Frederick Coutts

Our spiritual pilgrimage is living and vital only to the extent we recognize how much further we have to go to a perfect knowledge of the Son of God.

The Armoury Commentary — The Four Gospels
Frederick Coutts, Edit.

Man, although immersed in the realm of time and space, must raise his thoughts to ultimate issues. He cannot take things for granted and be content to live on the plans of instinct. Life seems contrived to raise questions in his mind, which is an indication of his greatness. A question mark epitomizes his whole life.

Reason to Believe
Harry Dean

It does not require a physician to discern that a sick man is well, or an electrician to observe that the streets are well lighted.

Christ's Cabinet
William McIntyre

New telescopes do not destroy ancient stars, and nothing new man can devise can dispense with the need for faith in God and sustaining prayer.

Meditations for the Ordinary Man
George B. Smith

116

Law

The law was given to define sin and to make it more sinful in man's sight, though not in God's sight.

More Than Conquerors
Milton S. Agnew

What the law tried to do by a restraining power from without, the gospel does by an inspiring power from within.

Aggressive Christianity
Catherine Booth

When the law ceases to have penalities, it ceases to be law, and becomes merely good advice or counsel.

Life and Death
Catherine Booth

Wherein does the law fail? It brings me right up, as it were, my schoolmaster leashing me right up to the cross, opening my eyes, creating intense desire after Holiness and efforts for it, and then it just fails me. Where? At the vital point. It cannot give me power.

Aggressive Christiantiy
Catherine Booth

Rules, laws, and regulations — what are they? Surely they are nothing more or less than the simple statement in words easily understood by everybody, of those plans and methods of doing things which are found, after thought and experience, and, we hope, divine revelation, to be most useful and successful.

The General's Letter
William Booth

Just as there are laws governing the life of the plant, and other and higher laws that govern the bird and beast, so there are higher laws for man, and still higher laws for man, and still higher for the Christian.

When the Holy Ghost is Come
Samuel Logan Brengle

Civil law judges overt action first, intention second; but spiritual law always reverses the two.

Peace Like a River
Sallie Chesham

As a mirror neither creates nor removes a blemish but reveals it, so the law cannot create or remove sin. The law only exposes the inherent evil of the human heart.

Search the Scriptures
Robert Hoggard

Laziness

If sinners perish through their own laziness, how many multitudes perish through the laziness of saints! Oh, this horrid attempt to delegate our responsibilities with regard to perishing men and women to others — to the minister, to the captain, to the sergeants — to anybody — to excuse this laziness!

The General's Letters
William Booth

Oh, how God must be nauseated by the people who, always confessing to divine drawings and callings to duty, have to be coddled, and coaxed, and courted into discharging it.

Salvation Soldiery
William Booth

There are men so incorrigibly lazy that no inducement that you can offer will tempt them to work; so eaten up by vice that virtue is abhorrent to them, and so inverately dishonest that theft to them is a master passion. When a human being has reached that state, there is only one course that can rationally be pursued. Sorrowfully, but remorsefully, it must be recognized that he has become a lunatic, morally demented, incapable of self-government, and that upon him, therefore, must be passed the sentence of permanent seclusion from a world in which he is not fit to be at large.

In Darkest England and the Way Out
William Booth

Leadership

The responsible leader should always prepare for his meeting by waiting upon God for needful wisdom and power.

Orders and Regulations for Officers

He strode into chapel purposefully, a leader, awaiting an Army, but prepared to begin with a platoon.

Blood and Fire
Edward Bishop

No sooner has any servant of God started up with any extraordinary gifts, or any successful spiritual enterprise, than a multitude of voices are to be heard — pouring forth their misrepresentations and calumnies and detractions as so many reasons to show why these benefactors of the race are not to be heard, or regarded, or believed, or supported or loved.

The General's Letters
William Booth

You must not wait for soldiers to find out what they can do, and to offer themselves; you must make the discovery, and hunt them out of their retirement, and bring them to the front, and use them to help you in the great conflict, for which you will require every agency on which you can possibly lay your hands.

Salvation Soldiery
William Booth

A mighty man inspires and trains other men to be mighty.

When the Holy Ghost is Come
Samuel Logan Brengle

It is openness of spiritual senses that makes and characterizes spiritual leaders. A spiritual leader is one who lives in the Spirit, who dwells in such constant and intimate closeness with God that he and his Lord commune with each other, giving and receiving messages. He has such confidence in the report of his spiritual senses that when God gives him a vision, he is not disobedient unto it — when God speaks, he rises up and follows. He knows the voice of his Shepherd and that voice leads him on.

Samuel Logan Brengle
At the Center of the Circle
John D. Waldron, Edit.

True leadership will not live for personal greatness but to make the occasion great.

In Good Company
Frederick Coutts

Every leader of God's people has to learn how to administer rebuke properly. He has, indeed, often to be a living rebuke.

The Silences of Christ
Albert Orsborn

The only time when a leader should not be in front of any army is when it is in retreat.

Meditations for the Ordinary Man
George B. Smith

Legalism

Have we not known people who kept all the rules, whose habits were faultless, and yet whose "sanctity" was cold and unattractive? They lacked a sense of the significant, giving priority to trivialities, putting procedure before people, and conformity before compassion. Their religion was all law and no grace.

The Armoury Coommentary — The Four Gospels
Frederick Coutts, Edit.

The quest for the best is admirable in many ways, but it is not without its perils. Perfectionists are notably hard to live with because, in their passion for the highest, they may fall victim to the temptation to fussiness, become impatient with the people less intense then they, and arrogantly critical of others.

Studies in Sanctification
Edward Read

Life

O Lord, keep me living while I'm still alive.

The Armoury Commentary — The Four Gospels
Frederick Coutts, Edit.

Many people live without giving life a thought.

Reason to Believe
Harry Dean

We have only one heart to give away; let us choose wisely where we invest.

A Sense of God
Peter W. Stine

Get away from it all! Lord, does a change of scenery change anything, really? Or does the servitude to material things become less binding at the beach or the mountain or with friends? The striving, the competition, the praise and approval of contemporaries is not slackened by a game of golf, or tennis, or scrabble. Getting away from it all seems like an expression of weakness. Life is living, Lord, and living is coping; and coping is knowing and using one's resources. We can escape the tyranny of care when we are wrapped in the cloak of Your peace. The pressures of working and striving will be relieved when gentled by Your touch.

Dear God
Virginia Talmadge

Liquor

The Salvation Army, recognizing present and potential spiritual and temporal dangers inherent in the use of alcoholic beverages, has historically required total abstinence of its soldiers and officers. While not condemning those outside its ranks who choose to indulge, it nevertheless believes total abstinence to be the only guarantee against overindulgence and the evils attendant on addiction — physical and mental debilitation, social conflict, economic waste and spiritual poverty.

The Salvation Army believes that experience has shown a direct connection between (1) the incidence of addiction and (2) the easy availability of alcoholic beverages and the increasing social acceptance of their consumption.

The Salvation Army believes that every individual who is addicted to alcohol may find deliverance from its bondage through submission of the total personality to the Lordship of Jesus Christ.

The Salvation Army also recognizes the value of medical, social and psychiatric treatment for alcoholics and makes extensive use of these services at its centers.

Position Statement
Commisioner's Conference, U.S.A
November, 1971

All who work among drink-addicts should constantly insist upon the uselessness of anything short of conversion, showing that making resolutions, signing pledges or even praying for help to overcome the drink habit is not enough.

Orders and Regulations for Officers

No person shall be received or continued as a member who shall keep a public house or brewery, or be engaged in the demoralizing traffic or sale of intoxicating drinks; or who shall frequent any public house or dramshop, except on business.

The History of the Salvation Army — Volume 1
Robert Sandall

Our Army boys don't want whiskey, beer, or gin;
    It has caused them already to fall into sin;
We mean to drive it out, and by God's help we can.
    We'll do our very best to restore fallen men.

Combat Songs of The Salvation Army
Sally Chesham, Edit.

Banish those who manufacture this distilled damnation, those who rob man of his reason, woman of her virtues, and children of the patrimony and bread. Cease to recognize, not only as Christians, but as men, those who feed on the weaknesses, wickedness, and sufferings of other. Hoist the flag of death over the brewers and dram shops. Christians of England, the time has come when to remain silent on this drink question is high treason to Christ. Tell us no more of charity to brewers and publicans. Your false charity has consigned millions to hell. Such charity favors the devil. Its speech betrays it. Arise and fight this foe!

Catherine Booth
The Officer's Review — 1933

Drunkenness is a physical, as well as moral disease, and if we could remove it, we must proceed on the same principle as we do with the insane; we must restore the reason before we can sanctify the heart. Some of our Christian friends object to this and say, "Then it is the gospel and total abstinence." We say emphatically, "Yes, Just in the same sense as in the case of a lunatic or a man raving with fever; it is the gospel and the physician."

Practical Religion
Catherine Booth

I told them that I should expect to hear the wails of widows and orphans mingled with their songs, and that I should expect the grass under my feet to be red with blood.
(Mrs. Booth's response to an invitation to a party sponsored by a brewer.)

Catherine Booth
Life of Catherine Booth — Volume 2
Frederick Booth-Tucker

We have no hesitation in affirming that strong drink is Satan's chief instrument for keeping the masses of many countries under his power. What is to be done? How shall we deal with the drink? We answer in the name of Christ and humanity – deal with it as with all other Satan-invented Christ-dishonoring, soul-ruining abominations. Wash your hands of it at once and forever, and give a united and straightforward testimony to the world that you consider it an enemy of all righteousness and the legitimate offspring of Satan. I submit that there is no other way for Christians to deal with strong drink. All other ways have

been tried and have failed. The time has come for Christians to denounce the use of intoxicating drinks as irreligious and immoral.

Catherine Booth
The Salvation Army – Its Origin and Development

We might adduce overwhelming evidence that strong drink is the natural ally of wickedness. Unquestionable statistics have been produced which show that its stimulus is essential to the plotting and commission of almost every kind of villainy. The gambler seeks it to aid him in the craft and cunning whereby he lures his victim on to financial ruin. The seducer has resource to its deceptive power to pave the way for his cruel licentiousness. The burglar braces his courage and hardens his conscience by its exhilarating fumes. The harlot drowns in the intoxicating cup of her sense of shame, and from it gathers strength to trample out the deepest, tenderest instincts of womanhood. The murderer is powerless to strike the fatal blow until maddened by its infernal stimulus.

Practical Religion
Catherine Booth

What would become of a man if he were to cook his own blood and eat his own flesh? How can a kingdom flourish that lives upon the destruction of its subjects, and that draws its revenues from their very graves?

Catherine Booth
The Life of Catherine Booth – Volume 1
Frederick Booth-Tucker

I feel great difficulty in speaking of the injury, misery, and death which the drink inflicts on the childlife of the nations. It is too horrible. Its horrors can only be exceeded by one thing – its wickedness. Thousands of children are cursed by drink before they are born! Thousands are drugged by it in the first months of life! Thousands are starved and neglected in their own mother's arms either because of her own or her husband's drinking habits! Thousands grow up polluted in the sources of their physical and moral well-being; thousands are robbed of innocence and virtue and thrown down to die in the mud of our great cities by this dark vampire! Thousands are turned into feebleminded and dependents, doubly cursed by this modern plague, inasmuch as they are first driven to distraction by its effects and then deprived of all that makes life bearable!

Likeness to God
Florence Booth

The Salvationist, says that the best side of a public-house is the outside.

The Army Uniform
Florence Booth

Many a man takes a beer, not from the love of beer, but from a nature craving for the light, warmth, company and comfort which is thrown in along with the beer. Reformers will never get rid of the drink shop until they can outbid it in the subsidiary attractions which it offers to its customers.

In Darkest England and the Way Out
William Booth

No amount of reasoning, or earthly or religious considerations, can have any effect upon a man who is so completely under the mastery of this passion that he cannot break away from it, although he sees the most terrible consequences staring him in the face. The drunkard promises and vows, but promises and vows in vain. Occasionally he will put forth frantic efforts to deliver himself, but only to fall again in the presence of opportunity. The insatiable crave controls him. He cannot get away from it. It compels him to drink, whether he will or not, and, unless delivered by an Almighty hand, he will drink himself into a drunkard's grave and a drunkard's hell.

In Darkest England and the Way out
William Booth

Still the mighty torrent of alcohol, fed by ten thousand manufacturers, sweeps on, bearing with it, I have no hesitation in saying, the foulest, bloodiest tide that ever flowed from earth to eternity. The Church of the Living God ought not to rest without doing something desperate to rescue all who are in the eddying maelstrom.

In Darkest England and the Way out
William Booth

The drink difficulty lies at the root of everything. Nine tenths of our poverty, squalor, vice, and crime spring from this poisonous tap-root. Many of our social evils, which overshadow the land like so many weeds, would dwindle away, and die if they were not constantly watered with strong drink.

In Darkest England and the Way Out
William Booth

We will have no mere teetotalism. We will have godly meetings, and we will teach all our people never to drink or touch the stuff, for Christ's sake.

William Booth
The History of The Salvation Army – Volume 1
Robert Sandall

The drink's been my undoing, it took all my cash,
You understand? We understand!
A drop too much, I'd stagger home my wife to bash,
You understand? We do!
But I have got salvation and it's changed my life,
Our home is filled with happiness in place of strife,
And if you don't believe it you can ask my wife,
You understand? We do!

Glory
John Gowans

If the drunkard ever needs anything to drive him to farther limits of despair, his treatment by his moral fellows will readily fill the bill. To endure the disgustful looks of men, the drawing aside of the skirts of women, the mocking jeers of children; to hear the slamming of doors in the face, to receive the curt and contemptuous refusals of aid; to walk on through the streets, on and on in a downpour of rain, slinking through slush and cold, a recipient of taunts and sneers, kicks and jeers – anything but a kindly word and a helping

121

hand...this experience can but harden the soul of man, turn his heart to granite and his blood to gall.

Out of the Depths
Clarence W. Hall

Loneliness

What a travesty that the last drop of the already overflowing cup of bitterness, the darkest hour of the darkest night, the crowning pain of the fiercest temptation, is the feeling that we suffer alone. The terror of spiritual darkness is that sense of isolation which envelops the soul like the chill autumn mist, shutting our every vision that could bring human comfort or consolation.

Messages to the Messengers
Catherine Bramwell-Booth

If you sometimes get the feeling that yours is "a voice crying out in the wilderness" remember that no worthwhile cause began as a mass movement.

It Seems to Me
Philip E. Collier

From this point Christ's loneliness becomes ever more acute until from a gaunt Cross there echoes into an empty sky the cry of ultimate desolation.

The Armoury Commentary – The Four Gospels
Frederick Coutts, Edit.

He does not promise we shall be spared from bereavement, but He does rescue us from the ultimate loneliness of a godless universe.

The Armoury Commentary – The Four Gospels
Frederick Coutts, Edit.

Love, God's

Love which conquered o'er death's sting,
Love which has immortal wing,
Love which is the only thing my broken heart to heal;
It bursts thro' the grave.
It brought grace to save,
It opened Heaven's gate.

I never knew such love could be –
This love He gave to me.

Songs of the Evangel
Evangeline Booth

I believe the rocks will turn gray with age. The forests will become unmoored in the hurricane. The sun will shut its fiery eyelid. The stars will drop like burned-out ashes. The hills will stagger and go over. The seas will heave their last expiring groan. The world will wrap itself in a sheet of flame. But God's love will never die.

Evangeline Booth
The General Was a Lady
Margaret Troutt

No miser ever loved his gold; no patriot ever loved his country; no mother ever loved her baby; no father ever loved his boy; no bridegroom ever loved his bride; no, not all the love of all the created beings on this earth put together would equal the love which God bears to you.

Purity of Heart
William Booth

There is no budding of the hillside, no murmur of the brook, no bird on the wing, no breath of the forest, no life on the sea, no cloudlet of the sky in which one cannot find God's touch of love. Love was the beginning of all things, and love will rush in and throb out the final climax of all, when in the day of the world's tribunal the heavy tramp of the nations is halted for love's sealing of every virtue, and crowning of all good.

Love is All
Evangeline Booth

God's love to me is wonderful,
That He should deign to hear,
The faintest whisper of my heart,
Wipe from mine eyes the tear;
And though I cannot comprehend
Such love, so great, so deep,
In his strong hands my soul I trust,
He will not fail to keep.

Sidney E. Cox
Salvation Army Song Book

Lord, I bask in Your love;
I drink it in like sweet wine to the thirsty
soul.
I revel in it like a child at a circus.
I marvel at it like a bride at her new hus-
band.

Eric Britcher
It's Beautiful
Dorothy Breen, Edit.

The Cross was to be the revelation of true
power, the power of light. The love we see
there is the only unbreakable power, for it
did not break then, when human sin had
done its utmost and manifested its utter
ugliness and shame. Here lies our confidence; always the final word is love.

Power and Glory
Harry Dean

To the north, south, east and west,
O wondrous love!
Some have heard, but tell the rest;
O wondrous love!
Vast the curse and great the fall,
Jesus Christ has died for all,
We will every nation call;
O wondrous love!

John Lawley
Salvation Army Song Book

Love divine, from Jesus flowing,
    Living waters rich and free,
Wondrous love without a limit,
    Flowing from eternity;
Boundless ocean,
    I would cast myself on Thee.

Love surpassing understanding,
    Angels would the mystery scan,
Yet so tender that it reaches
    To the lowest child of man.
Let me, Jesus,
    Fuller know redemption's plan.

Elizabeth MacKenzie
Salvation Army Song Book

That love could scan the deepest depths,
the highest heights and span all space till
love at last banishes hate.

The Creche and the Cross
Hulda C. Miller

When Adam sinned, the love which had
caused creation was also sufficient to
cause a remedy to spawn the ultimate solution to man's sinful inheritance.

A Sense of God
Peter W. Stine

The throne of God is not so much an aus-
tere emblem of sovereignty as it is a compassionate symbol of sacrificial love.

To the Point
Bramwell Tripp

Boundless as the mighty ocean,
    Rolling on from pole to pole,
Is the boundless love of Jesus
    To the weary sinful soul.

Waller
Salvation Army Song Book

Love, Human

The chief human need is to experience
love.

Chosen to be a Soldier

(The Salvationists) winning their way, by
force of simple love.

The Salvation Army – Its Origin and Development

What we want is more of this love which
touches, breaks, and melts hearts. It is the
greatest force in the universe. This love requires nothing for itself, it can live without
gratitude and die without a thank you. It
can endure, persevere, suffer. This love
hopes where everyone else despairs. Love
shuts the door on doubt and carries the
feeblest in its arms. It encourages when all
the world could discourage. Love is faithful; deaf to its own feelings; it warns comrades of their sin which so easily besets
them. The instinct of its affection is so true
that in order to avoid that the Savior's
heart should be wounded by the unfaithfulness of its comrade. It takes the trouble
to correct it.

The Officer – 1917

Every sun that has gone down has
strengthened my confidence in the power
of love.

Evangeline Booth
The General Was a Lady
Margaret Troutt

123

Let me love Thee, I am gladdest
    When I'm loving Thee the best;
For in sunshine or in sadness,
    I can find in Thee my rest.
Love will soften every sorrow,
    Love will lighten every care,
Love unquestioning will follow,
    Love will triumph, love will dare.

Herbert Booth
Salvation Army Song Book

I mean hearts made hot with holy love, such as will compel us to toil and sacrifice for the welfare of the object cared for. Such love as will make its possessor the servant of those beloved, and exercise a self-denying mastery over the heart that experiences it. Such love will be like our Master's. For "herein is love, not that we loved God, but that he loved us."

Purity of Heart
William Booth

If the flame of love burns low, the soul will be weak. If it dies out, the soul ceases to live.

William Booth
Chosen to be a Soldier

Show them the very essence of religion is love; the love that shows itself in benevolent effort for the salvation of others.

Salvation Soldiery
William Booth

The strength of The Army is built on two words; love and obedience.

William Booth
Peace Like a River
Sallie Chesham

There is lawful and unlawful love as regards the things of this life:
1. The love of the wrong things.
2. The wrong love of right things.

The Seven Spirits
William Booth

Love can bow down the stubborn neck,
The stone to flesh convert

Soften and melt and pierce and break
The very hardest heart.

Bramwell Booth
Trumpets of the Lord
Catherine Bramwell-Booth, Edit.

Love will not be barred by criticism, not bound by custom. It bursts forth and flows over in new ways every day. It seeks out its ends (never its "own") with a wisdom and patience that do not recognize failure as such, and find it dwells in a marred body and with a mind narrowed by ignorance; and seeing the beauty, love will deal tenderly, being careful because of old scars. The beauty, too, of the young not yet spoiled but with all the possibilities of a clear, upright life before them; and love, seeing by its own clear light so much further ahead than the young soul itself can see, will be inexhaustibly patient with youth's shortsighted ideas and changing desires, and persuade or compel with a power that is love's own, not less strong because it is always gentle.

Messengers to the Messengers
Catherine Bramwell-Booth

Love will teach our hands to serve and multiply our powers.

Messages to the Messengers
Catherine Bramwell-Booth

Divine love is the great test by which we are to try ourselves and all teachers and spirits.

When the Holy Ghost is Come
Samuel Logan Brengle

God requires me to love and serve Him with all my heart, and Gabriel can do no more than that.

Helps to Holiness
Samuel Logan Brengle

In cold weather men of all nations will gather around a stove in which there is fire, and so they will gather around Salvation Army officers and soldiers, and any others who are full of love.

The Soul-Winner's Secret
Samuel Logan Brengle

Love is a word that connotes what the giver wants,
Not what he bestows.

Walking with the Wind
Sallie Chesham

Basically to love God is to put His will first in our lives. To love our neighbor is to put his needs before our own. There may or may not be an emotional content in one or both of these relationships, but primarily these are twin expressions of an attitude of the will.

The Call to Holiness
Frederick Coutts

Christ wants nothing more than our love, which is the only guarantee of our loyalty. a father may have an otherwise perfect son, but if there is no love between them the father is wretched indeed. The rich young ruler brought to Jesus his moral goodness and his sincere religion, but not his love. If we do the same – and how easy it is to mistake this for Christian discipline – we actually crucify Jesus afresh.

The Armoury Commentary – The Four Gospels
Frederick Coutts, Edit.

Love– inspired religion alone is free from exhibitionism, unreality and compensatory harshness. We cannot produce this love; it is aroused when we recognize we are loved.

The Armoury Commentary – The Four Gospels
Frederick Coutts, Edit.

There are only two facts which men and women have to face. One is the fact of life, the other of death – and both are in the control of love. Whether we live or die, we are the Lord's.

The Call to Holiness
Frederick Coutts

Force can not command love.

Power and Glory
Harry Dean

Love can fertilize the arid soil
    Of disappointment, till again are seen
The shoots of promise in the stony ground;

Till for the bitterness is giv'n the oil
    of gladness; for the dustland, verdure green;
And, for the dirge, a song of gladsome sound.

James Gallatly
Book of Salvationist Verse
Catherine Baird, Edit.

A man unloved
Is not worth very much.
He hobbles through life
On a broken crutch.
But when he knows
That someone really cares,
He holds himself erect,
He acts, he dares!

Thanks for Your love;
It brings us hope again:
Makes beaten cripples
Into noble men!

O Lord!
John Gowans

I want, dear Lord, a love that cares for all.
A deep, strong love that answers every call;
A love like Thine, a love divine,
A love to come or go;
On me, dear Lord, a love like this bestow.

George Jackson
Salvation Army Song Book

The love which Jesus offers is measured only by our capacity to receive. And that capacity finds its limits in the love which we can offer Him.

Christ's Cabinet
William McIntyre

There is no piety without love, and love that is merely abstract is not love at all, but sentiment.

Marching to Glory
Edward McKinley

Love is a faculty which, if it is developed at all, will operate, though in varying degrees, in every relationship.

Our Rebel Emotions
Bernard Mobbs

As I am Thine by Thy pure love redeeming,
Let me be Thine by my pure love to Thee.

The Beauty of Jesus
Albert Orsborn

Choicest gifts are won by giving,
Truest gain springs out of loss;
There always is a blessing
In the shade of every cross.
Oh! lighter seems the burden
That we hear at love's behest;
For love lives by giving
Her choicest and best.

The Beauty of Jesus
Albert Orsborn

I must love Thee, love must rule me,
    Springing up and flowing forth
From a childlike heart within me,
    Or my work is nothing worth.
Love with passion and with patience,
    Love with principle and fire,
Love with heart and mind and utterance,
    Serving Christ, my one desire.

Albert Orsborn
Salvation Army Song Book

Love is a poor mathematician, and never knows how to set sensible limits to its ministry.

Studies in Sanctification
Edward Read

As long as one loves, one lives nobly.

Ruth Siegfried
My Best Men are Women
Flora Larsson

Help me understand when You let it rain for me and drench my life with a quiet shower of grief or criticism, of grayness, of trial, trouble or heartache. Then let love glide through my space – love that, when it is lovely, moves without a sound.

Dear God
Virginia Talmadge

There is one gift I'd like very much, Lord. It is the gift of loving. I'm not asking You for love, but for lovability – a feeling of love for everyone I meet along life's way; a love that is penetrating and so real that when I can't get through with love, I just give more love. You see, Lord, I'm asking for a love that will not tire; a love that sees the best and that loves that best into being; a lovability that is too brave to lie or to be unkind and too understanding to remember what should be forgotten and forgiven; a lovability that is not computerized but is "care-ability" and "share-ability."

Dear God
Virginia Talmadge

Since love's value is proved by love's test, Jesus, I'll give Thee the dearest and best.

Ruth Tracy
Salvation Army Song Book

Love that fails to respect a person, however it attends to his needs, is not enough.

The Desert Road to Glory
Clarence Wiseman

Unconditional love does not seek out the "deserving" poor – who is to be the judge? The healing, helping action comes first – the questions, if any, later, and they should be constructive! Christian love is not preferential since help is given only to those who fit into acceptable categories. Christian love knows no hours; it is always on call.

The Desert Road to Glory
Clarence Wiseman

Loyalty

Only those who are fully determined by God's help to be true soldiers of The Salvation Army till they die can rightly take the holy vows involved in the swearing-in ceremony.

Chosen to be a Soldier

The divided heart is often the real maker of mischief in the spiritual life.

Chosen to be a Soldier

We are not brought to God for an interview, but to remain with Him.

More Than Conquerors
Milton S. Agnew

I feel that, at this moment, I could put all
my children into their graves and go to a
workhouse bed to die, sooner than I could
see those first principles of The Salvation
Army, for which I have lived and struggled, traduced and undermined and sacrificed.

Catherine Booth
On the Banks of the River
Bramwell Booth

True love sticks to the Lord Jesus in the
mud, when He is fainting under His cross
as well as when the people are cutting
down the boughs and crying "Hosanna!"

Catherine Booth
Life of Catherine Booth – Volume 1
Frederick Booth-Tucker

God wants men and women that He can
reckon upon, who will be there at the very
time He wants them, and do the very work
He wants doing, whatever may stand in the
way.

Salvation Soldiery
William Booth

Oh, Builder of the City,
Make me a road without conclusion,
Winding out into the wilds but always
turning back.
Back to the fact, to the city –
You.

Walking with the Wind
Sallie Chesham

God has a place for everyone. He can use
all types: the believing, the doubting, the
sanguine, the phlegmatic, the optimistic,
the pessimistic. In the last analysis there is
but one thing needful – loyalty to Christian
service.

Christ's Cabinet
William McIntyre

Man

Man feels his own existence to be threatened by isolation on the one hand and absorption on the other. These are man's potential murderers.

Reason to Believe
Harry Dean

Man is greater than the stars he numbers, whose paths he plots and whose distances he estimates, because he can assess, evaluate and does in fact "transcend" them.

Reason to Believe
Harry Dean

Man is most God-like when he is most human.

Reason to Believe
Harry Dean

Marriage

A good marriage has to be worked at. It is an achievement, not a gift.

Orders and Regulations for Corps Officers

An engagement to marry is a transaction next in importance to the giving of oneself to God.

Orders and Regulations for Officers

Every salvation soldier must reject the godless mental reservation that if marriage is not a success, divorce is always possible.

Chosen to be a Soldier

Sharing is the essence of marriage.

Chosen to be a Soldier

May the Lord give you the grace to reject the gilded bait, preferring to suffer (if He will) loneliness and sorrow, rather than ally yourself with one who neither knows nor loves Him.

Catherine Booth
Mrs. Booth
W.T. Stead

The real ultimate Court of Appeal for all truly religious persons is not the husband, but God, whose authority is absolute. If the husband has any decisive voice, it is only given him to decide whether his or his wife's interpretation of the divine will is the more in accordance with the law of God, as revealed in Holy Writ, or as manifested in the leadings of Providence.

Catherine Booth
Mrs. Booth
W.T. Stead

I did not want to die for her, but to live for her. I wanted to put my arms around her, to comfort her, provide for her, protect her, bear her burdens, be her shield, and receive every blow of adversity or sorrow or misfortune that might befall her. I no longer thought of what she might bring or give me, but only of what I might give to and suffer for her.

Ancient Prophets
Samuel Logan Brengle

In the callow years of young manhood very small defects, which may not be defects at all, and would probably be unnoticed by older and wiser men, may cause "Cupid's darts to miss the mark."

Ancient Prophets
Samuel Logan Brengle

It is possible for a husband and wife to live together for many years, and instead of increasing, except in the most superficial way, in the knowledge of each other, to grow apart, until after many years they are heart strangers to each other, with separate interests, conflicting desires and tempers and alien affinities. To really know each other they must be bound together by stronger ties than mere legal forms; they must commune with each other, live in each other's hearts; enter into each other's joys, and share each other's sorrows, counsel each other in perplexity, seek the same ends and cultivate the same spirit.

Heart Talks on Holiness
Samuel Logan Brengle

It was while continuing my professional studies in an Eastern university that the conviction possessed me that my wife must not only have sweet womanly virtues, be adorned with refinement and the culture of the schools, but that she must be genuinely religious, must love God and His law supremely, for without this I realized we should fail in the highest fellowship. With this love and loyalty to God abounding, I knew that her love and loyalty could not fail.

Ancient Prophets
Samuel Logan Brengle

Marriage is a divine institution, is surrounded by divine sanctions, and should be entered into with a sense of its divine character and responsibilities and blessings, which, abused, can turn into the most fateful of curses; therefore, God's blessings should be sought in every step that leads it.

Ancient Prophets
Samuel Logan Brengle

If our religion means anything to us at all, it must have some bearing upon our attitude to marriage. If it can be ignored here, it can be ignored anywhere. If it is dismissed as irrelevant here, it is irrelevant everywhere. But for us our devotion to one another is expressed within the context of our dedication to God.

Essentials of Christian Experience
Frederick Coutts

I thank God no one was in a hurry to teach me, when a young man, about the mysteries and intimacies of sex. I learned all I needed to know in the best of schools – marriage with a pure lovely woman, founded on mutual respect, and sanctified by God's guidance and grace.

The House of My Pilgrimage
Albert Orsborn

Divorce is the defeat of God's intention for human happiness.

Meditations for the Ordinary Man
George B. Smith

Neither changing social conditions, fresh psychological insights, new lifestyles, a climate of moral permissiveness, nor any other thing can either diminish or destroy the holy obligations of Christian marriage.

A Burning in My Bones
Clarence Wiseman

The Christian home is still the foundation of the church and, therefore, the foundation of the nation. Such vows as "till death do us part" must never be neglected or set aside. We pray for all who enter into the sacred relationship of marriage that their union may be strengthened, their love for each other enriched, and their service to God increased through their union together.

Willard S. Evans
New Frontier

Mercy

Sinner, you are here. That is enough proof that God is good.

Life and Death
Catherine Booth

Mercy is not patronage, nor is it a form of proud forbearance which parades as a virtue rather than seeking to help a friend in need. It should be remembered that just as justice should be tempered with mercy, mercy should be tempered with justice.

The Armoury Commentary – The Four Gospels
Frederick Coutts, Edit.

Mercy Seat

No virtue attaches to the pentitent form as such, but coming there is a public confession of spiritual need, desire after God, or decision to do God's will. This act tests sincerity, helps to bring the seeker to that condition of soul in which God can deal with him, and assists him in breaking loose from evil habits. Moreover, the penitent form provides a place where spiritual guidance can suitably be given. Its use helps a leader to keep a definite aim before him in meetings.

Orders and Regulations for Officers

The penitent form must not be regarded as a place for the easing of a guilty conscience instead of a place for forsaking sin.

Orders and Regulations for Officers

There is no saving virtue in the Mercy Seat; but this act of kneeling there is a definite response to the divine urge to accept salvation there and then.

Chosen to be a Soldier

Which man is he? I ask,
The discontented one of yesterday?
Or this, with striving washed away,
Surveying now, with happiness complete,
Sinner kneeling at the Mercy Seat.

Reflections
Catherine Baird

The Salvation Army did not start with a band, a uniform, or poor men's hostels or slum corps – we started with a penitent form in the dark on Mile End Waste, London. The penitent form is not merely one of the institutions of The Salvation Army – it is one of the vitals that can never change. It is our communal rail, our baptismal font, where the fire of the Holy Spirit falls upon our soldiers. It is at the foot of the Cross of Jesus where the sinner lays down his burden; it is our altar – our cornerstone.

Evangeline Booth
The General Was a Lady
Margaret Troutt

The penitent form is dedicated to personal covenant-making between God and men; it is the place of decision. The Salvation Army was born at the penitent form.

Friendship With Jesus
Florence Booth

The Salvation Army was born, not in a cloister, nor in a drawing room, but on a spiritual battlefield — at the penitent form.

Love-Slaves
Samuel Logan Brengle

The penitent form is not merely a place but an idea. Its essential meaning is purely spiritual. The Mercy Seat is a meeting place set up by God. The influences of an Army meeting – the singing, the exhortation and prayer – are doubtless vehicles for the conveyance of God's message to the soul, but where the contract between God and man is made, there is the Mercy Seat. God marks the place. God knows the place.

The Mercy Seat
William Burrows

When a seeker kneels in true contrition at an Army penitent form, that form is holy ground; it is holy not because man has pronounced it such but because there the Savior and sinner meet.

The Mercy Seat
William Burrows

Every seeker comes alone
To make his prayers
But before one common throne
We bring our cares;
Coming with an inward awe,
Our Lord to meet,
We are not alone before the Mercy Seat.

Glory!
John Gowans

Come, then, at once; delay no longer;
Heed His entreaty, kind and sweet;
You need not fear a disappointment;
You shall find peace at the Mercy Seat.

Edward H. Joy
Salvation Army Song Book

Miracles

A miracle is the testimony of God; it is his own special witness to His own power.

Bramwell Booth
Trumpets of the Lord
Catherine Bramwell-Booth

We refer to these happenings as "miracles", but those who witnessed them knew nothing of such a term. To them they were "acts of power" or "signs".

Power and Glory
Harry Dean

Mission

In the gospel of Christ, as I have received it, in the Spirit of my religion as I teach it, may I ask that we all link hands in a solemn contract to press on. We must go on. While there is a land to Christianize, we must go on. While a lost girl wanders, we must go on. While there is a city or a home without a Bible, we must go on. Wherever the ship of life is in danger, there – death or life – we must go on!

Women
Evangeline Booth

Missionaries

Humanity, it is said, is far richer for the memory of the Crusaders, those men who followed the "way of the Holy Sepulchre" in the hope of eternal reward. But what can be said of the twentieth century crusaders who travelled not on gaily harnessed horses with men in richly engraved armor and bearing jeweled swords, but humbly and on foot through a dark continent: fighting not with lance or sword but with the Bible and song book, hypodermic needle and health chart; fighting devils and disease with indefatigable care and the ammunition of love?

Congo Crusade
Albert Kenyon

Every Christian should be a missionary, and it should be felt in every church that it is dishonorable to be idle.

William Booth
The History of The Salvation Army – Volume 1
Robert Sandall

What are the heathen? I sometimes feel and fear when I talk about them that some of my comrades regard them very much as they regard trees in a forest, or cabbages in a vast prairie, or, at the best, as a

race of monkeys of a little superior order to the ordinary run of creatures of the tribe. But has not the day come for us Salvationists to leave all those proud notions of superiority and those hateful race prejudices behind us?

International Congress Addresses
William Booth

We will accept Christ when He takes off his hat and trousers and boots.

Citizens of India
The General Next to God
Robert Collier

Missionary enterprise is not merely a Christian romance, or a thrilling option; it is indispensable to the life of any branch of the Christian church. To deny it is to perish.

The House of My Pilgrimage
Albert Orsborn

Moribund churches or stagnant Salvation Army corps provide no good ground for missionary zeal.

The house of My Pilgrimange
Albert Orsborn

Money

How is thrift to benefit those who have nothing? What is the use of the gospel of thirst to a man who had nothing to eat yesterday, and has not threepence today to pay for his lodging tonight? To live on nothing a day is difficult enough, but to save on it would beat the cleverest potitical economist that ever lived.

In Darkest England and The Way Out
William Booth

Money is the sinew of war; and, as society is at present constituted, neither carnal nor spiritual wars can be carried on without money.

In Darkest England and The Way Out
William Booth

No hope of doing good hereafter can justify the doing of worldly or doubtful things for the purpose of raising money.

Twenty-One Years Salvation Army
William Booth

We will wash it (money from publicans) in the tears of the widows and orphans and lay it on the altar of humanity.

William Booth
The General Next to God
Richard Collier

Do not let us even desire to be rich, either as individuals or as an organization. Let us choose to be poor. Let us fling the devil's golden bribes back in his face. This will give us power in dealing alike with rich and poor, whereas a spirit even wishing to be rich will cripple our influence and hinder our testimony.

Frederick Booth-Tucker
The Officer

Money is the rock on which many a good religious organization has made spiritual shipwreck. Though not recognizing certain root principles they have never been able to win the world with salvation. They have gone a certain distance and then they have come to the end of their financial rope and have stuck fast.

Frederick Booth-Tucker
The Officer – 1893

The majority of Protestant churches act as if it were a virtue to be rich, whereas in the eyes of God it is probably the greatest crime of which anybody can be guilty in the present age, with the anguished cry of famishing millions ringing in their ears – famishing not only for the Bread of Life, but even for the bread which perishes. Thank God, we are a poor people – poor as officers – poor as soldiers – poor as people. Long may we remain so!

Frederick Booth-Tucker
The Officer – 1893

Truly, wealth – ever hideous as a tyrant – never looks more comely than when it stoops to be the servant of the poor.

Life of Catherine Booth – Volume 2
Frederick Booth-Tucker

There are three ways of reaching a man's purse:
(1) Directly, (2) By way of his head with flattering words, (3) By way of his heart with manly, honest, saving words. The first way is robbery. The second way is robbery, with the poison of a deadly, but pleasing, opiate added, which may damn the soul. The third reaches his purse by saving his soul and opening in his heart an unfailing fountain of benevolence to bless himself and the world.

When the Holy Ghost is Come
Samuel Logan Brengle

Great wealth bred enormous poverty. No one yet related Christianity seriously to responsibility for the deprived and the depraved. Token gestures were made in the breadline, but the God who seemed to cajole the rich seemed not a blood relative to the waifs, widows, and wild eyed drunks who soiled the seam on the garment of silken Victorian society in America.

Peace Like a River
Sallie Chesham

In our Lord's judgment the power which wealth can bestow is a greater danger to its possessor than to those over whom it gives power.

The Armoury Commentary – The Four Gospels
Frederick Coutts, Edit.

Our prosperity tends to make us independent of God, even though our lips continue to pay homage to Him.

The Armoury Commentary – the Four Gospels
Frederick Coutts, Edit.

Money is amoral: it becomes what men make it.

The House of My Pilgrimage
Albert Orsborn

He deigned to see
That beyond the piece of silver
Good or evil worked their way;
One to make men cold and callous,
The other love's dear debt to pay.

Memoirs of Peter
Arthur Pitcher

The cry of thousands of precious souls going downward to destruction comes up with a mighty wail, which ought to pierce all our hearts. We cannot, we must not, we

133

dare not, we will not allow the work of God to stand still, for want of funds.

George Scott Railton
G.S.R.
John D. Waldron, Edit.

Morality

True morality begins, not with a quest for self-vindication, nor yet with a lament that such vindication is impossible; it begins when we respond to a love which raises us out of our self-concern altogether, including our self-esteem. This is what the gospel of God's love in Christ is able to do.

Our Rebel Emotions
Bernard Mobbs

Salvationists share with fellow Christians the conviction that true moral values are not derived from circumstances, nor the way we happen to feel at the moment, not by our particular genetic inheritance, not even by the interplay of social forces. They are rooted in the very nature of things, in God Himself.

A Burning in My Bones
Clarence Wiseman

Motherhood

Perhaps the greatest earthly blessing known to man is a godly mother. No other gift has so direct a bearing upon his present and everlasting well-being. She molds his future, gives his spirit a heavenly inclination, and imparts to it an impetus which, unless done violence to in the most determined manner, must secure for him in after days a full measure of earthly happiness and in the end everlasting life.

William Booth
The Founder Speaks Again
Cyril Barnes, Edit.

I see her as the light of our home, the inspiration of our childhood, the ideal of our ambitions, the repository of our confidences, the guardian angel of our souls, and now the beacon of our lives as we sail earth's sea toward the same blissful harbor in which she has dropped anchor forever.

Heart Messages
Emma Booth-Tucker

But it is to my darling mother I owe my deepest debt of love and gratitude. As I grew older, her gentleness and tenderness became the most powerful instruments of discipline to my wayward spirit, just as grace is more mighty to break and refashion hard hearts than law, and Mount Calvary more influential for redemption than Mount Sinai.

Ancient Prophets
Samuel Logan Brengle

From mother I unconsciously got a high ideal of gentle sweetness and purity, and all womanly virtues which adorn a home and make it a haven of rest and a center of inspiration and courage and noble ambition.

Ancient Prophets
Samuel Logan Brengle

He alone of all the children of men chose His mother, and He chose one who was poor and humble and unknown among men.

Heart Talks on Holiness
Samuel Logan Brengle

Here is the might and the responsibility of motherhood. She can hold her children to goodness and God, not by force, but by affection, not by the compulsion of command, but by the compulsion of high and holy character.

Ancient Prophets
Samuel Logan Brengle

The glory of motherhood is the glory of unfailing patience...of sacrifice....self-forgetful unselfishness...love that never faileth...unwavering faith and undying hope.

Ancient Prophets
Samuel Logan Brengle

We never see a blooming girl with rosy cheeks and laughing eyes and bewitching curls for whom some mother has not gradually faded and given her own bloom and beauty and youth.

Ancient Prophets
Samuel Logan Brengle

Long before I knew God in Christ, I saw Him and loved Him in my mother.

The House of My Pilgrimage
Albert Orsborn

Mother averred that while many things needed putting right in this untidy world, most of them would have to wait until after lunch.

The House of My Pilgrimage
Albert Orsborn

Motivation

Jesus Christ is going to be intensely practical in that day. He is not going to say, "Inasmuch as ye *thought* it," or "Inasmuch as ye *felt* it", or "Inasmuch as ye *intended*", or "Inasmuch as ye *promised* it" — but He is going to say, "Inasmuch as ye *did* it."

Life and Death
Catherine Booth

Even when we have the highest motives, a Christian must practice restraint.

Evangeline Booth
The General Was a Lady
Margaret Troutt

The world does not calculate that what I could not do for money, or from a sense of duty, or for the sake of success, yet for love's sake "I can do."

Messages to the Messengers
Catherine Bramwell-Booth

Jesus' teaching both here and elsewhere drives home the truth — unpalatable to all hypocrites — that every kind of conduct gets its reward on the plane of motive, and even the beautiful exercise of prayer can be marred by being used for the purposes of the old self-life.

The Armoury Commentary — The Four Gospels
Frederick Coutts, Edit.

Spiritual perception is always in proportion to our moral stature and purity of motive.

The Armouty Commentary — The Four Gospels
Frederick Coutts, Edit.

The Pharisees, making religion a matter of outward observance, were wholly concerned with their manner of life; Jesus, stressing the inwardness of religion, was concerned first with the motive of life.

The Armoury Commentary — The Four Gospels
Frederick Coutts, Edit.

No church is stronger than the convictions that motivate its people!

Search the Scriptures
Robert Hoggard

Great memories often give birth to great motives.

Soldier of Salvation
Wilfred Kitching

Have I worked for hireling wages,
Or as one with vows to keep;
With a heart whose love engages,
Life or death, to save the sheep?

The Beauty of Jesus
Albert Orsborn

Music

He (the corps officer) should encourage Army musicians to play and sing as efficiently as possible, in order the more effectually to bless and win their hearers; at the same time they should steadily resist the tendency to degenerate into mere performers, realizing the uselessness, for the Army's purposes, of music that is lacking in spiritual power.

Orders and Regulations for Corps Officers

The hymnal of the church is a reflection of its theology.

The Better Covenant
Milton S. Agnew

Who so worthy of a banner as our King? And to whom does all the music on earth belong, if not to Him? I contend that the devil has no right to a single note; and we will have it all away from him yet.

The Salvation Army in Relation to Church and State
Catherine Booth

No soldier should be given a bandsman's commission who does not show some proof of zeal for the salvation of souls.

Powers of Salvation Army Officers
Florence Booth

He (Satan) only allows us the crumbs that fall from his table, such as the old hundredth, and a few more funeral ditties. Of the soul and citadel of music he has taken possession...and with it he charms and chains and sways the world. But if the sensual worldly satanic music wields such a power, what might music not do when songs hand, hearts and voices were inspired and directed by the Holy Ghost...That is a problem that has yet to be solved...Let us swell louder and louder our triumphant songs, and to the sound of that victorious music let us go up to the conquest of the world for Jesus.

William Booth
The History of The Salvation Army — Volume 1
Robert Sandall

I would be willing to have the whole Army tried by court martial on the question of its singing alone, and I would like to see all the infidel philosophers of the age trying to find out what makes these people sing so well if it be not the love of God shed abroad in their hearts by the Holy Ghost given unto them.

Twenty-one Years Salvation Army
William Booth

Music has a divine effect upon divinely influenced and directed souls. Music is to the soul what wind is to the ship, blowing her onwards in the direction in which she is steered...Not allowed to sing that tune or this tune? Indeed! Secular music, do you say? Belongs to the devil, does it? Well, if it did, I would plunder him of it, for he has no right to a single note of the whole gamut. He's the thief!...Every note and every strain and every harmony is divine and belongs to us.

William Booth
The History of The Salvation Army — Volume 2
Robert Sandall

Perhaps some of you have heard me say in public that there will not be a note of music in hell; it will all be in heaven; and God ought to have it all here; but unfortunately God has not His rights here, and the church strangely lost sight of the value of music as a religious agency.

On the Banks of the River
Catherine Booth

The man must blow his cornet and shut his eyes, and believe while he plays he is blowing salvation into somebody, and doing something that will be some good, Let him go on believing while he beats the drum, or blows his cornet, and he will be just as anxious about the prayer meeting — he won't want to buckle up and rush off — he will say, "What is the use of all my beating, and blowing, if I do not see someone come to the penitent form?" All his beating and blowing is to get the people first into the barracks and then to the penitent form.

William Booth
The History of The Salvation Army — Volume 2
Robert Sandall

You cannot play a tambourine without feeling or at least showing a bold front to the foe.

Messages to the Messengers
Catherine Bramwell-Booth

Every great revival of religion results in a revival of singing and of the composition of both music and song.

The Guest of the Soul
Samuel Logan Brengle

Erik Leidzen would say that as far as Salvation Army musicians are concerned it seems at times that "Anything for Jesus" would suffice, that there was a mediocrity about our playing that he could not tolerate. We should strive to present in God's name the highest standards in music.

This Man Leidzen
Leslie Flossey

I would like to think that when the Almighty beckoned, "Let there be light!" He added tenderly, "Let there be sound!"

Erik Leidzen
This Man Leidzen
Leslie Flossey

There should be no dust of death on soul-saving music.

Stuff That Makes An Army
William G. Harris

The next time you hear a Salvation Army band, take off your hat.

John Philip Sousa
Marching to Glory
Edward McKinley

If we have given a song a different meaning, it was like giving a lovely lady a new dress.

The House of My Pilgrimage
Albert Orsborn

We are quite prepared to admit that our singing, especially in the open-air, may more closely resemble the blare of a military band than the melody of the sanctuary; but if the people who sing and the people who hear such singing — prefer it, in fact, to any other — what then?

Heathen England
George Scott Railton

The pain and anguish described in much modern music has no antidote; the hymns of Christ's church, on the other hand, bespeak that permanence and solidarity which God has promised.

A Sense of God
Peter W. Stine

Oh, the pow'r of holy song,
How it spurs our feet along,
On the upward way,
When weary with the pace,
How it keeps us doing well,
How it helps our ranks to swell,
How it oils the chariot wheels with heav'nly grace.

Ruth Tracy
Gems for Songster #1

Name of Jesus

I have sought a name for You,
But find nothing that will do
To describe what you mean to me
Though I search each titling cover,
And the beckoning book beneath,
And they vie with one another,
I simply can't discover
The Appropriate.

Wind Chimes
Sallie Chesham

I have no claim on grace;
I have no right to plead;
I stand before my Maker's face,
Condemned in thought and deed.
But since there died a Lamb
Who, guiltless, my guilt bore,
I lay fast hold on Jesus' name
And sin is mine no more.

The Beauty of Jesus
Albert Orsborn

Not till we knew our guilt and shame
Did we esteem the Savior's name.

The Beauty of Jesus
Albert Orsborn

Nature

Oh! Hateful guilty fright
That turned man's face from Him and made
A gloomy hiding place of some fair glade
In that all-radiant garden God had planned
For man's delight; giv'n him, that human hand
Might share with the Divine the living joy
Of making beauty.

Fighting for the King
Catherine Bramwell-Booth

We live in a stern universe where fire will not only bless us but burn us; where water will both refresh and drown us; where gravitation will either protect or destroy. We must not look at things sentimentally.

Love-Slaves
Samuel Logan Brengle

We see the sparrows feeding from the Heavenly Father's hand, the ravens and the young lions and every creeping thing looking to Him for daily food, the fox fleeing from enemies to his hole, the conies among the rocks, the wild goat among the mountain crags, the nesting bird, the busy ant, the swarming bees, the neighing war horse, the spouting whale, the bridal lilies, the rose of Sharon, green and smiling meadows, still waters, ice, snow and frost, the glowing fire, tempestuous wind and billowing seas, the lowering sky of the morning threatening rain and storm, the red sky of the evening presaging fair and smiling weather..

Ancient Prophets
Samuel Logan Brengle

Like sparrows in the winter
We dream of spring.

Wind Chimes
Sallie Chesham

Thank You, Master, for the tones,
    of dawn, and sunset glow,
    for myriad-shaded flowers, and evergreen grass;
for the riotous panorama of spring
only outdone by autumn's tints.

Between You and Me, Lord
Flora Larsson

If one tries to stick his puny hand in the great flywheel of God's creation, the consequences can be painful.

A Sense of God
Peter W. Stine

Needs

Unless there is a sense of need there cannot be the glory of possession.

Arnold Brown
The Privilege of All Believers
John D. Waldron, Edit.

The multitude had nothing to plead but its own need — and this is how men find their way into the Kingdom.
For need is often dangerous,
Not safe, nor simple;
It is vicious,
Or dirty,
Or sobbing,
Or threatening,
Or dreadfully repulsive,
Or I suppose,
Running at the nose.

Walking With the Wind
Sallie Chesham

The greatness of human need points to the greatness of the God who is.

Reason to Believe
Harry Dean

And what if strength should fail,
And heart more deeply bleed?
Or what if dark and lonely days
Draw forth the cry of need?
That cry will bring Thee down
My needy soul to fill,
And Thou wilt teach my yearning heart
To know and do Thy will.

Fannie Jolliffe
Salvation Army Song Book

Nurture

Every man should have his shadow, some one whose special business it should be to act the guardian angel to him, never letting him slip into sin, but following him patiently till he saw him safely landed in heaven. Can't we manufacture some shadows, especially for our weaker comrades? Can't we repeat the two by two business inaugurated by Christ with His disciples? Can't we leash our soldiers in couples, and make them responsible for each other's souls as well as for hunting the devil? Can't we make it impossible for anyone to drop out of the ranks for a single week unnoticed? Can't we have something on the cartridges like, "I am saved and so is my shadow?"

Frederick Booth-Tucker
The Officer — 1893

A soul can be led during the first weeks to a place which it may take years to reach, if the opportunity of those early days be neglected.

Messages to the Messengers
Catherine Bramwell-Booth

If the flock is to be preserved, the lambs must be shepherded. If babies are to live, they must be nursed with tender care. If the world is to be saved, we must have converts and they must be guarded with sleepless vigilance, and followed with ceaseless and loving care.

Ancient Prophets
Samuel Logan Brengle

Soul-winners are not spiritual incubators, but fathers and mothers in the faith with all the measureless responsibility not only of saving souls, but of keeping them after they are saved.

The Soul-Winner's Secret
Samuel Logan Brengle

Obedience

We believe that continuance in a state of salvation depends upon continued obedient faith in Christ.

Salvation Army Doctrine #9

Strength for what seems a formidable duty will not come until we first make the effort to obey.

The Officer — 1918

Every spark of light you get without obeying it, leaves your soul darker. Every time you come up to the verge of the Kingdom and don't go over, the less probability that you ever will.

Papers on Godliness
Catherine Booth

What does it mean to walk in obedience? Well, it does not mean searching the New Testament to find out how little of God's grace will get you to heaven!

Papers on Godliness
Catherine Booth

Any lingering disobedience, any lack of consecration, makes some of God's most precious messengers unsuitable for us. He could not speak to Peter of the call to suffer the agonies of the cross while he was unwilling to bear the chaff of a serving maid.

Likeness to God
Florence Booth

Go and get sure about God, and then you will have no difficulty in obeying Him — only get a proper idea of God, and you will be frightened enough of disobeying so great, and powerful, and holy a Being.

Salvation Soldiery
William Booth

If we secure His favor kneeling at His feet, can we retain it without following where those feet lead?

The General's Letters
William Booth

Obedience is only another word for the active side of religion.

Salvation Soldiery
William Booth

To obey God, then as now, meant often, if not always, to disobey men. To please God meant then, as now, to displease yourself and your neighbors and the devil, and to make things very unpleasant all round in a general sort of way. To keep right with God by doing His will was, as now, to get wrong and keep wrong with kindred and friends and fellow workmen, and many others with whom it is far more pleasant to keep right.

Salvation Soldiery
William Booth

What He wants is not reasons, but obedience.

Salvation Soldiery
William Booth

If a railway train could think or talk, it might argue that running on two rails over the same road year after year was very commonplace. But if it insisted on larger liberty and jumped the track, it would certainly ruin itself. So the man who wants freedom, and refuses to obey God's commands to be holy, destroys himself. The train was made to run on the tracks, and we were made to live according to God's commandment to be holy.

The Way of Holiness
Samuel Logan Brengle

Run away, O my brother, my sister, from the duty to which God in infinite wisdom and foreknowledge calls you, the path which He in boundless love marks out for you, and the devil will surely arrange to have a ship ready to carry you down to Tarsus. But He cannot insure you against a storm, and he would not if He could. Storms certainly await you, however softly the south wind may now blow.

Resurrection Life and Power
Samuel Logan Brengle

God is not concerned about the results we achieve so much as the obedience we offer!

The Armoury Commentary — The Four Gospels
Frederick Coutts, Edit.

The life controlled by the Spirit will not rebel at the place of service to which God appoints.

The Call to Holiness
Frederick Coutts

God will not call His people to a career but to a life of obedience.

Mildred Duff
Madge Unsworth

Give me obedience with a smiling face,
To go unwelcome ways with better grace.

O Lord!
John Gowans

Lord, if You bid me stand
Aside, while others fight,
If thus for me You planned,
I know it must be right;
I will not murmur, but only ask
For grace to do the harder task.

Matilda Hatcher
The Merchant of Heaven

In the unfolding affairs of men and nations there are two areas of authority — the thrones of men on earth and the thone of God in heaven. Wisdom and wealth are no substitutes to the sovereign will of God.

Search the Scriptures
Robert Hoggard

One must tread the path of holiness carefully, with a watchful eye, an ear always open to His voice and a spirit ever ready to obey.

Kate Lee
The Privilege of All Believers
John D. Waldron, Edit.

Part of an officer's obedience is listening to what he does not want to hear.

A Burning in My Bones
Clarence Wiseman

Officership

He must not only feel that he is responsible for commanding the corps, but that he is responsible to God for the salvation of the souls of every man, woman, and child in the town or district in which he is appointed.

Why and Wherefore
Bramwell Booth

Men! Men! Men! Oh, my God, send us men! Never mind if you do stammer, or if you have a wooden leg, or a weak chest, or if you have only one eye, or have no platform ability. If you are a Salvation Army soldier, and have brains, energy, tact and business ability, don't let this appeal haunt you till you write the Field Secretary straight away.

Bramwell Booth
The History of The Salvation Army — Volume 4
Arch Wiggins

The field officer, by virtue of his position, stands out before his soldiers more prominently than any other man. To them he is the ambassador and representative of God. He is their captain, their brother, their friend. Their eyes are constantly on him. They regard him as the pattern expressly set for them to copy, the leader who at all times it is their duty to follow.

Why and Wherefore
Bramwell Booth

The work of a Salvation Army officer is a sentence of hard labor for life.

Bramwell Booth
Mildred Duff
Madge Unsworth

What sort of soldiers are specially likely to be accepted? Those who are godly, and have a clear experience, and live a holy life; those who love souls, and are hard and energetic workers; those who have good health, and are loyal to the principles of the Army, and who appear to have sufficient gifts as are necessary to make efficient leaders.

Why and Wherefore
Bramwell Booth

Lay it to heart, my comrades, that an officer's success and power are manifest in the raising and maintaining of a fighting force. You will not be on the active list forever. Indeed, the year is fixed when your part in the rank will be played out. What we each can do in the fighting line to build up the Kingdom of God will soon be accomplished. Then other voices will issue the orders; other hands will wipe away the tears of the penitent, other brains and hearts will plan for the goodness and happiness of the soldier. Someone else will work for the holiness of the corps. But your works will follow you. It will be seen in the fighting qualities of the soldiers you have trained, in the power and spirit of the officers who replace you. The officers who will take the places of those now in command are being raised by their predecessors today.

Powers of Salvation Army Officers
Florence Booth

Our officers, each a personality, not dimmed but touched by grace into brightness, should be to The Salvation Army what the rainbow is to light.

Powers of Salvation Army Officers
Florence Booth

Here, young men and young women, you are thinking about this cadet business, and I am not surprised at it either. What is trade and shop keeping, and emigration, and marriage, and money making, and — and anything else compared with this business of war?

Salvation Soldiery
William Booth

I care not what the preaching abilities or other qualifications of a man of woman may be, if he does not succeed — if he does not get the people saved — he proves incontestably that he has missed his vocation, and he ought at once to turn over a new leaf and alter his plans, or inquire for some other walk of life in which he can succeed.

Salvation Soldiery
William Booth

Love, rightly directed, makes a good parent, a good husband, a good workman; and nothing short of love, and a great deal of it, will make a good officer.

Salvation Soldiery
William Booth

Make your will, pack your box, kiss your girl, be ready in a week.

Willliam Booth
The General Next to God
Richard Collier

WANTED ALWAYS
to become
OFFICERS IN THE SALVATION ARMY
men and women of God

Anxious to devote their lives to the work of souls,
Whose character will bear any amount of investigation;
Who can talk to a crowd of people out of doors and in, so as to wound sinners' hearts;
Who can lead a band of godly men and women to do something likely to win souls;
Who are perfectly ready to speak, pray, visit, sit still, travel a hundred miles, or die at a moment;
Who have given up drink, tobacco and finery, for Christ's sake, or are willing to give up anything and everything for Him;
Who are willing to be led and taught, and to be sent home again if they do not succeed.
Who are willing to be evil spoken of, hated and despised, and even to be misrepresented, misunderstood, and undervalued at headquarters.

143

THE FOLLOWING NEED NOT APPLY:

Persons, who, "being out of employment, desire to give themselves entirely, etc, etc.";
Who, "do not think they can be expected" to exhaust all their strength in laboring day and night to save souls;
Who, "if engaged, will endeavor to give satisfaction to their employers";
Who will take any notice of the fact of their going or living anywhere or doing anything they are asked to do;
Who desire "light employment", "find their work beginning to tell on them", etc. etc.;
Who would like to know "particulars as to salary, hours, home, etc., before being engaged";
Who "are sometimes troubled with doubts" about the inspiration of the Bible, the divinity of Christ, the Atonement, election, the possibility of falling from grace, eternal damnation, or the personality of the devil;
Who, "having had considerable experience" in our kind of work and think they know how to do it.

Heathen England
William Booth

We cannot offer you great pay, social position, or any glitter and tinsel of man's glory; in fact, we can promise little more than rations, plenty of hard work, and probably no little of worldly scorn; but if on the whole you believe you can in no other way help your Lord so well and bless humanity so much, you will brave the opposition of friends, abandon earthly prospects, trample pride under foot, and come out and follow Him in this new crusade.

In Darkest England and the Way Out
William Booth

Heralds of mercy and harbingers of hope, they (officers) link the palace with the garret, and heaven with both.

Life of Catherine Booth — Volume 1
Frederick Booth-Tucker

By and by such men leave the work that God calls them to do, because, as they say, they have not been treated well; while the fact is that, their minds being divided, they ceased to treat their work well. They no longer gave themselves wholly to it, and the people felt their lack of interest and power; hungry souls who looked for bread received a stone; poor sinners on the road to hell, and possibly on the very brink of ruin, went away from their cold and heartless services unawakened and unsaved. They lost their first grip of God, and then of the crowd; and their superiors, perplexed to know what to do with them, since the people no longer wanted them, were blamed. But blame others as they may, the blame really lies with themselves.

The Soul-Winner's Secret
Samuel Logan Brengle

As a stool needs three legs to stand evenly, an officer needs three firm bases for his life's work. He must be a man of God, a man of the Word, and a man of the people.

No Continuing City
Frederick Coutts

Any man who decried officership as a fit vocation for young people is unworthy of the trimming he wears.

A Godly Heritage
Wilfred Kitching

The enormous demand which the work makes upon body and mind and soul has always made it difficult to secure suitable agents, and has driven many who had for a season labored with us to relinquish their posts. This want of a sufficiently numerous staff of officers is more and more felt, as the increased number of our stations renders it necessary for us to have a larger force than ever in order to keep up the efficiency of each place. Resignation, while not surprising to those who know the nature of the work, has been a cause of serious difficulty, frequently putting the solidity of the work done to the test, weakening sometimes, in no small degree, the hands of those more faithful, who remain at their posts, and yet by the manifold grace of God continually overruled for our good.

Heathen England
George Scott Railton

144

To accomplish their mission Salvation Army officers must maintain a healthy and unbroken relationship with God, and also with the world of people and problems in which they serve. These two vital relationships are not contradictory but complementary, for only when they interact creatively in an officer's experience can the holy life of such a high calling be lived and practiced. In the Lord's High Priestly prayer for His disciples, He asked His Father not to take them out of the world, but to keep them safe from evil's power.

A Burning in My Bones
Clarence Wiseman

Omnipotence

Above the troubled tide of circumstances there is omnipotence.

The Officer — 1892
Herbert Booth

Earthly kingdoms rise and fall,
　Kings and nations come and go.
Thou, O God, art over all,
　None Thine empire shall o'erthrow.

Will J. Brand
Salvation Army Song Book

You spoke to me as the Almighty
　Ruler of earth and sea,
Yet One who condescends to
commune with a
simple human heart
without causing overwhelming fear.

Between You and Me, Lord
Flora Larsson

Omnipresence

If, then,
Incomprehensible,
You leap a million worlds
Your winged foot upon their arches
Can You still reign within the minute
Kingdom of my heart?

Walking With the Wind
Sallie Chesham

I bless because, however dense and chilling the mists, experience will prove that He was close at hand even when I could not see Him.

Essentials of Christian Experience
Frederick Coutts

God is not to be thought of as "out there" or "up there" but always as here.

Reason to Believe
Harry Dean

Open-air

Some people think we are too noisy,
　They say it's not cultured to shout;
And when the truth comes, close and searching,
　You'll see them get up and walk out.
The open-air gives them the shivers,
　For the old-fashioned way they won't stand.
Oh, where can they hide up in heaven,
　When they come face to face with this band?

Combat Songs of The Salvation Army
Sallie Chesham, Edit.

The Army's great mission is to take salvation to the people, and since many can be reached only thorugh the open air meeting, the importance cannot be overemphasized.

Orders and Regulations for Officers

It occurred to me that a day's open air services would be useful in arousing the town and in bringing under the Gospel a great number whom we cannot reach even with extraordinary means we are at present employing.

William Booth
Life of Catherine Booth — Volume 1
Frederick Booth-Tucker

Nothing is better calculated to wake up the officer for his work on the platform than a good open-air fight. Direct communion with the outer world in the streets and drinking saloons will move the soul to its very depths. Hearing the crowds blaspheme his Master and curse religion, and

145

seeing the multitudes rushing down to hell, will bring him to the front ready to do the very best that lies in his power.

William Booth
The Officer — 1893

Remember that you go out into the open-air to make people hear something about Jesus: and unless they do hear, the object of your going is defeated, no matter how much effort you may put forth, or how bravely you may endure persecution.

William Booth
The History of The Salvation Army — Volume 2
Robert Sandall

So far as I can see, the great battles of the future will be fought in the open-air.

William Booth
How to Preach
Charles Talmadge

The officer who does not believe in the value of the open-air will not be likely to get much out of it. If he only regards it as a calling-bird of the indoor services he will probably be content with little more than a performance. Whereas, the officer who goes for converting the people on the spot, appealing to them as they stand there, and arousing and awakening their consciences, will be likely to make his open-air a means of great blessing to soldiers and sinners alike. I always believe in the open-air — hence, perhaps, my success with it.

The Seven Spirits
William Booth

Late lie-a-beds awake; an unwashed child
Runs to a window and peeps round the blind.
For such the bush still burns; God may be found;
The Army ring is consecrated ground.

Frederick Coutts
Book of Salvationist Verse
Catherine Baird, Edit.

The Salvation Army would slowly die were our open-air meetings to cease: they are not merely one of our activities but are our life. Ours is religion with an outward thrust. To deny that is to die by slow paralysis.

The House of My Pilgrimage
Albert Orsborn

Open-air meetings must happen if the Army is to fulfill its God-given task of reaching the untouchables of our society. They must happen in small corps where the officer and family may have to stand alone with a portable amplifier and taped music. They must happen in the corps with large musical sections that have been locked indoors for years. They must happen if we are to remain true to the methods of Jesus and Booth.

Marching On!
Ted Palmer

The Salvation Army is a specialized vehicle for delivering the gospel; a compact, colorful, hard-hitting, open-air expert that makes the sky its Sistine Chapel and the walls of taverns, banks, brothels and 10-cent stores Westminster Abbey.

Marching On!
Ted Palmer

The Salvation Army is muscular Christianity. It was born in the streets and has always been healthiest when its lungs are stretched in the open-air. It is no pale-skinned, limp-wristed monastery of scribes, not a stain glassed, organ-soothed cathedral for pious ladies. It is a hairy-handed, bicep-bulging Peter standing on a street corner and preaching people into the Kingdom of God.

Marching On!
Ted Palmer

The open-air is the Army's picture window before the world.

Rediscovering the Open-Air
Lyell Rader

The Army would consider its open-air services a miserable failure if they caused no "obstruction" (especially to sin), or were not "a nuisance to the inhabitants," especially to such of them as are made rich upon the misery and ruin of others.

Heathen England
George Scott Railton

Opinion

If all religious opinions were of equal value, then none of them would be of any value.

The Person of Jesus Christ
John Morrison

Opportunity

Oh, my comrades, again I say what I have said before — when you see your duty, that is the moment for action. Don't let that moment slip, and so miss the power of it, for, perchance, you will never be as strong again.

Salvation Soldiery
William Booth

How perseveringly the devil tries to blind us to the possibilities of the present by the very tears we shed over the past!

Messages to the Messengers
Catherine Bramwell-Booth

I notice that, nearly always when I can see nothing ahead, if I look back I can see ever so clearly heaps of things I had either forgotten or else not noticed much when I was actually in them.

Messages to the Messengers
Catherine Bramwell-Booth

My wonder is not that I should have so slowly recognized that all is not gold that glitters but that I should have passed so much gold without seeing it glitter!

Messages to the Messengers
Catherine Bramwell-Booth

Tears for a past joy do not bring it back, and they often unfit one for present joys or duties.

Messages to the Messengers
Catherine Bramwell-Booth

We look ahead. We fill our days with resolves. We are always intending to do better and be better tomorrow, next week, next year, next corps instead of saying now.

Messages to the Messengers
Catherine Bramwell-Booth

There are two doors to every important spiritual work, the front door of opportunity, which we must open with humility, dependence and gratitude, and the back door of accomplished work, which we must close with prayer and praise lest in the former we fail through self-reliance or in the latter from self-esteem.

The Silences of Christ
Albert Orsborn

147

Pain

Yet I am richer since I lived with pain.
My list'ning ear, grown sensitive, receives
Deeper and higher and far sweeter tones
Than those I used to hear.

Book of Salvationist Verse
Catherine Baird

Feeling the cross isn't shirking it. Being weary isn't running away and to weep is not to sin. So that we need not be bashful contemplating our difficulties, especially when we do so with a view of getting round them, or through them, or over them, into a life more active in love and service for poor lost sinners than ever before.

Emma Booth-Tucker
The Officer — 1893

Flesh and blood does not bear pain as some may think.
The deepest wounded never shriek:
And there are no clenched fists;
It is only in the eyes where pain burns like twin martyr fires.

Walking With the Wind
Sallie Chesham

It is one thing to talk
About a broken heart
When your own has never
Broken been.
Of it,
And shape,
How it feels in the middle,
And taped back together
With quivering hands,
Then you leave talking
To other tongues,
To heaven the mending —
And simply go on walking
With the broken-hearted.

Wind Chimes
Sallie Chesham

Every pain that a human soul is capable of suffering is but a gateway through which it may pass to fuller joy.

Messages to the Messengers
Catherine Bramwell-Booth

Is there not a great harmony in pain?

Samuel Logan Brengle
Portrait of a Prophet
Clarence W. Hall

If our righteousness is worth anything it demands a willingness to be hurt, and in the place where we toil for our daily bread, we must be prepared for bruises.

Soldier of Salvation
Wilfred Kitching

Pain can teach me, Master.
It links me with humanity around the world.
Leveling all classes and all shades of color.
A groan is the same in all languages;
it unites us all.

I'm Growing, Lord!
Flora Larsson

Forgive me, Lord, for being so slow to thank You for this pain. Perhaps it was because I've really only felt thankful as the pain endured. At first, my faith was shining and I believed the pain would soon pass. Then when it lingered, when the night of pain was long and no star of healing gleamed, my faith seemed dim. But it was there in the darkness of the suffering that I saw how tenderly a star can glow. Lord, thank You for my pain that let me see the glory of Yourself. You came so close to me, Lord, and though I still hurt, the healing balm of Your love, bringing courage and strength to endure, is easing my pain.

Dear God
Virginia Talmadge

Perhaps hurt is the price for feeling, Lord,
and the more we feel, the more we will
hurt. I hate to hurt, but I would rather hurt
than not feel.

Dear God
Virginia Talmadge

Though Thy light some pain is bringing,
Thou art answering my prayer.

Ruth Tracy
Salvation Army Song Book

When care and sorrow meet me,
    Pain and grief and dark distress,
Still I cry, O give me Jesus,
    He alone can help and bless!

Ruth Tracy
Salvation Army Song Book

Patience

This waiting patiently for the Lord is the
way to His secret places of joy and communion. It lifts the soul up to the heights
where, by His love, the arrows of fear and
envy cannot strike us, where sin loses its
power to weigh down our spirits and
where the devil himself cannot disturb
our peace.

Bramwell Booth
Trumpets of the Lord
Catherine Bramwell-Booth, Edit.

All the roses on the rose bush do not
bloom at the same hour. Do not be depressed because some spiritual quality in
you is only a bud when you see the perfect
fruit in another. Thank the Lord there is
the bud, and let prayer and faith and effort
go on. There will be flower and fruit of
that particular kind in you one day.

Messages to the Messengers
Catherine Bramwell-Booth

It is often harder to suffer in the right spirit
than if one might blaze forth in righteous
anger toward the instrument of injustice.

Messages to the Messengers
Catherine Bramwell-Booth

If I were dying, and had the privilege of
delivering a last exhortation to all the
Christians of the world, and that message

had to be condensed into three words, I
would say, *"Wait on God!"*

Helps to Holiness
Samuel Logan Brengle

It is the inefficient and unskilled who
grow impatient — the school boy with his
homework, the learner at the piano, the
apprentice at the bench.

The Call to Holiness
Frederick Coutts

Peace

Thousands are looking for peace, are
working for peace, indeed, are praying for
peace. The truth is, peace is reserved for
the believer. This peace is effected by a
God given transformation of man's whole
disposition, through which the proper relation between the Creator and the creature is established.

More Than Conquerors
Milton S. Agnew

O strong and faithful, earnest Love,
Thy stillness points to stars above,
And 'mid abysmal dark there shines
Treasure once hid in secret mines;
By hill or vale I have no care,
No fear assails — for Thou art there.

Reflections
Catherine Baird

Man cannot forge a dart which can penetrate the soul that is at peace with God.

Life and Death
Catherine Booth

Peace is the universal want of man.
Everywhere and always the race is in a
state of unrest, "tossing like a troubled
ocean", seeking rest and finding none.
Consequently, men adopt many counter-
feits, and try to satisfy the aching void of
their souls with the opiates of Satan.

Life and Death
Catherine Booth

True peace, divine peace — the only
peace that will do to die with — arises out
of a settlement of our differences, and a
cessation of hostilities between the soul

and God, bringing assurance and quietness in view of both the past, present and future.

Life and Death
Catherine Booth

It is not your poverties, nor your persecutions, nor your afflictions, nor your ignorances, nor even so many other things that prevent your perfect peace. Sin is the enemy; and when malice and indolence, and ambition and unbelief, and every other evil thing has been cast out, your "peace shall flow as a river, and your righteousness shall abound as the waves of the sea."

Purity of Heart
William Booth

In this world the disciples of Jesus are the home of God, and that home is to be filled with sweet accord, not discord.

Ancient Prophets
Samuel Logan Brengle

Peace is the offspring of a faith that is ceaseless in its activity — an activity that is the most perfect, and the mightiest of which man is capable, for through it, poor unarmed men have subdued kingdoms, wrought righteousness, obtained promises, stopped the mouths of lions, quenched the violence of fire, escaped the edge of the sword, out of weakness were made strong, waxed valiant in the fight, turned to flight the armies of the aliens, women received their dead raised to life again.

Helps to Holiness
Sameul Logan Brengle

Any man is captivating who holds in the pocket of his heart the key to inner peace; and if he should have both the desire and the ability to share that treasure with others, his life is worth examining.

Peace Like a River
Sallie Chesham

Peace depends not on our relationship to circumstances but to the Father.

The Call to Holiness
Frederick Coutts

The peace which is of the Spirit is not necessarily peace with events but peace with God.

The Call to Holiness
Frederick Coutts

You give me inward joy
With outward strain;
You grant me peace of heart
With pangs of pain!
When outwardly
The pattern is perturbed,
Still deep within my depths
All undisturbed,
Tranquility holds court
And keeps her throne
When superficial joys
Are overthrown!

O Lord!
John Gowans

Not the stillness of a graveyard, a dead peace;
Not cloistered serenity, the peace of withdrawal;
Not the calm that narcotics give, a doped peace;
It's Your peace I want, Master.

Just a Moment, Lord
Flora Larsson

The benediction of Christ is upon the peacemaker, not the peace-lover.

The Christian Charter
George B. Smith

Persecution

Opposition has been the lot of God's people from the beginning, and the Bible foretells that it must continue to be so long as saints and sinners, holiness and wickedness, dwell side by side on earth.

Orders and Regulations for Corps Officers

It is a bad sign for the Christianity of this day that it provokes so little opposition. When the church and the world can go along comfortably together, you may be sure something is wrong.

Aggressive Christianity
Catherine Booth

151

One with my Lord, with His cross and His
shame,
With the mocking, the spear, and the
thorn;
I'm won by His love, I have taken His
name,
Should I leave Him because of earth's
scorn?

Herbert Booth
Gems for Songsters #2

Fifty years hence it will matter very little
indeed how these people treated us. It will
matter a great deal how we dealt with the
work of God.

William Booth
The General Next to God
Richard Collier

In face of aggression, the Christian does
not merely submit. He seeks to overcome
hatred by positive love.

The Armoury Commentary — The Four Gospels
Frederick Coutts, Edit.

Jesus never tried to hide from His disciples the probable costly outcome of their
faithfulness. They would be persecuted;
and this, He said, should not surprise
them, for the human heart's natural instinct is to destroy the light that reveals its
sinfulness.

The Armoury Commentary — The Four Gospels
Frederick Coutts, Edit.

Persecution is never easy, but it is triumphantly bearable if endured for a noble
cause.

The Armoury Commentary — The Four Gospels
Frederick Coutts, Edit.

Ridicule has caused more denials of faith
than danger.

The Armoury Commentary — The Four Gospels
Frederick Coutts, Edit.

Opposition always has been good for the
Christian Church. Its times of strength
coincide with its periods of persecution,
and it has been at its weakest when popular and prosperous.

Power and Glory
Harry Dean

Execution is but the doorway to corona-
tion.

Search and Scriptures
Robert Hoggard

I sometimes think that stoning the
prophets is crude and outmoded. They
can be just as surely slain by a too liberal
bill of fare. Don't stone them. Feed and fat-
ten them; that is the new technique. And
there are other means; flatter them, or ob-
lige them to attend too many social functions.

The House of My Pilgrimage
Albert Orsborn

Some days when persecution sore
Falls on His church, and o'er and o'er
The death knell calls
And saints must helplessly obey,
My heart takes courage still,
For I know that Jesus will
One morning drive the shadows away.
"'Tis time to rise", He'll say
And in the dawning day
The saints will smile at Him
And He at them.

Memoirs of Peter
Arthur Pitcher

Persecution is the world's testimony to the
power of the good life. A wolf will not
worry painted sheep, a cat will not seize a
toy mouse, nor will the world persecute a
counterfeit Christian.

The Christian Charter
George B. Smith

Perseverance

Must we give in? Must we decline to tread
in the blood-stained footsteps of the Captain of our salvation? Must we decline the
honor of being in the advance guard of the
Lamb's army because of the pain, because
of the conflict, because of the persecution?
Nay, nay; let us hold on, those who are
thus led by the Divine Spirit into paths
which involve conflict with everybody.

Paper on Godliness
Catherine Booth

You may suffer, you may bleed, you may break, but you shall go on.

Catherine Booth-Clibborn
My Best Men are Women
Flora Larsson

Every man who wants to really lead must be willing to grind.

The Seven Spirits
William Booth

"Go on," though tears bedew your cheek;
  "Go on", through flood and flame;
"Go on" the perishing to seek;
  To death "go on" the same!

Heart Messages
Emma Booth-Tucker

If one door seems hopelessly closed against you, undaunted you will hammer at another; if your way is blocked to Asia, you will be sure that there is a post for you in America. A post for you somewhere you are convinced there is, and you will never rest until you find it. If you cannot get at the crowds from the platform, you will plead with them in the street; if you are unable to speak with them in multitudes, you will the more zealously deal with the individual; in short, whether in train or car, at the back door or in your sick room, you will feel the instinct of the shepherd, your heart will go out in compassion, and you will be impelled to serve.

Heart Messages
Emma Booth-Tucker

To save the world is our desire,
For enemies we pray;
We'll never tire, we'll stand the fire,
And never, never run away.

William Pearson
Salvation Army Song Book

We'll tear Hell's throne to pieces,
And win the world for Jesus,
We'll be conquerors forever,
  For we never will give in.

William Pearson
Salvation Army Song Book

Therefore the more the door is shut the more we batter it. It is our business to go on.

George Scott Railton
G.S.R.
John D. Waldron, Edit.

I've found the secret of success,
'Tis holding on, 'tis holding on;
The way to every blessedness,
'Tis holding on, 'tis holding on.
Our warfare may be hard and fierce,
Oft Satan's arrows wound and pierce,
But still we get more smiles than tears
By holding on, by holding on.

Ruth Tracy
Salvation Army Song Book

Politics

Salvation soldiers must remember that the Army does not identify itself with party programs in politics and will not, therefore, endeavor to influence the voters within or without its ranks.

Chosen to be a Soldier

He entered into no secret cabals and councils. He belonged to no clique or party faction.

Ancient Prophets
Samuel Logan Brengle

The Salvation Army takes no part in party politics. It is indirectly, no doubt, a profoundly conservative force in the best sense of that term. But, in essence, it is an army of revolt. Every Salvationist is a soldier enlisted in a holy war against all that is opposed to God's will in the existing order.

Catherine Booth
W. T. Stead

Potential

The truth would seem to separate Jesus from men, and men from Him, but, in the light of the Gospel, is seen as a welcome truth for it demonstrates that a sinful condition is not God's intention for men. For in the bond of oneness with men Jesus gave Himself so completely for them that all separation was cancelled and a way made for them to become what they were always intended to be. Only thus can they in turn become "truly and properly" men.

Handbook of Doctrine

He went to the sinner, because He had a vision of the sinner saved. He went to the weary, because He had seen the posssibility of the weary at rest; to the unclean, for He saw them "clean every whit." In all He worked and toiled, not because of what there was, but because of what there might be.

Messages to the Messengers
Catherine Bramwell-Booth

Perhaps no real lover of souls has ever escaped the darkness of this kind of disappointment – the disappointment of failing to make people what we wanted them to be, and what we felt it was in them to be.

Messages to the Messengers
Catherine Bramwell-Booth

Real faith in Jesus, vital union with Him, will always make an interesting somebody out of a dull nobody.

Love-Slaves
Samuel Logan Brengle

We are now becoming what we shall ever be – lovers of God and the things of God, or haters of God and the things of God. We are now learning the sweet and heavenly art of loving, trusting and obeying God, fitting ourselves to live in eternity; or else by unbelief, disobedience and selfishness we are forming ourselves into vessels of wrath and dishonor, and hastening to endless darkness, loneliness and woe.

Resurrection Life and Power
Samuel Logan Brengle

Awed, I said, "Sure, I'm not too small?"
He said, "Not at all – for a beginning.
And there is no end
If I abide in you –
and you in Me."

Walking With the Wind
Sallie Chesham

God knows what we are, and yet still believes in what we can become.

The Armoury Commentary – The Four Gospels
Frederick Coutts, Edit.

Ideals become possibilities only when God creates them within men.

The House of My Pilgrimage
Albert Orsborn

Forgive us for the limit we place on love, Lord;
For drawing a line of demarcation where acceptance ends and rejection begins;
For having a dwarfed vision;
failure to see the potential of others;
For having prejediced attitudes which leave a chill on our relationships with our fellow men and a frost on our ability to reach out and genuinely love them for their highest good.

God's Whispers in My Heart
Shirley Pavey

Power

To have the most blessed desires for the will of God, but to have no power to fulfill it, would not only belie His majesty and belittle His might, but would be a positive torture for us. But God's response to the soul's preference for the right is power to fulfill that preference.

The Privilege of All Believers
John D. Waldron, Edit.

With an eye quick to see that souls are tottering on the brink of ruin, a brain alert to devise plans for their rescue, it is for you to estimate without a moment's hesitation that the Holy Ghost power is stronger than all the devil's forces.

Powers of Salvation Army Officers
Florence Booth

For strength to ever do the right,
For grace to conquer in the fight,
For power to walk the world in white,
Send the power!

William Booth
Salvation Army Song Book

The power of God cannot be dispatched, nor permanently dammed up, any more than the sunshine can be wasted or turned away from the earth. Always there is a breaking through, a reawakening, a return of the divine power, operating in the hearts of men. Given half a chance, this undying vitality comes down from the throne of God, and it is a work again! And it will be until all things are subject to our Lord and Savior, and the nations that are saved shall walk in the light of the glory of God.

Religion With a Punch
George Carpenter

Oh, don't pray for power to overcome or to do anything else! We are not to seek power but the Empowerer. God has no power to let like the property owners' long rivers and waterside. It was never known that He gave His power away. But He comes in Himself to the surrendered, believing human heart, and abiding there, exerts His power in us and through us. The command is not "seek ye power" but "seek ye Me."

Elizabeth Swift Brengle
Peace Like a River
Sallie Chesham

And what power is it? If it is physical power, then the power of a million Niagaras and flowing oceans and rushing worlds is as nothing compared to it. If it is mental power, then the power of Plato and Bacon, and Milton and Shakespeare and Newton is as the light of a firefly to the sun when compared to it. If it is spiritual power, then there is nothing with which it can be compared. But suppose it is all three in one, infinite and eternal! This is the power, throbbing with love and mercy, to which we are to bring our little hearts by living faith; and God will fill us with joy and peace and hope by the incoming of the Holy Spirit.

When the Holy Ghost is Come
Samuel Logan Brengle

It is not the river that just overflows all its banks that does the great work; it is the river that is confined that carries the commerce of nations and that which seems to be cramping you may be that which is necessary to enable you to carry on the most effective work. It is not the powder in the open that explodes and sends its missile afar – it is the powder shut up in the gun barrel.

Samuel Logan Brengle
Peace Like a River
Sallie Chesham

Power "over all the power of the enemy" is God's purpose for all His children. Power to do the will of God patiently and effectively, with naturalness and ease, or to suffer the will of God with patience and good cheer, comes with this blessed baptism. It is power for service or sacrifice, according to God's will.

When the Holy Ghost is Come
Samuel Logan Brengle

Some of us fail to recognize the gospel as "good news," viewing it rather as impossible idealism which makes life an insufferable burden. Christ is the power of God unto salvation, not the taskmaster of God unto distraction.

The Armoury Commentary – The Four Gospels
Frederick Coutts, Edit.

You will not feel lifted up when others come to you for help. You will not be cast down when others write and speak and act against you. You will know that it is not to you but to God they come, not at you but at God they are aiming. And you will be content to let God fight and win.

Mildred Duff
Madge Unsworth

Not the depth of my sin
But the breadth of His grace,
Not the darkness within
But the light of His face;
Not my weakness of faith
But the surge of His power.

From My Treasure Chest
Flora Larsson

In the new temptations that each day will bring,
Save me from self-confidence in every-thing,
Pardon I am sure of,
Make me sure of power,
Yours will be sufficient for the day, the hour.

Glory!
John Gowans

You will increase your own power by contributing fuel to the altar fires of others about you.

Fuel for Sacred Fire
T. Henry Howard

Spiritual power cannot exist without spiritual purity.

Allister Smith
The Privilege of All Believers
John D. Waldron, Edit.

Praise

Bless the Lord, we ought to get up and sing a song of praise before we go any further.

Life and Death
Catherine Booth

We have a right to rejoice, and we ought to do it. It is our highest privilege and our most solemn duty. And if we do it not, I think it must fill the angels with confusion and the fiends in the bottomless pit with a kind of hideous joy. We ought to do it for this is almost the only thing we do on earth that we shall not cease to do in heaven. Weeping and fasting and watching and praying and self-denying and cross-bearing and conflict with hell will cease. But praise to God, hallelujah, shall continue eternally.

Samuel Logan Brengle
Peace Like a River
Sallie Chesham

If You don't mind
I'll go right on
In praising You.
You see,
While it may not mean much
To You,
It means a lot
To me!

O Lord!
John Gowans

How wonderful it is to praise my God,
Who comforts and protects me with His rod;
How wonderful to praise Him every hour,
My heart attuned to sing His wondrous power!

Theodore H. Kitching
Salvation Army Song Book

I shall have to use picture language to tell you how I felt on reaching this new and dignified status. Had I been a bird I should have winged far up in the highest heaven and poured out my exultant song. Had I been a rosebud I should have opened instantaneously into a perfect flower, filling the room with my fragrance. Had I been a balloon I should have swelled until I burst!

From My Treasure Chest
Flora Larsson

Seconds or minutes? I don't know!
I only know that You have touched me,
that for a brief interval I have been
more spirit than body.
Now I not only believe, I know.
In exultation I rejoice in You.

Between You and Me, Lord
Flora Larsson

You may sing of the joys over Jordan
And the glories prepared for our sight,
But the soldier of Jesus rejoices
On the way to that city of light.

A. Saker-Lynne
Salvation Army Song Book

Prayer

During periods of prayer the leader should seek to help all to realize God's presence and to speak personally to Him.

Orders and Regulations for Officers

The salvation soldier must ever bear in mind that prayer is the chief means of keeping that contact with God in which His life fills the human soul and the Holy Spirit makes the presence of Christ living and real.

Chosen to be a Soldier

156

Prayer without desire is like a bird without wings; it cannot rise.

Bramwell Booth
Trumpets of the Lord
Catherine Bramwell-Booth, Edit.

There is no doubt that many people go astray in prayer because they are constantly asking God to deliver them out of trial and sorrow and temptation instead of praying for patience and grace to bear their trials and carry their sorrows and overcome their temptations.

Bramwell Booth
Trumpets of the Lord
Catherine Bramwell-Booth

No matter how much we may labor, our toil will be unblessed by God if it is not hallowed by prayer.

The Powers of Salvation Army Officers
Florence Booth

The soul that rises up to wrestle with God for His blessing on a forthcoming effort not only secures an answer in the direct pouring out of the Holy Ghost on his own soul, and the operating influences on the hearts of his hearers, but has all the latent energies of his own spirit roused up thereby.

William Booth
How to Preach
Charles Talmadge

We may pray ourselves black in the face, but if we do not comply with the conditions God will never move an inch to meet us.

William Booth
The Words of William Booth
Cyril Barnes

All great soul-winners have been men of much and mighty prayer, and all great revivals have been preceded and carried out by persevering, prevailing knee-work in the closet.

Helps to Holiness
Samuel Logan Brengle

Does not the Apostle teach that it is not by some desperate, dastardly deed that we quench the Spirit, but simply by neglect-ing to rejoice and pray, and give thanks at all times for all things?

When the Holy Ghost is Come
Samuel Logan Brengle

Four hundred devils cannot stand before the man who makes it the rule of his life to get up early to praise the Lord and plead for God's blessing on his own soul, and on the world. They will flee away.

Helps to Holiness
Samuel Logan Brengle

God meant the man He sent to speak His words, to sit at the feet of Jesus and learn of Him, to get alone in some secret place on his knees and study the Word of God under the direct illumination of the Holy Ghost, to study the holiness and righteous judgments of God until he got some red-hot thunderbolts that would burn the itching ears of the people, arouse their slumbering conscience, prick their hard hearts, and make them cry, "What shall we do?"

Helps to Holiness
Samuel Logan Brengle

In these days of organization, of societies, leagues, committees, multiplied and diversified, soul-saving and ecclesiastical machinery, we want "wrestlers with God" – men and women who know how to pray and who do pray. Not men and women who say prayers, but who pour out their hearts to Him, who call Him to remembrance and "keep not silence, and give Him no rest, till He establish, and till He make Jerusalem a praise in the earth."

Heart Talks on Holiness
Samuel Logan Brengle

Nothing that is of interest to us is too small to interest Him. Many people do not believe this, but it is true. They think God is interested only in big things; but the same God that made the flaming suns and mighty worlds made the tiny insect, fashioned the lenses of the eye and painted with brightest colors its dainty wings. He is interested in the little quite as much as in the great. Therefore, we may bring everything to Him in prayer.

The Way of Holiness
Samuel Logan Brengle

People who do not find God in prayer must hinder His cause instead of helping it.

Helps to Holiness
Samuel Logan Brengle

Prayer is a puzzle to unbelievers but a sweet privilege to us.

The Way of Holiness
Samuel Logan Brengle

Real prayer is something more than a form of words, or a hasty address to God just after breakfast, before the meeting, or before going to bed at night. It is an intense, intelligent, persistent council with the Lord, in which we wait on Him, and reason and argue and plead our cause, and listen for His reply, and will not let Him go till He blesses us.

Love-Slaves
Samuel Logan Brengle

The soul-winner must pray in *secret*.
The soul-winner's prayer must be *definite*.
The soul-winner's prayers must be *bold*.
The soul-winner's prayer must be *importunate, persevering*.
All prayer – the soul-winner's prayer – must be *for the glory of God*, and *according to His will*.
The soul-winner's prayer must be *mixed with faith*, must be believing prayer.
Finally, all our prayers must be in the *name of Jesus*.

The Soul-Winner's Secret
Samuel Logan Brengle

There is no conceivable difficulty that will not vanish before the man who prays to and praises God.

Helps to Holiness
Samuel Logan Brengle

Three great obstacles hinder mighty prayer: selfishness, unbelief, and the darkness of ignorances and foolishness.

When the Holy Ghost is Come
Samuel Logan Brengle

Prayer is so much more than saying of words or thinking of thoughts. It is the bringing of man into harmony with the spirit of God. It is the grand and essential

readjustment. That is why it is not easy to pray without the soul being deeply moved, either by some disturbing circumstances or by the outflowing of affection toward God.

Religion With a Punch
George Carpenter

Intercession is one way in which divine energies are released into the world, one method which we by no means released into the world; one method, which we by no means fully understand, by which man cooperated with God. That Christ intercedes for us is a thought of infinite encouragement; that our own intercessions are linked with His can keep us faithful in the place of prayer.

The Armoury Commentary – The Four Gospels
Frederick Coutts, Edit.

To pray together is to be shielded from evil, not only from the perils which beset the body but also from the dangers which assail the soul.

Essentials of Christian Experience
Frederick Coutts

We do not seek fellowship with God in order to avoid the demands of life, but to provide for them.

In Good Company
Frederick Coutts

We work for things that can only be accomplished by prayer, and pray for things that can only be obtained by work, life being undermined by over-busyness.

The Armoury Commentary – The Four Gospels
Frederick Coutts, Edit.

In prayer our weakness is linked to Almightiness, our ignorance to infinite wisdom, our need with the channel of unseen resources.

Footsteps to Calvary
Henry Gariepy

My praying has
A too familiar ring!
And You must sigh
To hear the same old thing.

0 Lord!
John Gowans

Anyone who is too busy to pray is too busy altogether.

Stewards of God
Edward J. Higgins

No other friend so keen to help you;
No other friend so quick to hear;
No other place to leave your burden;
No other one to hear your prayer.

Edward H. Joy
Salvation Army Song Book

We can never stock up a spiritual cupboard full of supplies, then cease to pray or seek God daily, feeling that we have plenty in our reserves to carry us through for a few weeks.

From My Treasure Chest
Flora Larsson

Many servants of God go away into solitude; but it is not the wilderness, the quiet retreat, that fortifies and reinforces the spirit – although silence itself is a wonderful restorative – but it is prayer in the silence that works the wonder.

The Silences of Christ
Albert Orsborn

Prayer will make the bitter sweet,
Smooth rough ways for weary feet;
Will shed within your life a radiance fair,
And heaven's sunshine upon your face!

The Beauty of Jesus
Albert Orsborn

If the knees have not been bent before the voice is lifted, or the sleeves rolled up, people don't get saved through our efforts.

Marching On!
Ted Palmer

The early Army was on the march because it was on its knees.

Marching On!
Ted Palmer

When prayers have seemed delayed,
And my heart is sore afraid,
'Tis not that God's forgotten my request;
But, while on the road to me,
His divinity may see
Other needs requiring healing grace.

Memoirs of Peter
Arthur Pitcher

Prayer ought not to be a struggle to overcome God's reluctance but a loving search to discover God's willingness.

Lyell Rader
When God Calls You
Edward Deratany

Prayer is not asking for things that are good – to attain the habit of goodness. Prayer calls God into alliance, not overcoming God's reluctance, but laying hold of His highest willingness.

The Christian Charter
George B. Smith

Prayer is sincere questing after God, and because it is the reverse of dictation, prayer in question form is highly appropriate!

The Desert Road to Glory
Clarence Wiseman

The place the Christian enters to pray is not only an oratory – that is, a place for prayer; it is also an observatory, a place of vision.

The Desert Road to Glory
Clarence Wiseman

Preaching

The message, if truly given by the Spirit, will be living and practical. It must be expressed in simple words which are not beyond the understanding of the listeners. A well chosen illustration will help stimulate their attention. The address should not be too lengthy. It is better to conclude while the hearers regretfully feel that they would have liked to hear more, than to go until they sigh with relief that the speaker has finished at last.

Chosen to be a Soldier.

Prepare as if you never prayed and then pray as if you never prepared.

Bramwell Booth
Peace Like a River
Sallie Chesham

A great deal of the truth preached nowadays would not cut the wings off a fly, much less pierce asunder the soul and spirit.

Life of Catherine Booth – Volume 2
Frederick Booth-Tucker

I will seek to preach among you the truth as it is in Christ Jesus. Not with faltering tongue, or unsound or questionable teaching, but I will preach it as the apostles of old taught it – the one controlling principle in life, the source of all morals, the inspiration of all charity, the sanctification of every relationship, and the sweetness of every toil.

Evangeline Booth
The Officer's Review – 1935

Preaching is the big job in the Army; it isn't sitting by a desk. It isn't delegating authority. It's the preaching. You've got to preach.

Evangeline Booth
The General Was a Lady
Margaret Troutt

Surely, a grieving of the Spirit is never more baneful than when officers, professing to be His mouthpiece, fail to deliver His message.

Powers of Salvation Army Officers
Florence Booth

The secret of power on the platform is the presence of God with the speaker. You may not have much ability as a speaker, or as much time to prepare as you would wish; but do not omit the essential – the Holy Presence with you.

Friendship With Jesus
Florence Booth

Be simple and understandable in your ideas. The way of salvation, and everything that has to do with walking in it, and with all the deep and experimental blessedness to which it leads, both in this life and in the next, is so simple that a fool, though a wayfaring man, can understand it if placed before him in a simple, straightforward and understandable manner.

William Booth
How to Preach
Charles Talmadge

By earnestness I mean that the soul of the officer should be on fire, and his whole energy engrossed with the importance of his topic.

William Booth
How to Preach
Charles Talmadge

I should think, if there is one sight which above another excites the deepest abhorrence of the angels, as they flit about this world on their errands of mercy, it is to see a man or woman doing the buffoon in the pulpit or on the platform while professing to represent suffering, agonizing Christ, whose death filled heaven with silence and awe.

William Booth
The Officer – 1893

I want to secure a harvest of souls for my Master. I want to effect the cure of the disease stricken people who sit before me, and to obtain a verdict from my audience in favor of truth and the claims of Jesus Christ, and it seems only reasonable that I should make such preparation beforehand as will enable me to gain my end and bring conviction to the hearts and conscience of those whom I have as my charge.

William Booth
The Officer – 1893

In order to speak effectively of the things of the Kingdom, the soul of the speaker must be wide awake to their importance, and to the responsibility of the opportunity presented at the moment when he endeavors to speak to them.

William Booth
How to Preach
Charles Talmadge

For an officer to speak effectively of the things of God he must be soundly converted, and either have experienced the blessing of perfect love or be on full stretch to find it, and have been baptized after a Pentecostal fashion with an all-consuming love of God and souls. He should know these things, seeing that they must constitute the chief theme of his preaching, and officers should mix up their own testimony with their explanations and exhortations. Paul, as a preacher, was a remarkable example in this respect. He was always giving his own experience.

William Booth
The Officer – 1893

No officer should be tempted to raise any merry and hilarious spirit in any audience without being able to immediately follow it up with some corresponding weighty truth. Before the smile has died away from the countenance the Sword of the Spirit should be plunged in the heart.

William Booth
How to Preach
Charles Talmadge

Oh, no! pleased or displeased, give his money or keep it, come again or stay away, your work is not to please but to profit, not to comfort but to convict, not to salve but to save!

Salvation Soldiery
William Booth

One of the first things absolutely essential to effective preaching is the personal realization on the part of the speaker of the things preached about. He must know in his own soul that the things proclaimed to others are what he declares them to be.

William Booth
How to Preach
Charles Talmadge

Preaching is not the performance of an hour. It is the outflow of a life.

William Booth
How to Preach
Charles Talmadge

Prepare as though there were no Holy Spirit; then preach with the conviction that there is.

William Booth
The Armoury Commentary – The Four Gospels
Frederick Coutts, Edit.

Words, whether many or few, committed to memory and repeated over and over again are, as a rule, hateful – especially on a Salvation Army platform, or, as far as that goes, anywhere else.

William Booth
How to Preach
Charles Talmadge

Your knowledge and education may be very imperfect – your voice and manner may be all unattractive, but a soul on fire will make the people listen wherever you may be or whatever you may have to say.

William Booth
The Officer – 1893

What we want is the truth poured out of a heart aflame with love – the Christianity of the Cross, which, while preaching hell, dies to save the people from it.

Frederick Booth-Tucker
The Officer – 1893

A cadet or humble soldier who is full of the Holy Ghost can tell more about the real, deep, spiritual meaning of the Bible than all the doctors of divinity and theological professors in the world who are not baptized with the Holy Ghost.

Helps to Holiness
Samuel Logan Brengle

I always feel that if I preach the truth in love, luminously, persuasively, with constant reliance on the Holy Ghost, the people will promptly yield to my invitations, and if they do not do so I feel the trouble must be with my spirit or manner of preaching.

Ancient Prophets
Samuel Logan Brengle

I find that often, with our friends at least, we drive the sort of truth into them and then we are tempted to say some right thing, something pleasant, agreeable, immediately, to save our own reputation for goodness or cleverness; or we are filled with fear lest we have unnecessarily offended them, instead of trusting God and leaving them alone with their own thundering consciences. We shoot the king's arrows into them, but instead of killing them outright, we at once pluck the arrows out with an apology and administer some balm of worldly wisdom that leaves the poor soul more alive with self-righteousness than it was before. It is a high state of grace that enables a man to deal faithfully with his fellow without flinching, and then leave him to meditate possibly to get saved, possibly to be filled with hate. It's about the severest test that ever comes to me.

Samuel Logan Brengle
The Officer's Review – 1935

If his own heart is broken, he can then break the hearts of others. If his heart is aflame, he can kindle a flame in other hearts.

Ancient Prophets
Samuel Logan Brengle

It is not the moral essay or the intellectual, or semi-intellectual kind of preaching that is most generally heard throughout the world today that is to save men; for thousands of such sermons move and convert no one. Nor is it a mere noisy declamation called a sermon – noisy, because empty of all earnest thought and true feeling; but it must be the kind of which Peter speaks when he writes of "them that preached the gospel…with the Holy Ghost sent down from heaven."

When the Holy Ghost is Come
Samuel Logan Brengle

My lifetime has been a preparation for preaching. But, more particularly, I prepare my sermons for others by preparing my own heart. When I read books other than the Bible, they are read not that parts of them might be included in my address, but to enrich my own thought and to quicken and inspire my faith. Thus, I spend a great deal of time preparing myself for preaching. Many make the mistake of giving more time to the preparation of their addresses than to the preparation of their own hearts, affections, emotions and faith; the result is often beautiful, brilliant words that have the same effect as holding up glittering icicles before a freezing man. To warm others – and is not that your purpose in preaching? – a man must keep the fire burning hot in his own soul.

Samuel Logan Brengle
Portrait of a Prophet
Clarence W. Hall

The best teacher in style of public speech is a heart filled to bursting with love to Jesus, and love and hope, and fear and faith for them.

The Soul-Winner's Secret
Samuel Logan Brengle

The speech may be without polish, the manner uncouth, and the matter simple and plain; but conviction will surely follow any preaching in the burning love and power and contagious joy of the Holy Spirit.

When the Holy Ghost is Come
Samuel Logan Brengle

We often see men with great natural powers, splendidly trained, and equipped with everything save this fiery baptism, who labor and preach year after year without seeing a soul saved. They have spent years in study; but they have not spent a day, much less ten days, fasting and praying and waiting on God for His anointing that should fill them with heavenly wisdom and power for their work. They are like a great gun loaded and primed, but without a spark of fire to turn the powder and ball into a lightning bolt.

When the Holy Ghost is Come
Samuel Logan Brengle

Pulpit occupiers are more numerous than pulpit illuminators.

It Seems to Me
Philip E. Collier

But they should know
The message isn't mine,
The word that heals
Just has to be
Divine.
And any truth
They recognize as true
Though I may speak it
Comes, of course,
From You!

O Lord!
John Gowans

Before sanctification, preaching meant honors for Brengle; now it was to mean glory for Christ. Hitherto preaching meant exaltation of self; now it would mean exaltation of a Savior from self. Previously he preached to please; now he would preach to disturb. Whereas his sermons made men say, "How beautiful is his oratory!", hereafter they would cause men to exclaim, "How black are my sins!" The same voice, the same tones, perhaps the same words, tickling the ears of the people, would now drop into an audience with the cleaving power of a sword, dividing his hearers into two opposite camps, compelling a choice of sides. For he had forsaken preaching as a profession, a medium for money making and fame-accruing, and adopted it again as a calling, a life passion, that would have as its only object the saving of men and women from lowest sinfulness to highest sainthood.

Portrait of a Prophet
Clarence W. Hall

It is one thing to sway the mind, it is quite another to touch the heart and lead a soul to God.

Out of the Depths
Clarence W. Hall

O is not the Christ 'midst the crowd of today
Whose questioning cries do not cease?
And will He not show to the hearts that would know
The things that belong to their peace?
But how shall they hear if the preacher forbear
Or lack in compassionate zeal?
Or how shall hearts move with the Master's own love,
Without His anointing and seal?

Albert Orsborn
Salvation Army Song Book

Praise only for the preacher is the true preacher's greatest disappointment.

The Silences of Christ
Albert Orsborn

To be a popular preacher may be the reward of faithful service, but it must never be an ambition. It must never be a cause for self-congratulation. Many a good man has mistaken the voice of his people for the voice of God, and rested content with the flatterer's applause, while true success lay for him far beyond and behind the cross, the shame and the despising!

The Silences of Christ
Albert Orsborn

I would not request of You, great profoundness of speech
Nor philosophical expression;
These may coat the hearts of men
But fail to turn the key and find entrance.

God's Whispers in My Heart
Shirley Pavey

How can lips catch fire unless prayer has first kindled the flame?

Rediscovering the Open-Air
Lyell Rader

REACHERS are needed more than PREACHERS.

Rediscovering the Open-Air
Lyell Rader

The officer or other person who leads the meeting is there to see that the truth as it is in Jesus, and that only it is set forth, and set forth in such a way as to inform the darkest mind present of the two great facts which alone we profess to propound: that every man is a guilty, hell-deserving sinner, and that there is a way of escape for him if he is willing to avail himself of it.

Heathen England
George Scott Railton

If we try to do God's work without delivering God's message we shall fail to achieve God's purpose.

The Desert Road to Glory
Clarence Wiseman

"The preacher preached," she explained simply, "and the Word of God attacked me in my heart."

The Desert Road to Glory
Clarence Wiseman

Prevention

It is easier and cheaper, and in every way better, to prevent the loss of home than to have to recreate that home. It is better to keep a man out of the mire than to let him fall in first and then risk the chance of plucking him out.

In Darkest England and the Way Out
William Booth

163

The Army has always subscribed to the theory that a fence at the top of the cliff is better than an ambulance at the bottom.

My Best Men Are Women
Flora Larsson

Presumption

The sin of the regular salvation hearer and of multitudes outside our ranks is that of presumption. They think that God is so anxious to save them that they do not need to have the slightest fear of being damned. They consider that they have to kneel down and offer a short prayer, or sit down and believe some passage of Scripture, in order to be made perfectly secure for both time and eternity.

William Booth
The Officer – 1893

Frequently in meetings and conventions the people all suppose Jesus is in the company, and yet there may not be one that is personally conscious of His presence. They take it for granted that He is with someone else, and lo! He may not be in their midst at all. He has not been perseveringly, importunately, humbly and believingly sought for and invited to come, and so He has stayed behind.

Heart Talks on Holiness
Samuel Logan Brengle

Pride

The Salvationist should recognize that he is in greater danger when all men speak well of him, and he may be lulled into self-satisfaction.

Orders and Regulations for Corps Officers

The love of applause is not an evil itself. All normally constituted men and women desire some sign that their efforts are approved by those whom they seek to serve; and a proper appreciation of such marks of approval is perfectly consistent with the most disinterested service on the part of a truly sanctified soul. It is the love of applause, the desire, the secret hunger for it which grows constantly with its indulgence, the having it as an end in view,

that makes a temptation which specially besets some people.

Bramwell Booth
Trumpets of the Lord
Catherine Bramwell-Booth, Edit.

When the devil sends somebody to flatter you, he has generally got somebody close behind with a daggar!

On the Banks of the River
Bramwell Booth

Stuck-up-ness is always an ugly form of the devil's family likeness, and never more hateful than when it shows itself in the converted member of the family.

Catherine Bramwell-Booth
The Officer – 1919

Lack of humility leads men into all kinds of sin, including the rejection of God Himself when He comes to us in some unexpected form.

The Armoury Commentary – The Four Gospels
Frederick Coutts, Edit.

The only antidote to pride, the saints unite to testify and illustrate, is to haunt Calvary.

The Armoury Commentary – The Four Gospels
Frederick Coutts, Edit.

The worth of a meeting does not depend entirely upon the leader. If a hearer cherishes a feeling of superiority – whether on account of his age or his fancied gifts – then the blessings of that meeting can pass him by. The oldest among us still need to pray, "O give me Samuel's ear."

The Armoury Commentary – The Four Gospels
Frederick Coutts, Edit.

Priorities

If I understand it, this is the fruit of the Spirit in the affections: God first. I am afraid, in a great many instances it is husband first, wife first, children first, and, I am afraid, in some cases business first, and then God may take what there is left, and be thankful for that! Now, anybody in this condition need not expect joy, peace, power. You will never get it. God will have to make you over again before you can get it, and to alter the conditions of His salvation.

Catherine Booth
Mrs. Booth
W. T. Stead

But beware, O my soul, beware of despising the day of small and feeble things. You won't get everything on a magnificent scale. Thousands will not comprise your audiences nor hundreds your flock every night. But let us be thankful for the bruised reed and the smoking flax, and mind that we do not break the one nor quench the other...and see to it that we do the work given us to do with all our might and that we do it well.

William Booth
How to Preach
Charles Talmadge

I might have carried out my consecration for the improvement of the community by devoting myself to politics. I might have turned Conservative, or I might have been a Radical, or a Home Ruler, or a Socialist, or have joined the Labor Party, or what is more probable, if the catastrophe had occurred, I might have formed another party. I saw something better than belonging to either party, and that by being the friend of every party I was far more likely to secure the blessing of the multitude and the end I had in view.

William Booth
The Founder Speaks Again
Cyril Barnes, Edit.

Rank, position, work, health, happiness, love, are all in a degree precious, but all nothing if the heart is not clean.

Messages to the Messengers
Catherine Bramwell-Booth

Men whom history acclaims, posterity reveres, and God crowns are the men who put first things first.

Ancient Prophets
Samuel Logan Brengle

Kneeling at the penitent form deals most effectively with pride, the parent sin of the human race – the first sin of that little egoist, the child, and the last infirmity of a noble mind.

The Mercy Seat
William Burrows

I needed the renewal and refreshment of
a time with You.
I needed the direct touch of Your
Spirit and Word.
I hadn't robbed You so much as myself,
of something vital and necessary.
Forgive my weak will, Master, my giving
into temptation,
my delaying tactics
that put second things first.

Between You and Me, Lord
Flora Larsson

Prison

While every prisoner should be subjected to that measure of punishment which shall mark a due sense of his crime both to himself and society, the main object should be to rouse in his mind the desire to lead an honest life; and to effect that change in his disposition and character which will send him forth to put that desire into practice. At present, every prison is more or less a training school for crime, an introduction to the society of criminals, the petrification of any lingering human feeling and a very Bastille of despair.

In Darkest England and the Way Out
William Booth

Prisons are often schools for burglary.

The Army Drum
Elizabeth Swift Brengle

Procrastination

There are some people who decide that they will accept Jesus at the eleventh hour and they die at 10:30.

Footsteps to Calvary
Henry Gariepy

165

On the margin of this river,
In your strains, why still delay?
Why not now be free forever
And the voice of God obey?

Richard Slater
Salvation Army Song Book

The souls that had put off salvation
"Not tonight, I'll get saved by and by
No time now to think of religion"
At last they had found time to die.

Richard Slater
Gems for Songsters #2

Promise

Some people never receive salvation because they never come to the point of believing that God will be as good as His word.

Handbook of Doctrine

Boundless as the starry heavens,
Filled with fiery orbs of light,
Are the promises of Jesus,
For the soul in nature's night.

Waller
Salvation Army Song Book

Public Relations

It is in the interest of the service to be in the columns of the newspapers as often as possible.

William Booth
The General Next to God
Richard Collier

Publicity means success.

Salvation Soldiery
William Booth

I would advocate the insertion of advertisement in every Sunday paper, in every sporting paper, in every vile print that is largely read by the people, where sinner's eyes go on a Sunday or any day.

George Scott Railton
G.S.R.
John D. Waldron, Edit.

166

Purity

A pure heart will make you a blessing to those around you, and that not merely as a result of what you do, but from the fact of what you are.

Purity of Heart
William Booth

What, then, is a pure heart? I reply that a pure heart is a heart that has been cleansed by the Holy Spirit from all sin and enabled to please God in all it does; to love Him with all its powers, and its neighbor as itself.

Purity of Heart
William Booth

When unsanctified men have a vision of God, it is not their lack of power, but their lack of purity, their unlikeness to Christ, the Holy One, that troubles them.

When the Holy Ghost is Come
Samuel Logan Brengle

If a water lily could grow in purity and beauty – in startling contrast to the foul waters around and below it – why could not the life of a man made pure and held by God blossom in the midst of a sinful and perverse generation?

Arnold Brown
The Privilege of All Believers
John D. Waldron, Edit.

Purity of heart involves purity of motive and imagination and secret desire. This depth of purity belongs to those who know the meaning of worship and who continually abide in Christ.

The Armoury Commentary – The Four Gospels
Frederick Coutts, Edit.

Even in places where beauty is rarest
Pure hearts can yet trace the finger of God.

Erik Leidzen
This Man Leidzen
Leslie Fossey

Of itself purity is not power, but it clears the way.

T. Henry Howard
The Officer – 1893

To be without blemish is to be without blame.

Studies in Sanctification
Edward Read

Purpose

Man's perfection lies not in accomplishment, but in spirit; not in performance, but in purpose.

The Holy Spirit – Friend and Counselor
Milton S. Agnew

Within the realm of God's great Kingdom faith never walks with aimless feet, love never labors in vain, nor is there ever waste in the crucible of suffering for the children of God.

Heart Messages
Emma Booth-Tucker

The Holy Spirit, dwelling within, turns our eyes from that which is temporal to that which is eternal; from the trial itself to God's purpose in the trial; from the present pain to the precious promise.

When the Holy Ghost is Come
Samuel Logan Brengle

R

Race

The Salvation Army from its inception has been concerned with the spiritual and social needs of all people. Its services in all parts of the world have been developed in recognition of the Biblical principle that "God hath made of one blood all nations of men for to dwell on all the face of the earth" (Acts 17:26).

In 1898 The Salvation Army stated in its Orders and Regulations for Social Officers that "none shall be debarred from any of its benefits...because they are of any particular nationality, race or color." This policy has not changed through the years. In the present age when Christians everywhere are called to a more vital witness to the love of God by supporting the cause of racial justice, it is felt that a re-affirmation of the Army's administrative and operating policy is needed.

The Salvation Army opposes discriminatory practices related to race, age, sex, or national origin at all levels of operation and administration, and seeks to promote inter-group understanding and give full support to the imperatives of human and civil rights, in housing, education, and employment, and in cultural and religious activities, sharing that spiritual affinity which makes all men brothers. More specifically:

1. All positions in The Salvation Army to be filled by employees are open to persons who have the necessary qualifications and skills, without discrimination by race, age or sex, except where age or sex is a bona fide occupational qualification.
2. Qualified persons of any race or sex may apply for training for Salvation Army officership, and no one shall be debarred from such training on the basis of race or sex.
3. Advisory organizations shall include in their membership interested citizens who will reflect the racial and cultural composition of the community.
4. Membership requirements in character-building and religious groups associated with The Salvation Army are not based on race or national origin.
5. Salvation Army social services to individuals or families are given without regard to race, sex or creed according to the capacity of the organization to serve in meeting the needs of those involved; and all institutional services shall be equally available to clients on the basis of need and capacity to benefit from the program of the institution.
6. Salvation Army worship services shall be open to persons of any race, age or sex and spiritual ministrations shall be made available to all.
7. Salvation Army membership (soldiers) shall be open to all qualified persons without discrimination by race or sex.

Commissioners' Conference —
United States of America
May, 1964; Revised May, 1973

The Supreme Court's historic decision outlawing segregation in the nation's public facilities is heartily endorsed by The Salvation Army.

A ruling so soundly based on Christian principles cannot but receive understanding and cooperation from all Salvationists dedicated to the ideal that in Christ all are one.

We accept our full Christian responsibility to work earnestly and sympathetically to the end that a practical implementation of the decision may be successfully effected.

The Commissioners' Conference —
United States of America
November, 1954

An officer must never forget that the Army is international, a brotherhood of many nations and peoples, God is the Father of all mankind and every officer, as His child, should love all men of all races.

Orders and Regulations for Officers

Reading

I carefully kept novels of every kind from my children, and am certain that many of the troubles which afflict and divide families have their origin in works of fiction. Not only are false and unnatural views of men and women, and of life in general, presented, but sentiments are created in the minds of young people which produce discontent with their surroundings, impatience of parental restraint and a premature forcing of social and sexual instincts, such as must cause untold harm. Not only so, but they lead to the formation of relationships and companionships that cannot but be injurious, while the mind is filled with pernicious and vain ambitions destined never to be fulfilled.

Catherine Booth
Life of Catherine Booth — Volume 1
Frederick Booth-Tucker

Never *expect* to find Jesus while your mind is preoccupied with the husks and trash of foolish worldly literature. The fact that you can relish such stuff proves that you are far too worldly and indifferent to seek in such a way as to be likely to find the Pearl of Great Price.

Life and Death
Catherine Booth

What were all the novels compared with the story of my Savior? What were the choicest orators compared with Paul?

William Booth
The Words of William Booth
Cyril Barnes

I would say never read fiction, except on furlough, and then choose it wisely. There is so much that is helpful, soul-nourishing, and heart-inspiring in the experiences, thoughts and doings of real men and women, that the Salvation Army officer is the last person who in the midst of his work should live in an imaginary world.

Messages to the Messengers
Catherine Bramwell-Booth

Imagine a sea chart, made purposely incorrect. Though well-drawn, attractively colored, yet it shows the word "harbor" where in fact sandbanks exist; the marking "good channel" above hidden rocks, and the coast lights given for guidance all confused. You'd throw such a map away. So you should do with some books!

Mildred Duff
Mildred Duff
Madge Unsworth

Reality

God wants not ecstatic dreamers, but practical men and women.

Fuel for Sacred Flame
T. Henry Howard

Lord, save me from postcard mentality,
always expecting the glamorous,
the super-colored, the glossy,
and comparing it to the detriment of
my more plain and human life.
Keep me from imagining that the exotic is real life
and my usual duties a treadmill to
be escaped from.
Let me find joy, Lord, in the everyday.

Between You and Me, Lord
Flora Larsson

To him beauty is not the petals of flowers, music not the instruments, thought is not the braincells of man, love is not clasping arms, prayer is not the bended knee; the real things in his existence are the spiritual forces behind the flowers, instruments, brain cells, clasped arms and bended knees.

Meditations for the Ordinary Man
George B. Smith

Rebellion

There is a time in the history of every sinner (certainly of every one who hears the gospel) when he chooses to remain away from God, and the choice to remain away is equivalent to positive departure.

Life and Death
Catherine Booth

While there is a vestige of insubordination to the requirements of conscience and of God, there can be no peace. On this point thousands of Christians mistake. They allow themselves in things which they feel to be unlawful, and then strive and pray to obtain a sense of acceptance through Christ. They want the Spirit to witness with their spirits that their eyes please God, while they know that their ways are such as cannot please Him: Therefore they want the Spirit to witness to a lie, which is impossible.

Practical Religion
Catherine Booth

Jesus Christ may leave heaven, and come down to the stable, the manger, the wilderness, and a life of suffering and scorn: Jesus Christ may go down into the darkness of the grave, intercede at the right hand of the Father, and, by His Spirit, knock at the door of their hearts, pleading for admission; but they will not consider His claims or consent to give up their sins, or cast themselves on His mercy, and believe unto the enjoyment of His salvation. They will not humble themselves to acknowledge Him before men, or deny themselves by bearing His cross, or fighting for His cause.

The Founder's Messages to Soldiers
William Booth

When we say that Jesus' death was the supreme evil we do not simply mean that it was an unjust and fearfully painful death. In those respects it was not unique. It was the supremely evil act because it meant the rejection, the most violent and irrevocable rejection possible, of God's love towards us and His claim upon us as these were made flesh in the person of Jesus. Moreover, this rejection of God was also the rejection of the highest possibility of our own human nature. The murder of the Son of God was also the murder of the ideal son of man.

Reason to Believe
Harry Dean

In the final analysis all spiritual ruin, in this life and the next, issues from one cause alone; the rejection of Christ can be so constant as to harden the heart against every overture of divine mercy. It is such rejection that is a sin unto death.

Search the Scriptures
Robert Hoggard

The revolt of modern youth is not against goodness, truth and beauty; it is against the failure of the world to realize them.

Meditations for the Ordinary Man
George B. Smith

For a Christian to assert his own will in opposition to the mind of Christ is not just crazy; it is high treason.

When God Calls You
Edward Deratany

Religion

The more I see of fashionable religion the more I despise it; indeed, how can fashionable religion ever be other than despicable? The same classes of character this age presents were in Jerusalem when Jesus lived and died.

Catherine Booth
Mrs. Booth
W.T. Stead

Religion becomes the enemy of Christ when its picture of God ceases to grow and expand. We must beware of worshiping a god who is simply the guardian of all we cherish, the justification of all our ways of life and the protector of our group.

The Armoury Commentary – The Four Gospels
Frederick Coutts, Edit.

Reluctance

What hosts of people there are who are continually coming up to sacrifice, and consecration, and service, and they know what the great God wants from them, and they don't get any further. They believe in God. They love Him very much. They want His blessing so that they may be the means of life and salvation to multitudes. They would like that, they would love it very much, but there is some duty – some Isaac to be offered – some work to be done.

They get the message from God concerning this duty. They know it is from God; they see they ought to obey – they want to obey – they make up their minds to obey, cost them what it may, but they won't do it just now.

Salvation Soldiery
William Booth

Our reservations are the damnations of our consecrations.

William Booth

Reservation is one secret of the weakness prevalent among God's children, and the cause of three-fourths of the failures in this higher walk of the divine life.

Salvation Soldiery
William Booth

Don't have a "but" in your consecration.

Messages to the Messengers
Catherine Bramwell-Booth

Reservations have power to spoil all.

Messages to the Messengers
Catherine Bramwell-Booth

Renewal

It has not been an easy job. It has oftentimes been lonely, and wearying to the point of exhaustion. It has taxed my mind, challenged my will and utmost devotion, drunk up my spirit, drained me to the dregs when there seemed to be no virtue left in me, and I have had to slip away into solitude, like my Master, to the mountains, for quiet communion, for the replenishing of exhausted reserves of power and the renewing of all life's forces.

Ancient Prophets
Samuel Logan Brengle

The world wants the "water of life" carbonated; the Christian seeks the "still waters" of the soul.

The Christian Charter
George B. Smith

Repentance

The genuine penitent will therefore be willing to confess his sin, to renounce his sin and, where necessary, to make restitution for his sin.

Orders and Regulations for Officers

Where there is true repentance, there is always free forgiveness.

Orders and Regulations for Officers

God never left a truly repentant soul in the dark.

Life and Death
Catherine Booth

By repentance, I mean the renunciation of all sin, and the unreserved surrender of the soul to God, which is not only a condition of pardon in the first instance, but of continued salvation all the way through.

Salvation Soldiery
William Booth

I saw the humility of Jesus, and my pride; the meekness of Jesus, and my temper; the lowliness of Jesus, and my ambition; the purity of Jesus, and my unclean heart; the faithfulness of Jesus, and the deceitfulness of my heart; the unselfishness of Jesus, and my selfishness; the trust and faith of Jesus, and my doubts and unbelief; the holiness of Jesus, and my unholiness. I got my eyes off everybody but Jesus and myself, and I came to loathe myself.

Samuel Logan Brengle
Portrait of a Prophet
Clarence W. Hall

Genuine repentance always results in God granting forgiveness and restoring the broken relationship between Himself and the forgiven.

The Armoury Commentary — The Four Gospels
Frederick Coutts, Edit.

Pardon is not granted to those who convince themselves they are comparatively guiltless; it belongs to those who have ceased to trust in their own righteousness and have all their faith in God's mercy.

The Armoury Commentary — The Four Gospels
Frederick Coutts, Edit.

Repentance means a radical change of mind, of outlook and attitude. This surely is also a happy experience, being the gateway into a new relationship with God and our sinful past. But it can only begin when a man ceases to be concerned about himself in his interest in others and in the consequences to them of what he has done. That is noble and creative sorrow, not another expression of self-centeredness.

The Armoury Commentary — The Four Gospels
Frederick Coutts, Edit.

Reputation

Everybody has settled it that we are fools, if not a great deal worse; therefore we can go into a town and do exactly what we think best, without taking the least notice of what anybody may say or wish. We have only to please God and get the people saved, and that is easily done.

Twenty-one Years Salvation Army
William Booth

You see, we have no reputation to lose.

William Booth
The General Next to God
Richard Collier

A man's reputation and character are sacred in the sight of God, and just as He forbids one man to rob another of his property, or take his life, so He forbids him to lie about another, or rob him of his good name.

Heart Talks on Holiness
Samuel Logan Brengle

Surely there is nothing more pitiable on earth, more mourned in heaven, more scoffed at in hell, than the sight of a worker in holy things wholly eaten up not with zeal for the sanctuary, but with concern for his own reputation.

The Silences of Christ
Albert Orsborn

You take care of your character and God will take care of your reputation.

Clifton Sipley

Respect

Respect for personality is essential to Christianity.

Reflections
Catherine Baird

More than love is needed. There must also be respect. Love that fails to include respect is unhealthy. A sincere regard for the dignity of a person is one of the distinguishing traits of Christian love, which is invariably unselfish and never makes light of others.

A Burning In My Bones
Clarence Wiseman

Respect is one of the greatest builders of confidence. A man or woman who has respect is rich.

Andrew S. Miller
Soldiers' Seminar

Responsibility

The babe in Christ must be made to feel his individual, untransferable responsibility. He must be taught that labor is the law of life, spiritual as well as natural, and that to increase in wisdom and stature and in favor with God he "must be about his Father's business".

The History of The Salvation Army — Volume 1
Robert Sandall

The promised baptism was not seen to be a great reality, not something that would relieve men and women from personal responsibility, but something which, on the contrary, would greatly increase it. It was felt to be something that would make it a serious thing to live — and living, to be a still more tremendously serious thing to be a disciple of Jesus Christ.

Visions
William Booth

While using all material means, our reliance is on the co-working power of God. We keep our powder dry but we trust in Jehovah.

In Darkest England and The Way Out
William Booth

The measure of revelation is always the measure of responsibility.

The Call to Holiness
Frederick Coutts

I have occasionally heard of officers of various ranks, expressing the opinion that the Army is not as spiritual as it used to be, and blaming somebody, unnamed — and, I think, unknown — for such a condition, without once questioning themselves as to their own share of responsibility for the supposed declension.

Stewards of God
Edward J. Higgins

Resurrection

The Risen Savior is the supreme antagonist and conqueror of sin.

Handbook of Doctrine

If He did not rise again from the tomb, it would, after all, be only a dead thing like a splendid specimen of carved marble in some museum: exquisite to look upon, and of priceless value, but cold and cheerless, lifeless and dead.

Bramwell Booth
Trumpets of the Lord
Catherine Bramwell-Booth, Edit.

It was a death that made an end of death, and a burial that buried the grave.

Bramwell Booth
Trumpets of the Lord
Catherine Bramwell-Booth, Edit.

In the presence of the resurrection of Jesus all other miracles pale as do the stars before the rising sun. It is the crowning evidence that He is the Son of God.

Resurrection Life and Power
Samuel Logan Brengle

On Easter morning new hope came thrilling the world again. Here was not only assurance that the cause was not lost, but that it was timeless.

All Things New
William Burrows

What happened changed Christianity from a moral code to a moral dynamic. The Resurrection not only lifts our horizons, enabling us to live in "the eternal dimension", It assures us that goodness ultimately triumphs.

The Armoury Commentary — The Four Gospels
Frederick Coutts, Edit.

What is the alternative to belief in the Resurrection? It is to believe in the defeat of good, to hold that Calvary is the end, so that man has forever frustrated God's purposes. This is a philosophy of despair.

Power and Glory
Harry Dean

In wondrous love and might arrayed,
Today our Savior left the tomb;
He burst the chains that death had made,
To save the world from endless gloom.
Now none need find a sinner's grave
Since Jesus lives, and lives to save.

Julia Peacock
Salvation Army Song Book

Today He closed the gates of hell,
And opened wide the doors of heaven;
O help our songs of praise to swell,
And join the ranks of those forgiven.

Julia Peacock
Salvation Army Song Book

Revelation

Every advance in divine revelation has an enriching effect on the revelation that preceded it. With the coming of greater light, values not previously perceived are seen to have been there from the first.

Handbook of Doctrine

As it is only by the light of the sun that we see the sun, so it is by Jesus that Jesus is best revealed.

Bramwell Booth
Trumpets of the Lord
Catherine Bramwell-Booth

Man does not discover God; God reveals Himself to man. God seeks men before men seek God. God reveals His wisdom and power through nature. He reveals His holiness through His judgments. He reveals His redeeming love through faith. We see the power of God in the starry heavens, the stormswept sea, the flooding, rushing river, the lofty mountains, the flaming volcano, the devastating tornado, the silent forces resistlessly lifting mighty forests from tiny seeds, and holding them aloft in columnar strength and beauty against wind and storm from century to century.

Ancient Prophets
Samuel Logan Brengle

Revival

Revivalism may be defined as Christianity in earnest — impatiently in earnest to produce an immediate impression on the hearts, and consciences of men. Revivalism differs from the ordinary conventional methods of religious teaching in that it concentrates all its efforts upon the supreme point of inducing individuals to take the fateful decision upon which their whole future depends. To rouse men from apathy and indifference, to compel them to face squarely the eternal alternative, to bring to bear upon hesitating souls the pressure necessary to induce a definite acceptance of the service of Christ — this is revivalism.

Catherine Booth
W.T. Stead

Find out those who will join you. Tell your captain how you feel, if you are not a Captain: if you are one, tell your corps how you feel. Let others whose blood is fired and whose hearts are melted after the same fashion join hands with you. Make a Mount Carmel of some ante-room, of barracks, or kitchen, and offer yourself up as a sacrifice, body, soul and spirit, and believe and wait until you receive the holy fire.

The General's Letters
Willliam Booth

Great revivals among God's people and awakenings among the ungodly never begin in a great way.

Ancient Prophets
Samuel Logan Brengle

In the lonely and still night, while others sleep, He stirs some soul to sighs and tears and strong cryings and wrestling prayer. He kindles utter, deathless devotion in that soul, a consuming jealousy for God's glory, for the salvation of men, for the coming of the kingdom of God; and in that lonely and still night and out of that travail, that agony of spirit, mingled with solemn joy, a revival is born.

The Guest of the Soul
Samuel Logan Brengle

The revival is born in the heart of some lonely, ongoing, wrestling, believing, importunate man or woman who will give God no rest, who will not let Him go without His blessing. Bright-eyed, golden haired, rosy cheeked dolls can be made by machinery and turned out to order, but living babies are born of sore travail and death agony. So revivals may be simulated, trumped up, made to order, but not so do revivals begotten by the Holy Ghost.

The Guest of the Soul
Samuel Logan Brengle

Righteousness

It is not what people eat but what they digest that makes them strong; it is not what they gain but what they save that makes them rich; it is not what they read but what they remember that makes them learn; and it is not what they profess but what they practice that makes them righteous.

The Officer — 1919

His blood defines the ground of righteousness.

More Than Conquerors
Milton S. Agnew

The Christian who lives under the imputed righteousness of Christ is living under less than his heritage offers, namely the imparted righteousness of Christ.

More Than Conquerors
Milton S. Agnew

O take Thy plummet and Thy line,
Apply them to this heart of mine,
And thus reveal each crooked place
But contrast with true righteousness!
Let holy truth condemn each sham;
Show what Thou art, and what I am.

Arthur Booth-Clibborn
Salvation Army Song Book

If a man is not hungry, he doesn't want to give more than 5 or 10 cents for a loaf of bread, but as he gets very hungry — hungry enough, and that is possible, he'd give the whole world for a loaf of bread. So if a man isn't very hungry after righteousness he'll quibble over every little thing and compromise and dodge in all sorts of ways to escape the Cross, but let him get desperately hungry to be right, and he'll stop arguing and trying to justify himself, and he will be willing to do anything, suffer anything, in order to get right, to be holy.

Samuel Logan Brengle
The Officer's Review — 1935

Righteousness is conformity to the divine law, but holiness in conformity to the divine nature.

Heart Talks on Holiness
Samuel Logan Brengle

Self-righteousness is seen to be a sheet too short to cover us; our moral and spiritual nakedness is exposed.

Samuel Logan Brengle
At the Center of the Circle
John D. Waldron, Edit.

176

Sacraments

It is important to note that none of the company receiving the bread and wine that Jesus Himself blessed and dispensed experienced any inward change. In Gethsemane they failed to watch and pray. At the betrayal they fled. From that time to the Resurrection they were without faith or hope and Peter, fresh from the influences of the Upper Room, was soon denying his Lord with oaths.

Handbook of Doctrine

Although water baptism, signifying the dedication of one's self to Christ, may indeed be a picture of the spiritual experience, it is not the reality of that experience. It is only a testimony to it.

More Than Conquerors
Milton S. Agnew

Another mock salvation is presented in the shape of ceremonies and sacraments...Men are taught that by going through them or partaking of them, they are to be saved...What an inveterate tendency there is in the human heart to trust in outward forms, instead of seeking the inward grace! And when this is the case, what a hindrance rather than help have these forms proved to the growth, nay, to the very existence of that spiritual life which constitutes the real and only force of Christian experience.

Catherine Booth
The History of The Salvation Army — Volume 2
Robert Sandall

When a husband goes overseas and leaves his wife behind, then his photograph which she has in remembrance is precious to her; she has it on her work table by day and under her pillow at night. But when he returns she throws away the picture or gives it to the child to play with, and she embraces the husband. Tell the questioner that the Bridegroom, the Holy Ghost, has come, and now that you have Him — the substance — the picture has lost its charm.

William Booth
Mildred Duff
Madge Unsworth

Our witness is simply that the presence of Christ may be fully realized, and His grace freely received, without the aid of any material elements. Our testimony is not against the sacraments — and never has been, but to the truth that the unsearchable riches of grace can be communicated by the Holy Spirit, and received directly by the believer, who comes to the throne of grace in faith.

In Good Company
Frederick Coutts

Would it not be out of character if our Lord — who came to open up a new and living way to God which, as the author to the Hebrews plainly saw, superseded the Jewish sacrificial system lock, stock and barrel — imposed any new and obligatory ceremony as an intregal part of the new covenant which He inaugurated by His life, His death and His rising again? When He called for wholehearted love to God and man as the twin essentials, did He not say that on these hung "all the law and the prophets"?

In Good Company
Frederick Coutts

Baptism wihtout water, but with the Holy Ghost, is far more scriptural than baptism with water, but without the Holy Ghost.

Closer Communion
Clifford Kew

Sacrifice

There is no such thing as greatness made easy, glory at half price, achievement at the bargain counter.

The Officer — 1918

In the simplest terms, a sacrifice is a gift to God — a gift which has basic values to us and Him.

The Better Covenant
Milton S. Agnew

Love without sacrifice is like a fire without a flame.

Emma Booth-Tucker
The Officer — 1892

Each one who would be a savior must face alone Gethsemane, must carry alone the cross. It is not ours to take away or even diminish your sacrifice, for in so doing should we not take from you the abundant reward?

Frederick Booth-Tucker
The Officer — 1893

They bleed that we may be blessed; they keep watch that we may take rest and sleep; they suffer and oftimes die that we may live.

Ancient Prophets
Samuel Logan Brengle

Does violent retaliation cure injustice? Obviously not. It is the "one cheek", the giving up of the coat only, the going of one mile that reveals the weakness. By turning the "other cheek also", offering the cloak as well, and going the second mile we wrest the initiative from our antagonist and assume moral command of the situation.

Power and Glory
Harry Dean

The gospel is free, but it is not cheap.

Power and Glory
Harry Dean

The reward for sacrifice may be more sacrifice; for service, more service.

Stuff That Makes an Army
William G. Harris

Our officers rarely speak of personal sacrifice and not at all while their eyes rest steadily upon the wounds of God. Yet, should sacrifice be implicit in our consecration, look for it not in the purse, though that be slender enough; not in the world's pity and patronage, though by some we still be accounted fools; not in any physical hardship or family inconvenience, though these must be faced. Look rather in the realm of personality, where spirits, as individualistic and ambitious as any in this world, choose to be submissive to the demands and discipline of a cause when they identify with the Cross of Christ. Look also in that kingdom of the mind, where so many of our officers would delight to follow their individual tastes in cultural pursuits. They feel that the wisdom that cometh from above requires of them not merely the negation of the evil things, but also the submission of the good things, their gold and frankincense and myrrh, to the absolute all-comprehending service of their Lord and Master.

The House of My Pilgrimage
Albert Orsborn

When the success of the salvation warfare is at stake, sacrifice is the standing order of the day.

Marching On!
Ted Palmer

Although self-preservation is acknowledged to be the first rule of nature, self-sacrifice remains the greatest rule of grace.

Manpower for the Master
Bramwell H. Tillsley

Salvation

We believe that repentance toward God, faith in our Lord Jesus Christ, and regeneration by the Holy Spirit are necessary to salvation.

Salvation Army Doctrine #7

Praise God, I'm saved!
    Praise God, I'm saved!
All's well, all's well!
    He sets me free!

Salvation Army Song Book

This meant deliverance from the deepest and most penetrating sin. This meant hope for the most profligate sinner. But...it meant the unlimited heights to which His salvation would lift, the penetrating completeness of this salvation, the holy life to which He would commit those for whom He prayed.

The Better Covenant
Milton S. Agnew

God's great work is the making of men in His own image — the restoration of the dismantled temple to the likeness of its Maker.

Bramwell Booth
Trumpets of the Lord
Catherine Bramwell-Booth, Edit.

How many orders of beings and how many myriads of beings His goodness has enriched, and will enrich to all eternity, we cannot tell. We do know that it has peopled heaven with glorious happy beings, and that it is trying to save and rescue from earth those who have fitted themselves to become vessels of destruction. We know that it flowed out to man in Eden, where the Father placed him in innocence and purity, and surrounded him with all possible facilities for temporal and spiritual happiness; and we know that the Fall did not even interrupt its flow, but that immediately the divine plan for man's restoration and salvation was launched, and salvation means cooperation with God all the way through, from the first ray of light till He bids you come up higher.

Life and Death
Catherine Booth

The wounds of Christ are open,
  Sinner, they were made for thee;
The wounds of Christ are open,
  There for refuge flee.

Songs of the Evangel
Evangeline Booth

Much of what this world can boast,
I have learned to count as dross;
And the sight that charms me most
Is a sinner at the cross.

Sounds of rapture, earthly glee,
Thunders roll and oceans wave,
These I've heard but give to me
Sinners asking Christ to save.

Charms and joys once felt and known,
Backward through my life I trace;
Backward this joy stands alone
Sinners found and saved by grace.

Herbert H. Booth
Gems for Songster #1

O boundless salvation! Deep ocean of love,
O fulness of mercy, Christ brought from above,
The whole world redeeming, so rich and so free,
Now flowing for all men, come roll over me!

O ocean of mercy, oft longing I've stood
On the brink of Thy wonderful life-giving flood!
Once more I have reached this soul-cleansing sea,
I will not go back till it rolls over me.

William Booth
Salvation Army Song Book

The worst man that ever walked will go to heaven if he obtains it (salvation) and the best man that ever lived will go to hell if he misses it. Oh, publish it abroad!

Salvation Soldiery
William Booth

To get man soundly saved it is not enough to put on him a pair of new breeches, to give him regular work, or even to give him a university education. These things are all outside a man, and if the inside remains unchanged you have wasted your labor. You must in some way or other graft upon the man's nature a new nature, which has in it the element of the divine.

In Darkest England and The Way Out
William Booth

We may only hope of the permanent deliverance of mankind from misery, either in this world or the next, in the regeneration or remaking of the individual by the power of the Holy Ghost through Jesus Christ. But in providing for the relief of

179

temporal misery I reckon that I am only making it easy where it is now difficult, and possible where it is now all but impossible for men and women to find their way to the Cross of our Lord Jesus Christ.

In Darkest England and The Way Out
William Booth

What is the use of a doctor who cannot cure, a life boat that cannot rescue, an overseer who cannot relieve? And what would be the value of a Savior who was not good and gracious and strong enough to save the vilest and worst, and to save them as far as they need?

William Booth
The Founder Speaks Again
Cyril Barnes, Edit.

Thou art the Way!
Can my rebellious feet
Find them a way more sweet?
Or wandering wide
From early morn to eventide
Trace out a way more straight
From gate of hell to heaven's gate?
From fleshly cold
To heart of God?

Fighting for the King
Catherine Bramwell-Booth

God's holiness demands the condemnation of sin; God's love and mercy demand the salvation of the sinner.

Samuel Logan Brengle
Portrait of a Prophet
Clarence W. Hall

It is a folly to preach the infilling of the Spirit to those who have not been to Calvary.

Arnold Brown
The Privilege of all Believers
John D. Waldron, Edit.

"This fellow welcomes sinners", said the Pharisees of Jesus. What on their lips was a malicious slander has become the glory and impelling attraction of the Christian Gospel.

The Armoury Commentary — The Four Gospels
Frederick Coutts, Edit.

We all know that there is a plain difference between a place of worship and an industrial plant, though the balance of life requires our attendance at both. But to suppose that what goes on in the one — but not the other — is of interest to God, is to put limits to true religion and to deprive man of his only hope of a salvation which can redeem the whole of his life.

Essentials of Christian Experience
Frederick Coutts

It's the work of a moment,
It's the work of a lifetime,
It begins in an instant,
It may take eternity,
But the work of the Spirit,
Of the world – changing Spirit,
Can begin at this moment in me.

Glory
John Gowans

When Jesus calls me from the crowd, Ellen,
I know what my answer will be.
I'll laugh and I'll shout it out aloud;
The Blood of the Lamb cleanses me.

The Blood of the Lamb
John Gowans

Here is the greatest truth of all: God saves man.

Evangeline Booth
Out of the Depths
Clarence W. Hall

"Behold, God is my salvation," exclaimed Isaiah. "I know whom I have believed," said Paul. Yes, the personal factor in our relation to the Lord is indispensable. It is not a case of "what", but "whom", not "it" but "Him".

Fuel for Sacred Flame
T. Henry Howard

"Lord, take the big knife and remove all my sins".

Congo Crusade
Albert Kenyon

"You all know that I've been different this week", she said, "and I'll tell you why. I used to be mates with Satan but now I"'ve gone mates with God."

My Best Men are Women
Flora Larsson

What pen can portray the full tragedy of broken lives, noble even in their ruin? What speech can convey the plowing miracle of rescue and renewal?

Albert Orsborn
The History of The Salvation Army — Volume 3
Robert Sandall

No! No! Nothing do I bring,
But by faith I'm clinging,
To Thy Cross, O Lamb of God!
Nothing but Thy Blood can save me.

Richard Slater
Salvation Army Song Book

Boundless as eternal ages,
 As the air we breathe is free,
Is the boundless, full salvation
 Jesus purchased on the tree.

Waller
Salvation Army Song Book

The experience of being "born of the spirit" is no fleeting euphoria. It does not rely for permanence on favorable feelings or congenial circumstances, but rather on faith that holds in the dark, prayer that says "Amen" to God's will whatever it may be and obedience to the Lord that ignores the cost.

The Desert Road to Glory
Clarence Wiseman

The Salvation Army

The Mission, time after time, sends out one or more evangelists into a town, where they are perfect strangers, but where, laboring in the same spirit of confident dependence upon the power of the Holy Ghost, they soon form a force, recruited from the most abandoned of the people for the further prosecuting of the same work.

Christian Mission Pamphlet

The Christian Mission, under the superintendance of the Rev. William Booth, is a Salvation Army recruited from among the multitudes who are without God and without hope in the world, devoting their leisure time to all sorts of laborious efforts for the salvation of others from unbelief, drunkenness, vice and crime.

Christian Mission Pamphlet

How many queer folks in the Army you see,
Good old Army!
And but for the Army where would they all be?
Good old Army!
Some of them oft used to wear ragged clothes,
Some of them too used to wear a red nose;
How the Army got hold of them nobody knows,
Good old Army!

The penitent-form is the Army's delight,
Good old Army!
Turning poor sinners from darkness to light;
Good old Army!
Some come to weep and to cry and to sob,
To get them to pray is a difficult job,
And sometimes a boozer comes out for a bob——
Bad old boozer!

Gems for Songsters #1

The Salvation Army is composed of persons who, having experienced forgiveness of sins and conversion by divine power, are enlisted under its banner as soldiers, fighting for God and souls.

Orders and Regulations for Officers

The Salvation Army is a fellowship of people who have accepted Jesus Christ as their personal Savior and Lord and whose common aim is to induce others to subject themselves to the lordship of Christ.

Chosen to be a Soldier

The word "salvation" indicates the purpose of the Movement; namely, to induce all men to submit to God, embrace the salvation provided for them in Christ, accept

God the Father as their supreme ruler, obey His laws, and spend their lives in the loving service of those about them, thereby enjoying the favor of God both here and hereafter. The word "army" indicates that the Movement is a fighting force constantly at war with the powers of evil and also that, in certain features of its construction and government, it resembles a military army.

Orders and Regulations for Officers

Here is a witness from the world itself that the first great outstanding feature of The Salvation Army, that which impressed itself first and foremost upon the mind of the multitude, is not that we are humanitarian, or social, or philanthropic — although we are all these put together — but that we are religious.

Bramwell Booth
Trumpets of the Lord
Catherine Bramwell-Booth, Edit.

I can imagine some holy being just arrived from another world asking "What is The Salvation Army?" and being answered in terms according to his own understanding, "The Salvation Army is love for souls".

Bramwell Booth
Trumpets of the Lord
Catherine Bramwell-Booth, Edit.

Our very title, The Salvation Army, is an expression of the fact that we are fighting men and women! If it be true — as, thank God, it is for most of us — that we receive a divine call to this work, then we may truly say that God brought us into the world to fight!

Bramwell Booth
Trumpets of the Lord
Catherine Bramwell-Booth, Edit.

The Salvation Army exists not so much for the Salvationist as for the whole world. So that the safety and continued life of the Army depend not upon our guarding and shepherding what we have won, but upon our uttermost devotion to help and bless and save mankind. This is the grand message of the Army of the past to the Army of the present.

Bramwell Booth
Trumpets of the Lord
Catherine Bramwell-Booth

The Salvation Army is a force of men and women knit together in holy love and fellowship for the purpose of inducing mankind to submit to God and embrace the salvation provided for them in Christ. Because it is organized and governed after the manner of the great standing armies of the world; but with this difference, that its object, instead of slaying men, is to bring them to a saving knowledge of the truth as it is in Christ Jesus.

Bramwell Booth
Why and Wherefore

The whole spirit and purpose of The Salvation Army are exerted in the direction of peace and brotherly kindness. The Army fights evil and error of every description. In its operations discipline is tempered with love; sacrifice and service are freely given for the highest purposes.

Bramwell Booth
Why and Wherefore

We had to build the ship while we were at sea, and not only build the ship but master the laws of navigation.

Bramwell Booth
The General Next to God
Richard Collier

My father and mother kissed each other and in that kiss was conceived The Salvation Army.

Evangeline Booth
The History of The Salvation Army — Volume 6
Frederick Coutts

The Army's objective has not altered. Its call is to save. Its tactics and maneuvers may change, but they must always aim without compromise directly at undermining the Devil's kingdom by aggressive means.

Powers of Salvation Army Officers
Florence Booth

The Salvation Army — we shall never lose that title! It is for you to see that the meaning does not cease to be apt. It is for you to protect that title from becoming as a tombstone over what was once a living and breathing body.

Friendship with Jesus
Florence Booth

As to such details affecting the continuance of the Movement, it does not appear to me that they will do so in the least, seeing that the real power is the life and Spirit of God; but even if they did it must be our concern to serve our generation according to what we conceive to be the will of God, leaving the future with Him. We have no ambition for this work to live any longer than He desires. Therefore, if it ever loses its spirit and life we are content for it to die.

Catherine Booth
The Life of Catherine Booth — Volume 2
Frederick Booth-Tucker

You want a real, living embodiment of Christianity over again, and if The Salvation Army is not going to be that, may God put it out! I would be willing to pronounce the funeral oration of the Army if I did not believe it was going to be that.

Papers on Godliness
Catherine Booth

God in His good providence had led us unwittingly, so to speak, to make an army. We called it an army, and seeing that it was an army organized for the deliverance of mankind from sin and the power of the devil, we called it an army of deliverance; an army of salvation — The Salvation Army.

William Booth
The History of The Salvation Army — Volume 1
Robert Sandall

I want to say to every Salvation soldier, let us not trust in The Salvation Army, but in the mighty God Who has made The Salvation Army. Our strength is not in our banners, nor our colors, not our comrades,

apart from the almighty power of God, the Holy Ghost.

William Booth
The History of The Salvation Army — Volume 2
Robert Sandall

My first idea was simply to get the people saved, and send them to the churches. This proved at the outset impracticable.
1st — They would not go when sent.
2nd — They were not wanted.
3rd — We wanted some of them to help us in the business of saving others.

Twenty-one Years Salvation Army
William Booth

What a strange name! What does it mean? Just what it says — a number of people joined together after the fashion of an army, and therefore it is an army, and an army for the purpose of carrying salvation through the land.

Salvation Soldiery
William Booth

The only reason for which the organization exists being war, common sense requires that it should be framed after that pattern which mankind, in all ages, has found to be, not only the most effective but the only one possible for an army.

William Booth
God's Army
Cyril Barnes

Your Salvation Army has been made to accomplish the impossible, and conquer that which to human calculations cannot be overcome.

Salvation Soldiery
William Booth

Just so far as the Army still stands apart in its love and desperate devotion to the one goal — the glory of God and the salvation of sinners — just so far as it is prepared to suffer loss and ignominy, to toil and sacrifice, to live and die for the fulfillment of that end — just so far will all the floods and the flames of earth's opposition or the devils and deluges of hell's bitterest hate prove powerless to hinder its onward march.

Emma Booth-Tucker

183

The great fact remains that, unless we are saving sinners, our very existence as an Army is not justified.

Messages to the Messengers
Catherine Bramwell-Booth

The longer my experience grows the more truly do I feel that the Army is worth sticking to. It is a big thing and a joyful thing to have a share in it, and to be a part of it.

Messages to the Messengers
Catherine Bramwell-Booth

What is the use of being young and re-sourceful, if you are not succeeding in get-ting hold of big sinners? That is why God made The Salvation Army — to win souls and the worst.

Messages to the Messengers
Catherine Bramwell-Booth

Society has been for years trying to "ele-vate the masses" by the leverage for Chris-tianity, but ignoring for the most part, the simple and fundamental fact that a lever must go under the mass to be raised. The Salvation Army has been raised from the under stratum of society by the leverage of a Christianity which came to it; and now, in turn, it has hold of the lever. It only asks a place whereon to stand, to move the world.

The Army Drum
Elizabeth Swift Brengle

If love leaks out we shall lose our crown. We shall have a name to live and yet be dead. We may still house the homeless, dole out food to the hungry, punctiliously perform our routine work, but the minis-try of the Spirit will no longer be our glory. Our musicians will play meticulously, our songsters will revel in the artistry of song that tickles the ear, but leave the heart cold and hard.

Ancient Prophets
Samuel Logan Brengle

There are three things in which I cannot see much difference, a column of The War

Cry, a page of Wesley's Journal and a chap-ter of the Acts of the Apostles.

Mr. Brunlow (Independent Methodist Magazine)
The History of The Salvation Army — Volume 2
Robert Sandall

It is an Army out to fight another army; to wrestle, to conquer, to take prisoners and to establish and govern territories. The salvation fight demands the best a man and woman can give of heart and mind, of sacrifice and service.

The Angel Adjutant
Minnie Lindsay Carpenter

The Army had spanned the globe for the very reason that it was mobile, single-minded and defied convention.

The General Next to God
Richard Collier

The Salvation Army's war was against human distress, not against another army.

A Gentle War
Lawrence Fellows

To definitely get a sinner converted and enrolled and in fighting form is a greater victory than putting a dozen people on the rolls who are members of churches and missions.

T. Henry Howard
The Officer

The Salvation Army was not planned in ad-vance by any man or body of men. William Booth never claimed to have invented or created it; indeed, no hint can be found that he, his devoted wife, or his zealous and undauntable followers dreamed to what they were proceeding — until they found established an Army of which they were soldiers.

Albert Orsborn
The History of The Salvation Army — Volume 1
Robert Sandall

Take away the military paraphernalia — uniforms, badges, officers, barracks, or-ders from headquarters — and you still have our raison d'etre: getting people saved. But take away the militant evangelism for which God raised us up and you are left with no more than an expensive and complicated adult version of toy soldiers.

Marching On!
Ted Palmer

We are a Salvation Army. Not a bed and board army. Not a musical army. Not a money collecting army. Not a recreation center army. Not a hospital army.
These are but the battlefields, the weapons and the logistics of the fight.

Marching On!
Ted Palmer

The Salvation Army is the stained-glass window of the Christian church. It is this world's most colorful expression of the light and life of Christ.

Marching On!
Ted Palmer

Joy! Joy! Joy! There is joy in The Salvation Army!
Joy! Joy! Joy! In the Army of the Lord!

William Pearson
Salvation Army Song Book

O Thou God of every nation,
    We now for They blessing call;
Fit us for full consecration,
    Let the fire from heaven fall.
        Bless our Army!
With Thy power baptize us all.

William Pearson
Salvation Army Song Book

There is not anywhere today another organization professing to undertake throughout the whole world a scheme of evangelization specially directed to meet the need of the most abandoned and godless of the community; and surely, therefore, we may fairly claim to be the Lord's special force raised up for the emergency.

Heathen England
George Scott Railton

I intended carefully to instuct my children that if at any time they see The Salvation Army a wealthy respectable concern, the majority of whose "soldiers" simply go when they please to attend its "ministrations" and leave the godless to perish; that

if they see another set of people, however they may be clothed and despised, who really give up all to go and save the lost, they must not for a moment hesitate to leave the concern their old dad helped to make and go out among those who most faithfully carry out what the Founder of the Army laid down in his writings.

George Scott Railton
G.S.R.
John D. Waldron, Edit.

Our cathedral is the open-air, our college is the prayer room, our library the Bible.

Heathen England
George Scott Railton

The genius of The Salvation Army has been to use effectively a force made up — for by far the greater part — of ordinary people, first and foremost, because they have been inspired by an unexcelled devotion to the cause, having been moved to give themselves unreservedly to it by the conviction that they have been called thereto by God.

The History of The Salvation Army — Volume 2
Robert Sandall

If The Salvation Army were wiped out of London, five thousand extra policemen could not fill its place in the repression of crime and disorder.

Charles Spurgeon
The History of The Salvation Army — Volume 3
Robert Sandall

From the moment that the Army had received its title its destiny was fixed. The whole organization was dominated by the name.

W.T. Stead
The History of The Salvation Army — Volume 2
Robert Sandall

The Salvation Army is a miracle of our time. It is the latest revelation of the potency of the invisible over the visible, the concrete manifestation of the power of the spirit over matter.

Mrs. Booth
W.T. Stead

The Salvation Army is essentially autocratic, but the authority of the General is exercised only by the continually renewed voluntary consent of his soldiers. There is no Mutiny Act in The Salvation Army. There is before every Salvationist the open door, through which he can go out whenever he pleases.

Mrs. Booth
W.T. Stead

1878 was the turning point in the history of The Salvation Army. In thirteen years it had established a beachhead, developed a fighting spirit and trained its shock troops. Henceforce it would fan out in all directions taking the world by surprise.

William Booth's First Gentleman
Harry Williams

As a tree grows by the hidden thrust of nature, so the Army grows by the hidden power of God.

A Burning in My Bones
Clarence Wiseman

The Salvation Army exists for those who do not belong to it as much as for those who do.

A Burning in My Bones
Clarence Wiseman

The salvation of human beings in their totality is its primal passion, and its religious faith is the source of its coherence and the dynamic of its evangelical and social work. Were that faith to diminish with a consequent impoverishment of the corps which give the Army both vitality and manpower, all parts would suffer; Christian witness and social concern alike would gradually wither away. Those who imagine the Army is only, or even primarily, a social service agency, reveal appalling ignorance of its authentic nature.

A Burning in My Bones
Clarence Wiseman

The Salvation Army must be God's voice calling the wayward, the lonely, the destitute into the circle of His love.

General Jarl Wahlström
The Officer – 1981

Salvationism

The Army spirit is a fighting spirit. It recognizes that precious souls are dying and asks to be nerved for the fight. It scorns the plush comfort of the cushioned pew and acknowledges that "in the open-air our Army we prepare." It has a vibrancy, a vitality that makes an irresistible appeal to those whose blood courses warmly through their veins. As with Isaiah in the temple, it leads the man who sees the holiness of God not only to seek cleansing and healing but to hear God's voice calling him to action on behalf of his brothers, and to respond, "Here am I, send me."

Will Pratt
New Frontier

Every officer should possess, and be possessed by, what is frequently described as "the Army spirit". That is to say, he will devote himself without reserve to the purpose for which The Salvation Army exists — the salvation of the people.

Orders and Regulations for Officers

What sometimes we call the spirit of the Army is that union of holy love and fiery zeal and practical common sense which produces wherever it is found the fruits of salvation by the power of Christ.

Bramwell Booth
The Angel Adjutant
Minnie Lindsay Carpenter

The life of a Salvationist is a life of interruption. Wherever he goes there are "lions in the way". Telegrams and letters follow him to every retreat. Seclusion, privacy, and the quietude supposed to be necessary for literary enterprise — the words have been obliterated from his dictionary, the very ideas have almost faded from his mind. His table is a keg of spiritual gunpowder, his seat a cannon ball; and he writes as best he may amid the whiz and crash of flying shot and shell, the rush and excitement of a never ending battle, in which peace and truce are words unknown, and rest, in the ordinary sense of the word, is relegated to heaven.

Catherine Booth
Life of Catherine Booth — Volume 1
Frederick Booth-Tucker

Salvationism is the harmony diffused through the whole man when the principles of The Salvation Army are struck true and clear on the strings of the heart. Salvationism is not a matter of externals, though it pervades externals, and draws from them an indispensable note in its concord.

Powers of Salvation Army Officers
Florence Booth

Salvationism means simply the overcoming and banishing from the earth of wickedness.

William Booth
The Officer — 1893

We are a salvation people. This is our specialty, getting saved, and then getting somebody else saved and then getting saved ourselves more and more, until full salvation on earth makes the heaven within, which is finally perfected by the full salvation on the other side of the river.

William Booth
Blood and Fire
Edward Bishop

The spirit of the Army, sometimes called salvationism, is an endowment from God for the Army's peculiar and special work in His plan for mankind.
It is a precious spirit — warm and flaming with love, born in heaven, and is one, just one, of the great revelations of the loving heart of God the Father, centered in Jesus Christ, to a needy, helpless and in many cases hopeless human race.

Stuff Than Makes an Army
William G. Harris

Shall we be satisfied with going on as hitherto, picking up one here and one there, gathering together a more or less select congregation, forgetful meanwhile of the Master's command, "Go ye out into the highways and hedges, and compel them to come in?" The Salvation Army has taught us a higher lesson than this. Whatever may be its faults, it has at least recalled us to His lost ideal of the work of the church — universal compulsion of the soul of men.

Dr. Lightfoot
The History of The Salvation Army — Volume 2
Robert Sandall

Satan

Satan has put men fast asleep in sin, and that it is his great device to keep them so. He does not care what we do, if he can do that.

Life and Death
Catherine Booth

How much there is of the past recorded on the page of history, and how much we see in the present, turn which way we will, to justify the assertion of Satan that he is really and truly in possession of the bodies and souls of men and of the very world they dwell in.

Salvation Soldiery
William Booth

He will suggest his own evil wishes and desires, and then seek to persuade you that they are from your heart. He will say, "How can you be sanctified and have such sinful thoughts as those?" Disown his foul productions. Tell him they are not yours. Tell him they belong to him.

Purity of Heart
William Booth

It must be remembered that it is not merely intellectual ignorance that we have to fight; it is the natural darkness and pollution of the human heart, and the devices, excuses and misrepresentations which the devil only too often whispers into one ear while we in the name of Jesus Christ are speaking to the other; for Satan fights with us for the souls of men at every turn.

William Booth
How to Preach
Charles Talmadge

One of my miseries has always been that the enemy of souls knows so well how to take advantage of my valleys and hills!

Messages to the Messengers
Catherine Bramwell-Booth

Religion has not lost its power to interest the people, nor have the needs and sorrows of others ceased to appeal to the hearts of those who do love God; but the devil succeeds too well in keeping the sinner and the saint apart.

Messages to the Messengers
Catherine Bramwell-Booth

Satan ever seeks to destroy holy love and divine unity. When he comes he arouses suspicions, he stirs up strife, he quenches the spirit of intercessory prayer, he engenders backbitings and causes separations.

When the Holy Ghost is Come
Samuel Logan Brengle

The devil knows and understands how to waste time and stop progress.

William Booth
The Armoury Commentary — The Four Gospels
Frederick Coutts, Edit.

Cleverly and strategically he maneuvers from one to the other. If he cannot catch us in unwariness, he tries to overwhelm by wearing down our resistance. If he cannot trap with the unknown, he nettles with an itch that can't be scratched.

Refuge in the Secret Place
Edward Deratany

He takes the lovely thing
And twists
Its beauty to his will.
Distorts the very
Word of God
His purpose to fulfill.

O Lord!
John Gowans

If the devil comes into this office, throw inkpots at him.

Elijah Cadman
The House of My Pilgrimage
Albert Orsborn

At times as an angel of light he appears,
  At times lion-like he comes to our fears;
By gains and by losses, by praise and by jeers,
  He seeks to entrap us in sin.

Richard Slater
Combat Songs of The Salvation Army
Sallie Chesham, Edit.

In the laboratories of invention he is inspiring weapons of destruction; in peace conferences he is fostering fear and hatred among nations; in industry he is generating strife among masters and men; in our colleges, youth camps and schools he is propagating false theories; on platform and in the press he is subverting truth, making evil seem good; on stage, screen, and through the medium of broadcasting, he is twisting and distorting morals, and in a thousand ways he is corrupting human nature.

The Christian Charter
George B. Smith

Science

Unless there is a raising of the world's standards in man's treatment of his brother, the very advance in scientific knowledge will convert this earth into a place of death; for every advance in scientific knowledge arms the evil as well as the good in human nature; and man may increase his power in certain directions without increasing those powers which are associated with his moral development or his spiritual life.

Powers of Salvation Army Officers
Florence Booth

We have only admiration for science. We fully recognize the wondrous discoveries and inventions of uplift and helpfulness that human knowledge and scientific research have given to the world. We praise God for them. But we do contend that the efficiency which comes of knowledge has not superseded the gospel which is all victorious divine love.

Evangeline Booth
Out of the Depths
Clarence W. Hall

Second Coming

And now there are thousands talking about His second coming who will neither see nor receive Him in the person of His humble and persecuted followers. Christ manifested in flesh, vulgar flesh, they cannot receive. No: they're looking for Him in the clouds! What a sensation there would be if He were to come again in a carpenter's coat! How many would recognize Him then, I wonder!

Catherine Booth
All Things New
William Burrows

Christ did say that the Christian's primary responsibility was to be ready for the Second Coming. People who spend their time in idle speculation are denying the spirit of His words. In speaking of His coming again, Christ was calling men to live — to work out their values and make all their decisions — against the background of the eternal. Only then could they always be ready.

The Armoury Commentary — The Four Gospels
Frederick Coutts, Edit.

When He comes
In power and glory,
Passing through time's tethered
Clouds,
Shrouds will shrivel,
Graves dissemble,
As I join earth's acclamation
For the King of all creation!

Wind Chimes
Sallie Chesham

Security

The simple condition of eternal security is faithfulness — obedience and continued love toward God on the part of the Christian. As long as he continues to exhibit these, he is safe.

The Security of the Believer
Milton S. Agnew

Find a tiny place for me,
Under Your shadow, Rock!
Thrust me not
Into the scorching sun.

Lock me under Your
Mightiness,
Lest I fall again
When the winds
Begin to seek me out.

Wind Chimes
Sallie Chesham

Just hold me, Lord,
Tight-fisted,
With a grip like all eternity.

Walking With the Wind
Sallie Chesham

Spiritual security is a hopeless problem apart from divine union. It is so in all stages of religious life, and the most advanced saint is no less dependent on God than is the soul of the new convert.

Fuel for Sacred Flame
T. Henry Howard

Seeking

When we hunger we are prepared to do our part and to take that food for our souls which we need. This illustration applies closely in the spiritual realm, for you know that appetite is a good sauce; making the very simplest food delicious. Dry bread, if you are hungry or have missed a meal or two does not need margarine on jam to make it sweet. Just so the spiritual appetite keeps alive the desire for those simple yet important things by which the soul lives.

Florence Booth
The Officer — 1918

Do you ask, how can we get the fire? I answer, not by feasting, but by fasting; not by playing, but by praying; not by sleeping and slothfulness, but by watching and by diligently seeking God and the souls that wander from Him; not by skimming The War Cry once a week and reading newspapers and devouring the comic sections and sporting news, but by searching the Scriptures.

Resurrection Life and Power
Samuel Logan Brengle

189

The truth that saves the soul is not picked up as we would pick up the pebbles along the beach, but it is obtained rather as gold and silver, after diligent search and much digging.

Helps to Holiness
Samuel Logan Brengle

On, come on,
Quit climbing the steeple,
to find Him
We've got to play people,
Not God.

Walking With the Wind
Sallie Chesham

The trouble is that our "hunger" for God is frequently more a passing whim than a sustained longing. But still we find only what we seek; for spiritual discoveries can never exceed spiritual desires.

The Armoury Commentary — The Four Gospels
Frederick Coutts, Edit.

Who comes to Me, the Savior said,
Shall constantly partake,
The stream that from the fountainhead
Alone his thirst can slake.
Who seeks in faith that fountain pure,
His freshness shall retain.
Shall peace and happiness insure
And never thirst again.

William Kitching
Salvation Army Song Book

Vainly I seek a cure for my soul's ailing,
Vainly aspire to reach the life divine,
Slave of myself, myself forever failing,
Helpless am I until Thy grace be mine.

Albert Orsborn
Salvation Army Song Book

No one will get far with God unless he gets thoroughly dissatisfied with himself.

Studies in Sanctification
Edward Read

Just outside the land of promise
You have waited many years,
And your life has been o'erclouded
With a host of haunting fears.
There is victory in Jesus,
Come to Him without delay;

Seek just now a full salvation
And the voice of God obey.

Walter H. Windybank
Salvation Army Song Book

Self

A false charity begins in self, and ends on earth.

Papers on Godliness
Catherine Booth

To accept Jesus only on our terms amounts to a rejection.

The Armoury Commentary — The Four Gospels
Frederick Coutts, Edit.

Self-Denial

Man needs to beware lest in claiming his rights he loses his witness.

Transformed Christians
Milton S. Agnew

The power of self-denial to work good fruit in us is often dependent upon our silence about it.

Powers of Salvation Army Officers
Florence Booth

Self-denial is the first law of grace.

William Booth
The Christian Charter
George B. Smith

Self-denial will prove your love to Christ.

Catherine Booth
Words of Catherine Booth
Cyril Barnes

Denial that is not self-imposed is not self-denial.

Heart Talks on Holiness
Samuel Logan Brengle

Now, when the Christian whose heart throbs with love for the Savior realizes that Jesus puts Himself in the place of the prisoner in his lonely, dark cell; the slave toiling without recompense under the lash, with the galling, clanking chain; the sick one on the bed of sleeplessness and pain; the heathen, in his blindness and ignorance and superstition and fear; the helpless orphan and the poor widow, and the outcast sinner, and says, "Inasmuch as ye have done it unto one of the least of these my brethren, ye have done it unto Me." He must deny himself.

Heart Talks on Holiness
Samuel Logan Brengle

We deny ourselves only when we voluntarily give up that which we like, and which we might lawfully keep. And I have no doubt that God often allows us luxuries and abundance, not that we may consume them upon ourselves, but rather that we may deny ourselves joyfully for His dear sake, and the sake of the needy ones about us.

Heart Talks on Holiness
Samuel Logan Brengle

By going without pudding every day for a year, I calculate I can save 50 shillings. This I will do and will remit the amount named as quickly as possible.

Carleton
The General Next to God
Richard Collier

A life of abstention is not of necessity a life of holiness.

Peace Like a River
Sallie Chesham

Selfishness

To act selfishly is the denial of true love.

Chosen to be a Soldier

Ah! I fancy sometimes that the selfishness of the human heart can be manifested as truly in religious things as in anything else, and that the spirit of grab can be shown even amidst the holiest surroundings and influences. Does it not seem as if some people say, "Let me get all I can out of Christ; let me have all I can out of The Salvation Army; let me rejoice and enrich myself with the happiness which flows from its services, from the prayers and attentions of its officers, from its music and song and from its comradeship and sympathy; but I am not going to give anything very much back again.

Bramwell Booth
Trumpets of the Lord
Catherine Bramwell-Booth

There are many people who seem to be ever reckoning how much they can get out of God for as little as possible in return.

Salvation Soldiery
William Booth

Faith is lost when love leaks out and living becomes selfish.

Ancient Prophets
Samuel Logan Brengle

Fear is a fruit of selfishness. Boldness thrives when selfishness is destroyed.

When the Holy Ghost is Come
Samuel Logan Brengle

Strictly speaking, sanctification does not destroy self, but selfishness — the abnormal, mean and disordered manifestation and assertion of self.

When the Holy Ghost is Come
Samuel Logan Brengle

Self-acceptance may be nothing more than laziness; unwillingness to make an effort at effecting a remedy in circumstances, character and conduct.

The Armoury Commentary — The Four Gospels
Frederick Coutts, Edit.

Selfishness is never happier or more firmly entrenched than when parading as piety, which is one reason why our selfish prayers are far less conscious than our selfish deeds.

The Armoury Commentary — The Four Gospels
Frederick Coutts, Edit..

The "I want" outlook is made no less self-centered and bigoted and evil by being dressed up in religious garments.

The Armoury Commentary — The Four Gospels
Frederick Coutts, Edit.

My case was just,
But my bulldozer way
Of getting what I want
Was wrong You say?

And is that why
My vict'ry can't be sung?
And its sweet taste
Is sawdust on my tongue?

John Gowans

You were planning in the shadows
while I demanded in the light of the day.

I'm Growing, Lord!
Flora Larsson

Once I wanted to hug life to myself and
stash away my blessings for times of need,
but it never worked. Hoarding my blessings never filled my life. It impoverished
it.

Dear God
Virginia Talmadge

Separation

Separation is never isolation; it is insula-
tion.

More Than Conquerors
Milton S. Agnew

Love is a fire, and we know that fire can
burn up much rubbish — even the poor
rubbish of selfishness it can consume: but
that which is foreign to the fire like the
clinker among the coals, must be taken
out and cast away, otherwise the fire will
become choked and clogged.

Likeness to God
Florence Booth

Our separateness will not be a separateness from people, however sinful, which
is Pharisaism; but a separation from sin
unto God and a dedication to people
which is Christian holiness..

Frederick Coutts
The Privilege of All Believers
John D. Waldron, Edit

Service

An officer is first of all the servant of all.

Orders and Regulations for Officers

"Here I abide," she vowed; "you recom-
pensed
My hate with love and clothed my nakedness

With all you owned. You're nearer God
than I;
For God is love, and loveless innocence
Is like a clean, white platter without food,
To set before the hungry and sick."

Reflections
Catherine Baird

This is how God's servant pays
For the gift of His employ:
Bleeding hands and wounded feet
Empty purse and hallowed heart!

Reflections
Catherine Baird

You don't get real joy from jewels. The joy
from social attainments is nice but it soon
passes. The joy of service to the poor and
unfortunate is lasting and blessed.

Evangeline Booth
My Best Men are Women
Flora Larsson

They need to be brought to see that they
are not only called to the adoption of sons,
but to the work of servants — not only to
feel the privileges of the Kingdom but to
be actual co-workers for God in bringing
others to share these blessings. Even
when Christians are brought to discern
this duty they require to be taught how to
discharge it.

William Booth
The History of The Salvation Army — Volume 1
Robert Sandall

Not as slaves to master
Ever yielding lives,
But as love enraptured
To lover gives;
Thus would I be
Servant of Thee
Lord of my life forever.

Fighting for the King
Catherine Bramwell-Booth

The fact is, God is using everybody that he
can, and using them to the full extent of
their fitness for His service. So, instead of
praying so much to be used, people
should search themselves to know
whether they are usable.

Helps to Holiness
Samuel Logan Brengle

To those who have entered into the secret of the Master, His yoke is the badge of freedom, and His burden gives wings to the soul.

Love-Slaves
Samuel Logan Brengle

You have visions of glory and rapturous delight, and so count yourselves filled with the Spirit. Do these visions lead you to virtue and to lowly, loving service?

When the Holy Ghost is Come
Samuel Logan Brengle

How can I better serve Thee, Lord,
   Thou who hast done so much for me?
Faltering and weak my labors have been;
   O that my life may tell for Thee!

Bramwell Coles
Salvation Army Song Book

Genuine holiness will find its expression in unrewarded service to the last, the least and the lost.

The Splendour of Holiness
Frederick Coutts

In the economy of the Spirit the higher a man's place, the humbler his duties.

The Armoury Commentary — The Four Gospels
Frederick Coutts, Edit.

People want Christ's healing, but not His lordship. They seek privilege without responsibility; to receive from God without corresponding service.

The Armoury Commentary — The Four Gospels
Frederick Coutts, Edit.

The church of Christ is perfect when she is fulfilling her intended end as the body of Christ, acting as His eyes to search out human need, His feet to run to meet that need, His hands to succor need, His lips to speak comfortable words to those in need. Thus behaving, His church is a glorious church, without spot or wrinkle, perfect in the Father's sight because she is fulfilling His purpose for her.

The Call to Holiness
Frederick Coutts

The ideal is a balanced life — prayer, and perspiration; silence and service; worship and work.

The Armoury Commentary — The Four Gospels
Frederick Coutts, Edit.

The servant of God goes on working for God by good report, by evil report and — hardest of all — without being reported at all!

The Call to Holiness
Frederick Coutts

The hallmark of the Christian is service to others. But service which is not inspired by the indwelling Spirit of Christ degenerates into a subtle form of self-advertisement. Only service motivated by divine love rises up to Him as a sweet-smelling savor.

Search the Scriptures
Robert Hoggard

In recent years I have crossed and recrossed high mountains where great rivers have their courses. The little streams meeting and blending and swelling into rivers have interested me; but I have remembered that the value of these rivers lies not in the fact of their having springs in high places, but that they send their sweet, fertilizing waters down the valleys and across the prairies and plains where the multitudes live and labor. So while the springs of spiritual life must be in heavenly places, they are of little value unless the experiences flow down to the levels where men strive and cry, and through the places where the multitude live and toil and suffer.

Fuel for Sacred Flame
T. Henry Howard

I don't ask for a front line position
Lord,
(though even as I say it my ego raises an eyebrow and coughs importantly)
but I do want to feel I'm needed and useful.

Between You and Me, Lord
Flora Larsson

O make my life one blazing fire
Of pure and fervent heart-desire
The lost to find, the low to raise,
And give them cause Thy name to praise.
Because wherever I may go
I show Thy power to every foe!

T.C. Marshall
Salvation Army Song Book

Give direction to my loving and my working so that my serving will make sense.

Dear God
Virginia Talmadge

Christians cannot move beyond the first word of the Lord's Prayer without sensing a stirring of soul to report for duty to help a neighbor in need. God is our Father, as well as my Father.

A Burning in My Bones
Clarence Wiseman

Sex

The Salvation Army as a Christian movement believes that human sexuality is a gift of God, and that the Bible presents sex and its proper use as a privilege, created, ordained and blessed by God.

The Salvation Army, is however, keenly aware that a sexual revolution is taking place in today's society which has brought about, to an unprecedented degree, a lowering of social mores, a decline in family stability, and an increase in sexual promiscuity among both youth and adults. To counter the disastrous efforts of this situation, The Salvation Army strongly affirms that the complex physical, psychological and social dimensions of human sexuality must be governed by spiritual and moral considerations derived from our Judeo-Christian heritage.

The Salvation Army recognizes that the battle between flesh and spirit is never easy but believes that the sex drive is designed by God to lead to the highest expression of human love only within the holy estate of matrimony, and that when it is expressed outside of that relationship, it inevitably leads to misery of self and others.

Therefore, The Salvation Army reaffirms

that the Bible gives the clearest teaching to guide human behavior and reveals that it is God who gives man the capacity for responsible sexual expression. The Army deeply deplores the practice of indiscriminate sexual activity under any circumstances, and wholeheartedly subscribes to the high moral standards exemplified and taught by Jesus Christ, the Son of God.

The Commissioners' Conference — United States of America
November, 1971

The Salvation Army, concerned that the dignity of mankind should be preserved, deplores the increasing pornography infecting books, magazines and newspapers, and the pornography and blasphemy infecting theaters, cinemas, radio and television.

The Salvation Army believes that attitude reflects widespread feeling against blasphemy and the commercialization of sex in ways which ensure financial gain for the exploiters and the creation of false values in the lives of the exploited.

The Salvation Army maintains its stand against evils which threaten the quality of personal and national character and seeks to arouse public conscience against such evils.

The Salvation Army wholeheartedly supports the proper education of the young on matters relating to the sanctity of right human relationships based on the teaching of Christ.

Above all, The Salvation Army believes that the wholesomeness of society depends upon the conversion of men and women everywhere to the Christian way of life in which high standards of morality are established.

International Headquarters — London
March, 1974

An officer will not allow himself to be influenced by any lowering of moral standards in the society in which he lives. If a soldier or recruit fails to live up to the standards of sexual morality which are the Army's declared and cherished standards,

194

based upon the truth and spirit of Christ's teaching, such failure cannot be ignored.

Orders and Regulations for Officers

Sexual misconduct is an offense against the law of love, since it is a gratification of selfish desires without Christian respect for the personality of the other party.

Chosen to be a Soldier

The Salvation Army accepts a natural and Biblical interpretation of sex. This emphasizes a unity between physical and spiritual dimensions in human personality. It also lays specific stress on sexual relationships as interpersonal ones requiring responsibility for another. It removes thought and deed from the area of guilt and disgust which so many men and women sadly experience. Convinced that the sex act belongs exclusively in marriage, the Salvationist cannot accept the concept of unfettered sexual experimentation.

Chosen to be a Soldier

Humanity is composed of two sexes, and woe be to those who attempt to separate them into distinct bodies, making of each half a whole!

In Darkest England and The Way Out
William Booth

The profession of the prostitute is the only career in which the maximum income is paid to the newest apprentice.

In Darkest England and The Way Out
William Booth

One of the guards of my adolescent years, during those lonely periods after mother died, was the thought of a wife to whom one day I wanted to give myself as pure and unsoiled as I hoped to find her. When tempted to run after forbidden pleasures, that thought was one of the great restraints in my life — one of the supreme protective influences. I wanted so to live that I could open my heart and tell my wife my whole life without shame.

Samuel Logan Brengle
Peace Like a River
Sallie Chesham

The instinct and power of reproduction is the noblest physical gift God has bestowed upon man; it makes man a partner with God in the creation of the race, and therefore the prostitution of that noble instinct and power is the vilest and worst of all crimes, and has brought into the world more sorrow, shame, ruin, and woe than probably all other crimes combined.

Love-Slaves
Samuel Logan Brengle

To rob a man of money is bad, but to rob a woman of her virtue is worse. To debauch the future mothers of the race, and so to rob unborn children and generations yet to be, of the noblest of all rights — the right of pure, sweet, holy, reverent motherhood — seems to me to be like poisoning the wells and springs from which cities must drink or perish, and hence one of the greatest crimes.

Love-Slaves
Samuel Logan Brengle

Silence

Don't you see that while the devil kept me silent, he kept me comparatively fruitless.

Catherine Booth
W.T. Stead

And may not silence lie as well as speech?

Fighting for the King
Catherine Bramwell-Booth

The very silence of a holy man is with power. I have known such silence to still the voice of slander and foolishness, and hush the laugh of silliness and folly.

The Way of Holiness
Samuel Logan Brengle

It is the very courtesy of God which is the reason why so often we miss Him. He comes to us in such unobtrusive ways in the person of someone in need, in the goodness of those we take for granted, in beauty we are too preoccupied to notice, in a quiet moment we are too busy to use.

The Armoury Commentary — The Four Gospels
Frederick Coutts, Edit.

195

Sometimes silence speaks louder than thunder; sometimes her cries are sharper than a two-edged sword; sometimes she is more powerful than marching troops, more formidable than a marching army. Have we not all had those deeper moments of life when only silence was appropriate? To speak a word would seem almost profane in such moments.

Footsteps to Calvary
Henry Gariepy

Simplicity

Simplicity, parent of reality, offspring of sincerity, how great a charm! how unfailing an appeal to the heart of God! how invincible a weapon in the battle for souls!

Heart Messages
Emma Booth-Tucker

Sin

We believe that our first parents were created in a state of innocency, but by their disobedience they lost their purity and happiness, and that in consequence of their fall all men have become sinners, totally depraved, and as such are justly exposed to the wrath of God.

Salvation Army Doctrine #5

The most serious aspect of the nature of sin is that it is anti-God, inspiring not only movement away from Him, but hostility toward Him.

Handbook of Doctrine

The unpardonable sin is more an attitude than a single act. As long as one persists in it he has no pardon. But forgiveness is immediately available, as for any sin, if this attitude is discarded. He who fears lest he has committed such a sin has not. His concern prohibits that possibility.

The Holy Spirit — Friend and Counsellor
Milton S. Agnew

One of the remarkable facts about wrong of every kind is that it so quickly joins forces with other wrong. Sin is the grand support of sin.

Bramwell Booth
Trumpets of the Lord
Catherine Bramwell-Booth, Edit.

See how the drinking places, the degenerate stage, the immoral literature, the nasty talk of the street, combine to inflame the baser nature and make the animal in man the master of his destiny! So that this wonderful creature, the noblest of God's works, sinks lower than the swine, and finds at last the only joys of life in the gratification of a depraved appetite and in the corruption of a filthy lust. Labor is a necessary nuisance! The service of his generation, a sign of servitude! The life of restraint, of temperance, of noble aspiration — why, it is all fudge as compared with the joys of quenching a depraved thirst, or of lascivious mirth, or of licentious indulgence!

Bramwell Booth
Trumpets of the Lord
Catherine Bramwell-Booth

Human nature is degenerate soil; and it is not necessary to sow in it directly the seeds of self-will, rebellion, and worldliness, but only to leave it to itself, unsubdued, unpruned, and unrenewed by the grace of God, and the harvest is sure to be one of bitterness and sorrow.

Catherine Booth
Life of Catherine Booth — Volume 2
Frederick Booth-Tucker

It is not the surroundings that make people happy, but the state of their hearts; and I fancy we should feel worse in the insufferable light of the Gloryland, with a sense of moral impurity, than we should in the darkness of hell itself.

Life and Death
Catherine Booth

Let us see how infinitely preferable it is that sin should be destroyed here than damned hereafter; how much better it is to get it into the fountain, where it can be annihilated, than into the lake of brimstone and fire, where the smoke of its torment must ascend forever and ever.

The General's Letters
William Booth

Oh, how sin will plead for life! how it will retreat to be spared! Oh, what plausible arguments Satan will bring to move you to pity, and at least postpone for a season the putting it away! And oh, how friends near and dear will join to entreat you not to be too severe on yourself, not to be legal, not to be a melancholy fanatic!

William Booth
The Founder Speaks Again
Cyril Barnes, Edit.

Sin is a real thing, a damnable thing. Don't care what the scientists call it, or what some of the pulpits are calling it. I know what it is. Sin is devilish. It is sin and sin only prevents the world from being happy. Sin! Go into the slums of the great cities, pick up little girls six years of age, sold into infamy by their own parents. Look at the drunken mother murdering her own child. Look at the father, strapping his crippled boy. Sin! That's what I call sin...something beastly and devilish!

William Booth
The General Next to God
Richard Collier

When man reaches the age of accountability, grace finds him with a heart completely and thoroughly depraved — deprived of grace without God, and under the power and domination of his selfish and sinful appetites. This condition is thorough — entire.

Salvation Soldiery
William Booth

With uncleanness there is a sense of perpetual unworthiness for the task.

Salvation Soldiery
William Booth

And look at those in the shade of life's approaching night. Have they learned better? Is the spell broken? No! Their setting sun reveals but a seared conscience, a life far spent, a life, it may be, of toil and suffering, but toil for naught, labor for that which satisfieth not. And still their eyes are blinded, and still they stumble on.

Heart Messages
Emma Booth-Tucker

Oh, the anguish, the humiliation, the marring of the souls of men, because in the beginning of their relationship with God there was no hand wise, strong, and tender enough to put in the knife and deal with the deadly thing!

Messages to the Messengers
Catherine Bramwell-Booth

He will find a big, dark something in him that wants to get mad when things are against him; something which will not be patient; something that is touchy and sensitive; something that wants to grumble and find fault; something that is proud and shuns the shame of the Cross; something that sometimes suggests hard thought against God; something that is self-willed and ugly and sinful.

Heart Talks on Holiness
Samuel Logan Brengle

It is not necessary to blot the sun out of the heavens to keep the sunlight out of your house; just close the blinds and draw the curtains. Nor do you pour barrels of water on the flame necessarily to quench the fire — just shut off the draught. You do not dynamite the city reservoir and destroy the mains and pipes to cut off your supply of leaking water — but just refrain from using the tap. So you do not need to do some great evil, some deadly sin, to quench the Spirit.

Samuel Logan Brengle
Peace Like a River
Sallie Chesham

Sin does not leap upon us fully armed. It steals in through a look, a swift silent suggestion or imagination, but love and loyalty to Jesus will make you watchful and swift to rise up and cast out the subtle enemy.

Ancient Prophets
Samuel Logan Brengle

The devil accuses us of sin. The Holy Spirit condemns us for sin.

Helps to Holiness
Samuel Logan Brengle

The great hindrance in the hearts of God's children to the power of the Holy Ghost is inbred sin — that dark, defiant, evil something within that struggles for the mastery of the soul, and will not submit to be meek and lowly, patient, forbearing and holy, as was Jesus; and when the Holy Spirit comes, His first work is to sweep away that something, that carnal principle, and make free and clean all the channels of the soul.

When the Holy Ghost is Come
Samuel Logan Brengle

The most startling thing about sin is its power to enslave. Jesus said, "Whosoever committeth sin is the servant of sin", and everyday life and experience prove the saying to be true. Let a boy or a man tell a lie and he is henceforth the servant of falsehood unless freed by a higher power. Let the bank clerk misappropriate funds, let the business man yield to a trick in trade, let the young man surrender to the clamor of lust, let the youth take an intoxicating glass, and henceforth he is a slave. The cord that holds him may be light and silken, and he may boast himself free, but he deceives himself; he is no longer free; he is a bondsman.

Heart Talks on Holiness
Samuel Logan Brengle

We may choose the path in life we will take; the course of conduct; the friends with whom we will associate; the habits we will form, whether good or bad. But, having chosen the ways of sin, we are then swept without further choice with a swiftness and certainty down to hell, just as a man who chooses to go on board a ship is surely taken to the destined harbor, however much he may wish to go elsewhere. We choose and then we are chosen. We grasp and then we are grasped by a power stronger than ourselves — like the man who takes hold of the poles of an electric

battery; he grasps, but he cannot let go at his will.

Heart Talks on Holiness
Samuel Logan Brengle

While sin lasts, misery lasts.

Love-Slaves
Samuel Logan Brengle

"The people will think I have done something terrible," is the natural retort of the unregenerate soul. "But you have," is the reply, "You have thrown the goodness of God back in His face. You have misused the body or the talents or the opportunities God has given. You have been thoroughly selfish and have given no time or thought to helping others."

The Mercy Seat
William Burrows

Still in the way of my choosing,
Still heav'nly guidance refusing,
Friendships I deemed were enduring
Failed me when greatest my need of a friend,
Treasures seemed dross as I gained them,
Pleasures lost charm as I drained them,
Satan the while still alluring me on
That way which in darkness must end.

C. Collier
Gems for Songsters #2

An experience of continually sinning and repenting is no more normal spiritually than a life of falling ill and getting well again is normal physically.

The Splendour of Holiness
Frederick Coutts

Sin lies in the will, not in the instincts.

The Call to Holiness
Frederick Coutts

The concept of the "unpardonable sin" is not a single word or act, but an established attitude of mind and way of life. How can God do anything for men who deliberately and persistently falsify spiritual facts by calling evil one of those things that makes a man a man, and if he willfully corrupts and destroys this part of his nature he robs himself of his eternal hope.

The Armoury Commentary — The Four Gospels
Frederick Coutts, Edit.

There are no sinful things, only sinful people. Adverse circumstances are not sinful in themselves, but possibly provide an easier excuse for sinful hearts to reveal themselves.

The Armoury Commentary — The Four Gospels
Frederick Coutts, Edit.

The capacity for holiness is the same as the ability to sin and it is literally true that it is a man's desire for the highest that, misdirected, can lead him to the lowest depths of human shame.

Reason to Believe
Harry Dean

The sin of man in its totality has introduced elements of chaos and evil into the whole of life and, seeing life is run on a family basis, all men everywhere share in the disastrous results of human depravity.

Reason to Believe
Harry Dean

Sin is both wickedness and weakness; from its wickedness we are separated by the blood of the dying Christ, for its weakness we have the strength of the risen Christ.

Studies in Sanctification
Edward Read

Sin is horrid; chuck it up!

The History of The Salvation Army — Volume 2
Robert Sandall

As he did with Adam and Eve, Satan likes nothing better than to make us believe that what we are doing is in our best interests, whether or not God is served. However, after he has convinced us to eat of the forbidden fruit, he will inevitably crawl off, leaving us exposed in our own weakness.

A Sense of God
Peter W. Stine

Whether sheltered in an elegant mansion or exposed in a shabby slum, sin is the same foul spiritual disease whose inward corruption eventually breaks out in revolting sores for all to see and smell.

To the Point
Bramwell Tripp

Social Work

When a cab horse falls upon the street,
   No matter who's to blame,
If carelessly he missed his feet,
   They lift him just the same.
The sunken of our fallen race,
   A tenth is not a few,
We'll lift them up in every case,
   When the General's dream comes true.

Early Salvation Army Song
Combat Songs of The Salvation Army
Sallie Chesham, Edit.

Social services...a league of what is best in the world to fight what is worst.

Bramwell Booth
The History of The Salvatin Army — Volume 6
Frederick Coutts

Here is one of the foundation principles of our social work. From the beginning we have said openly that our love and labor are for all. It is not necessary to have a good character to secure our compassion and help. We do not make it a condition of being blessed and comforted that a man should belong to a union or go to church or join The Salvation Army. We make, so far as we can, our sun, like our Father's, to shine on what are called the "undeserving", the "worthless" poor as well as on the others; and our rain to descend on the bad and idle, as well as on the good and industrious.

Bramwell Booth
Trumpets of the Lord
Catherine Bramwell-Booth

We shall make but little further progress until it has been recognized that the lapse in morals is a moral lapse and can only be really rectified therefore by moral influences. You can no more heal a moral disorder by physical remedies than you can cure smallpox by reciting the Ten Commandments! Shutting people up in institutions, giving them employment there, forcing them into religious services, will of themselves never restore what has been lost. Nor can you, by such means, induce in them that all-important factor — without which no efforts for their deliverance can be of any permanent value — the desire and the will to be delivered.

Florence Booth
Maiden Tribute
Madge Unsworth

I must assert in the most unqualified way that it is primarily and mainly for the sake of saving the soul that I seek the salvation of the body.

The Darkest England and The Way Out
William Booth

I must assert unhesitatingly that anything which dehumanizes the individual, anything which treats a man as if he were only a number of a series or a cog in a wheel, without any regard to the character, the aspirations, the temptations, and the idiosyncrasies of the man, must utterly fail as a remedial agency.

In Darkest England and The Way Out
William Booth

I propose to go straight for these sinking classes, and in doing so shall continue to aim at the heart. If we help the man it is in order that we may change him.

In Darkest England and The Way Out
William Booth

It is no doubt better than nothing to take the individual and feed him from day to day, to bandage up his wounds and heal his diseases; but you may go on doing that forever, if you do not do more than that; and the worst of it is that all authorities agree that if you only do that you will probably increase the evil with which you are attempting to deal, and that you had better let the whole thing alone.

In Darkest England and The Way Out
William Booth

It isn't wicked to be reduced to rags. It is not a sin to starve, to pawn the few sticks of furniture to buy fuel and pay the rent. It is a misfortune that comes to people, honest and good people, in hard times, or when work is hard to get. It is such people that the social scheme means to help.

William Booth
The General Next to God
Richard Collier

Legislation may do much to counteract the mischief, but the spread of religious feeling will do more. The true Christian is a real self-helper. In bringing the truth of religion before the suffering masses we are also assisting in the great work of social reform. When we have taught people to be religious, half the battle has been won.

William Booth
The History of The Salvation Army — Volume 1
Robert Sandall

No one gets a blessing if they have cold feet, and nobody ever got saved while they had a toothache.

William Booth
The History of The Salvation Army — Volume 1
Robert Sandall

Our social operations are the natural outcome of Salvationism, or I might say, of Christianity as instituted, described, proclaimed, and exemplified in the life, teaching, and sacrifice of Christ. Social work, in the spirit and practice which it has assumed with us, has harmonized with my own personal idea of true religon from the hour I promised obedience to the command of God.

William Booth
The History of The Salvation Army — Volume 3
Robert Sandall

Social service is only the expression of life which abides in the soul and forces into activity the desire to take religion upon one's self the burdens of humanity. It is only when we get more soul into our lives that we are able to do any good. All the social activity of the Army is the outcome of the spiritual life of its members. All social service must be based on the spiritual, or it will amount to little in the end.

William Booth
The History of The Salvation Army — Volume 3
Robert Sandall

Take a man, hungry and cold, who does not know where his next meal is coming from; nay, who thinks it problematical whether it will come at all. We know his thoughts will be taken up entirely with the bread he needs for his body. What he wants is a dinner. The interests of his soul must wait.

In Darkest England and The Way Out
William Booth

1. The first essential in every program is that it must change the person.
2. The services to be effectual must change the circumstances of the individual when they are the cause of the problem.
3. Any solution worthy of consideration must be on a scale commensurate with the problem with which it proposes to deal. (It is no use trying to bail out the ocean with a pint pot.)
4. Not only must the program be large enough, it must be permanent.
5. While the program must be permanent it must also be immediately practicable.
6. The indirect features of the program must not be such as to produce injury to the persons who seek to benefit.
7. While assisting one class of the community, the program must not seriously interfere with the interests of another..

William Booth
Stuff That Makes An Army
William G. Harris

The first essential that must be borne in mind as governing every scheme that may be put forward is that it must change the man when it is his character and conduct which constitutes the reasons for his failure in the battle of life.

In Darkest England and The Way Out
William Booth

The Salvation Army stands for hope; that, when every other light is extinguished, and every other star has gone down, this one gleam shines steadily and clearly out in the darkened sky: "If I could only get The Salvation Army, they will do something for me."

International Congress Addresses — 1904
William Booth

Any scheme of Social Salvation is not worth discussion if it is not as wide as the scheme of Eternal Salvation set forth in the gospel.

In Darkest England and The Way Out
William Booth

Why all this apparatus of temples and meeting houses to save men from perdition in a world which is to come, while never a helping hand is stretched out to save them from the inferno of their present life?

In Darkest England and The Way Out
William Booth

But what is the use of preaching the gospel to men whose whole attention is concentrated upon a mad, desperate struggle to keep themselves alive? You might as well give a tract to a shipwrecked sailor who is battling the surf which has drowned his comrades and threatens to drown him. He will not listen to you. Nay, he cannot hear you any more than a man whose head is under water can listen to a sermon. The first thing to do is to get him at least a footing on firm ground and to give him room to live. Then you may have a chance. At present you have none. And you will have all the better opportunity to find a way to his heart, if he comes to know that it was you who pulled him out of the horrible pit and the miry clay in which he was sinking to perdition.

George Carpenter
Social Evils the Army Has Challenged
S. Carvosso Gauntlett

If we ourselves, for want of a better way of speaking, refer to our evangelical work and also our social work it is not that these are two distinct entities which could operate one without the other. They are but two activities of the one and the same salvation which is concerned with the total redemption of man. Both rely upon the same divine grace. Both are inspired by the same motive. Both have the same end in mind. And as the Gospel has joined them together we do not propose to put them asunder.

Frederick Coutts
God's Army
Cyril Barnes

Since social work philosophy basically believes in the sanctity of the individual personality, with a common goal to help each person served to become a happier and more useful person, why should not the Army's ideal of the marriage of its happy religion with its useful social work be approved and more widely adopted by social workers everywhere?

Ruth Pagan
Stuff That Makes An Army
William G. Harris

Social work of The Salvation Army kind can be accomplished only by the type of individual who is produced by its evangelical work. Through continuous new consecrations, through the growth of spiritual perception, through an ever-widening compassion, she (or he) becomes qualified for the cure of souls.

Maiden Tribute
Madge Unsworth

We sallied forth on a crusade of house-to-house visitation, Bible in one hand and welfare order book in the other, for the Army had established a central welfare fund to help the city's destitute. We knew both books had to be together, for they represented evangelism as the Army knew it.

A Burning in My Bones
Clarence Wiseman

Sorrow

Grief needs to be expressed. Too firm a control of feelings can lead to difficulties later on.

Orders and Regulations for Officers

In grieving there are often four fairly clearly defined states: numbness, pining, depression and recovery.

Orders and Regulations for Officers

The Christian does not sorrow without hope, but he does sorrow.

Orders and Regulations for Officers

The pain of grief is part of life; it is the price we pay for love.

Orders and Regulations for Officers

Once we realize that sorrow, though not a gift from God, is an experience we can offer Him, He will purify our emotions, causing darkness with Him to be brighter than light without Him.

Reflections
Catherine Baird

Sorrow is sanctified, not by silence alone, but by service.

Woman
Evangeline Booth

When sorrow's hazy path I tread,
    When I am tried by sore affliction,
When darkest shadows round me spread,
    Then I have full conviction
That all I do, and all I say,
    Is pleasing to my Savior;
And soon my sorrows melt away
    Beneath His love and favor.

Herbert H. Booth
Salvation Army Song Book

The heart must be bruised and by sorrow infused,
    'Ere the soul will its blossoms release.
To bring joy to others fear not to mourn,
    There are riches in loss for others borne.

Poems
Evangline Booth

There is no waste in the crucible of suffering to the children of God. Sorrow never walks at our side with aimless feet.

Heart Messages
Emma Booth-Tucker

202

While some smile, others weep; perhaps not openly, yet the tears are none the less bitter because hidden, and the anguish none the less bitter because unrevealed. Sorrow never tires, never sleeps, never dies. It is always there, and its shadows seem the gloomier from the brilliant contrast presented by the light and glow of Christmas cheer.

Heart Messages
Emma Booth-Tucker

It is often the case that heaven's choicest gifts are wrapped up in our darkest troubles. Indeed, sorrow is frequently God's ambassador — the chosen herald of some special blessing. At the moment we may be disappointed with the mournful appearance and melancholy uniform of the messenger. We may be tempted even to close our hearts against his entrance, and to reject the message that he bears. We had pictured to ourselves the dazzling brilliance of an archangel, and behold the funereal robes and solemn linaments of woe! It is long, perhaps, before we discover that he is in very truth an angel, but an angel in disguise. We unfold with trembling, hesitating hand the scroll of destiny. But our tears and sighs are at length changed to songs of joy when we decipher in every word and line the assurances of a Father's love.

Life of Catherine Booth — Volume 1
Frederick Booth-Tucker

Perhaps none but the hand of grief can cause those heart chords to vibrate which produce the tender harmonies so captivating to the human ear, and which doubtless find their echo in the divine heart!

Life of Catherine Booth — Volume 1
Frederick Booth-Tucker

Those who possess the highest joys are open to the keenest sorrows.

Life of Catherine Booth — Volume 2
Frederick Booth-Tucker

Great grief is like a furnace — it either refines or destroys; like a mighty wind, it either tears up by the roots the faith of years, or sweeping over it, leaves it strengthened and established.

Messages to the Messengers
Catherine Bramwell-Booth

If now you turn your eyes on yourself, on your loss, on your own broken hopes, you will walk in the shadow, and every other way will seem brighter than yours; every other beast's burden less heavy than your own. But if you turn your eyes away from yourself to God, you will walk in the light, leaving the shadow behind all the way, and seeing, with eyes that ears have made keen, the shadows that fall across some one else's way, and the burden that is breaking another heart.

Messages to the Messengers
Catherine Bramwell-Booth

Oh! The pain of sorrow!
It robs hope of tomorrow.

Fighting for the King
Catherine Bramwell-Booth

Your spirit must not dwell in the darkness of the grave, but in the light of heaven.

Messages to the Messengers
Catherine Bramwell-Booth

I have seen His face in blessing
When my eyes were dimmed with tears;
I have felt His hand caressing
When my heart was torn by fears,
When the shadows gathered o'er me,
And the gloom fell deep as night,
In the darkness just before me,
There were tokens of His light.

I have stepped in waves of sorrow
Till my soul was covered o'er,
I have dreaded oft the morrow,
And the path which lay before,
But when sinking in my sadness
I have felt His helping hand,
And ere the day dawn came His gladness,
With the courage to withstand.

William McAlonan
Gems for Songsters #1

203

The grief of others had invaded my heart;
Their pangs at death's door
Made a knot in my stomach
Which could not be dismissed
With some philosophical jargon.

God's Whisper in My Heart
Shirley Pavey

A man is poor indeed whose only inheritance from yesterday is a legacy of regret.

A Sense of God
Peter W. Stine

Soul-Winner/ Soul-Winning

Without personal dedication to soul-winning no one can be a good Salvationist.

The Salvation Army — Its Origin and Development

The only consolation for a Salvationist on his dying bed is to feel he has been a soul-winner.

Catherine Booth
Life of Catherine Booth — Volume 2
Frederick Booth-Tucker

I think I can say that from the day of my conversion to God I have never read a biography, heard an address, or attended a meeting, without asking myself the question: "Is there anything here from which I can learn how better to fulfill my own mission in enforcing the claims of my Lord; and saving the souls of men?"

William Booth
How to Preach
Charles Talmadge

If you cannot go to the rescue one way, go another.

Salvation Soldiery
William Booth

Some men's ambition is art,
Some men's ambition is fame,
Some men's ambition is gold,
My ambition is the souls of men.

William Booth
The General Next to God
Richard Collier

We must have more men and women for the business whose hearts God has touched, whose tongues the Holy Ghost has fired, and whose lives are consecrated to the highest possible ends to which our being, human or divine, can be offered up — the helping of Christ to save the world.

The General's Letters
William Booth

"If I thought I could win one more soul to the Lord by walking on my head and playing the tambourine with my toes, I'd learn how."

William Booth
The History of The Salvation Army — Volume 4
Arch Wiggins

How many a heart, waiting often not for the light of convincing truth, not for the rains of God's preparing warnings, not for the thunders of His pent up wrath, not for the long sowing of patient love, but rather for the harvest scythe of a pointed word, of a kind entreaty, of a drawing into the garner, and the sheaf of wheat would fall at our feet, and the Kingdom of Heaven would be richer and a soul would be won!

Heart Messages
Emma Booth-Tucker

We have no hobbies — at least, not that we are aware of — unless it be a hobby to want to save the largest possible number of souls with the highest possible salvation in the quickest space of time by the best imaginable methods. That is the bullseye of our target — the end for which we exist — the sum and substance of our mission.

Frederick Booth-Tucker
The Officer — 1893

People are worth saving from their wretched surroundings; from themselves; above all, from their sins.

Messages to the Messengers
Catherine Bramwell-Booth

The more ignorant, the more halting, the more weak, the more sinful they are, the more surely will you know that you are sent to them — to them, the sinners (they may be soldiers as well), not to the righteous. The soldiers at P---- were all righteous! You are sent to the lost, not the found; to the weak, not the strong; sent to gather them into the Kingdom — the lame, the halt, and the blind.

You are indeed sent to these people with the gossipings, deceptions, superstitions and backslidings. Their sins call for your holiness; their weakness for your strength; their coldness of heart for your love and zeal. All these claim you. The people's need cries out in unmistakable accents. I know your heart cries out, too: "Who is sufficient for these things?"

Messages to the Messengers
Catherine Bramwell-Booth

But standing here in spirit on Mount Calvary, we see and feel that to be like Him we must spend ourselves as unreservedly in His cause as the worlding is spent in the cause of self; that we must toil for Him as the miser toils for himself; sacrifice for Him as the explorer does for science.

Heart Messages
Emma Booth-Tucker

As certainly as like begets like, so certainly will the soul-winner put the mark of his own spirit and consecration on the people he influences; and if he is himself not more than half won to the cause of his lowly Master, he is not likely to do more than half win others. The soul-winner is dealing with fundamentals. His object is to change not merely opinions and conduct, but the characters; to work a moral revolution in the affections, dispositions, the wills of men; to turn them from temporal things which they see, to eternal things which they do not see; from all vices to all virtues; from utter selfishness to utter self-sacrifice, and that often in spite of ever present self-interest, and that often is spite of ever present self-interest, and in the face of the combined opposition of the world, the flesh and the devil.

The Soul-Winner's Secret
Samuel Logan Brengle

He that is anxious about his dinner, and eager to get to bed at a reasonable hour, or concerned about his salary, or over solicitious about his health, or querulous about his reputation and the respectability and financial condition of his appointment, or is afraid of weariness and painfulness, and headache is not a great soul-winner.

The Soul-Winner's Secret
Samuel Logan Brengle

If we would put first things first, we must be ready at any moment to lay aside our books, our music, our studies, our business, our own pleasure and profit, to save souls.

Ancient Prophets
Samuel Logan Brengle

Someone, no longer trying to save himself or to advance his own interests, dies to self, to the world, to the praise of men, to the ambition for promotion, for place, for power, and lives unto Christ, lives to save men. Then the awakening of sinners comes.

Ancient Prophets
Samuel Logan Brengle

The soul-winner must not despise the day of small things.

Ancient Prophets
Samuel Logan Brengle

There are many who are interested in the cause of Christ, and who are pleased to see it prosper in their corps, their church, their city, their country. But there are but few who bear the burden of the world upon their souls day and night, who make His cause in every clime their very own, and who, like Eli, would die if the ark of God were taken; who feel it an awful shame and a consuming sorrow, if victory is not continually won in His name.

Heart Talks on Holiness
Samuel Logan Brengle

So the worker for souls may read ten thousand books, may be able to quote poetry by the yard, may be acquainted with all the facts of science and history, and may even be a profound theologian, but unless he be a diligent student of the

Bible, he will not permanently succeed as a soul-winner.

The Soul-Winner's Secret
Samuel Logan Brengle

To save a soul is better than to command an army, to win a battle, to rule an empire or to sit upon a throne.

The Way of Holiness
Samuel Logan Brengle

While harshness and severity will only harden the wanderer from God on the one hand, a gospel of gush will fill him with indifference or contempt on the other. The soul-winner then, must not have the hardness and brittleness of brass or cast iron, not the malleability of wrought iron or putty; but rather the strength and flexibility of finest steel that will blend, but never break; that will yield, and retain its own form.

The Soul-Winner's Secret
Samuel Logan Brengle

The penitent form worker is like a doctor; he must make a right diagnosis to be able to point out the cure which God waits to effect.

The Mercy Seat
William Burrows

Where a more restrained atmosphere obtains, there is sometimes a deplorable lack of persistence in a prayer meeting. The spirit of expectation is absent, for often it is assumed that those present are already converted and living a life of victory. But we are presumptuous if we assume that souls will be saved without labor.

The Mercy Seat
William Burrows

Oh, what a wretchedness exists in the world around
Caused by sin in every form, woe and pain abound;
Wanted, men and women who will stop the dread decline;
Savior, what we all want is a love like Thine.

W.H. Howard
Gems for Songsters #2

I am willing — even at sunset — to abandon preaching, as such, if any man can show me a better way to get souls saved.

The House of My Pilgrimage
Albert Orsborn

The life of a soul saver is the grandest, merriest, strangest life that can be lived on earth — the life of Jesus lived over again in us. It will cost you all, but it will be a good bargain at that!

George Scott Railton
G.S.R.
John D. Waldron, Edit.

It is significant that Christian character and compassion thrive most vigorously in the lives of those who seek to lead others to the Lord.

A Burning in My Bones
Clarence Wiseman

Sovereign

God retains His power over man as a sovereign, not by coercing his will, but by rewarding or punishing according to the use he makes of his freedom — according to his *willing* and *acting*.

Life and Death
Catherine Booth

His idea of God's sovereignty is that it asserts itself in legislating how man ought to act and in punishing him for disobedience, and not in divesting him of his freedom in order to prevent disobedience.

Life and Death
Catherine Booth

Spouse Abuse

Jim Jones had a brute of a temper,
    It caused lots of trouble and strife,
When someone downtown would not please him,
    He'd go home and thrash his poor wife.
But the Mrs. is now very happy,
    And the kiddies shout, "Hip, hip, hooray!"
For instead of his wife, now he's beating
    The drum in the Army today.

Combat Songs of The Salvation Army
Sallie Chesham, Edit.

206

I came to feel that was part of the mission of my life, one of the objects of my being, to make some one little woman happy; while to injure a woman, to mar her life and blast her happiness seemed to me the supremest cursedness and treason against the most sacred rights and claims of humanity.

Ancient Prophets
Samuel Logan Brengle

Statistics

The Salvation Army has a vital interest in religious statistics, in a way both practical and broad; it is concerned to know how many saints and how many sinners there are in any given area of town or country, with a view to converting the latter into the former as speedily as possible, and it keeps in mind always, as a stimulus to hastened effort, the growing population in those states which we Christians call hell and heaven.

The Army Drum
Elizabeth Swift Brengle

Statistical measurements of a work that can't be measured, a numerical evaluation of work beyond human values.

Marching to Glory
Edward McKinley

Stewardship

As stewards of God each soldier of a corps must feel individual responsibility for financing the work. Each corps is expected to be self-supporting to the highest possible degree as well as raising money for the work in general.

Chosen to be a Soldier

Each member shall contribute, when convenient, not less than one penny per week, and sixpence per quarter, and as much more as he or she can afford towards the support of the preachers employed by the Mission. Those meeting in class shall give their weekly offering to the leader at the close of each meeting; but those who do not attend the weekly believer's meeting shall be provided with collecting boxes in

which they shall store their weekly offerings, and such offerings shall be collected quarterly.

Christian Mission Pledge
The History of The Salvation Army — Volume 1
Robert Sandall

It is incumbent upon all Salvationists to give, as they are able, for the support of the salvation war. This giving is both a duty and a privilege. Ony the sacrificial giving of Salvationists allows us the right to seek the monetary aid of the public in financing the Army's work. Every Salvationist should understand and accept the principle of stewardship.

Orders and Regulations for Officers

Search your heart and then your pocket;
  In them both you're sure to find
Ammunition for the fight
  We are waging for the right.
Oh, there's power when purse and heart are both combined.

Combat Songs of The Salvation Army
Sallie Chesham, Edit.

The possessions of a consecrated Salvationist all belong to God in the sense that they are available for use as God wishes; this means that the Salvationist provides for his own needs economically, in order that he may give liberally to God's work.

Orders and Regulations for Officers

We will contribute according to our ability offerings to assist the Society in its operations.

Christian Mission Pledge
The History of The Salvation Army — Volume 1

Who can estimate how many beautiful blossoms are blighted, how many noble natures spoiled, by being abandoned to a ceaseless association with unsuitable or careless inferiors? In what a multiplicity of cases are the lambs left to the hireling, while the one whom God intended to play the part of the shepherd is busying himself with a thousand trivialities such as will matter little enough when his stands with his flock to give an account of his stewardship before the Throne!

Life of Catherine Booth — Volume 1
Frederick Booth-Tucker

Checks on the Bank of Futurity I account gladly enough as a free gift, but I can hardly be expected to take them as if they were current coin, or to try to cash them at the bank.

In Darkest England and The Way Out
William Booth

How far is it right or moral, how far is it Christian, for one who professes to love his Savior and is a member of His Blood-bought Church, and who may up to a point recognize the pressure of Christ's call and command to carry the Gospel to all the world, to withhold God's part of His money — the holy tithe — from God?

Soldier of Salvation
Wilfred Kitching

There are three kinds of givers represented by the flint, the sponge and the honeycomb. It takes a blow of steel to get anything out of the flint, and then it gives only a vicious snap. It takes a squeeze to get anything from a sponge, then it gives only that which it has absorbed. The honeycomb is but a cover for sweetness, and with only a tiny puncture it yields its sweetness.

The Christian and His Money
Edward Laity

True worship springs from the heart and flows through the pocketbook.

The Christian and His Money
Edward Laity

We say to a congregation, "You cannot spend ten minutes in a public-house or music hall without paying dearly for it; and we are sure, if you like to come here, you will also like to help us meet the expenses."

Heathen England
George Scott Railton

Strength

Faint not, thou gallant warrior,
When the black fumes of grim discouragement
Would suffocate the hope within the breast,
Look up! See where the gathering clouds
Are pierced by burning radiance — His Cross —
The Great High Priest touched with the feeling
Of our poor infirmities.

Reflections
Catherine Baird

The cross that He gave may be heavy,
But it ne'er outweighs His grace;
The storm that I feared may surround me,
But it ne'er excludes His face.
The thorns in my path are not sharper
Than composed His crown for me;
The cup which I drink not more bitter
Than He drank in Gethsemane.

Ballington Booth
Gems for Songsters #1

I bring to Thee my heart to fill;
    I feel how weak I am but still
    To Thee for help I call.
In joy or grief, to live or die,
For earth or heaven, this is my cry,
    Be Thou my all in all.
I've little strength to call my own,
And what I've done before Thy throne,
    I here confess, is small.
But on Thy strength, O God, I lean,
And through the Blood that makes me clean,
    Thou art my all in all.

Herbert Booth
Salvation Army Song Book

It is better to be strengthened to bear the burden than to be spared the burden. It is better to be succored in the fight than to be shielded from the fight.

Samuel Logan Brengle
At the Center of the Circle
John D. Waldron, Edit.

His life should speak — that goes without saying. But it cannot tell the whole truth because Christ is always greater than the best any can achieve.

Reason to Believe
Harry Dean

I do not ask Thee, Lord,
    That all my life may be
An easy, smooth and pleasant path;
    'Twould not be good for me
But O I ask today
    That grace and strength be given
To keep me fighting all the way
    That leads to God and heaven!

Fannie Jolliffe
Salvation Army Song Book

Success

Soldier — where courage lives,
there also lurks defeat,
Whene'er defeat, a chance to rise
again!

Poems
Catherine Baird

Whatever your seeming success may be today, your success in God's eyes is determined by the degree of your likeness to Himself.

Likeness to God
Florence Booth

And, Salvation Army cadet, if you bring the giants down, and keep on bringing them down, God and men will believe in you; and neither God nor man will believe in you if you don't.

Salvation Soldiery
William Booth

Comrades, whatever other gifts you have, if you are to succeed, you must have hearts and minds that can feel.

Salvation Soldiery
William Booth

Uttermost success implies first, uttermost consecration, which grows and changes and grapples with each new cross as it presents itself, and then it implies uttermost faith, which stretches out its hands to grasp and appropriate every new gift and grace that its eye discovers.

Frederick Booth-Tucker
The Officer — 1893

Real success is giving the achievement of noble ends priority over the enjoyment of present pleasures.

The Armoury Commentary — The Four Gospels
Frederick Coutts, Edit.

To be a good loser is often less demanding than being a good winner.

The Armoury Commentary — The Four Gospels
Frederick Coutts, Edit.

Suffering

Everyone has seen a mother suffer in grateful silence, both bodily pain and heart anguish, in her child's stead preferring that the child should never know. Suppose it should turn out, hereafter, that many of the afflictions which now seem so perplexing and so grievous have really been given us to bear in order to spare and shield our loved ones and make it easier for them — tossing on the stormy waters — to reach Home at last?

Bramwell Booth
Trumpets of the Lord
Catherine Bramwell-Booth

Pitiful followers of Him should we be, if we wished to have only joy when He had only suffering.

Bramwell Booth
Trumpets of the Lord
Catherine Bramwell-Booth

God's way to exaltation is through the Valley of humiliation.

Aggressive Christianity
Catherine Booth

Suffering is the only ladder long enough to lift us from our low levels on earth to thrones in heaven.

Love is All
Evangeline Booth

The power of the first witnesses to Jesus lay in what they suffered for Him.

Friendship With Jesus
Florence Booth

Going meant suffering to Christ; it meant this to the Apostles. They went to the world; this meant going to scorn, poverty, stripes, imprisonment, death — cruel death. If you go you will have to suffer; there is no other way of going. One of the most common delusions is that people studiously avoid the suffering, pick and choose the sort of work which is agreeable to them, persuade themselves they are "called" to that specially, and then reckon they are going to the world. Suffering and saving are terms of almost the same significance in the Christian's career. If he suffers for Christ he saves, and if he saves he suffers. These men suffered for Christ, and saved with a vengeance. If they had dodged the suffering they would never have saved at all.

The General's Letters
William Booth

Many of the real injuries we are called upon to suffer are made by our imaginations to appear far more serious than they really are. Molehills are magnified by gloomy imaginations until they appear next door to crucifixions.

The Founder's Messages to Soldiers
William Booth

A wilderness with Jesus cannot be lost time; and in the fruits and flowers of the Canaan experiences which are following on, we shall fully recognize the value of the sowing days of suffering.

Heart Messages
Emma Booth-Tucker

We could not give you back your earthly treasures but sorrow's seed, planted in sanctified soil, brings greater things than those — things immortal, things more powerful, things more lasting, things more consoling, things eternal, things triumphant; yes, they are born out of the seed which is dying, yielding an ever more abundant harvest!

Heart Messages
Emma Booth-Tucker

Do not make the mistake of wanting to choose how you shall suffer!

Messages to the Messengers
Catherine Bramwell-Booth

His greatest servants have often been the greatest sufferers. They have gathered up in themselves and endured all the pains and woes, sorrows and agonies, fierce and cruel martyrdom of humanity, and so have been able to minister to all its vast and pitiful needs, and comfort its voiceless sorrow.

Samuel Logan Brengle
Peace Like a River
Sallie Chesham

I have found it so, and so will you. It is like taming a colt. It saves much pain when it gets full grown to have been broken young. Our afflictions are our yoke. They are God's way of training us.

Samuel Logan Brengle
Peace Like a River
Sallie Chesham

Storm succeeds sunshine, and darkness the light; pain follows hard on the heels of pleasure, while sorrow peers over the shoulder of joy; gladness and grief, rest and toil, peace and war, intermittently intermingled, follow each other in ceaseless succession in this world. We cannot escape suffering while in this body.

When the Holy Ghost is Come
Samuel Logan Brengle

Weeping becomes wonder.

Excursions in Thought
Jean Brown

No great thing has ever been done without suffering. The Salvation Army is not wrong in taking for its device the words "Blood and Fire": revolutionists for God and for purity must be ready to go through blood and fire.

Josephine Butler
Maiden Tribute
Madge Unsworth

The cynic is often a man who has made the wrong reaction to suffering, who has projected his own darkness outwards so that life itself is hateful and all goodness "too good to be true".

The Armoury Commentary — The Four Gospels
Frederick Coutts, Edit.

This world is blighted, and suffering is one of the bitter consequences of its waywardness.

Power and Glory
Harry Dean

I do not ask Thee, Lord,
   That tears may never flow,
Or that the world may always smile
   Upon me as I go.
From Thee fell drops of blood;
   A thorn-crown pressed Thy brow;
Thy suffering brought Thee victory then,
And Thou canst help me now.

Fannie Jolliffe
Salvation Army Song Book

In many lives I have seen the exhibition of patience in suffering to be a greater miracle than the power of healing, knowing that the sick have not taken their lot as a meaningless stroke of fate, but as a God given occasion to share in the vast fellowship of human suffering.

A Goodly Heritage
Wilfred Kitching

Let us remember that we are called not to comfort, but to a cross; not to security, but to suffering; not to immediate triumph, but, maybe, to tribulation.

Soldier of Salvation
Wilfred Kitching

At times 'tis hard for flesh and blood,
To say: Thy will be done, my God;
But if my grief means others' gain,
O what to me are loss and pain!

W. Elwin Oliphant
Salvation Army Song Book

Jesus was silent on the subject of His pain, teaching us how to consummate the value and beatuy of one's consecration by the overwhelming power of love stronger than death. All the charm of our self surrender seems to disappear when the pain and sorrow of our sacrifice cause us undue concern. Let it be ours henceforth, O Lord, not only to share Thy dying, but also Thy silent dignity.

The Silences of Christ
Albert Orsborn

Let cowards seek an easy way
And win the praise of men;
Cross bearing, dying day by day,
Is still the conquering plan.

George Scott Railton
Gems for Songsters #1

It is an honor that my husband has been wounded for the cause of Jesus Christ.

Kiye Yamamuro
The General Next to God
Richard Collier

Suicide

Can anything be done to prevent the suicidal tide from rising? That is the practical question. And it seems to me that we must supply the friendless, the dazed, bewildered creatures with a guide, the momentarily maddened slaves of folly with thoughts and homes that will steady them, and above all lead them to the arms of Him who is still saying, "Come unto Me, all ye that labor and are heavy laden, and I will give you rest."

William Booth
The History of The Salvation Army — Volume 3
Robert Sandall

And youngsters in their teens, ignoring all life's joys,
Die by their own hands! Their lovely bodies left like broken toys
Upon life's refuse heap.
Dear children, choosing at life's dawn, death's night, thus reap

The harvest of their unbelief
For all who love them multiplying grief!

Fighting for the King
Catherine Bramwell-Booth

Supernatural

A religion robbed of the supernatural element is an insipid thing.

Out of the Depths
Clarence W. Hall

Surrender

God requires me to abandon all I can, as a condition of salvation, and then, when He saves me, He will give me power to abandon all that I could not before.

Aggressive Christianity
Catherine Booth

It is not the quality of the instrument you place in the hands of God which determines its usefulness; it is the full surrender you make of it; it is not the quality of the agent, but it is God's having the full disposal, the undisputed sway, in using Him.

Life and Death
Catherine Booth

We want people who can go through with things, no matter who, or what, comes in the way, who can literally offer up the love of father and mother, and houses and land, and sea, aye! and life itself, who can put all on the altar, and stay and see it burn to ashes, if it comes between them and duty.

Salvation Soldiery
William Booth

Before we can be filled we must be emptied. Before we can have the "life more abundant" we must die to sin.

Ancient Prophets
Samuel Logan Brengle

No great work has ever been accomplished without utter abandonment to it.

The Soul-Winner's Secret
Samuel Logan Brengle

WE MUST DIE! We feel that we must live, must live for the sake of some, for the people of God whom we love as our own souls, and for the perishing sinners about us. We are prone to magnify our own importance, to think no one's faith is so mighty, no one's industry is quite so fruitful, no one's love quite so unfailing, no one's presence quite so necessary as ours. But after we die the blessed God will still live. His years fail not, and He will bless our sons and carry on His work. Glory to God!

Heart Talks on Holiness
Samuel Logan Brengle

God's service demands costly self-giving. Virtue goes from us whenever we give ourselves to people; and anything less than the giving of ourselves, as distinct from the giving of our service, is camouflaged selfishness, perhaps self-protection. Christ was not play acting when He agonized at Gethsemane; and really to follow Him is to serve at similar personal cost.

The Armoury Commentary — The Four Gospels
Frederick Coutts, Edit.

The coming of His reign we are to pray, "Thy Kingdom come". Often it must mean "my kingdom go".

The Armoury Commentary — The Four Gospels
Frederick Coutts, Edit.

The first word in the Christian vocabulary is not struggle — but surrender; not one more try — but yield to the divine will; not one more effort and this time you will make it — but to submit to one another.

The Splendour of Holiness
Frederick Coutts

Submit to the hand of the Divine Potter, become as clay in His hands, and out of the ugliness and distortion of the past He will make for Himself a vessel of honor.

Search the Scriptures
Robert Hoggard

Much has been written about "living life at its best". This appeal for a full surrender of ourselves to Jesus Christ brings us not only into the sphere of high thinking, but of high living.

Fuel for Sacred Flame
T. Henry Howard

Have it Your own way, Lord.
You've won!
I lay my weapons down.
You would not give me blow for blow,
no steel met mine.
And yet I am as vanquished.

From My Tresure Chest
Flora Larsson

Lord, let me share that grace of Thine
    Wherewith Thou didst sustain
The burden of the fruitful vine,
The gift of buried grain.
Who dies with Thee, O Word divine,
    Shall rise and live again.

Albert Orsborn
Salvation Army Song Book

Men made in the likeness of God, even in his fallen state may, with ill reverence, still find in his own gratification some indication of what must be the "delight" of the Lord when men and women, humble or of high degree, so yield themselves to Him that they of their own free will issue of His plans for mankind of His Fatherhood and love.

The History of The Salvation Army — Volume 2
Robert Sandall

Accomplishment can come only by surrender; true liberation comes by submission.

A Sense of God
Peter W. Stine

Now is my will resigned,
    Struggles are quelled;
Clay on the wheel am I,
    Nothing withheld.
Master, I yield to Thee
Crumble, then fashion me,
Flawless and fit to be
    Indwelt by Thee.

Leslie Taylor-Hunt
Salvation Army Song Book

How couldst Thou smile on me if, in my heart,
I was unwilling from treasures to part?
Since my redemption cost Thee such a price,
Utmost surrender alone will suffice.

Ruth Tracy
Salvation Army Song Book

213

Talent

No matter how great your talent, He won't practice your violin for you, and He will seldom even purchase it.

Peace Like a River
Sallie Chesham

Talent, unaided by exacting toil, does not carry one far.

Out of the Depths
Clarence W. Hall

Tears

How many compassionate tears does this perishing world get from you?

The Founder's Messages to Soldiers
William Booth

One tear will often do more to unlock the hardest heart than a bushel full of arguments.

Frederick Booth-Tucker
The Officer — 1893

Such are the strange contradictions of spiritual life, that tears have a place in our highest happiness.

Messages to the Messengers
Catherine Bramwell-Booth

And though no more they're visible
Tears keep me clean —
Inside.

Walking with the Wind
Sallie Chesham

Tears can be a signature of awe,
A miracle in the raw
The stuff of courage, not self-pity;
Signifying an aria,
Not a woeful ditty.

Walking with the Wind
Sallie Chesham

The sun won't always shine,
Sometimes the rain clouds form,
And from the clearest sky
May fall a thunderstorm;
The unexpected stress
Awakens sleeping fears,
And faith must find its way
Through mist of bitter tears.

Glory
John Gowans

Let's be hurt by the hunting of others. Let's shun anything and everything that might stain our holy Movement, except the stain of a tear.

Marching On!
Ted Palmer

Temptation

The words "in all points" go to the root of the matter, for all temptation is basically a conflict between God's will and self-will. All men are thus tempted though not of necessity by the same form of enticement. The nature of temptation will vary with the nature and circumstances of the one who is tempted. But the root choice which Jesus had to make was between the pressure of His own desires and the will of God for Him. In this He is one with us.

Handbook of Doctrine

Fresh from the creative genius of God and created in the image and likeness of God, Adam was tempted. Retaining the divinity of the Godhead, but clothed with the vulnerable humanity of mankind, Jesus was tempted "in all points" like as we ever may be. And this immediately after His anointing with the Holy Spirit. The most holy of God's children face temptation. It is the constant evidence that Satan never gives

215

up his desire and effort to reclaim those who were once his.

The Holy Spirit — Friend and Counsellor
Milton S. Agnew

As the storm and whirlwind, which twist the roots and toughen the fibers of an oak, also help in its growth and development; as occasional struggle with furious hurricanes and wild waves is a part of the discipline of a sailor; as bloody battles and fierce danger are a portion of the soldier"s lot; as difficult problems and hard lessons enter into the training of a student, so temptation is a part of our lot as moral beings in this state of probation.

Resurrection Life and Power
Samuel Logan Brengle

Infirmities and temptations are incorporated by our Heavenly Father into His educational and disciplinary plans for us, and are overruled for our highest good and widest usefulness; we need not expect to be entirely free from them while we are in the body. If we were free from them we could not enter into the fellowship of Jesus, nor sympathise with our brethren, and that would be an immeasurable loss to us.

Heart Talks on Holiness
Samuel Logan Brengle

It is no sin to be tempted. It is sinful to yield.

Ancient Prophets
Samuel Logan Brengle

For the richer a man's personality, the more there is of him to be tempted. We need not be surprised — as occasionally we are — at the collapse of some outstanding figure. The wonder is that such occurrences are as rare as they are. The lone climber on the exposed mountain ridge feels the fury of the gale of which the pedestrian, content to plod placidly along in the valley below, is ignorant.

In Good Company
Frederick Coutts

Immunity from temptation is nowhere promised.

The Call to Holiness
Frederick Coutts

Many of us know little of Satan's real power because we yield so easily. He has no need to exert himself unduly. We fall so quickly for so little. Only he who resists steadfast in the faith knows how powerful can be the tempter's pull.

The Call to Holiness
Frederick Coutts

The subtlest temptations come, not at the allurement of what is wrong in itself, but as an inclination to us of what is good in itself for wrong purposes, or to try to get things which God intends us to have by methods that He cannot bless.

The Armoury Commentary — The Four Gospels
Frederick Coutts, Edit.

We are betrayed by what we are, and never more swiftly is a man totally undone than by that which is his strength.

The Call to Holiness
Frederick Coutts

Curiosity has been the parent of many a subtle temptation.

Out of the Depths
Clarence W. Hall

No outside temptation or pressure makes a Christian do the things of which he is ashamed; it is a saboteur within.

Studies in Sanctification
Edward Read

Three temptations usually assail the Christian; the temptation to recline, the temptation to shine and the temptation to whine.

Meditations for the Ordinary Man
George B. Smith

We are each tempted along the line of our powers and personalities.

Meditations for the Ordinary Man
George B. Smith

216

He saw the dangers of modern Gomorrah, but could not resist the temptation of pitching his own tent in the midst of the flame.

A Sense of God
Peter W. Stine

Thanksgiving

As lilies of the valley pour forth perfume, so good hearts pour forth thanksgiving. No mercy is too small to provoke it, no trial too severe to restrain it. As Samson got honey from the carcass of the lion he slew, and as Moses got water from the flinty rock, so the pure in heart are possessed of a sort of heavenly alchemy, a divine secret by which they get blessings out of all things, and for which there is giving of thanks.

Heart Talks on Holiness
Samuel Logan Brengle

Theology

Knowledge without God is like a man learned in all the great mysteries of light and heat who has never seen the sun. He may understand perfectly the laws which govern them, the results which follow them, the secrets which control their action on each other — all that is possible, and yet he will be in the dark.

Bramwell Booth
Trumpets of the Lord
Catherine Bramwell-Booth

Sound doctrine will of itself never save a soul. A man may believe every word of faith of a churchman or a Salvationist and yet be as ignorant of any real experience of religion as an infidel or an idolator. And it is this merely intellectual or sentimental holding of the truth about God and Christ, about holiness and heaven, which makes the ungodly mass look upon Christianity as nothing more than an opinion or a trade; something with which they have no concern.

Bramwell Booth
Trumpets of the Lord
Catherine Bramwell-Booth

No man can have the heart, even if he had the head, to preach the gospel fully, faithfully and constantly unless he has the experience.

When the Holy Ghost is Come
Samuel Logan Brengle

There is a sense in which every thoughtful, studious, prayerful Christian becomes his own theologian; works out, under the leading of the Holy Spirit, his own theology, and discovers what he believes to be the true doctrines of the Bible. He may accept the teachings or doctrines of his parents and religious leaders, and hold them intellectually but his theology is really limited to those articles of faith which vitalize his life, guide and inspire his conduct, mold his spirit, comfort and guard his heart, purify his nature, and kindle his hope of the future.

Resurrection Life and Power
Samuel Logan Brengle

In theology we are not so much enquiring about God, as confronted by Him. Strictly speaking, God should only be enquired from. He is never object, always subject.

Reason to Believe
Harry Dean

We cannot measure spiritual force by rules of philosophy or definitions of theology any more than by a carpenter's rule or chemist scales. It is "with the heart man believeth unto righteousness". And yet, the character of a man's thoughts has much to do with success or failure in the spiritual life. He is influenced by what he thinks.

Fuel for Sacred Flame
T. Henry Howard

Unfortunately, not all Christians display a commendable humility in their approach to the greatest reality of all — God. Listening to them one gets the distinct impression that God has been caught in their net, analyzed at the laboratory, classified and annotated finally and for all time. If you ask them about God and His ways they produce a large volume and then proceed to spell it all out in amazing detail. It would seem that God has been captured between the covers of a book, and has been neatly reduced to a string of propostions.

Doctrine Without Tears
John Larsson

Time

Time is so precious that, unless it can be spent in sleeping or working, every minute of it is begrudged, and my feeling whenever I seat myself in a tram — be the journey long or short — is, "Now, engine driver, do your best, and fly away!"

The General's Letters
William Booth

God who heals the brokenhearted can also bridge the broken past.

Heart Messages
Emma Booth-Tucker

The devil's purpose is to rob us of now.

Messages to the Messengers
Catherine Bramwell-Booth

The past was mine, the future may be mine, and the present is mine.

Messages to the Messengers
Catherine Bramwell-Booth

Diamonds and gold nuggets are not so precious as minutes.

The Soul-Winer's Secret
Samuel Logan Brengle

What? So soon? Another year? It seems impossible that a year could have passed so swiftly, and yet the return of this day assures me that once more the earth has run her wondrous race through the lanes of light, and vast voids of space, and deep abyss of the night, amid the silent pomp and splendor of starstrewn heavens, completing another of her ceaseless cycles around the sun, ending another year and bringing me to this day.

Resurrection Life and Power
Samuel Logan Brengle

Due appreciation of the value of time lies back of the proper use of opportunity.

Stewards of God
Edward J. Higgins

We carefully hoard our coins of base metal and we throw away our golden hours.

From My Treasure Chest
Flora Larsson

Yesterday is an old garment, Lord,
  creased, stained and threadbare.
Help me to throw it off,
  casting it into the coffers of the past,
  done with, laid aside and forgotten.

Let me not walk in my yesterdays;
  not live again the used-up hours,
  regretting the misspent moments,
  brooding over the rebuffs,
  fingering the tattered glory-rags,
  clutching them close to my eager breast.

Just a Moment, Lord
Flora Larsson

And dost Thou ask a gift from me;
  The gift of passing time?
My hours I'll give, not grudgingly,
  I feel by right they're Thine.

Richard Slater
Salvation Army Song Book

I could open a rosebud, Lord, but I would spoil the flower; I can move the hands of the clock but I can't change the time.

Dear God
Virginia Talmadge

Tobacco

The Salvation Army, as a branch of the Christian Church, and as a recognized community agency, concerning itself with the development of the spiritual life, the enrichment of social and cultural interests and the safeguarding of the health of those it serves, historically has discouraged the use of tobacco in any form.

Recognizing the body to be the temple of God which must not be defiled (I Corinthians 3:16, 17), The Salvation Army requires total abstinence from tobacco on the part of its soldiers and officers.

Salvationists encourage the dissemination of authoritative and reliable medical research reports on the health hazards associated with the use of tobacco.

Commissioners' Conference — United States of America
March, 1965; Revised October, 1976

There's people who love their terbacker,
    Who never will purity see
Till they lay down their pipe and their
    snuff box
And holy and sanctified be.
There'll be no spittoons up in Glory,
    The air ne'er with smoke will be blue.
There only the pure ever enter;
    How can you expect to get through?

Combat Songs of The Salvation Army
Sallie Chesham, Edit.

Tongues

All the great prayers in the Bible were clearly spoken and recorded in a known language. Neither "tongues" nor "other languages" are even mentioned in the prayer life of David, Ezekiel, Isaiah — upon all of whom the Spirit came in power. Nor do we find it in the prayers of Jesus, of John, of Elizabeth and Mary, of Zacharias and Anna — all of whom were "filled with the Holy Spirit." The mighty, moving prayers of Paul are recorded in the language of the day. Then through the centuries great men of the church, filled with the Holy Spirit, men of impressive prayer life, have not been known for ecstatic utterances, but for simple prayer petitions. Must the pattern change now?

The Holy Spirit — Friend and Counsellor
Milton S. Agnew

This is exactly what God's people must emphasize — not tongues but cleansing, not charisma, but sanctification, not gifts but evangelism.

The Holy Spirit — Friend and Counsellor
Milton S. Agnew

A man may be longing after the "gift of tongues" and neglecting the tongue he already has; thinking how much good he could do if he could suddenly speak the German language, while all the time he is comparatively neglecting the use of English, which he can speak.

The General's Letters
William Booth

If you have not had the gift of tongues in the miraculous fashion I have described, you certainly have had the gift of that Tongue of tongues which speaks the language of the heart, the Tongue which not only speaks out of the heart of the speaker, but right into the heart of the listener; and verily, verily, is the Tongue of Fire.

Visions
William Booth

Trials

Darkly hangs the threatening gloom
O'er my trembling soul
No voice cheers me midst the breaker's
roll,
Tis my soul's Gethsemane
Tis my darkest hour, Savior, help,
For I trust in Thy great power.

Gems for Songsters #2

Difficulties are the stones out of which God's house are built.

The Officer — 1917

Within the thicket of difficulty blossoms the rose of love.

The Officer — 1918

Tribulation is God's molding chisel.

More Than Conquerors
Milton S. Agnew

This world is not a place of rewards, but of trials.

Bramwell Booth
Trumpets of the Lord
Catherine Bramwell-Booth

You ask me did I ever feel so? Yes, I think, just as bad as any mortal could feel — empty inside and out, as though I had nothing human or divine to aid me, as if all hell were let loose upon me! But I have generally felt that worst before the best results, which proves it was satanic opposition.

Catherine Booth
Mrs. Booth
W.T. Stead

There will always be winds — when on your knees, in lectures or meetings, while visiting people to take your mind off what you are doing, but don't go with the wind. People become weak by never going against anything.

Evangeline Booth
The General Was a Lady
Margaret Troutt

If all were easy, if all were bright,
Where would the cross be, and where the fight?
But in the hardness, God gives to you
Chances of proving that you are true.

Lucy Booth-Hellberg
Salvation Army Song Book

The unexpected trial is often, I believe, the call to greater things; and if, instead of being alarmed, we were more ready to respond, we should find the new demand had led us into an altogether different conception of our own strength and knowledge, as well as having given us another token of how much God can do.

Messages to the Messengers
Catherine Bramwell-Booth

The trial of the sinner, manifesting his wickedness, becomes the commencement of his punishment. The trial of the saint reveals his character to all the world, proves that he is genuine, and measures the "how much" of his love to God and Man.

Life of Catherine Booth – Volume 2
Frederick Booth-Tucker

It is not God's purpose to take us to heaven on flowery beds of ease, clothe us in purple and fine linen, and keep a sugar plum in our mouths all the time. That would not develop strength of character, nor cultivate simplicity and purity of heart; nor in that case could we really know Jesus, and the fellowship of His sufferings. It is in the furnace of fire, the lion's den, and the dungeon cell that He most freely reveals Himself to His people.

Heart Talks to Holiness
Samuel Logan Brengle

It is the work of the Holy Spirit to guide the people of God through the uncertainties and dangers and duties of this life to their home in heaven.

When the Holy Ghost is Come
Samuel Logan Brengle

Manifold trials call for manifold grace; manifold grace works for us manifold experience; manifold experience gives us a manifold testimony, enabling us to meet manifold needs.

Samuel Logan Brengle
Portrait of a Prophet
Clarence W. Hall

Sooner or later the heavenly vision comes to all men. It comes in the whisperings of conscience, in the strivings of the Spirit, in the calls of duty, in the moments of regret for an evil past, in moments of tenderness and sorrow, in the crises of life, in the entreaties of God's people. It comes in the afflictions and losses, in the thunders of the law, the death of loved ones, in crushed hopes, disappointed plans and thawed ambitions.

Heart Talks on Holiness
Samuel Logan Brengle

There is no possible evil that may befall us from which God cannot deliver us.

The Way Of Holiness
Samuel Logan Brengle

If human fatherhood at its best thinks first of its children's character, not their comfort, we should not be surprised if God our Father refuses to listen to our cries for exemption from the trials of life.

The Armoury Commentary – The Four Gospels
Frederick Coutts, Edit.

People who normally appear to be much the same are often seen to be utterly different when facing unexpected trials; the storms of life reveal the values by which they have lived and in which they have trusted.

The Armoury Commentary – The Four Gospels
Frederick Coutts, Edit.

No matter how difficult, diabolical or disastrous the trials and troubles that beset the path of a Christian, they can never outreach the gracious hand of our Heavenly Father.

Search the Scriptures
Robert Hoggard

I have seen His face in blessing
When my eyes were dimmed with tears;
I have felt His hand caressing
When my heart was torn by fears.
When the shadows gathered o'er me,
And the gloom fell deep as night,
In the darkness just before me
There were tokens of His light.

William Mc Alonan
Salvation Army Song Book

Having Jesus with you does not mean
A journey without storm;
But when your last resources have all failed,
When before the howling storm gust you have quailed,
One word from Him and, lo, the storm will cease,
The tempest in the soul will yield to peace.

Memoirs of Peter
Arthur Pitcher

Jesus' holiness did not exempt Him from trial; rather, it put Him on the battlefield.

Studies in Sanctification
Edward Read

What a blessed moment it is when, with a fragment of God-given insight, we can discern precious jewels or value gleaming in what we had previously seen only as intimidating obstacles to our happiness.

A Sense of God
Peter W. Stine

Trinity

We believe that there are three persons in the Godhead – the Father, the Son and the Holy Ghost – undivided in essence and co-equal in power and glory.

Salvation Army Doctrine #3

I heard of a theologian who asked a missionary laboring among the so-called primitive people if he had taught them the doctrine of the Trinity. "I can't teach them about the Trinity until they learn to count to three."

A Burning in My Bones
Clarence Wiseman

Trust

Take the final leap into the arms of a crucified Savior.

Aggressive Christianity
Catherine Booth

Trust makes you the heir of every promise. Unbelief destroys your claim to any.

Catherine Booth
Life of Catherine Booth – Volume 2
Frederick Booth-Tucker

Where they could not trace, they trusted; where they could not feel, they believed; where they could not see, faith lent them sight.

Love is All
Evangeline Booth

No tempest can my courage shake,
My love for Thee no pain can take,
No fear my heart appall;
And where I cannot see, I'll trust,
For then I know Thou surely must
Be still my all in all.

Herbert H. Booth
Salvation Army Song Book

Beginning as I did, so to speak, with a sheet of clean paper, wedded to no plan, and willing to take a leaf out of anybody's book that semed to be worth adopting, and, above all, to obey the direction of God the Holy Spirit, I have gone on from step to step.

William Booth
The History of The Salvation Army – Volume 1
Robert Sandall

Jesus' holiness did not exempt Him from trial; rather, it put Him on the battlefield.

Studies in Sanctification
Edward Read

Do not take yourself out of love's way; but trust the wisdom and the power of the Father to change the course of the stars before He allows a sanctified soul to be in the wrong place.

Messages to the Messengers
Catherine Bramwell-Booth

For your heart, as for mine, the question is not do I understand God, but do I trust Him? Not do I agree with God, but do I obey Him? Not do I see God, but do I love Him?

Messages to the Messengers
Catherine Bramwell-Booth

God would rather let the stars drop out of the firmament than fail you.

Heart Messages
Emma Booth-Tucker

But though worlds, like drunken men, tumble from their orbits, and though the universe crash into ruin, the childlike confidence of the man who trusts God will enable Him to sing with the Psalmist, "God is our refuge and strength, a very present help in trouble. Therefore, will not we fear, and though the earth be removed, and though the mountains be carried into the midst of the sea; though the mountains shake with the swelling thereof."

Heart Talks on Holiness
Samuel Logan Brengle

Trust is not a state of lazy indifference, but of the highest activity of heart and will.

The Way of Holiness
Samuel Logan Brengle

We are never sure of self, but quietly, unwaveringly, sure of our Redeemer and Lord.

Ancient Prophets
Samuel Logan Brengle

Trustful and watchful: these are typically Christian attitudes. The believer knows that Christ will ultimately weave all the tangled threads of his life and of human history into a satisfying design.

The Armoury Commentary – The Four Gospels
Frederick Coutts, Edit.

How wonderful it is to walk with God
Along the road that holy men have trod;
How wonderful it is to hear Him say:
Fear not, have faith, 'tis I who lead the way!

Theodore H. Kitching
Salvation Army Song Book

Though thunders roll and darkened be the sky,
I'll trust in Thee!
Though joys may fade and prospects droop and die,
I'll trust in Thee!
No light may shine upon life's rugged way,
Sufficient is Thy grace from day to day.

John Lawley
Salvation Army Song Book

I was feeling my way upward and forward in that high and wide country of the soul, where there are no main roads and few beaten tracks, but only the footprints of earnest seekers, learning how to dwell "in the secret place of the Most High God."

The House of My Pilgrimage
Albert Orsborn

Next to working for God with a pure motive, the most important thing seems to be to leave our work in God's hands, without anxiety.

The Silences of Christ
Albert Orsborn

Sanctify Thy name, O Lord,
By Thy people here,
For the altar or the sword
Save us from our fear!
When the battle rages fast
Help us in the fiery blast
Let us not be overcast,
Prove Thy greater things.

The Beauty of Jesus
Albert Orsborn

The ability to cope ought to be a peculiarly Christian strength; a Christian recognizes that there is a pattern in the tapestry, the hand of God is indeed present in what seems to be a muddle, and His light is in the midst of the darkness.

A Sense of God
Peter W. Stine

Truth

That truth which is most uncommon will be most useful.

William Booth
How to Preach
Charles Talmadge

Love the true. Walk, act, speak, think the truth. Despise the lie wherever you find it, however well disguised, however advantageous the point at which it promises to bring you out; short cuts to a desired end which necessitate a deviation from the way of truth involve you in unknown dangers; and, even if they were safe, they degrade the soul that travels them.

Messages to the Messengers
Catherine Bramwell-Booth

We increase our grasp upon the truth as we share it with others.

The Armoury Commentary – The Four Gospels
Frederick Coutts, Edit.

Such vital principles as truth and righteousness can never change. What is truth today will be truth in a hundred years to come. What is pure today will be pure then. The things that are impure will ever remain impure. There may be transitions in human thought but those have to do with man; the great principles of religion have to do with God, and He is the same yesterday, today, and forever.

Stewards of God
Edward J. Higgins

And when I do wrong, something tells me it is wrong. I know downright well there is falsehood and there is truth, there is justice and there is injustice, there is ugliness and there is beauty.

A Burning in My Bones
Clarence Wiseman

Tyranny

You cannot make disciples using totalitarian methods.

Reason to Believe
Harry Dean

U

Unemployment

The workless man is the whole social problem in the concrete. He is the coming pauper; he is the potential criminal; he is the would-be suicide. And more than this he is the scion of a miserable house. He and his children after him even to the third generation will under existing conditions eat the bread which has been earned by the sweat of somebody else's brow, and he will die twenty years before he ought to die, leaving behind a legacy of misery and shame in the children who will follow his example, and do their part to impoverish the world they might have done something to enrich and improve.

Work in Darkest England
Bramwell Booth

Uniform

The uniform of The Salvation Army is not intended to isolate its wearer from other people, but is rather the dress of "a servant of all." It does not imply a rebuke to sinners, but rather a loving greeting from the Heavenly Father. It is no claim to superiority and no attempt to proclaim Salvationism as a condition of salvation, but is a testimony about the grace of God in Christ.

Chosen to be a Soldier

The clerk at his desk, the hawker with his barrow, the washerwoman over the tub, the child at school, the statesman at the council chamber – each may be an overcomer and wear the white garment here and now. The man burdened with unemployment, the one desperately beset with temptation which he is manfully resisting, the woman bereft of all earthly comfort and joy, can this very day, and

every day, walk in white and have sweet council from Him. Uniform wearing, because we love Jesus and desire to bear witness for Him, is one way of letting our light shine.

The Army Uniform
Florence Booth

The soldier who is only willing to wear uniform when at the meetings, and in the presence of Salvationists, is as much an anomaly as would be a military soldier only willing to wear uniform when on parade.

The Army Uniform
Florence Booth

The uniform was not designed merely to secure outward uniformity. The uniform, like every other distinguishable mark of The Salvation Army, was designed to be an expression of our great soul-saving purpose. Our uniform was introduced so that the man in the street should know the Salvationist, so that the Salvationist, wherever he went, should be labeled as set apart for Jesus, marked as one eager to pray with and to help others.

Friendship With Jesus
Florence Booth

Never allow yourself in any place where you could not go in uniform because the uniform would reproach you for being there.

Messages to the Messengers
Catherine Bramwell-Booth

I would like to wear a suit that would let everyone know I meant war to the teeth and salvation for the world.

Elijah Cadman
The History of The Salvation Army – Volume 2
Robert Sandall

Our uniforms count for more than a millionaire's millions.

Holland French
The General Next to God
Richard Collier

The bonnet has become a world symbol of service for Christ under the Army flag. It has outlived both scorn and caricature. In early days it was spat upon, smothered with bad eggs, and dented with stones hurled by savage antagonists of the movement. But it has triumphantly recuperated from every attack.

My Best Men Are Women
Flora Larsson

A person who wore an Army uniform had to believe in heaven; he could be promoted to Glory at any time.

Marching On!
Ted Palmer

I looked upon this question as most important in settling who should belong to the expedition, for I felt sure no woman would consent to wear such a uniform unless it was her single aim to seek the salvation of souls.

George Scott Railton
The History of The Salvation Army — Volume 2
Robert Sandall

A thousand diligent and skillful artificers of headgear for women have devised a thousand new fashions in the last fifty years. But the only type that lasts is the bonnet of the Hallelujah Lass. Although never worn by more than a small minority of the population, it is one of the few fixed elements in the kaleidoscope of hats, bonnets, and other headdresses. The worse we may think of the Salvation bonnets, the more we must respect the force wielded by the woman who, by her will, can make that particular headgear at once familiar and constant in every continent.

Mrs. Booth
W. T. Stead

Unity

Faith in Him depended on the brotherly love and unity of His disciples. So it did, and so it does to this day. When there is unity, there is faith. Where there is division there is doubt.

Samuel Logan Brengle
At the Center of the Circle
John D. Waldron, Edit.

The religion of Jesus is social. It is inclusive, not exclusive. We can have the glory only as we are united. We must be one in spirit with our brethren. Let division come and the glory departs. Let the unity of brotherly love continue, and the glory abides.

Samuel Logan Brengle
At the Center of the Circle
John D. Waldron, Edit.

Few things make a mockery of Christianity more than disunity among believers.

The Armoury Commentary — The Four Gospels
Frederick Coutts, Edit.

Just as the oneness of a piece of mineral or vegetable life is surpassed by the oneness of animal life, which in turn is surpassed by the richer oneness of human life, so that in turn is transcended by the unimaginable richness of Him whom we call Father, Son and Holy Spirit.

In Good Company
Frederick Coutts

"Unity" forms the red line of Calvary love.

Evangeline Booth
The General Was a Lady
Margaret Troutt

Urban Life

Our troubles in large towns arise chiefly from the fact that the massing of the population has caused the physical bulk of society to outgrow its intelligence. It is as if a human being had suddenly developed fresh limbs which were not connected by any nervous system with the gray matter of his brain.

In Darkest England and The Way Out
William Booth

V

Victory

Now to be more than conqueror is not merely to put down the enemy, but to rise to higher heights upon his prostrate form. To be more than conqueror not only to withstand the blows of the weapons in the enemy's hand, but to seize these same weapons and use them in an aggressive attack upon the enemy.

More Than Conquerors
Milton S. Agnew

But I see laurels resting there,
More lovely than the crown I wear,
For he has learned to love with kingly grace
To triumph though he did win the race.

Reflections
Catherine Baird

Victory for you will mean victory for others.

Bramwell Booth
Friendship With Jesus
Florence Booth

No retreating, hell defeating,
Shoulder to shoulder we stand;
God, look down, with glory crown
Our conquering band.
Victory for me
Through the Blood of Christ, my Savior;
Victory for me
Through the precious Blood.

Herbert H. Booth
Salvation Army Song Book

Sometimes there stirs in you a spirit that magnifies every sense of strength of which you are conscious. The actual burdens and sorrows of life's little day are only as the dust under your feet. Your spirit rises to another atmosphere. Faith joins you to the infinite powers of Everlasting God. You are not of the dust returning to dust, but of the immortal looking for a new heaven and a new earth; and finding, in the dear earth of the present, daily opportunity for triumphing over every degrading and selfish impulse. Consciously strong, you step forth almost eagerly: no sin shall soil your soul, no sorrow break your spirit, no hope deferred to make your heart sick. You triumph in temptation, and rejoice in sacrifice, with a joy that cannot be explained.

Messages to the Messengers
Catherine Bramwell-Booth

He took hold of one end of the promise, and the devil got hold of the other end, and they pulled and fought for the victory.

Helps to Holiness
Samuel Logan Brengle

The spirit of Jesus is the spirit of conquest.

Ancient Prophets
Samuel Logan Brengle

I am convinced that where there has been unbroken trust there has been final victory. It has not always seemed to be victory, judged by human standards, but the individual has had the inward sense of conquest; "I have overcome the world."

All the Days
George Carpenter

So may we
Huddled in our little hells,
Do more than dream of wholeness;
We may stroke
The hem of heaven –
And win release.

Sallie Chesham
It's Beautiful
Dorothy Breen, Edit.

227

Victory always comes where a man, having poured out his heart in prayer, dares to trust God and express his faith in praise.

Helps to Holiness
Samuel Logan Brengle

In our aim for holy living we are not promised immunity from temptation, God having provided some better victory by His grace.

The Call to Holiness
Frederick Coutts

The victories of holiness can be won in our factories and kitchens and back streets. Indeed, that is where they must be won if an unbelieving generation is to be persuaded of the truth of this Christian doctrine.

The Call to Holiness
Frederick Coutts

Jesus lives to keep me –
O what wondrous love!
In the Father's presence,
Advocate above;
Keeps me when sin's tempests blow;
This one thing I know!

Sidney Cox
Salvation Army Song Book

Confronted with the Lord of life, man had made a show of power, but what is eternal cannot be blasted out of existence, and God cannot be defeated by man.

Power and Glory
Harry Dean

His victory over death, and in history, His lesser victories in our lives, are pledges of a greater victory yet to be.

Power and Glory
Harry Dean

We are assured that the final word always is with God and not with evil.

Power and Glory
Harry Dean

In the end, Christ prevails over Antichrist, the church over the world, Jerusalem over Babylon, the angels of God over the angels of satan, deity over the dragon, light over darkness and holiness over sin.

Search The Scriptures
Robert Hoggard

When first, as His follower, I saw the world mock, defy, abuse, scorn, bargain away, condemn and crucify my Lord, my nature cried out, "Smite, Lord! For Thy glory's sake, lest the world should read weakness in Thy surrender, smite the smiters!" But no. He dies. Down into the gulf He goes alone, followed by the curses of His enemies and the doubts and disappointed love of His friends. Is meekness, then, the conqueror, not might? Yes, assuredly; the Lamb will finally triumph over the beast.

The Silences of Christ
Albert Orsborn

To worldly pomp make Thou my vision blind,
From thoughts of self, dear Lord, release my mind;
Break ev'ry tie which still to earth would bind,
Then set my spirit free
That it may strive for Thee –
Victoriously.

Kaare Westergaard
The Merchant of Heaven

Virgin Birth

The doctrine of the virgin birth does not imply that there is anything inferior about the normal process of human birth. Nor is it, in itself, the foundation of our belief in the Incarnation. This doctrine affirms that the coming of Christ was at God's initiative.

The Armoury Commentary – The Four Gospels
Frederick Coutts, Edit.

The virgin birth of Christ did not trouble the early church. They could do no other than reason that such a sinless life, such a sacrificial death and such a triumphant resurrection required such a supernatural beginning.

Search the Scriptures
Robert Hoggard

Visitation

Visitation means personal contact with people in their own homes – or other places where they are to be found – with a view to furthering their spiritual interests.

Orders and Regulations for Officers

I esteem the work of house to house visitation as next in importance to the preaching of the Gospel itself...This is the work which most needs doing of any work in the vineyard. There are teeming thousands who never cross the threshold of church, chapel or mission hall, to whom all connected with religion is as an old song, a byword, and a reproach. They need to be brought into contact with a living Christ in the characters and persons of His people. They want to see and handle the Word of life in a living form. Christianity must come to them embodied in men and women, who are not ashamed "to eat with publicans and sinners"; they must see it looking through their eyes, and speaking in loving accents through their tongues, sympathizing with their sorrows, bearing their burdens, reproving their sins, instructing their ignorance, inspiring their hope, and wooing them to a fountain opened for sin and uncleanness.

Catherine Booth
Friendship With Jesus
Florence Booth

He has many advantages in visiting. First, they know as he is a busy man, and nobody expects that he can stop to hear small talk, and so they never think of offering it to him; and then, second, they know he is after their souls, and they expect that he will go for them as soon as the first words are out of his lips. This makes it easy for him to talk religion, and they all expect, if there's a chance at all, that he'll want to pray; and that makes it seem the right thing for him to get on his knees, and to be off again as soon as he gets up.

Sergeant-Major Do-Your-Best
William Booth

I cannot tell exactly how it is, but I know that no men are so beloved as those who visit; and a call, a few loving words and an earnest prayer, will be remembered for some time to come.

Salvation Soldiery
William Booth

Better, therefore, to go and fetch a convert to the meeting, even if you do less well in your talk, than to prepare the most careful address and not have him there to hear it.

Messages to the Messengers
Catherine Bramwell-Booth

The quicker you turn up the greater effect your visit is likely to have either on the convert or on his relations.

Messages to the Messengers
Catherine Bramwell-Booth

I succeeded in the work. Did it by visiting mainly; that's when you get at the hearts of the people.

The Army Drum
Elizabeth Swift Brengle

Avoid all occasions for gossip. When you visit, enquire about their souls, about their children, about their health, then read a promise, pray and go on. Never stay in a house more than 10 or 15 minutes. Don't appear to be rushing but say what you have to say and be gone. Many officers spoil their visitation by staying too long.

Samuel Logan Brengle
Peace Like a River
Sallie Chesham

When you visit, always mark a promise in their Bible before you leave and tell them to meditate upon it. Get the young people to the meeting and mark promises for them. Teach them to pray also.

Peace Like a River
Sallie Chesham

VISITATION

Don't fail to visit among the poor too, and let them know you are there to minister and bless them. They are the people who need you and that you can make into soldiers.

Samuel Logan Brengle
Peace Like a River
Sallie Chesham

The War Cry

War Cry, War Cry, come and buy a War Cry,
Very cheap, five cents each – won't you
come and buy?
War Cry, War Cry, come and buy a War Cry!
News of our salvation war – Oh, come and
buy!

Early Salvation Army Song
Combat Songs of The Salvastion Army
Sallie Chesham, Edit.

I say they will have a copy of "The War Cry"
up there, in the celestrial language, and I
shall read it to Abraham, Noah, David, Job
and Paul, and to the angels, and I shall
make them listen to the stories, if they
don't know them all, and we shall have an
extra song!

Catherine Booth
Life of Catherine Booth – Volume 2
Frederick Booth-Tucker

There must be no outside advertisements.
Salvation is not to be made a stalking
horse for traders to trot out their money-
making schemes upon.

The History of The Salvation Army – Volume 2
Robert Sandall

Are you feeling sad and blue,
Sure that no one cares for you?
Well, here's something you can do –
Sell the War Cry!
'Twill your drooping spirits cheer,
As you journey far and near,
Brighten up the pathway drear,
With The War Cry.

Angel Lane
Combat Songs of The Salvation Army

Warfare, Earthly

Many young Salvationists have served, and
are serving, with distinction in the armed
forces (some as chaplains), and The Salvation Army has always sought to bring them
a ministry of help and guidance. We owe
an equal ministry to others who, by reason
of conscience, are opposed to military service. We respect the right of every individual to arrive at his own decision in this
matter, based on his Christian conscience.
We teach respect for properly constituted
civil authority and loyalty to our "nation
under God." Therefore, we counsel those
of our constituents who object to military
service to take advantage of the legal
means provided for alternate service. We
join with fellow Christians around the
world in praying that all men may learn to
live together in the love and power of the
Lord Jesus Christ, which takes away the occasion for war and strife.

Commissioners' Conference – United States of America
April, 1971

The Salvationist will regard war as an evil
and will condemn the use of force as a
means of settling differences between nations.

Chosen to be a Soldier

The war is hideous – a fierce and hellish
tragedy. The earth is red with blood and
the sky dark with the wrath of God. War-
like preparations and wicked ambitions,
whenever they have been found together
in the history of the world, have always
produced abominable consequences.
War violates almost every rule God has
laid down.

Bramwell Booth
The Officer's Review – 1933

But against all this, modern Christianity which professes to believe the teaching of Him who taught us not to resist evil, but to love our enemies, and to treat with the utmost benevolence hostile nations, has nothing to say. All the devilish animosity, hardhearted cruelty, and horrendous consequences of modern warfare are not only sanctioned but held up as an indispensible necessity of civilized life, and, in times of war, patronized and prayed for in our churches and chapels, in as much impudent assurance as though Jesus Christ had taught, "But I say unto you, an eye for an eye, a tooth for a tooth, and return evil for evil, hate your enemies and pursue them with all the diabolical appliances of destruction which the devil can enable you to invent."

Catherine Booth
The Officer's Review – 1933

What is the duty of Salvationists at such a crisis? I cannot answer such a question fully now, but I can give a guiding word. One thing is plain – every true soldier of The Salvation Army would cry day and night to God to avert so dreadful a calamity. Let him shut his ears to all the worldly, unscriptural, unchristian talk about war being a necessity. It cannot be a necessity before God that tens of thousands of men should be launched into eternity with all manner of revengeful passionate fellings in their souls, and too often, according to the testimony of these who know all about it, with dreadful blasphemies on their lips. Whatever may be the right method of settling human disputes and preventing earthly calamities, this cannot be the divine plan. This cannot be the will of God.

The General's Letters
William Booth

The wartorn world has plunged into such a raging sea as it has never known before, and mighty nations are tossed like storm-beaten ships on its wild waves. The hearts of men are troubled. The minds of men are perplexed. The faith of men is tried. The patience of men is taxed to the uttermost while the accumulated wealth of the world is thrown with wild haste into the bottomless pit of war, and the young manhood of the world is being swept away in storms of steel and torrents of blood. The eyes of courageous men and weeping women are strained and wearied, trying to peer through the darkness to discover a rift in the black clouds of war. It is a perilous time! The old order changes, yielding place to the new and we are sweeping into an era the character of which no man can forecast, yet which we hope will be more glorious than any former time.

Resurrection Life and Power
Samuel Logan Brengle

Mankind still insists that force is a moral weapon, that "might" can sometimes be "right." Why we will not learn the lessons of history that worldly power and glory is doomed to fail, and that finally only divine love will prevail?

Power and Glory
Harry Dean

Over and over again it is the same teaching – much misunderstood, often ridiculed, rarely believed – that violence makes no worthwhile conquests, and nothing matters save love.

Power and Glory
Harry Dean

Any thoughtful person possessed by deep reverence for the Christian ethic finds it extremely difficult to come to terms with war.

A Burning in My Bones
Clarence Wiseman

That war is wicked is indisputable from the moral and especially the Christian point of view, which finds the problem complicated by its understanding of the irrational and evil forces operating within history. Though these forces will continue to operate until "the kingdoms of this world are become the kingdoms of our Lord," Christians are not absolved from responsibility for doing all possible to reduce the risk of war.

A Burning in My Bones
Clarence Wiseman

Warfare, Spiritual

Light is no more opposed to darkness, nor fire to water, than are the principles and practices of the Army to the principles and practices prevailing among the ungodly. War against the enemies of God naturally supposes that they will, in return, hate and seek to injure, in one form or another, all who are on His side and seeking His interests.

Orders and Regulations for Corps Officers

The Salvation Army is engaged in aggressive warfare against the power of evil. Therefore, to be successful its action must be forceful, vigorous, prompt and decisive.

Orders and Regulations for Officers

The underlying purpose of Salvation Army activities still is to raise up, from the slaves of sin and circumstance, a people of God who shall take their places as soldiers in the fighting line and form part of a great force attacking evil.

The Salvation Army – Its Origin and Development

While activity is impossible without life there can be no strong life, whether bodily or spiritual, without plenty of activity, and there can be no strong salvation without plenty of fighting.

Orders and Regulations for Corps Officers

After the war is over, after the fighting's done,
After the foe is vanquished, after the victory's won,
Every soul you've rescued will be a jewel, a star,
Set in your crown by the Savior, after the war.

Jack Addie
Combat Songs of The Salvation Army
Sallie Chesham, Edit.

The man who is "holy and blameless before Him" is a warrior, combating the powers of darkness and evil in a godless age, but with God-given power, panoply, and prayer.

Transformed Christians
Milton S. Agnew

We're in God's Army and we fight
Wherever wrong is found;
A lowly cot or stately home,
May be our battle ground.
We own no man as enemy,
Sin is our challenged foe;
We follow Jesus, Son of God,
As to the war we go.

Catherine Baird
Salvation Army Song Book

The day of victory's coming, 'tis coming by and by,
When to the Cross of Calvary all nations they will fly;
O comrades in the Army, we'll fight until we die,
For the day of victory's coming by and by.

James C. Bateman
Salvation Army Song Book

Never must we lose sight of the fact that the spirit of attack is one of the distinctive features of The Salvation Army. Was it not, in fact, this that brought the Army into existence? There were already churches and chapels and mission halls. There was probably more religious observance than now, an abundance of preaching, any amount of routine business of what is called Christian service. That which was lacking – that which gave birth to the Army – was desperate unflinching assaults on the strongholds of evil outside.

Trumpets of the Lord
Catherine Bramwell-Booth, Edit.

What are our soldiers for if not to fight? And how can they fight if they never come up with the enemy and force him to stand, and see their leader strike home with the truth? The fact is that some corps – and fine bodies of men and women they are – make little or no impression on the great mass of people in their district, or outside the comparatively small circle of their own people and their families and a fringe of regular hangers-on outdoors and in, just because they do not stand up to the enemy and provoke a proper battle.

Bramwell Booth
Trumpets of the Lord
Catherine Bramwell-Booth

God cannot make heroes except by conflict, anymore than man can. Whoever
heard of a hero who never fought?

Catherine Booth
Life of Catherine Booth – Volume 2
Frederick Booth-Tucker

Be an enemy – a fighting enemy of the
world, the flesh, and the devil. Be an ag-
gressor; carry the war into the enemy's
camp. Be a fighter, a soldier, a man or
woman who has the fire of war against sin
in blood and bone.

Evangeline Booth
The General Was a Lady
Margaret Troutt

Prejudice sometimes tells us, "You never
saw Christ on a wheel." But neither did
you ever hear of Him speaking through a
telephone. The opportunities of today are
wide and God-given, and we should be
blind indeed if we failed to recognize and
seize the greater facilities they give our
holy fight.

Evangeline Booth
The General Was a Lady
Margaret Troutt

Our plan of action has not changed; it is to
lead an army to warfare and victory. If we
hoped to bless and save the people
through the preaching, and visiting, and
personal work of the officer alone, we
should no longer be an Army.

Friendship with Jesus
Florence Booth

The effect was electric! This assault
seemed to dispel my fears. I interpreted it
to mean opposition, and knew that the
devil does not waste his ammunition.

Florence Booth
Maiden Tribute
Madge Unsworth

If we are to conquer we must fight, and
the more fighting we get the better, and,
so far as that goes, the more profitable it
will be, and the more we shall enjoy it if
we are sure our fighting will bring victory.

Salvation Soldiery
William Booth

Let me say – to you who are soldiers of The
Salvation Army – you are embarked in this
war – to you it is the great question of life,
the responsibility for success or failure is
upon you. However interested the civilian
may be in any conflict that happens to be
going on, either at home or abroad, he
feels that the great responsibility of it is
upon the shoulders of the soldiers. It is
they who have to run the risks, and gain
the victories, and wear the medals, and it
is they who have to bear the odium of defeat; just so here, you are the soldiers of
salvation, and the responsibilities of the
war are all upon your head.

Salvation Soldiery
William Booth

Throw yourself into the fight regardless of
anything and everything. Never mind what
sort of a spectacle you make. Give yourself
up to the task, of securing victory, and you
will be very likely to gain it.

William Booth
How to Preach
Charles Talmadge

We are sent to war. We are not sent to
minister to a congregation and be content
if we keep things going. We are sent to
make war — and to stop short of nothing
but the subjugation of the world to the
sway of the Lord Jesus.

William Booth
The Words of William Booth
Cyril Barnes

While women weep as they do now, I'll
fight; while little children go hungry as
they do now, I'll fight; while men go to
prison, in and out, in and out, as they do
now, I'll fight; while there is a drunkard
left, while there is a poor lost girl upon the
streets, while there remains one dark soul
without the light of God, I'll fight – I'll fight
to the very end!

William Booth
The Founder Speaks Again
Cyril Barnes, Edit.

Christians! We are on the battlefield. The
powers of evil are ranged against us in
deadliest array. Humanly speaking, our foe

in invincible, his number is legion; armies of drunkards, millions strong; armies of the fallen, destroyed and destroyers; armies of infidels, daily gaining ground; armies of professors, filled with worldliness; armies of children, cursed from birth; armies of oppressors, heartless and brutal; armies of the oppressed, whose cries pierce heaven; armies with tears in their eyes, wounds in their hearts, but bound to their own interests; armies from every land, of every people, armed to the teeth by every device of Satan; armies of destruction; armies of hell!

Heart Messages
Emma Booth-Tucker

Whether war in the interests of nations be a necessity or not, the great Calvary struggle for the redemption and reclamation of mankind in which we are engaged, is an eternal needs-be.

Heart Messages
Emma Booth-Tucker

It seems only reasonable to suppose that if old ships which have been riddled with the devil's bullets and cannon balls in the past can be so far repaired and rendered watertight as to sail the seas and engage the enemy, still greater will be the success of the brand new men-o-war which are turned out spic and span from the Heavenly dockyards.

Frederick Booth-Tucker
The Officer

Those who are to lead in the fight must be prepared to see their comrades fall, and run as well as the enemy, and must be willing to stand alone, if need be, grasping the standard even in death.

Life of Catherine Booth Volume 2
Frederick Booth-Tucker

And why more war? Because the cry of slaughtered millions rises up louder and louder to heaven, crying to our inmost souls, with irresistible violence, to rise and fight more furiously than ever for the salvation of our fellows from the forces of evil which are dragging them drunken, befouled, degraded, wretched down to an eternity of woe. Because Jesus our King,

the dying Jesus of Calvary, still looks weeping on doomed cities and multitudes wandering without a shepherd and begs us to lay down our lives for them as He laid down His life for us. Because, following in His footsteps, despised, troubled, persecuted, opposed, we have by His continual help tasted victory, seen crowds of captives set at liberty and because we still hear that great voice high above all the noise of many waters bidding us go to overcome the world.

Commissioner Catherine
Catherine Bramwell-Booth

Press on with the duties of the Kingdom; march with songs upon your lips, with patience, and, if the need call, with tears, but ever without halting, until we march through the Gates into the City.

Messages to the Messengers
Catherine Bramwell-Booth

Our warfare is more complex and desperate than that between nations and its issues are infinitely more far-reaching, and we must equip ourselves for it; and nothing is so vital to our cause as a mastery of the doctrine and an assured and joyous possession of the pentecostal experience of holiness through the indwelling Spirit.

When the Holy Ghost is Come
Samuel Logan Brengle

We are to rescue the slaves of sin, to make a people, to fashion them into a holy nation, and inspire and lead them forth to save the world. How can we do this? Only by being in the forefront of God's spiritual hosts; not in name and in titles only, but in reality; by being in glad possession of the deepest experiences God gives and the fullest revelations He makes to men.

When the Holy Ghost is Come

WAR! WAR!
IN WHITBY
2,000
MEN AND WOMEN
Wanted at once to join the Hallelujah Army, That is making an attack on the Devil's Kingdom every Sunday in ST. HILDA'S HALL at

11 AM, 3 and 6:30 PM
And every week night in the Old Town Hall
at 7:30
To be led by CAPTAIN CADMAN from
London
Evangelist of the Christian Mission

Elijah Cadman
The History of The Salvation Army – Volume 1
Robert Sandall

Let no one imagine that, because of divine aid, life for me is merely like riding an escalator up to mansions in the skies. Life is a warfare. I have to struggle. I know the effects of unceasing strain upon brain and heart and body. Often I am compelled to cry out, "Who is sufficient for these things?" The flight of time appalls me, the battle with human sins and frailties burdens me. But in the darkest hour there is still the unquenchable conviction that if I trust God and seek only to do His will I shall come out all right and the great responsibilities thrust upon me will be carried to the credit of God's Kingdom.

George Carpenter
The Privilege of All Believers
John D. Waldron, Edit

We have a birthright tenderly to cherish!
We have a charge no language can define!
Systems may fail, and things ignoble perish
But not the cause aflame with fire divine.
Great are our victories won on many a field,
But greater far our victories unrevealed.

George Carpenter
The History of The Salvation Army – Volume 6
Frederick Coutts

Since I have been converted
And the devil's ranks deserted,
I've had such joy and gladness in my soul.
For Jesus I've been fighting,
And in the war delighting,
And now I'm pressing on toward the goal.

W. G. Collins
Salvation Army Song Book

The accomplishment of Christ was of such magnitude as to tip the scales decisively in the conflict between good and evil. In Him God's love shines forth convincingly to assure mankind that compassionate concern, not careless indifference, is at the heart of things.

The Armoury Commentary – The Four Gospels
Frederick Coutts, Edit.

Of necessity, in any army there must be generals and other commanding officers. However, they are all part of the fighting force. God never delegates only those in command to do the fighting, nor does He maintain a standby army. He has no reserves and there is never a discharge from the ranks.

When God Calls You
Edward Deratany

We go forth not to fight 'gainst the sinner, but sin;
The lost and the outcast we love.

Fred W. Fry
Salvation Army Song Book

Great battles have been won
By quiet men
Who bring a sense of peace
And priestly poise
Win battles with no bloodshed
And no noise!

O Lord!
John Gowans

Combativeness is, I grant you, part and parcel of human nature – and a most valuable quality when exercised for humane and morally sound purposes. And what is there to prevent the fighting instinct instead of applying itself to the destruction of human wealth and life, being directed to the destruction of everything that now jeopardizes the happiness and peace of mankind? Imagine the young men of all nations enlisted to fight the moral evils threatening our social life...the best scientists of the world to fight disease...the womanhood of the nations to fight everything inimical to family life...dedicated to a high ideal the fighting instinct can become most powerfully beneficent.

As witness The Salvation Army has succeeded in uniting men and women of almost every race and color and tongue in a passionate and sustained crusade against every form of social and moral evil.

Edward J. Higgins
The History of The Salvation Army – Volume 6
Frederick Coutts

We're a band that shall conquer the foe
If we fight in the strength of the King;
With the sword of the Spirit, we know,
We sinners to Jesus shall bring.

William Hodgson
Salvation Army Song Book

Our strength for warfare is Thy might,
Our hope of guidance is Thy light.

Mandell
Salvation Army Song Book

A meeting without a prayer meeting is a battle without a wound, or slaughter or death.

Commissioner Nicol
The Officer – 1893

War it was, in word and in deed. War with all its sacrifices, and separations, costly in blood and tears, and even to the price of death.

The House of My Pilgrimage
Albert Orsborn

The Salvation Army has had some minor Waterloos, but never a Watergate.

Marching On!
Ted Palmer

Come, join our Army, to battle we go.
Jesus will help us to conquer the foe;
Fighting for right and opposing the wrong,
The Salvation Army is marching along!

William Pearson
Salvation Army Song Book

Neath Thy sceptre foes are bending,
And Thy name makes devils fly;
Captives' fetters Thou art rending,
And Thy Blood doth sin destroy.
For Thy glory,
We will fight until we die.

William Pearson
Salvation Army Song Book

We're marching on to conquer all,
Before our God the world shall fall;
We'll face the foe, to battle go,
And never, never run away.

William Pearson
Salvation Army Song Book

In our work, as in war, daring disobedience is sometimes the best faithfulness.

Heathen England
George Scott Railton

Whatever treaties may be signed or broken, we shall keep advancing.

Heathen England
George Scott Railton

I'll gird on the armor, and rush to the field,
Determined to conquer and never to yield;
So the enemy shall know,
Wheresoever I may go,
That I am fighting for Jehovah.

Mark Saunders
Salvation Army Song Book

Steadily forward march!
To Jesus we will bring
Sinners of every kind,
And He will take them in.
Rich and poor as well,
It does not matter who,
Bring them in with all their sin;
He'll wash them white as snow.

J. Slack
Salvation Army Song Book

Tin hat for a halo! Ah! She wears it well! Making pies for homesick lads. Sure is "beating hell"! In a region blasted by fire and flame and sword. This Salvation lass battles for the Lord!

From "Stars and Stripes"
The General Next to Good
Richard Collier

It was an Army in which there was to be more guerilla warfare than pitched battles by rigidly drilled battalions.

William Booth's First Gentleman
Harry Williams

Weakness

There is a spiritual bankruptcy, just as there is a pecuniary one. I may become so eager to help the poor that I indiscriminately give away all my property and so become a pauper myself. Likewise I may be so eager to help souls that I give away all my spiritual capital.

Samuel Logan Brengle
At the Center of the Circle
John D. Waldron, Edit.

Will

You have not absolute power over your intellect, but you have power over your will.

Life and Death
Catherine Booth

In the very nature of things there can be no union with Jesus without this union of will. That is really all he can call his own. His mind, with all its splendid powers and possibilities, may be reduced to idiocy; he may be robbed of his property. His health, and even his life may be taken away from him, but who can enter into the domain of his will and rob him of that?

Heart Talks on Holiness
Samuel Logan Brengle

It is not my feelings, but the purpose of my heart, the attitude of my will, that God looks at, and it is that to which I must look.

When the Holy Ghost is Come
Samuel Logan Brengle

Wisdom

Wisdom is the right use of knowledge

Chosen to be a Soldier

Wisdom is a thing of the heart more than of the brain, and the wisdom of God is really a revelation of the love of God.

Bramwell Booth
Trumpets of the Lord
Catherine Bramwell-Booth

So often when human wisdom is found wanting, the Holy Spirit provides the right word to say; the important thing is to say what you have to say in love, and also be prepared to listen as well as speak.

A Burning in My Bones
Clarence Wiseman

Witnessing

Because it has always been the conviction of The Salvation Army that those who have experienced the salvation of Christ are called to be witnesses for Him, right from the moment of his conversion the convert should be prepared to witness by his word of testimony.

Chosen to be a Soldier

Today it is necessary to remind ourselves that, important as good platform addresses undoubtedly are in The Salvation Army, the principle avenue through which to reach other souls is that of testimony – by definite word of mouth and also by the witness of a consistent life.

The Salvation Army – Its Origin and Development

It is nothing less than a miracle that we have been able, out of every nation and from every class, to raise up workers – people with the spirit to endure as well as to strive. In this is to be seen one of the great achievements of the Army; we have turned the sufferers themselves into saviors and have made for our messengers an unparalleled opportunity.

Bramwell Booth
The Salvation Army – Its Origin and Development

If any business man were to talk and act as many Christians do, he would be set down as having a screw loose.

The Salvation Army in Relation to Chuch and State
Catherine Booth

We say the world is dying; what for? Sermons? No! Periodicals? No. Dying for discussions? No! For fine-spun theories? No! For creeds and faith? Oh, you might have them by the dozen! What is it dying for? Downright, straight-forward, honest, loving, earnest testimony about what God can do for souls; that is what it wants.

Catherine Booth
Friendship With Jesus
Florence Booth

I wanted to find them, to go to them. I wanted to tell them as quickly and as simply as I could the greatest fact of all the ages – the dying love of God.

Evangeline Booth
The General Was a Lady
Margaret Troutt

The so called Salvationist who cherishes a solitary religion is an artificial bloom in a garden of flowers.

The Army Uniform
Florence Booth

There is no glow in an unholy heart to kindle a flame of holiness in another heart.

Likeness to God
Florence Booth

When the life is in harmony with the lips, the testimony of the humblest child of God is as the sure stone aimed from David's sling.

Friendship With Jesus
Florence Booth

And now, Hallelujah! the rest of my days
Shall gladly be spent in promoting His praise
Who opened His bosom to pour out this sea
Of boundless salvation for you and for me.

William Booth
Salvation Army Song Book

God wants men and women to walk about the world so that those around, believers and unbelievers alike, shall see the form and hear the voice of the living God; people who shall be so like Him in spirit and life and character as to make the crowds feel as though the very shadow of God had crossed their path. Will you be a shadow of God?

The Seven Spirits
William Booth

What is the use of a sun that does not shine?

The Seven Spirits
William Booth

The world today, perhaps more than ever before, needs apostles of the com-monplace, the living of the life of Jesus in the ordinary insignificances that go to make up an average day.

Messages to the Messengers
Catherine Bramwell-Booth

Don't limit the power of testimony by unbelief. A torch loses no light and heat by lighting a thousand other torches.

Heart Talks on Holiness
Samuel Logan Brengle

If I am cured of a terrible cancer, it will do no good (in helping others) for me to go around living my good health. I must tell you who cured me and how, if I would honor my physician and do good to other sufferers. "Ring out the good news all over the world! If a man will be holy, he must give God all the glory. And if he does he must 'Tell the great things God has done for Him!'"

Samuel Logan Brengle
Peace Like a River
Sallie Chesham

Like a good many soldiers, who are tremendously brave when there is a "big go" and everybody is favorable, or who can even stand an attack from persecutors, where muscle and physical courage can come to the front; but who have no moral courage to wear the uniform alone in their shop where they have to face the scorn of their mates and the jeers of the street urchin. These are soldiers who love dress parade, but do not want hard fighting at the front of the battle.

Helps to Holiness
Samuel Logan Brengle

We may be sweet singers, eloquent and moving preachers, skillful organizers, masters of men and assemblies, wizards of finance, popular and commanding leaders, but if we are not soul-winners, if we do not make men and women see the meaning of Jesus, and hunger for His righteousness and purity, and bow to Him in full loyalty, then one thing, the chief thing for an Army officer, we lack.

Ancient Prophets
Samuel Logan Brengle

I must not sit back and pray that others will do something; or complacently watch someone else sharing his faith. I must demonstrate my faith, and I must do even more. I must persuade for Christ.

Excursions in Thought
Jean Brown

The chief weapon in the Christian armory is the eloquence of example.

Christ is the Answer
Frederick Coutts

There are times when the Christian's duty is to stand, at whatever cost. At other times he should "flee" that his witness may be given elsewhere. The criterion is "the furtherance of the gospel."

The Armoury Commentary – The Four Gospels
Frederick Coutts, Edit.

It is not part of true religion to make a man grovel, not even before God. The call is to bear and share the terrible freedom of love.

Reason to Believe
Harry Dean

Christianity as a creed may be subjected to argument. Even the Biblical record of wonderful things may be challenged. But when Christianity is met with in the form of a human, living, walking, breathing miracle...well, it is just a trifle harder to dispose of or even to debunk.

Out of the Depths
Clarence W. Hall

The new life in Christ always longs to impart itself. The wonderful things which Christ whispers in a man's ear in secret burn within him until he can tell them to others.

Christ's Cabinet
William Mc Intyre

Witnesses to God's message in this sin-stained world are not sent forth to court praise or to fear blame, but to cry aloud – "Ye must be born again!"

The Silences of Christ
Albert Orsborn

We are witnesses for Jesus,
In the haunts of sin and shame,
In the underworld of sorrow
Where men seldom hear His name;
For to bind the broken-hearted
And their liberty proclaim,
We are witnesses for Jesus,
In the haunts of sin and shame.

William D. Pennick
Salvation Army Song Book

Witnessing can only be accomplished by using everyone who places himself or herself under our direction to testify publicly for Christ, or, in other words, by making every Saul of today who is converted under our ministrations a Paul of tomorrow.

George Scott Railton
The History of The Salvation Army – Volume 2
Robert Sandall

The saints indeed make it easier to believe in God.

Studies in Sanctification
Edward Read

To share either the shame or the glory of one's secret soul is always costly, but that is what makes it vital.

Studies in Sanctification
Edward Read

Woman

An officer should firmly and judiciously insist upon the women having opportunity for active service, according to their ability, equal to that enjoyed by men.

Orders and Regulations for Corps Officers

It is a principle of Salvationism that, in God's plan, the highest interests of men and women stand or fall together; that, whenever any attempt is made to separate these interests, injustice must follow. The Salvation Army emphatically declares that no laws can be good in effect which profess to care for and guard the interests of one sex at the expense of another.

The Salvation Army – Its Origin and Development

The Salvation Army has been happy in its women officers. The lessons of experience undoubtedly teach us that they are fully qualified for all the work of the ministry of Christ.

Bramwell Booth
The Angel Adjutant
Minnie Lindsay Carpenter

Did not God, and has not nature, assigned to man his sphere of labor, "to till the ground, and to dress it"? And if exemption is claimed from this kind of toil for a portion of male sex, on the ground of their possessing ability for intellectual and moral pursuits, we must be allowed to claim the same privilege for women; nor can we see the other or why God in His solitary substance has endowed a being with powers which He never intended her to employ.

Practical Religion
Catherine Booth

God holds you responsible, just as He holds any other being. He has not got two codes – one for men and one for women. There will be no two judgment seats, whatever men do here.

Papers on Godliness
Catherine Booth

Until the position and mission of women are properly estimated and cared for, in vain shall we look for perfect oneness in parents, and real worth in children. Never until she is valued and educated as man's equal will unions be perfect, and their consequence blissful.

Catherine Booth
Words of Catherine Booth
Cyril Barnes

If she has the necessary gifts, and feels herself called by the Spirit to preach, there is not a single word in the whole Book of God to restrain her, but many, very many to urge and encourage her. God says she shall do so, and Paul prescribed the manner in which she shall do it, and Phebe, Junia, Phillip's four daughters, and many other women actually did preach and speak in the primitive churches. If this had not been the case, there would have been less freedom under the new than under the old dispensation.

Practical Religion
Catherine Booth

If woman loves, she worships. If she champions a cause, she will fight for it. If she gives, she gives all. If she lives for, she will die for.

Woman
Evangeline Booth

We women have made many homes in the world, but we have now the task of changing the world into a home. We have seen many fathers of families. We have now to realize the Fatherhood that includes all families, the Fatherhood of God in Christ. The housekeeping that we have now to undertake is housekeeping on the grand scale; it must include all nations, all people in a nation, the rich and the poor, the saints and the sinners – come ye to the waters; come and be reconciled to God in His heaven and man upon earth.

Woman
Evangeline Booth

All I ask is – let us find out the powers of our women comrades, whether they belong to our own families or not, and give them the chance to use those powers for the promotion of the glory of God and for the salvation of the world.

The Founder's Messages to Soldiers
William Booth

First and foremost, I insist on the equality of woman with man. Every officer and soldier should insist upon the truth that woman is as important and valuable, as capable, and as necessary to the progress and happiness of the world as man.

The Founder's Messages to Soldiers
William Booth

If God has given her the ability why should not woman persuade the vacillating, instruct and console the penitent, and pour out her soul in prayer for the sinners?

Catherine Booth
Words of Catherine Booth
Cyril Barnes

In externals nothing is more remarkable in the recent progress of the Mission than the great advance of our female ministry. It has sometimes been said that female preachers would be the ruin of the Mission. But on the contrary, it turns out that the prosperity of the work in every respect just appears most preciously at the very times when female preachers are being allowed the fullest opportunity.

William Booth
The History of The Salvation Army – Volume 1
Robert Sandall

My best men are women.

William Booth
My Best Men are Women
Flora Larsson

To many men, woman is little more than a plaything for their leisure hours. To others she is like a piece of property, a slave in everything but name, ofttimes being treated with less consideration as to health and confort than the horses that run the omnibus, or the beasts that are fattening for slaughter.

The Founder's Messages to Soldiers
William Booth

When the prophetesses disappear you may look out and tremble, for the prophets will be in great danger of going as well.

Salvation Soldiery
William Booth

Because the Bible declares it, and because the Spirit within us urges it, and because conscience, the experience of others, and our own past efforts all prove that something by women can be done, that therefore we can and must do something for the dying world.

Heart Messages
Emma Booth-Tucker

The rights of woman – what are they?
The right to labor and pray;
The right to lead the soul to God,
Along the path her Savior trod.

The Army Drum
Elizabeth Swift Brengle

Long denied the right of public testimony as well as the opportunity to proclaim the truth of the Savior's mission, women have in the history of our Movement fully proved that they may be as effective, as acceptable and as successful as their brethren, both as teachers and rulers in the Kingdom of Christ on earth. The extraordinary theory that the gifts of the Holy Spirit are confined to those who have taken part in a certain ecclesiastical ceremonial, narrow and mistaken as it may be, is surely mild and simple form of error compared with the appalling notion that those gifts are confined to men, and are to be forever withheld from the other half of the human family.

Bramwell Booth
The Angel Adjutant
Minnie Lindsay Carpenter

With all the record of opposition to Jesus in the Gospels, there is no instance where a woman ever opposed Christ. No women ever forsook, betrayed or in any way expressed enmity against Christ. Rather they followed Him, opened to Him their homes and hearts, bathed His feet with their tears, anointed His head with spikenard, and now as men were hounding Him to death, they showed the compassion of their tears and sorrow and with Him went weeping to His martyrdom.

Footsteps to Calvary
Henry Gariepy

God has given to women a graceful form and attitude, winning manners, persuasive speech, and above all, a finely toned emotional nature, all or which appear to us eminent qualities for public speaking. I believe that one of the greatest boons to the race would be women's exaltation to her proper position, mentally and spiritually. Who can tell its consequences to posterity? If indeed there is in Jesus Christ "neither male nor female" but in all touching His Kingdom they are one, who shall dare thrust woman out of the church's operations or presume to put any candle which God has lighted under a bushel? Why should the swaddling bands of blind custom be wrapped around the female disciples of the Lord?

Catherine Booth
My Best Men are Women
Flora Larsson

It is more difficult for women to reach the higher positions than for men. To be advanced, a man requires hardly more than average gifts. A woman must be superior.

Laura Petri
My Best Men are Women
Flora Larsson

If The Salvation Army ceased to exist today, it would have amply justified its past career and covered its originator with glory, if only because it has brought forward again to the light that chosen instrumentality of the kingdom of heaven, female ministry, and allowed the demonstration of its utility and power – its divine right.

Heathen England
George Scott Railton

The double-faced devil will consent to advancement to the most public position possible if it be but to lead precious souls to hell. The stage! Oh, yes, by all means go on to the stage. Dance there half-dressed, if you like. Take part unblushingly in the representation of the vilest iniquity before the dense crowd of the highest and most learned in the land. Sing, speak, perform, be shameless, be a great, public, constant lie, and you shall be worshipped by whole nations for it all. Nobles shall pour their wealth at your feet for the honor of your hand. The greatest monarchs of the earth will bow to you, the whole press of every Christian people shall laud you. The "religious papers" reserve a little quiet column on purpose for such names as yours! Every kingdom of the world shall be yours if you like to take the foremost part in leading men down to the pit. But to stand upon that very same stage to lead men to heaven! To speak, or sing, or pray there! Oh, horrible! Abomination! Degradation of your sex! Disgrace to religion! Outrage to society! Society! – the very society that would gloat over your performance as an actress and shut you out of its circles because you were one. And as to appearing in the open-air, at the street corners, addressing men, braving insult, and standing amidst the godless multitudes to speak aloud for God – why, you must be demented – lost to every sense of propriety, utterly without respect for yourself, to dream of anything of the sort! Surely, you will not make such an exhibition of yourself, and disgrace family and friends forever!

Heathen England
George Scott Railton

We do not argue for the employment of any one in any task they are not fully qualified for; but we insist that disqualification must be proved – not merely asserted – in every case, and that a woman who is duly qualified to manage shall be allowed to do so.

Heathen England
George Scott Railton

With the divine commission to disciple all nations in its present miserably imperfect state of execution, to forbid any willing worker because she does not happen to belong to our sex, is one of those fantastic and horrible offenses against God and man which may justly be described as a mystery of iniquity and the abomination of the earth.

Catherine Booth
Mrs. Booth
W. T. Stead

Work

To the salvation soldier the first consideration in regard to employment should not be money, holidays, free time, the likelihood of promotion, etc., for in all honorable walks of life Christians are servants of Christ and must therefore make the question of His will and His interests their foremost concerns.

Chosen to be a Soldier

I don't remember the houses I have lived in, the people I have known, the things of passing interest of the moment. They are all gone. Nothing stands out before my mind as of any consequence but the work I have done for God and for eternity. That is all that there is to rejoice in.

Catherine Booth
Mrs. Booth
W. T. Stead

"A dirty job," do you say? Granted, and so, I suppose, is digging silver and gold and diamonds; but men reckon that it pays.

Salvation Soldiery
William Booth

This and better will do.

International Congress Addresses – 1904
William Booth

Your best! What's the good of that? Your best won't be any good to the Army and the sinning world. Anybody can do their best. Don't you see that's the difference between having God by the Holy Spirit help you and just doing what you can do? What you can do is no good to anybody, anybody can do their best at something. You are going to rely upon the help of God. And you're going to be able to do better than your best.

William Booth
Commissioner Catherine
Catherine Bramwell-Booth

If the conditions of our work make it impossible to fulfill our duty to the sinner and to the Army, I believe we ought to find a plan which would change our conditions of work.

Messages to the Messengers
Catherine Bramwell-Booth

If to you, work done merely for gain can ever be on the same level as work done for love, then it simply means you have never raised your work to the right standard.

Messages to the Messengers
Catherine Bramwell-Booth

It is not for you and me to be deciding what shall prosper – whether this or that. Our business is to do the sowing well.

Messages to the Messengers
Catherine Bramwell-Booth

Other people's estimate of your work cannot change its quality.

Messages to the Messengers
Catherine Bramwell-Booth

We human creatures seldom exert ourselves unduly, unless necessity be laid upon us. If we can succeed – find what we need or want – without great efforts or sacrifice, why make it? The fact is, we are mostly blind to the result of effort and sacrifice in us, and are generally thinking only of results outside ourselves.

Messages to the Messengers
Catherine Bramwell-Booth

Wonder always represents work.

Messages to the Messengers
Catherine Bramwell-Booth

Jesus was a working man, and as such understands working men. He knows their weakness. He has been pinched with their poverty. He can sympathize with them in their long hours of toil that bars them from that culture of mind which, no doubt, many crave. He understands.

Heart Talks on Holiness
Samuel Logan Brengle

Most people divide the work of the world into what they call sacred and secular work. Preaching, praying and reading the Bible, conducting meetings and the like, they consider to be sacred work but washing and ironing and learning, building houses and making shoes, practicing law of medicine, working in mines and mills, in shops and stores, and on shipboard; that they call secular work. But why make such a distinction? It is not the work, but the heart and purpose behind the work at which God looks.

The Way of Holiness
Samuel Logan Brengle

Superior proficiency comes with superior practice.

Samuel Logan Brengle
Peace Like a River
Sallie Chesham

We know not what part of our work God is going to use in His plans for saving the world; therefore, let it all be good and true.

The Way of Holiness
Samuel Logan Brengle

A willing pair of hands may be a greater blessing than a witty tongue.

The Call to Holiness
Frederick Coutts

Everyone who is working for Jesus is working for us as well.

The Call to Holiness
Frederick Coutts

The ideal is a balanced life – prayer and perspiration; silence and service; worship and work.

The Armoury Commentary – The Four Gospels
Frederick Coutts, Edit.

The truth is that the work of the Kingdom has to be done most often in unspectacular ways.

The Armoury Commentary – The Four Gospels
Frederick Coutts, Edit.

Working for God is no substitute for living with God.

The Armoury Commentary – The Four Gospels
Frederick Coutts, Edit.

Works

You are sowing to the flesh; but do you see what the harvest must be? For God has so made you, that if there were no material hell, while you exist and remain guilty, you must be a hell to yourself.

Life and Death
Catherine Booth

All the memories of deeds gone by
Rise within me and Thy power defy;
With a deathly chill ensnaring,
They would leave my soul despairing.

Herbert Booth
Salvation Army Song Book

Good works must be self-forgetful to be of real value.

The Armoury Commentary – The Four Gospels
Frederick Coutts, Edit.

The attempt to earn credit with God is doomed to failure. Free forgiveness is our only hope – and that is exactly what is offered.

The Armoury Commentary – The Four Gospels
Frederick Coutts, Edit.

The best that overanxious man can do falls below the least of the works of God.

The Armoury Commentary – The Four Gospels
Frederick Coutts, Edit.

We tend to credit ourselves with our possessions – financial, intellectual, social or moral, in such a way as to lose our humanity.

The Armoury Commentary – The Four Gospels
Frederick Coutts, Edit.

Greatness does not consist merely in doing great things but rather in doing little things in a great way.

Manpower for the Master
Bramwell H. Tillsley

World

I do here and now and forever, renounce the world and all its sinful pleasures, companionships, treasures and objects, and declare my full determination boldly to show myself a soldier of Jesus Christ in all places and companies, no matter what I may have to suffer, do or lose by so doing.

Articles of War

The sinful world was not ready and is not now ready to be sanctified; it must first be saved.

The Holy Spirit – Friend and Counselor
Milton S. Agnew

What a valley of dry bones the world appears to the man whose eyes have been opened to see the truth of things. Verily, verily, it is one great cemetery crowded with men, women, and children dead in trespasses and sin. Look for a moment at this graveyard, in which the men around you may be said to lie with their hearts all dead and cold to Christ, and all that concerns their salvation. Look at it. The men and women and children in your town are buried there. The men and women in your city, in your street. Nay, the very people who come to your hall to hear you talk on a Sunday night are there.

The Seven Spirits
William Booth

Snowflakes come down no faster than the tears fall in this weeping wilderness. Thorns are more numerous than roses, tares than wheat. Sickness, disappointment, and death walk every street and visit every home. Winter comes to every heart. Ah, yes! The scarcity of sympathy speaks no lack of sorrow! There is sorrow enough and to spare!

Heart Messages
Emma Booth-Tucker

Where do human kingdoms lead? To despair, destruction and death. We need the courage to pray "Thy kingdom come," even though its coming will be at the expense of human pretensions, including our own.

Power and Glory
Harry Dean

Worldliness

A worldling is a person who is taken up with himself and applies a false scale of values, unrelated to the will of God.

Chosen to be a Soldier

Contempt of others, coupled with self-satisfaction, is worldliness in essence.

Chosen to be a Soldier

God's plan is not that His men be removed out of the world, but that the world should be kept out of His men.

Transformed Christians
Milton S. Agnew

Worldliness is the spirit that says, "This is the age that is important. Indeed, there may not be another age at all. So live it up.

'Eat, drink, and be merry, for tomorrow you will die.'." There is not eternal tomorrow. Again it says, "This is the age of self-sufficiency in mind, will, morals," disavowing man's lost condition and the need of man's repentance, faith, surrender, and of God's mercy and grace. "This is the age of self-pleasing," not allowing for self-denial, self-restraint. Worldliness is the spirit that, at its best, says, "This is the age we must serve humanity and improve the world," forgetting that our first duty and first love must be to God. It substitutes manmade goodness for godliness.

Transformed Christians
Milton S. Agnew

Alas, and has it come to pass that there is no strictly Christian social intercourse and enjoyment? Have the topics of our glorious Christianity become so stale and uninteresting? Have the themes of gospel enterprise and individual effort lost all their inspiration? Have the songs of Zion lost their enchanting and inspiring influence? Has the voice of social prayer become quite silent? Has every spark of enthusiasm in religion gone out, that when Christians want to find interest and enjoyment, they must seek it in themes and things peculiarly belonging to the god of this world, and his votaries? Has it come to pass that Christians have so little confidence in the God of the Bible, and the religion of Jesus, that they must seek an alliance between Christ and the world in order to interest their children and save them from open profligacy and vice?

Practical Religion
Catherine Booth

Christians are nowhere taught, either directly or indirectly, that it is any part of their duty to provide amusement for the children of this world; nay, the direct teaching of Scripture goes to prove that it is their duty to seek to alarm and convict them. There is not a line in the whole Bible on which an argument can be built for amusing people while yet in their sins.

Practical Religion
Catherine Booth

246

Are not Salvationists in danger of a similar evil? Does not their faith for congregations, and money, and souls and other successes often rest in their officers, or their buildings? Do they not trust in their singing, or their praying, or something else that they do themselves, or get done for them by others, rather than in the direct work of the Holy Spirit, and the active cooperation of God?

The Founder's Messages to Soldiers
William Booth

While eschewing fripperies and fopperies ourselves, there is a danger lest the last remnant of the "carnal mind" should manifest itself in the way we dress our children. True, there are reasons which make it advisable under certain circumstances to avoid putting them in uniform. Nor is it necessary on the other hand to make frights and sights of them. We are no advocate for the charity child system, which would make speckled birds of our little ones. But this is very different to tricking them out in laces and gewgaws, with all the colors of the rainbow, thus fostering in their hearts the seeds of vanity and worldliness.

Frederick Booth-Tucker
The Officer – 1898

My concern has not to do so much with the attacks made upon our faith from without as with its betrayals from within. The promise is that the gates of hell shall not prevail against the church of God, and on that promise we can rely. But it is when Christians are less than Christian that the citadel is opened from within to an enemy who, left to his own strategems and devices, could never capture it from without.

Essentials of Christian Experience
Frederick Coutts

Never again tempt me with worldly pleasure.
Vain, empty all, as bubbles on the wave.

C. Fry
Gems for Songsters #1

Slowly but surely, Solomon substituted the things of the flesh for the things of the spirit. He chose to live his life under the sun rather than the other side of the sun, the sphere in which the soul finds satisfaction in the living God.

Search the Scriptures
Robert Hoggard

What are possessions but ties that bind one to earth, cords that hamper the soul's free movement?

Just a Moment, Lord
Flora Larsson

Worry

Worry is a great foe to holiness, and perfect trust puts an end to worry.

The Way of Holiness
Samuel Logan Brengle

Worship

It a serious mistake to be so preoccupied with living *for* God as not to have time for living *with* God, adoring Him, listening to Him, worshipping Him, and consciously resting in His love.

Chosen to be a Soldier

The commandment "Thou shalt have no other gods before Me" did not introduce religion and worship to men; it was an attempt to correct already existing religious ideas and practices.

Handbook of Doctrine

The highest form of worship is when God is honored for what He is, without petition for benefits other than that of communion with Him.

Handbook of Doctrine

I believe the Lord is not only grieved and disappointed but I believe He is angry when His people meet, and talk, and sing, and pray, and then go away without any definite result having been reached – without ever having given anything to Him, or received anything from Him. I believe He feels with respect to us, just as He felt with respect to His people of old, when He said, "Why come ye and cover my altar with tears?"

Papers on Godliness
Catherine Booth

The Christian engages in worship in order to clarify the action he must undertake in everyday life, to reinforce his spirit so that he becomes a co-worker with the God who is at work in human affairs.

The Armours Commentary – The Four Gospels
Frederick Coutts, Edit.

Worship carries us away from the mundane and sublunary life we lead. One reason worship is successful in doing this is that time, as we ordinarily consider it, is not an ingredient of worship. There is a great timelessness about the creeds, for instance, or about the prayers, or even the great hymns. The attitude of quiet and waiting before God in worship is anticipatory of that future hour (note how time is inescapable even in our language) "when the trumpet of the Lord shall sound and time shall be no more."

A Sense of God
Peter W. Stine

Worship is as close as we can come on earth to experiencing the Kingdom. When we come together to share in the praising of God – whether this takes place in cathedrals or in a storefront with broken glass – we are part of a microcosm within which hours and minutes should have no meaning.

A Sense of God
Peter W. Stine

Writing

Writers should –
(a) Aim at getting someone saved, sanctified, or set to work for the salvation of the bodies or souls of men.
(b) Be alive, on fire, in earnest.
(c) See that their papers are short, pointed, and interesting.
(d) Write in the plain, everyday language of the common people.
(e) Write clearly, on one side of the paper only.

(f) When writing songs, compose them to well-known tunes, commonly sung in the Army, or the popular tunes of the street.
(g) See that their tunes have some go and fire in them, and be such as can be easily learned.

Why and Wherefore
Bramwell Booth

The purpose of every publication in the Army shall be the same as that for which the Army itself exists, namely, the glory of God in the salvation of the people, the sanctification of the soldiers, and the inspiration of each and all, officers and soldiers alike, with the Spirit which brought Jesus Christ from heaven to live and suffer and die for the salvation of the world.

William Booth
The History of The Salvation Army – Volume 2
Robert Sandall

The pen and the tongue are the two axles on which the world revolves. Of the two it is difficult to say which has the greater influence. True there is subtle magic about the tongue which the pen can never quite get hold of. But there are multitudes of hearts whose eyes are reached by the written word, whose ears are deaf to the tongue of the charmer, charm he ever so wisely. And not only does it get at such, but it usually reaches them when they are alone, and thus most accessible to the shafts of truth.

Frederick Booth-Tucker
The Officer – 1893

It is not easy to write, at least not for me. I sweat and agonize over everything I write, but when it is written and published and goes on its way to bless others, then my heart bursts with song. It is much like a mother's agony in childbirth, I suppose, only it's mental and spiritual.

Samuel Logan Brengle
Peace Like a River
Sallie Chesham

Mere words could not describe God, and even if they could, they would have been open to misunderstanding and misinterpretation, for they lack compelling power. If words had been equal to the task, a book could have saved mankind.

Power and Glory
Harry Dean

In my case, my own spiritual condition, my inner harmony, my contact with God, was the first source and fount of anything I could write. I must be at peace with myself, no inner contradictions. I must be in touch with God, not merely with facts about Him.

The House of My Pilgrimage
Albert Orsborn

Surely poetry is not mere abstract thought, but is woven of the very stuff of living, all the colors, all the tones, sombre and gay, combining in its form and beauty.

The House of My Pilgrimage
Albert Orsborn

Youth

The supreme purpose of the Army's work among young people has been from the beginning to bring the young to Jesus Christ and to develop them as fighters in the ranks of The Salvation Army.

The Salvation Army – Its Origin and Development

Children brought up without love are like plants brought up without sun.

Catherine Booth
Life of Catherine Booth
Frederick Booth-Tucker

It has been a special joy to me to know that there are so many young in the ranks, who may have but acted as our armourbearers hitherto, but who, when we have left the field, will leap into our places and go on with this War, and I congratulate you all a thousand times upon your remaining opportunities for usefulness.

Catherine Booth
On the Banks of the River
Bramwell Booth

Under some of the conditions of modern industry, children are not so much born into a home as they are spawned into the world like fish, with the results which we see.

In Darkest England and The Way Out
William Booth

It is a glory among us that our youth may lead, but you must so act toward the elders under your direction that your youth may never be your shame.

Messages to the Messengers
Catherine Bramwell-Booth

Accept my youth, my strength, my prime,
Accept each moment of my time;
Earth's choicest joys I sacrifice
And choose Thy smile at any price.
I hear and now obey the call.
And leap by faith doubt's highest wall;
I cannot give Thee less than all
Lord, take it all, take it all!

Frederick Booth-Tucker
Salvation Army Song Book

Zeal

I would go on an errand to hell if the Lord
would give me the assurance that the devil
would not keep me there.

Catherine Booth
On the Banks of the River
Bramwell Booth

Have I the zeal I had
When thou didst me ordain
To preach Thy word and seek the lost
Or do I feel it pain?

Herbert H. Booth
Salvation Army Song Book

The secret of success is often inquired for.
Here it is: it is not in natural gifts, or
human bearing, or exceptional opportunities, or earthy advantages, but in a
heart consumed with the flame of ardent,
holy, heavenly love.

Salvation Soldiery
William Booth

A man full of God cannot be thrust aside.

The Soul-Winner's Secret
Samuel Logan Brengle

The zeal of other people blazes up, burns
low and often dies out, but the zeal of a
man with a clean heart, full of the Holy
Ghost, increases year by year.

The Way of Holiness
Samuel Logan Brengle

Boldness is a fruit of righteousness, and is
always found in those who are full of the
Holy Ghost. They forget themselves and
so lose all fear. This was the secret of the
martyrs when burned at the stake or
thrown to the wild beasts.

When the Holy Ghost is Come
Samuel Logan Brengle

True zeal is from above. Its source is in the
mountains of the Lord's holiness, and its
springing fountains in the deep, cool valleys of humanity.

The Soul-Winner's Secret
Samuel Logan Brengle

We can either be like a rousing fire on a
cold day, or like a wet blanket on a
winter's night.

T. Henry Howard
The Officer – 1893

I want, dear Lord, a soul on fire for Thee,
A soul baptized with heavenly energy;
A willing mind, a ready hand,
To do whate'er I know,
To spread Thy light wherever I may go.

George Jackson
Salvation Army Song Book

The people have been taught, not so much
to seek for rhapsodies of delightful feeling, or sweet, comfortable calm (though
these have been preciously enjoyed) as
for that perfect love which casteth out fear
and fits people for desperate warfare
against sin – for that consuming zeal
which uses up in the Master's service
every faculty and hour.

Heathen England
George Scott Railton

We're fanatics and fools, too, they tell us
We don't understand what we say;
We'd rather be fools for the Savior
Than fools for the devil for aye.

J. Russell
Gems for Songsters ;2

ZEAL

Don't let the fire in your heart go out,
The fire that the Savior built
When you came to Him and He saved your
soul
And pardoned your sin and guilt;
With joy you could sing and shout.
Don't let the fire go out!

Down in its depths has your heart turned
cold?
The fire must be burning low.
Oh, set it aflame with an earnest prayer
And keep it for Christ aglow,
Dispelling all fear and doubt.
Don't let the fire go out!

More Poems of a Salvationist
Irena Arnold

Bibliography

Original publishers listed, with some books no longer available, and others reprinted by other publishers.

AGNEW, MILTON S. — *Better Covenant, The,* 1975. Beacon Hill Press, Kansas City
Holy Spirit, The – Friend and Counsellor, 1980. Beacon Hill Press, Kansas City
More Than Conquerors, 1959. Salvation Army, Chicago
Security of the Believer, 1974
Transformed Christians, 1974. Beacon Hill Press, Kansas City

ARNOLD, IRENA — *More Poems of a Salvationist,* 1945, Salvation Army, Atlanta

AVERY, GORDON — *Companion to the Song Book,* 1961. Salvation Army, London

BAIRD, CATHERINE — *Banner of Love,* Salvation Army, London
Book of Salvationist Verse, 1963. Salvation Army, London
Poems, 1933. Colonial Press, Clinton, Massachusetts
Reflections, 1975. Salvation Army, London

BARNES, CYRIL — *God's Army,* 1978. David C. Cook Pub. Elgin, Illinois
Founder Speaks Again, The, 1960. Salvation Army, London
Words of Catherine Booth, 1981. Salvation Army, London
Words of William Booth, 1975. Salvation Army, London

BISHOP, EDWARD — *Blood and Fire,* 1965. Moody Press, Chicago

BOOTH, BRAMWELL — *On the Banks of the River,* 1926. Salvation Army, London
Why and Wherefore, Salvation Army, London
Work in Darkest England – 1894, 1894. Salvation Army, London

BOOTH, CATHERINE — *Aggressive Christianity,* 1880. Salvation Army, London
Life and Death, 1883. Salvation Army, London
Papers on Godliness, 1890. Salvation Army, London
Practical Religion, 1885. Salvation Army, London
Salvation Army in Relation to Church and State, The, 1889. Salvation Army, London

BOOTH, EVANGELINE — *Love is All,* 1935. Salvation Army, London
Poems
Songs of the Evangel, 1927. Salvation Army, New York
Woman, 1945. Fleming H. Revell, Co., New York

BOOTH, FLORENCE — *Army Uniform, The,* Salvation Army, London
Friendship With Jesus, 1922. Salvation Army, London
Likeness to God, Salvation Army, London
Powers of Salvation Army Officers, 1924. Salvation Army, London

BOOTH, WILLIAM — *Founder's Messages to Soldiers,* 1921. Salvation Army, London
General's Letters, The, 1886. Salvation Army, London
In Darkest England and The Way Out, 1890. Salvation Army, London
International Congress Addresses – 1904, 1904. Salvation Army, London
Purity of Heart, 1902. Salvation Army, London
Salvation Soldiery, 1889. Salvation Army, London
Seven Spirits, The, 1907. Salvation Army, London
Sergeant-Major Do-Your-Best, Salvation Army, London
Visions, 1906. Salvation Army, London

BOOTH-TUCKER, EMMA — *Heart Messages,* 1904. Salvation Army, New York

BOOTH-TUCKER, FREDERICK — *The Life of Catherine Booth – Volume 1,2,* 1910. Salvation Army, London

BRAMWELL-BOOTH, CATHERINE — *Commissioner Catherine,* 1983. Dartman, Longman and Todd, London
Fighting for the King, 1983. Hodder and Stoughton, London
Messages to the Messengers, 1921. Salvation Army, London
Trumpets of the Lord, 1947. Hodder and Stoughton, London

BREEN, DOROTHY — *It's Beautiful,* 1984. Salvation Army, New York

BRENGLE, ELIZABETH SWIFT — *Army Drum, The,* 1909. Salvation Army, London

BRENGLE, SAMUEL LOGAN — *Ancient Prophets,* 1929. Salvation Army, London
Guest of the Soul, The, 1934. Marshall, Morgan and Scott, London
Heart Talks on Holiness, 1897. Salvation Army, London
Helps to Holiness, 1896. Salvation Army, London
Love-Slaves, 1923. Salvation Army, Atlanta
Resurrection Life and Power, 1925. Salvation Army, London
Soul-Winner's Secret, The, 1903. Salvation Army, London
Way of Holiness, The, 1902. Salvation Army, London
When the Holy Ghost is Come, 1909. Salvation Army, London

BROWN, FRED — *Salvationist at Work, The,* 1960. Salvation Army, London

BROWN, JEAN — *Excursions in Thought,* 1980. Salvation Army, London

BURROWS, WILLIAM — *All Things New,* Salvation Army, London
Mercy Seat, The, 1951. Salvation Army, London

CARPENTER, GEORGE — *Religion With a Punch,* 1943. Salvation Army, London

CARPENTER, MINNIE LINDSAY — *Angel Adjutant, The,* 1921. Salvation Army, London

CHESHAM, SALLIE — *Peace Like a River,* 1981. Salvation Army, Atlanta
Walking with the Wind, 1969. Word Books, Waco, Texas
Wind Chimes, 1983. Salvation Army, Altanta

COUTTS, FREDERICK — *Armoury Commentary – The Four Gospels, The,* 1973. Hodder and Stoughton, London
Call to Holiness, The, 1957. Salvation Army, London
Christ is the Answer, 1977. Salvation Army, London
Essentials of Christian Experience, 1969. Salvation Army, London
History of The Salvation Army, The – Volume 6, 1973. Hodder and Stoughton, London
In Good Company, 1980. Salvation Army, London
No Continuing City, 1976. Salvation Army, London
Splendour of Holiness, The, 1983. Salvation Army, London

COLLIER, PHILIP — *It Seems to Me,* 1983. Salvation Army, Atlanta

COLLIER, RICHARD — *General Next To God, The,* 1965. William Collins and Son and Co., Glasgow

DEAN, HARRY — *Power and Glory,* 1956. Salvation Army, London
Reason to Believe, 1970. Hodder and Stoughton, London

DERATANY, EDWARD — *Refuge in the Secret Place,* 1971. Gospel Lite, Glendale, California
When God Calls You, 1978. Thomas Nelson, Nashville, Tennessee

DITMER, STANLEY E. — *I'm In His Hands,* 1985. Salvation Army, Atlanta

FELLOWS, LAWRENCE — *Gentle Way, A,* 1979. Macmillan, New York

FOSSEY, LESLIE — *This Man Leidzen,* 1966. Salvation Army, London

GARIEPY, HENRY — *Footsteps To Calvary,* 1977. Fountain Press, Harrison, Arkansas

GILLIARD, ALFRED J. — *All the Days,* Salvation Army, London

GOWANS, JOHN — *Blood of the Lamb, The,* 1979. Salvation Army, London
Glory!, 1977. Salvation Army, London
Jesus Folk, 1973. Salvation Army, London
O Lord!, 1981. Salvation Army, London

HALL, CLARENCE W. — *Out of the Depths,* 1930. Fleming H. Revell, New York
Portrait of a Prophet, 1933. Salvation Army, London

HARRIS, WILLIAM G. — *Storm Pilot,* 1981. Salvation Army, London
Stuff That Makes an Army, 1962. Salvation Army, New York

HIGGINS, EDWARD J. — *Stewards of God,* Salvation Army, London

HOGGARD, ROBERT — *Search the Scriptures,* 1981. Salvation Army, Atlanta

HOWARD, T. HENRY — *Fuel for Sacred Fire,* 1924. Salvation Army, London

ISELEY, GUSTAVE — *First Called Christians,* 1952. Salvation Army, London

JOY, EDWARD H. — *Old Corps, The,* 1944. Salvation Army, London

KENYON, ALFRED — *Congo Crusade,* 1955. Salvation Army, London

KEW, CLIFFORD — *Closer Communion,* 1980. Salvation Army, London

KITCHING, WILFRED — *Goodly Heritage, A,* 1967. Salvation Army, London
Soldier of Salvation, 1963. Salvation Army, London

LAITY, EDWARD — *Christian and His Money, The,* Salvation Army, Atlanta

LARSSON, FLORA — *Between You and Me, Lord,* 1975. Shaw, Wheaton, Illinois
From My Treasure Chest, 1981. Salvation Army, London
I'm Growing, Lord, 1978. Shaw, Wheaton, Illinois
Just a Moment, Lord, 1973. Hodder and Stoughton, London
My Best Men are Women, 1974. Salvation Army, New York

LARSSON, JOHN — *Doctrine Without Tears,* 1974. Salvation Army, London

McINTYRE, WILLIAM — *Christ's Cabinet,* 1937. Salvation Army, Atlanta

McKINLEY, EDWARD — *Marching to Glory,* 1980. Harper and Row, San Francisco

MILLER, HULDA C. — *Creche and the Cross, The,* 1977. Salvation Army, New York
Merchant of Heaven, Epworth Press, London

MOBBS, BERNARD — *Our Rebel Emotions,* 1970. Hodder and Stoughton, London

MORRISON, JOHN A. — *Person of Jesus Christ, The,* 1966. Salvation Army, Atlanta

ORSBORN, ALBERT   *Beauty of Jesus, The,* 1947. Salvation Army, London
                     House of My Pilgrimage, The, 1958. Salvation Army, London
                     Silences of Christ, The, Salvation Army, London

PAVEY, SHIRLEY   *God Whispers in my Heart,* 1982. Salvation Army, Toronto

PALMER, TED   *Marching On!,* 1981. Salvation Army, Toronto

PITCHER, ARTHUR   *Memoirs of Peter,* 1981. Salvation Army, Atlanta

RADER, LYELL   *Rediscovering the Open Air,* Salvation Army, London

RAILTON, GEORGE SCOTT   *Heathen England,* 1882. Salvation Army, London
                        Twenty-One Years Salvation Army, 1886. Salvation Army, London

READ, EDWARD   *Studies in Sanctification,* 1975. Salvation Army, Toronto

SALVATION ARMY   *Articles of War*
                     Christian Mission Annual Report – 1877
                     Chosen to be a Soldier, 1977. London
                     Gems for Songsters I, 1922. London
                     Gems for Songsters II, 1937. London
                     Officer, The, London 1892, 1893, 1898, 1917, 1918, 1919, 1923
                     Officer Review, The, London 1932, 1933, 1936
                     Handbook of Doctrine, 1969. London
                     New Frontier, Rancho Palos Verdes, California
                     Position Statements, Commissioners' Conference, New York
                     Position Statements, International Headquarters, London
                     Sacraments, The, London
                     Salvation Army Song Book, 1954. London
                     Southern Spirit, The, Atlanta
                     This Was Their Call, 1977. London
                     War Cry, The, Verona, New Jersey

SANDALL, ROBERT   *History of the Salvation Army, The – I-III,* 1947-1955. Thomas Nelson and Sons, London

SMITH, ALLISTER   *Made Whole*

SMITH, GEORGE B.   *Christian Charter, The,* 1972. Salvation Army, London
                     Meditations for the Ordinary Man, 1961. Salvation Army, London

SMITH, J. EVAN   *Booth, the Beloved,* 1949. Oxford University Press, Oxford

STEAD, W.T.   *Mrs. Booth,* 1900. James Nisbet, London

STINE, PETER W.   *A Sense of God,* 1980. Baker Book House, Grand Rapids, Michigan

TALMADGE, CHARLES   *How to Preach,* 1979. Salvation Army, New York

TALMADGE, VIRGINIA   *Dear God,* 1981. Salvation Army, Atlanta

TILLSLEY, BRAMWELL   *Manpower for the Master,* Salvation Army, Toronto

TRIPP, BRAMWELL   *To the Point,* 1963. Salvation Army, Chicago

TROUTT, MARGARET   *General Was a Lady, The,* 1980. A.J. Holman Co., Nashville

UNSWORTH, MADGE   *Maiden Tribute,* 1954. Salvation Army, London
                     Mildred Duff, 1956. Salvation Army, London

WALDRON, JOHN D.   *At the Center of the Circle,* 1976. Beacon Hill Press, Kansas City
                     G.S.R., 1981. Salvation Army, Toronto
                     O Boundless Salvation, 1982. Salvation Army, Toronto
                     Privilege of All Believers, 1981. Salvation Army, Toronto
                     Salvationist and the Atonement, The, 1982. Salvation Army, Toronto

WIGGINS, ARCH   *History of The Salvation Army, The, Volume 4,5,* 1964. Thomas Nelson, London

WISEMAN, CLARENCE D. *Burning in My Bones, A,* 1979. McGraw-Hill Ryerson, Ltd., Toronto
                     Desert Road to Glory, The, 1982. Kebra Books, Toronto

WILLIAMS, HARRY   *William Booth's First Gentleman,* 1980. Hodder and Stoughton, London.

Index